Gregory Bull would like to dedicate  *other articles to the unmentioned heroes of the peace punk movement tists, the squatters, the young punks who put gigs on in the local village aid out their 'no more than' to get into a gig or to buy a record.*

Its also dedicated to David and Shelagh Bull - without them this wouldn't be in your hands.

Mike Dines would like to dedicate this book to Sam, Molly, Spike and the Magoo

If you find any artwork in this book which was created by yourself and you wish it to be removed or you would like to be credited please contact gregorybull1@gmail.com

No part of this publication may be reproduced, stored in or introduced into a retrieval system, or transmitted, in any form or by any means (electronic, mechanical, photocopying, recording or otherwise), without the prior written permission of the copyright owner, except by a reviewer who may quote brief passages in a review.

This book is sold subject to the condition that it shall not, by way of trade or otherwise, be lent, re-sold, hired out or otherwise circulated without the author's prior consent in any form of binding or cover other than that in which it is published and without a similar condition including this condition being imposed on the subsequent purchaser.

Published by Itchy Monkey Press 2016.
All work copyrighted to the original author or artist 2015.

This book is dedicated to the memories of Paco Carreno and Dickie Hammond

SOME OF US SCREAM SOME OF US SHOUT

Edited by Gregory Bull and Mike Dines

Stig Miller [Amebix]

Jacky Smith

CONTENTS

The Name is Crass, Not Clash....	Matthew Worley	12
Red leb. Black leb. Sticky black.	Greg Bull	24
Am I an Anarchist? A Tale of Anarcho Curiosity.	Russ Bestley	29
Mindful Token Tantrums/Anarcho In Action	Darren Johns	33
From Crass to Thrash to Squeakers	Otto Sompank	60
Chumbawamba - A Retrospective	Chris Butler	63
Conflict!	Chris Butler	66
Fuck War	Paul Davies	81
Antisect Live Gig Review and In Darkness... Album Reviews	Tony Drayton	86
Antisect	Caro Wallis	89
Antisect - The Buck Stops Here	Lance Hahn	90
Antisect - Postal Interview for Unknown Fanzine	Persons Unknown	99
Antisect - Another Postal Interview	Persons Unknown	106
Hex	Darren Pike	109
On Tour With Crass	Vincent Learoyd	111
Punk Was Once An Answer	Anth Palmer	113
The Snatcher (Remix)	Marcus Blakeston	118
Gifts of the Garden	Andrew J Wood	121
Always Another Door	Gerard Evans	128
To End Up on Your Table…	Alastair 'Gords' Gordon	141
I Changed My World	Stephen Spencer-Fleet	148
The Nouveau Hippies	Paul Platypus	154
Publish And Be Damned	Nick Hydra	157
Why Do You Think That They Are Laughing?	Rich Cross	165
Well, Sir. I Might	Willie Rissy	173
Memories	Tim Voss	178
Tumbleweeds.	Ted Curtis	184
The Squatting Year	Gail Thibert	191
Poetry	Ruth Harvey Gasson	203
The Last of the Mohawks	Tom Lainer-Read	210
Protest, Resist, Live: An Interview with SLUG	Mike Dines	218
How I Learnt To Love Grindcore...	Matt Grimes	243
A Haunting	Lucy Robinson	252

Foreword

Gregory Bull

I always liked the number three.

I like a trilogy.

I like the idea that there was too much for two, and not enough for four.

The triptych is a wonderful thing.

And so this is kind of the third in a series of books I have helped to co-edit focusing on the anarchist punk scene of the 1980s – a project which started with *Tales From The Punkside*, continued with *Not Just Bits of Paper* and now, at least for the time being for me, concludes with *Some Of Us Scream, Some Of Us Shout...*

But, like Douglas Adams, the editorial cabal who've compiled this series reserve the right, at some future date, to make this a trilogy comprised of more than three parts.

It has been an intense two and a half years of reading, researching, editing, cajoling, blagging and generally sniffing out the memories of our collective dim and distant past.

A past which grows ever distant each passing day. And a past which deserves to be written about. A time when it really was about Do It Yourself.

This series of books, one co-edited with Mickey Penguin and two with Mike Dines, was born out of that same DIY ethic.

I had asked someone to make up a book of flyers to highlight all the lesser known bands, helpers, artists and others who had taken a part in the anarcho-punk scene, but who had never been thanked or heralded.

No one answered the call.

Sure there are some great books out there on the subject, and there is, allegedly, a definitive book coming out of Dial House which will tell the whole tale; it will include many many flyers, handouts, pamphlets and more...

But I wanted "ordinary" people to have a voice. Oral, living history, real recollections [if a little embellished at times] and real histories and tales. It's what I like to read. The opinion of us is just as valid as the opinion of them. There really was no them and us back then, there was only you and me. We all helped in our own way, many of us were in bands, even if we never played a gig, released any vinyl or toured.

So I was left in the position of looking around and finding out how to do this publishing thing. It was a very swift learning curve.

And so this journey ends for now with this book you hold in your hands. Hopefully it helps tell the tale of those young men and women who wanted to create a better place for us all to live in.

And hopefully we achieved a little space for ourselves and we continue to struggle for what's right.

Peace and freedom,

Greg Bull

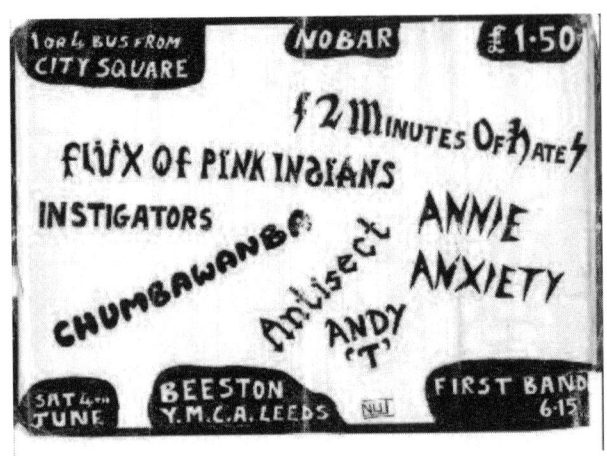

Introduction

Mike Dines

Some of Us Scream, Some of Us Shout: Myths, Folklore and Epic Tales of the Anarcho is the second in the *Tales From the Punkside* series. Whereas the self-titled first volume encompassed the wider punk scene, *Some of Us Scream…* brings together the stories, the artwork and the inspiration of the anarcho-punk scene from the 1980s to the present day.

As with *Tales…* stimulus has come from the everyday, from those who were 'there' and from those who have personal accounts to convey. Too often a 'scene' such as anarcho-punk becomes defined by its canon, its key players. In this case, they are often (amongst others) Crass, Conflict, Rudimentary Peni, the Subhumans and Flux of Pink Indians (of which, ironically, the editors would like to thank for the title of this book). The editors do not wish to detract from their stories but merely add to them, to document those who were inspired by the music, those who (in their own ways) further contributed to the scene.

Many would argue that anarcho-punk remains the apotheosis of the personal. It meant a way-of-life, a call-to-arms and a collectivity of musicians, artists, agitators and malcontents. It took as its standing point a diversity of the subversive. From so-called 'new age travellers' to the Animal Liberation Front; from Class War anarchism to the pacifism of Greenham Common; and from the women's rights movement to the politics of freedom-for-all. Anarcho-punk meant an egalitarian approach to lifestyle. In addition, the underpinning political cause that united all these was the movement's succinct critique of Thatcherism and the highly politicized 1980s in the UK. It is through this current volume that many of these tales are told.

In The Revolution of Everyday Life: The Perspective of Power (2012), Raoul Vaneigem notes that, 'today there is not an action or a thought that is not trapped in the net of received ideas. The slow fall-out of particles of the exploded myth spreads sacred dust everywhere, choking the spirit and the will to live.' For Vaneigem, 'the most certain chances of liberation are born in what is most familiar…this commonplace creature roams naked in railway stations and vacant lots; it confronts you at each evasion of yourself, it touches your elbow, catches your eye; and the dialogue begins. You must lose yourself with it or save it with you' (PM Press, pp. 7-8). With a personal fascination for the everyday I find some of this in *Some of Us Scream…* From the learning of Subhumans lyrics on the bus to the tragedy of squatting, and from the protests at RAF Cottesmore to the aesthetic backdrop of tortured animals and Falklands War survivors, these are tales from the familiar, the 'known.' The nakedness of expression and poignancy of the personal is evident throughout the anarcho. The homemade posters depicting laboratory animals, the cutback music production of songs about poverty, alienation and despair: anarcho-punk became a repository of reflection, critique and just plain desperation in the face of an oppressive and violent Thatcher government.

On an academic basis, I am fully aware of the issues surrounding oral history as being more 'authentic' or 'real.' Although oral testimony has become an acceptable source for much research in this area, I also realize the issues surrounding having such testimony stand alone as a source, let alone as a definitive narrative. As such, the reader must be aware that a construction of the narrative such as this book offers, is without problems surrounding neutrality and methodology. As this is not a purely academic piece of work, this should not impact on its reading or distribution. Yet the reader should also be aware of the editors' intention in collating such a book. As anarcho-punk was accused for having overbearing ideals (you must be vegetarian, you must be a pacifist) so the reader is asked to be critical of anarcho-punk itself.

Indeed, without this critical self-reflection, anarcho-punk becomes stagnant. It becomes static, caught up in a wave of nostalgia that ironically wishes for the return of 1980s Thatcherism. It becomes a movement that is defined only by its discernable features (vegetarianism, anti-Thatcher, anti-vivisectionist viewpoints) instead of the dynamics of political dissent and the individual. It is highlighted in my own chapter that the term/label 'anarcho' seems, at times, almost redundant. The label is unable to reflect the diversity and dynamism of the movement whilst at the same time restricting its thoughts and ideas within a label. 'Anarcho-punk' is a useful way of formalizing what many of us did in the 1980s, but this was, and is, by no means the end of it.

Although I have written an introduction for this current volume, much of the credit for *Some of Us Scream…* must go to Greg Bull. Indeed, it is a privilege to be called a co-editor next to an individual who did most of the legwork in this volume. The excellent design, painstaking collation of work and obvious enthusiasm in these pages belong to Greg. I'm afraid I'm like a mere bystander. I would also like to say a big thank-you to Alastair 'Gords' Gordon for the inspiration behind the *Punkside…* title (the connotations of which are not lost on those fluent in Japanese punk), to each of the contributors to this volume and of course to Sam, Eric, Molly and Spike.

And dedications? Shall I dedicate the book to those who were there? Shall I buck against the academic and be a romantic old sod? Why not. So yeah, I dedicate this book to those who were lucky enough to be part of the anarcho-punk scene. And for the future? In the inimitable words of Culture Shock, Onwards and Upwards!

Mike Dines

September 2015

Legendary Punk Drummer - Fransisco "Paco" Carreno 12.12.1965 – 20.02.2015

Maria Carreno

September 2015

One of the greatest punk drummers of all times, part of something iconic, he was the stitch work that completed the chain, fighting for what he felt was right, telling others, 'this is how it is.

Through his music, his songs and the beat of his drums, he inspired and supported throughout, never aloof nor condescending, he helped others fulfil music goals, but above all he was clever, amazing and funny and a brother to us all.

From the tender age of 12 years old his passion for drumming grew.

He joined Conflict at the age of 15 years old, then Experiment and Inner Terrestrials, they journeyed on together, each one played their part, in Paco's life, the family of punks and comrades close to his heart.

Paco was many things to many people, especially from his family of punk but to mum and I, he was simply Pax, big brother and loving son, a big man in every respect of the word, he has left a gaping hole in our lives and the lives of so many others. We cherish every memory of him, his laughter, his life, his passion and the beat of his drums, may they live on and on…. to give us comfort from the loss.

A wonderful son, brother, friend to all and Oh yes what a drummer! RIP Paco, Always in our hearts

We'll play our music in respect of Paco….as it echoes in the street, remembering his beat, his trademark style, no other could imitate….

Always in our hearts
Maria Carreno

Fransisco "Paco" Carreno 12.12.1965 – 20.02.2015

WE'RE ALL CONDITIONED TO THINK TEN TELLIES ARE BETTER THAN ONE
AND TO BLOW THIS WORLD UP TEN TIMES IS BETTER THAN TO BLOW IT
UP ONCE
BILLIONS SPENT ON DESTROYING THE WORLD WHILE MILLIONS STARVE,
WHERE DID WE GO WRONG?
WHERE DID WE GO WRONG? MAYBE YOU DON'T THINK THAT THIS IS
WRONG?

WE AS ONE ARE SAYING
FEED STARVING PEOPLE
FUCK YOUR BOMBS

ALL THROUGH OUR LIVES WE ARE SHOVED ABOUT
SOME OF US SCREAM, SOME OF US SHOUT
SOME OF US COMPLAIN, PROTEST
WHILE OTHERS SMILE IN ECSTASY
WHY IS IT ACCEPTED AS THE WAY TO LIVE
OUR BODIES FALLING THROUGH ONE BIG SIEVE
WE'RE SORTED OUT, BRUSHED AND COMBED
SOME SMILE, SOME FROWN
SOME REJECT THIS WAY TO LIVE
AND PAY THE PRICE TO HOW THEY EXIST

WHO ARE YOU?
WHAT ARE YOU?
WHAT DO YOU DO?
WHAT ARE YOU DOING?
WHAT ARE YOU DOING IT FOR?
WHAT ARE YOU DOING IT FOR?

WE CAN'T ACCEPT THEIR DISRESPECT
THEIR EYES AND BOMBS THAT WATCH OVER US
THEIR SYSTEMS CREATING WAR
WHILE SOCIETY BREEDS HATE
AND THEY MAKE OUT THAT IT'S NORMAL
FOR PEOPLE TO FIGHT AND HATE
THEY SHOVE TOY GUNS ON IMPRESSIONABLE CHILDREN
THEIR FUTURE SOLDIERS OF WAR?
IS IT TOO LATE FOR US ALL TO CHANGE?
HAVE WE GONE TOO FAR?

WE AS ONE ARE SAYING
WE DON'T WANT YOUR LIFE NO MORE
FUCK OFF

SOME OF US SCREAM

FLUX OF PINK INDIANS

Colin Jerwood and Paco Carreno [Conflict]

Irene Frizzera

Colin Jerwood and Paco Carreno [Conflict]

Irene Frizzera

The Name is Crass, Not Clash ...

Matthew Worley

When the Sex Pistols succumbed to their inglorious end, at San Francisco's Winterland Ballroom on 14 January 1978, British punk did not so much die as detonate like a cultural nail bomb. A range of musical styles and subcultural forms emerged in the aftermath, each rising from the debris to stake claim to punk's 'true' meaning and purpose. In Britain, a flowering of subcultural revivals appeared across inner-city estates and along the hedge-lined streets of suburbia, each one – be they mods, skinheads, rockabillys or rude boys – endeavouring to return to the moment *before* pop had been lost to the pretensions of *Sgt Pepper* and the muso-dawdling of progressive rock. The Clash, meanwhile, manoeuvred to embed themselves more firmly in the canon of 'classic rock' (eventually being touted as heirs apparent to The Who, who they supported in the US), while punk's Bowie-lineage evolved via new romanticism and positive punk towards what would eventually become goth. Some tried to freeze the punk moment forever; developing a generic punk sound and a generic punk look that produced flashes of brilliance as it burrowed deeper into the rubble of diminishing returns. Others took punk's promise to 'question everything' to its logical extreme, experimenting with sound and composition or eschewing pop lyricism in favour of short-hand treatises on the politics of personal relationships, consumerism and capital. Still more explored the gaping abyss that opened up on the other side of 'No Future', producing dark sounds and dark words to weigh heavy on the shoulders of the country's disaffected youth. Through punk came new mod, new pop, new romantics, post-punk, posi-punk, Oi!, industrial and 2-Tone. And then there was Crass ...

Crass inspired the most politically significant and influential fragment of punk's cultural devastation, taking up McLaren and Westwood's repositioned Anarchy-symbol to forge a recognisable alternative to the Sex Pistols' threat of 'No Future'. As the skies darkened over the post-war 'consensus', through which the dead-hand of Thatcherism emerged to reshape and redefine Britain's socio-economic structures and sense of purpose, so Crass strived to resist the blows sustained by those who did not subscribe to – or were not deemed to fit into – the Tories' 'new beginning'. Following Crass' example, countless punk bands, fanzines, collectives, squats and campaigns emerged across the UK's hinterlands: residues of hope struggling to find peace and freedom in a country at war with itself and mired in a morass of self-loathing.

Crass formed in 1977; a band that grew into a collective around the nucleus of Penny Rimbaud and Steve Ignorant. They were based at Dial House in Epping Forest on the edge of London's sprawl; an old farm-house that Rimbaud, Gee Vaucher and others renovated in the late 1960s to provide a creative hub that served as a working alternative to mainstream social structures and expectations. From therein Crass cultivated a unique sound, image and worldview that sought to transform punk's rhetorical anarchy into a viable political and cultural opposition. Across a series of LPs, EPs, and 7" singles, the band launched an aural assault on everything from Christianity ('Reality Asylum') and the inequities of 'the system' ('Big A Little A') to patriarchy (*Penis Envy*) and the rigid orthodoxies of leftist politics ('Bloody Revolutions'). Where the Sex Pistols embraced chaos, Crass devised a design for life best summed up in their slogan 'there is no authority but yourself'. In other words, Crass took punk seriously: they recognised within it an extension of pre-existing counter-cultures and sought to mould its values of autonomy and anti-authoritarianism into a potent political weapon. A legion of bands and artists emerged in their wake, holding firm to the punk banner before Crass finally unravelled in 1984, buckling under internal strains but simultaneously complementing the Orwellian countdown that had loomed over their activities from the outset. The catalogue numbers on the records – from *The Feeding of the Five Thousand*'s '621984' to 'Your Already Dead's '1984' – ticked off the years until the imagined boot stamping on a human face forever laid into the miners, trade unionists, travellers, peace campers, single mothers and riotous youth attempting to resist.

In terms of music, Crass tended towards a harsh, discordant reading of punk. They quickly developed an immediately recognisable sound based around Rimbaud's skitterry (almost military-style) drumming and an incessant buzz of guitar noise that buried standard chords beneath feedback, amp hum and speed. Songs bled into one another as the band's politically charged lyrics spewed forth from the mouths of Ignorant, Eve Libertine, Joy de Vivre and Pete Wright; each song written to a specific brief and a focused intent. Authority figures were besmirched, institutions undermined, and punk's own cultural development was subjected to a critical meta-narrative that questioned its compromises and exposed its contradictions. As this suggests, Crass songs were designed to provoke and confront, tackling topical issues such as the Falklands War (1982) whilst also placing contemporary events within a wider critique of prevailing political ideologies and systems. The music, therefore, served as a medium for political communication; it provided a frame within which Crass could agitate and propagate. To this end, the various 'spaces' provided by the culture of popular music – and, by extension, punk – were utilised to disseminate information, initiate protest and stimulate debate. Crass' records, for example, came in black-and-white fold-out sleeves crammed with essays, lyric sheets, points of contact, information and imagery. Crass gigs, most of which were benefits for an array of progressive causes, served both as a good night out AND a forum of political engagement. Film, fanzines, posters, prints and pamphlets accompanied the music. And though the band's image of plain black clothes was designed to reject punk's being understood as mere fashion, it simultaneously gave the group a look of collective identity that soon found favour across an expanding punk audience.

Indeed, for many a young punk, Crass provided a *way into* politics. The late 1970s had seen the New Jerusalem promised by Labour snag on the faultlines of global economics and political compromise. The left, still bound to a Leninist mind-set or competing to assert different identities as the dominant 'vanguard' of social change, appeared fractured and on the back foot. The far right, as always, offered prejudice, imagined pasts and violence as a conduit to fascism; Thatcherism bore hope for middle England and the entrepreneurial – it did little for anyone with a soul or a conscience. But anarchism, especially the DIY anarchism cultivated around Crass, navigated paths in-between. In a pre-internet age, where the media's reach was wide but concentrated, so Crass, the Poison Girls and soon-to-be others offered an alternative media that did not just report and document, but provided a counter narrative: an alternative reality.

The politics of Crass – and anarcho-punk they helped inspire – are best understood as a totality. On the one hand, anarcho-punk embraced a broad range of progressive campaigns, including anti-militarism, pacifism, feminism, eco-politics, atheism, animal liberation and vegetarianism. Many of these fed out of long-standing counter-cultural concerns, while others were very much a product of a post-war world cast in the shadow of Auschwitz and Nagasaki. In particular, Crass became synonymous with the Campaign for Nuclear Disarmament (CND), particularly once the Cold War reignited in 1979–80 as a result of Soviet intervention in Afghanistan, the Iranian revolution and the political shift in the West occasioned by the rise to prominence of Margaret Thatcher and Ronald Reagan. Yet such concerns were more broadly integrated into an overarching worldview in which the global power structures that maintained state authority and prevailing socio-economic relations presaged only war and oppression. War, the band maintained in the sleeve notes to *Christ The Album* (1982), was simply 'confirmation of the imposed reality in which we exist'.

On the other hand, Crass embodied a lived politics that anarcho-punk forever aspired to. Their records, fanzines, pamphlets, films and artworks were all self-produced from within the Crass collective. The mainstream music press was rejected in favour of independently produced fanzines; independent labels and distribution were preferred over the established music industry infrastructure. Money raised was utilised to release the music of allied bands or to facilitate further Crass activity. Most importantly, the band's members were active. Not only did they support and raise awareness of movements such as CND, but Crass and their associates were involved in the squatters' movement, the maintenance of anarchy centres in London, animal liberation initiatives and the Stop the City campaigns of the mid-1980s which served as precursors to the poll tax demos of 1990 and the anti-globalisation demonstrations of more recent times. It was Crass, moreover, who mobilised the most high-profile opposition to the Falklands War in 1982, releasing singles such as 'How Does it Feel to be the Mother of a Thousand Dead', which provoked questions in the British parliament, and disseminating the infamous 'Thatchergate' tapes. These comprised a cut-and-spliced 'conversation' between Reagan and Thatcher relating to the deployment of US missiles in Europe, the ramifications of which led the band to receive overtures from the KGB and a burgeoning MI5 file.

Crass also engaged with the movement they helped inspire. Handwritten letters replied to the thousands that began to arrive at Dial House by the early 1980s; badges, information and advice were duly dispatched. The band's rejection of the standard gig circuit ensured they relied on people to help set up gigs off the beaten track – in church halls, scout huts and community centres. Subsequently, the band tended to stay with those who helped organise the gig, extending their already standard practice of engaging with the audience before and after the performance. If punk blurred the lines between those on the stage and those off, then Crass sought to rub them out completely – a concept extended via the release of three *Bullshit Detector* albums compiling tracks from the thousands of demo tapes that found their way to the band.

Not surprisingly, perhaps, the politics of anarcho-punk were contentious. Crass were often criticised for preaching, for lacking humour and displaying a patronising – maybe even a misanthropic – attitude towards the wider population. The band's songs and writings tended to portray mainstream society as comprising a brainwashed mass in denial about the abject horror of nuclear devastation and kept in check by a complicit media and the platitudes of corrupt politicians. Amongst sections of the punk fraternity, too, Crass were criticised for their espousal of supposed hippy ideals – their utilisation of the peace sign, the rural ideal of their 'communal' living. For all their apparent libertarianism, the strictures that came hand in hand with a commitment to vegetarianism, feminism etc., soon mounted up. The band, and those inspired by them, could appear judgemental and exclusive, leading some to see them more as a cult than part of punk. In the music press, a spat between Rimbaud and *Sounds'* Garry Bushell, pushed a wedge between the anarchist bands and those who saw themselves – and punk – in class-terms or eschewed *all* politics. The Exploited, led by Wattie Buchan, took umbrage with Crass' 'Punk is Dead' (a song critiquing the commercial appropriation of punk's 'first wave'), naming their debut LP *Punk's Not Dead* and further fuelling intra-punk tensions (before later making amends with a joint gig at the 100 Club). Worst of all were Special Duties, who's Steve Arrogant made a desperate attempt to gain notoriety on the back of a Crass-slagging press interview and a single, 'Bullshit Crass', that needs to be heard to be believed. Ironically, the band's drummer later played in Dirt.

To be sure, Crass also raised the heckles of political parties on the left and right. By late 1979, their gigs – more often than not, played alongside Poison Girls – hosted regular confrontations between members of Britain's neo-fascist organisations and anti-fascists gathered on the revolutionary left. It was, moreover, in an attempt to distance themselves from the politics of left and right that the band adopted anarchism and the anarchy symbol to designate their refusal to commit to any fixed ideology. The politics of anarcho-punk were the politics of individual freedom and collective responsibility; they rejected fascism but also the class-based analysis of the Marxist left. Even then, however, such a position opened Crass up to criticism amongst punk's anarchist milieu. For some in and around the London Autonomy Centre (which Crass helped to fund), syndicalist ideas and a more assertive anarchist influence fanned disapproval of the band's pacifism and, again, their disavowal of class. The Apostles, in particular, took a critical view of Crass in the early 1980s.

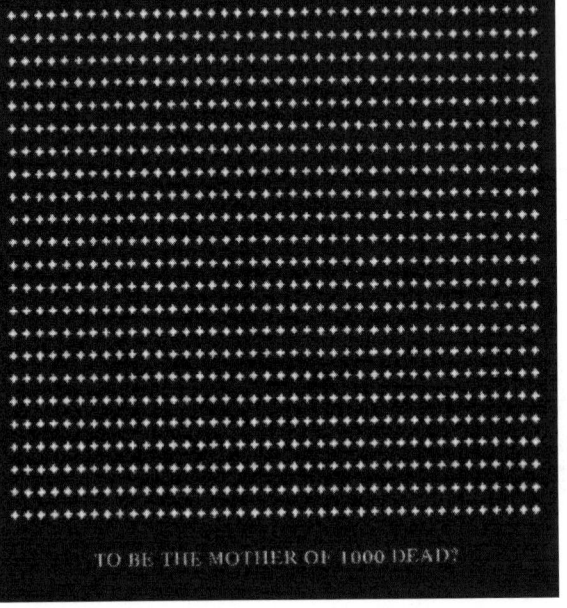

TO BE THE MOTHER OF 1000 DEAD?

But despite such tensions and the many over-heated wars of words, the influence of Crass on 1980s British punk (and 'alternative' music more generally) is difficult to underestimate. Not only were the band's records a permanent fixture at the top of the then-important 'alternative charts' published in the music press of the time, but Crass' politics and methods informed an expansive network of bands, collectives, labels and fanzines inspired by their example. Many bands, including Conflict and Flux of Pink Indians, released their first EPs on the Crass label before going on to set up their own labels and release their own records. As anarcho-punk expanded, so equivalent scenes developed across the country. London, in particular, boasted a vibrant milieu that comprised bands from the capital's surround attracted by anarchist squats, centres and politics. Though some, such as Dirt, were born very much in the Crass mould, others took anarcho-punk off into more varied musical and political directions. Where the Poison Girls applied an anarchist spin to feminism, so Conflict welded the boot-boy aura of Oi! onto the anarchist politics of Crass to forge a confrontational punk that revelled in the promise of riotous assembly and encouraged the direct action approach of organisations such as the Animal Liberation Front. For others, anarcho-punk simply offered a valid alternative to the blunt class-consciousness of Oi! or the violent reportage of bands such as Blitz. It is notable, too, that anarcho-punk bands often emerged from smaller, even rural, outposts in the UK. Anarcho-bands were generally more varied in terms of gender and class background than their other punk equivalents. As Ian Glasper's survey makes clear, the likes of Alternative, Andy T, Antisect, Chumbawamba, Disrupters, Hagar the Womb, Icons of Filth, The Mob, Part 1, Rubella Ballet, Rudimentary Peni, The Sinyx, Subhumans, Zounds and countless others form an integral part of any Crass-inspired story (not to mention the countless fanzines, posters and pamphlets that spread the word far and wide).

Overall, the history of Crass and anarcho-punk is one that has only recently emerged from the shadows of broader punk and rock narratives. Anarcho-punk revelled in its establishing a working alternative to mainstream music and popular culture. It was, by its nature, located outside and against society. This enabled anarcho-punk to avoid appropriation by the mechanisms of capital that it so forcibly derided, facilitating a vibrant political culture centred on music but providing entry to myriad worlds of militant and radical opposition. To this end, Crass did what punk always promised it would: it taught people how to say NO.

DURING THE 'CRISIS' IN THE FALKLANDS BETWEEN 950 AND 1450 WERE MURDERED BY THE STATES OF BRITAIN AND ARGENTINA.

Crass

Photo by Willie Wit

Crass

Photo by Willie Wit

```
CRASS/POISON GIRLS NORTHERN TOUR
OCTOBER 1980

Tues 7  ROCHDALE
                The Tropical Club
Wed 8  HALIFAX
                Lee Mount Club
Thurs 9  HULL
                Blind Institute
Fri 10  HUDDERSFEILD
                Cleopatras
Sat 11  MIDDLESBROUGH
                Rock Garden
Mon 13  BRADFORD
                The Sweat Box
Wed 15  LIVERPOOL
                Gatsbys '2'
Thurs 16  NOTTINGHAM
                Ad Lib Club '2'
Fri 17  MANCHESTER
                Mayflower Club '2'
Sat 18  EDINBURGH
                The Nite Club
Sun 19  CLEATOR MOOR
                Civic Hall

£1.00 entry to all gigs
Dates marked '2' with ZOUNDS
(to be confirmed).
Doors open (generally) at 7.30p.m.
matinée & evening performances
in Edinburgh-5p.m. & 9p.m.
```

IN ALL OUR DECADENCE PEOPLE DIE

THIS IS A SAMPLE OF SOME OF THE SPRAYS THAT WE USE FOR VARIOUS GRAFFITI PROJECTS. IF YOU CUT THIS STENCILS OUT, PERHAPS IT WOULD BE BETTER TO COPY THEM ONTO THIN CARD FIRST, YOU COULD USE THEM FOR DECORATING CLOTHING, IN WHICH CASE SILVER SPRAY IS THE BEST TO USE IF IT'S ONTO BLACK CLOTHES, OR IF ITS ONTO ANY OTHER LIGHT COLOUR ANY CAR SPRAY PAINT WILL DO. YOU CAN BUY ALPHABET STENCIL KITS IN MOST SHOPS THAT SELL ART MATERIAL. YOU CAN ALSO BUY CRAFT KNIVES WHICH ARE THE BEST TYPE FOR CUTTING STENCILS. SOME OF THESE STENCILS ARE THE ONES THAT WE USE ON POSTERS ETC. TO LET PEOPLE KNOW THAT WE DON'T AGREE WITH THE SHIT THAT THEY PROMOTE. IT'S A GOOD WAY OF SPENDING AN EVENING, BUT DON'T GET CAUGHT. GRAFFITI IS A REALLY EFFECTIVE WAY OF LETTING YOUR OPPINIONS BE SEEN. IF ALL THE ARMY RECRUITMENT OFFICES IN THE COUNTRY WERE SPRAYED WITH A FIGHT WAR STENCIL MAYBE THE MESSAGE WOULD GET THROUGH A LITTLE. GOOD LUCK WITH THEM.

WHO DO THEY THINK THEY'RE FOOLING: YOU?

WEALTH IS A GHETTO

IF YOU STOP ME AND ASK "WHAT NOW?WHERE NOW?"
DO YOU REALLY EXPECT AN ANSWER?
IS IT NOT SIMPLY YOUR OWN CONSCIENCE FROM WHICH YOU SEEK A REPLY?
I CAN ONLY SAY THIS OR THAT
AND HOPE THAT WE MIGHT STRIKE A COMMON CHORD.
MEANWHILE WE LEARN MORE OF OURSELVES
AND PARTS OF EACH OTHER.

WHERE THE SEA BEATS MERCILESSLY ON THE SHORE
THERE IS THE SECURITY OF THE LAND.
AT THE SEA'S DEEPEST POINT THERE IS OFTEN A STRANGE CALM.

It is no longer enough for our actions to be dictated to by reason that perhaps ten years ago had some relevance,we are no longer living in a society that will be swayed by reason,(perhaps we never were),and even if we were,do you really believe that those who stand in authority above and beyond our society are ever going to listen to that reason?we are living in a police state where any illusion of democracy that might once have existed has now become clearly defunct and remoulded into an (as yet) benevolent form of fascism.We are quite simply powerless if we continue to follow logic and reason that has its roots in a past era,IT IS TIME TO ACCEPT THAT THE PEACE MOVEMENT MUST BE AND IS BY NATURE A REVOLUTIONARY MOVEMENT.

No real peace will be achieved as long as any of the institutions of the State remain intact because the State is the WAR MOVEMENT and is by nature a REACTIONARY MOVEMENT.Politely asking,or even reasonably demanding peace and the conditions that will make it possible from a State in which the whole policy is one of oppression,is blatantly absurd.OUR JOB IS THE COMPLETE DISMANTLING OF THE STATE,A WILLINGNESS TO FIGHT FOR THAT END AND A COMPLETE REFUSAL TO PARTICIPATE IN MINDLESS HALF-UNDERSTOOD POLICIES OF REFORM.Surely it is obvious that the most that could reasonably be expected through reform is a liberalisation by the State and its agents,but the POWER WOULD STILL BE THEIRS.Is that what we want?That is precisely what we've had throughout this century and now, in 1984,can you honestly say that it has worked?The State will ALWAYS make concessions to the people,not for any other reason than to maintain their control.It is our job to ACCEPT OUR OWN AUTHORITY,it is no longer enough to beg that others make concessions on our behalf.The struggle IS by no other name a 'CLASS WAR',not one defined by stale leftist jargon of 'workers and bosses',nor feminist jargon of 'men and women',these are glib complications,the divisions are more easily defined....the rich and the poor,the State and the people.

It is time to realise that the State will not be swayed by reason or by quasi-mystical escapism disguised as action.Of course we should as individuals develop reason,should respond to our own spirit (mystical or otherwise),nurture compassion and love,BUT to apply those realisations as a political force is unrealistic and naive,as a personal strength it is fine,politically,however,it is not enough,not enough by far.We are involved in REVOLUTION,not a university debate.

It is time to realise that in fact the Peace Movement is no movement at all,it is a loose term thrown around an enormously diverse group of individuals.It encompasses Ex Servicepeople Against The Bomb on the right,to militant activists on the left.My own sense of comradeship wears thin just left of center,I'm prepared to work alongside individuals from Labour voting liberals to anarcho militants because,fundamentally,I believe the goal is,if not actually stated,there as potential....ie.OVERTHROW OF THE STATE.Anyone further right than the Labour voter I view with suspicion and caution.Right wingers are drawn to the Peace Movement, as they are to the A.L.F.,not because they are aware of global problems,not because they operate for humanitarian purposes,but simply because they want to protect what is THEIRS,their traditions,their positions,their self interested greed.IT IS NOT OURSELVES THAT WE ARE TRYING TO SAVE,IT IS OUR WORLD.

From the Labour voter to the anarcho militant (and beyond) is a huge and diverse range of individual motive,reason and rationalisation.When a miner says that he's striking to protect his job and at the same time manage,if not destroy,Thatcher's regime,I am prepared to support his struggle EVEN IF I do believe that NO ONE should have to work in the terrible conditions that miners are expected to tolerate to earn the pittance they're paid by their wealthy overlord (the State).I am prepared to support that struggle because it is a part of the whole pattern of dissent that will eventually give way to mass insurrection.

When the Greenham Women say that their action is exclusively a women's action and that it is primarily 'symbolic' with the purpose of informing public oppinion with,presumably,the hope of forcing governmental reform,I am prepared to support their action, all be it passively),not because I support seperatism,to me seperatism is devicive and ultimately self defeating (the struggle is no more unisex than the enemy),nor do I support their struggle because I believe that symbolic action can or will bring about any real change,I don't and it won't.I support their struggle because they demonstrate the potential of a revolutionary lifestyle which is a part of the whole pattern of dissent that will eventually give way to mass insurrection.

If the miners and the Greenham Women could realise their shared oppression and look for the similarities and common denom-
inators in their struggle,rather than the differences,we would be now witnessing the creation of a REAL Peace Movement.The links are obvious.Pits are being closed because coal fired power stations are not in line with Government policies of nuclear expansion.Nuclear power stations produce the raw materials for nuclear bombs and that's REAL POWER.So,as the pickets stand outside their fence to protect their world and the Greenham Women stand outside their fence to protect their world,the State smiles on benignly.As long as the connections aren't made and operated on the State will be laughing.Isn't it time TO DROP OUR DIFFERENCES AND TO UNDERSTAND THAT ALL OF OUR INDIVIDUAL ACTIONS ARE POTENTIALLY MASSIVELY POWERFUL IF ONLY WE CAN LEARN TO ACCEPT THAT OUR STRUGGLE IS SHARED,WE ARE NOT ALONE.

How much longer do we have to tolerate the action numbing debates about pacifism versus activism?How much longer are we going to tolerate moralistic clap-trap about how this group or that group OUGHT to behave?Surely we MUST understand that the struggle of oppressed people throughout the world is our struggle and that the methods employed to make that struggle effective are as diverse as the individual struggles and the individuals involved in them.It is my view that many of the policies of the Non Violent Direct Action movement are essentially obsolete.I am not prepared to be a victim of State violence and I am not prepared to suggest that others should be.I believe that 'symbolic' protest exposes people to very Unsymbolic treatment at the hand of the old bill,the number of arrests at demonstrations over the last year runs into thousands.The 'fill the jails' philosophy is in my view a philosophy of the victim,if others choose to follow that course I shall support them ONLY in that their actions are a part of the whole pattern of dissent that will eventually give way to mass insurrection.I,for my part,will not accept such twelve a role.I am no sheep to be led to State slaughter.

Except for the extremely few so called 'psychotic' individuals that I have met in my lifetime,(and the large numbers of a-cho robots who I am aware are drawn to a life of army or police),I know of NO ONE who would wish to hurt their fellow human being. Those who do only do so because the State,and the society that it controls and manipulates,have been so hideously perverted by its unthinking, uncaring oppression.Yet,for how much longer do we have to tolerate firstly the spectacle of our comrades being brutalised by agents of the State and secondly moralistic criticisms from within the Peace Movement of those who feel it necessary to fight back?We are TOGETHER in the struggle but I am NOT prepared to accept that the State and its figurehead Thatcher,who quite mercilessly murdered over three hundred sailors aboard the Belgrano,is going to be in the least effected by policies like 'fill the jails'.Do we really believe that such policies stretch the resources of the State?It is blatantly obvious that they DO stretch OUR resources.JUST HOW MANY COMRADES ARE WE PREPARED TO GIVE TO THE STATE?When is it that we are going to realise that what ever sense of decency we have grasped as individuals is NOT mirrored in the persons who inhabit the corridors of power?We have,each one of us, had to struggle against almost impossible odds to find some little part of ourselves that cries out 'this is wrong,I will not be a part of it'....is it morally desirable that we should allow ourselves to be punished for possessing that little ray of light?

    I once visited a friend who was serving a sentence in one of Her Majsty's Psychiatric Hospitals.I pleaded with him to listen to my plans for his escape.I implored him to prepare himself for a break-out.He replied that they could take his possessions,that they could take his body,that they could abuse him in whatever way that they liked,but that they would never extinguish the little piece of light,the radiant truth that was within him.Three months later he was dead.Some would argue that the light still shines, others that he at least died with his integrity and dignity intact.In my view that is stupid and empty rhetoric.I should have liked to have shared this beautiful spring day with my friend,but for the malicious and violent arrogance of the State he would have been here today and I might not be wrapped as I am in the grey gloom of THEIR REALITY.I KNOW THAT THERE ARE COLOURS AND THAT THERE IS BEAUTY AND WONDER.I KNOW THAT THIS LIFE IS PERFECT,THAT IT IS UNIQUE,YET FOR EVER IT SEEMS THE BLACK CLOUDS WILL DARKEN ALL THAT IS GOOD,NOBLE AND PURE.I KNOW,BUT I CAN NOT FEEL.We can not afford to be martyrs (if only because it is perhaps easier for the martyr than for those who are left behind).The struggle is one that we have to make together,OUTSIDE THE FENCE and,indeed,I believe,AWAY FROM THE FENCE.The spectre of thousands of jailed comrades does nothing but confirm the frightening cynicism of the enemy.We must not allow ourselves to become victims in the twentieth century witch hunt.Those dark prisons cast black clouds upon the radiant skies of our future.LET US RISE ABOVE THIS DARKNESS.LET US STAND ABOVE THE CLOUDS AWAY FROM THE CHAINS OF BONDAGE THAT HOLD US HERE SO INEFFECTIVE.

    I am making these points not because I wish to disassociate myself from those who support N.V.D.A.,but because I do not wish them to disassociate themselves from me and other 'militants'.We are ALL on the outside and ALL have a part to play in the struggle.I firmly believe in pacifism in the broadest meaning,that is I abhor any form of violence towards any living being and believe that no disagreement can be resolved through the use of force be it personal or global,BUT I will not stand by and see my comrades suffer at the callous hand of the State.WE HAVE THE RIGHT TO PROTECT OURSELVES,IT IS THE COMMON RIGHT OF THE INDIVIDUAL. Now,I am not stupid enough,nor am I sufficiently macho,to believe that I can save a comrade from arrest or brutalisation if there's large numbers of old bill around,but if there's a good chance of a save,and my comrade hasn't been programmed to accept arrest like a passive robot,I believe the chance is worth taking and if it involves a bruise or two either way,that's fine because a bruise or two in the street is infinitely preferable to the obscene treatment that's possible within the confines of the nick.I would extend this scenario to ANY situation where people take it upon themselves to physically violate my comrades.For too long we have passively stood by as rightist idiots desecrate so much of what we have created.It is too precious to allow our gains to be lost without a fight.But,more importantly by far,how much longer are we going to involve ourselves in suicidal policies of mass public demonstration?Is it not time to very carefully analyse the validity of such actions?The Peace Camps are fine,but are they the most effective deployement of people?Are they enough?Stop The City is fine,but does it stop the City?Is it enough?Could it not be that the strategy of centralised protest actions is now defunct?There are of course values in such actions,but nearly all those values are personal ones.Personal development is fine,is essential,but at what point do we stop developing our personalities and start USING them?That large numbers of potentially disruptive individuals are conveniently located around the various U.S. bases can be nothing but a source of satisfaction to the State.As long as we're THERE we're nowhere else.Do you really believe that playing cowboys and indians with cruise missile convoys actually concerns the State?They LOVE it.Do you really believe that the 'thin blue line' minds demonstrations like Stop The City?They LOVE it.They positively REVEL in the chance to flex their ugly muscles against those who they know will very rarely reply in kind.Unlike us,they have NO INHIBITION AT ALL ABOUT USING FORCE.Come the time that I strike out,it will be because I care.They strike out for precisely the opposite reason,because they don't care,and why should they?What threat are we to their supremacy?Like the Ukranian guards who rode the cattle trucks,they KNOW THAT THEY HAVE THE POWER.It is my view that passive resistance,rather than challenging that power,actually reinforces it.If passive acceptance of abuse makes the burden lighter,it is arguably worth adopting,but as a de facto policy it is madness.HOW MANY CHRISTS HAVE TO DIE UPON THE CROSS OF OUR FEAR BEFORE WE REALISE THAT WE ARE NOT THE VICTIM,BUT THE EXECUTIONER?

    For some reason I am led to think of the limbo dancer who squeezes beneath the locked door of a public toilet and concusses herself on the toilet bowl on the way out.I'm not quite sure what the parrallel is,but it's been with me all day.

    So,I do not believe in pushing for reform,or being a fish in the State fishtank,or passively accepting State violence,or being a member of the State's debating society,or that developing one's own awareness is enough.None of that is going to create any worthwhile changes.I am however broadly prepared to support those positions because I do believe that they are essential ingredients for what I believe is the inevitable insurrection,(it might not come in my lifetime,BUT IT WILL COME).

    Within all this,I have not clearly stated MY position,that may be partly because it is one of ambivalence.On the one hand I profoundly believe in the power of the word,on the other,the power of action,they can and do work together,but they can be,and frequently are,mutually destructive.Just as my words can invalidate my actions,so my actions can invalidate my words.Rarely are they in TOTAL accord.But let me say what I _believe_ is the right course of action and let me in my own quest for inner strength judge my own ability to live up to those words.I am prepared to let my words be public,my actions I shall share with few people and in that sense shall remain private.

    I believe that the Peace Camps,mass demonstrations etc. have their limited uses but that it is time to deploy ourselves more usefully and more discretely.The policy of massing together in a show of numbers is enabling the old bill to see us and document us as just that,numbers.We are far too willingly allowing ourselves simply to become numbers on their files.It is important to remember that having a criminal record can and will inhibit your movements for life,SO DON'T GET CAUGHT.At any one of the U.S. bases there is at this moment individuals employed in 'criminal acts' of sabotage,be they wire-cutting,tresspassing, observing and noting State secrets,conspiring to cause damage etc.etc.My argument is that the majority,but not all as that would leave the bases unattended,would be better employed committing 'criminal acts' further afield.Why risk arrest at public demonstrations of sabotage (Greenham wire cutting etc.) when far more damage could be done to State institutions that are not so well guarded and are not in the glare of public view.There are inumerable institutions worthy of our attentions,from social security offices and schools,to council offices and police stations,in fact any and all the institutions of the State.

    I believe that there are only two possibilities for the future of our planet.One is that the State is allowed to continue its oppression and abuse of the people until,for its own ends and because of its unutterable arrogance,it exterminates all life with its obsession for war.We live in an insane situation where we risk nuclear devastation every day be it in the form of the inevitable nuclear war or the inevitable nuclear plant disaster.I use the term inevitable because it IS inevitable that this will and must happen unless WE STOP IT FROM HAPPENING,which is possibility two.Possibility two involves the TOTAL disarming of the State and ALL its institutions.It is a race against time.I believe that those who assert 'evolutionary reformist' logic are effectively accepting possibility one.We can no longer depend on sanity.Has sanity ever prevailed?Thus I believe that nothing short of all out revolution can change our planet into a safe home.

Inevitably in a short article such as this,it is necessary to localise issues,but I realise that if any revolution is to be successful it MUST be international.It is not for me to define the type of struggle that others should follow in their own nation, they are informed of the issues and I have to trust that their considerations have been made to suit the locale.WHAT I MUST TRY TO ACCEPT IS THAT THEIR STRUGGLE IS MINE EVEN IF I DON'T WHOLLY SUPPORT THE METHODS.

Although I have considered myself a pacifist for as long as I can remember,my belief in pacifism has,perhaps because of the manner in which others have manifested it,worn thin.How can seperatism be seen as pacifist?How can deliberate provocation and then deliberate servitude,as in blockade philosophy,be seen as pacifism.WE ARE ALLOWING OURSELVES TO BE PASSIVE VICTIMS,THIS IS NOT HOW I BELIEVE PACIFISM SHOULD BE PRACTISED.I no longer believe that mass protest will achieve anything but,at the best,mild reforms. I no longer believe it to be morally acceptable to see my comrades picked on and abused by agents of the State.I no longer believe that by demonstrating my own sense of awareness and love that it will have any effect whatever on those who have been brainwashed by the State to hate and hurt.By taking polarised positions WITHIN the Peace Movement we are conforming to the State's divide and conquer policy.More than any other philosophy,I believe that the feminist/N.V.D.A. faction is responsible for forcing the wedge of divide into the Peace Movement.How is it that actions that I might take are dismissed as macho where actions such as the Greenham fence pulling are heralded as demonstrations of a new spirit of womanhood.AREN'T WE JUST PEOPLE?Isn't anarchism the practice of self awareness,isn't pacifism the practice of self awareness,isn't feminism the practice of self awareness?WHERE IS THE PLACE FOR THE DIVISIONS THAT I FEEL ARE IMPOSED UPON ME AS AN INDIVIDUAL BY THOSE WHO ARE AFRAID OF THEIR OWN INDIVIDUALITY.I AM TIRED OF THE EXCLUSIVE GROUPS,TIRED OF THE WEDGES,TIRED OF BEING ALONE WHEN I FEEL TOGETHER.

I believe that it is time to AGREE amongst ourselves that DIVERSITY is DESIRABLE and that our various actions should be presented to the State AS A UNIFIED BLOCK.Might it not have been an act of generosity and love for the slogan to be 'Greenham PEOPLE are everywhere' and might it not have been MORE EFFECTIVE?Or is it too late to agree amongst ourselves?

I believe that it is time to diversify our actions,that we should form small groups who plan their own actions ranging from the now almost 'socially acceptable' form of vandalism,graffiti and super glue attacks,to the less acceptable ' vandalism' of bricks,paint bombs,wire cutters and matches.Now,I'm not so naive as to think that a paint bomb attack on an Army Recruitment office is going to bring the State to its knees,IT ISN'T.I do believe,however,that constant,widespread actions against ALL the institutions of the State could act as signals,or catalysts to a much broader dissent.Hand in hand with increased activity,there MUST be a wider distribution of information.If we sabotage a nuclear power station,we MUST make sure that as many people as possible know WHY.Of course we will have to be discreet,but the State MUST KNOW WHY IT IS BEING ATTACKED if it is to eventually fall.It is our job to INFORM ourselves of the workings of the State and to UNDO IT.We must match our actions with our intelligence and LET THEM KNOW THAT WE KNOW.Our art and our creativity are,I believe,our most powerful weapons.We must use that creativity to predict futures,we must start to prepare for a new world.No revolution is worthwhile unless there is a clear plan of what is desirable beyond it.Isn't it time to start stating WHAT WE'RE FIGHTING FOR?Isn't it time to start creating policies for debate concerning our future.We are so often forced into regression.We hide in our dark pits peering at the light far above us,isn't it time TO START REACHING FOR THAT LIGHT.

I AM NOT A WORM.

Now,perhaps,I have come to the hardest section of this article,the meanest test of my essentially pacifist nature.......... I believe that as the public become aware of the possibilities of real change,they will firstly passively support and then,given the right impetus,actively support the struggle.BUT the State,its agents and the agents of 'friendly' States,(hence the need for an international movement),will NOT be prepared to stand by and allow the people the freedom that they demand,but by then the people will not only have glimpsed that freedom,THEY WILL NOT BE SATISFIED UNTIL THEY HAVE ACHIEVED IT.So,for those of us who were a part of the great Peace Movement revival of the late 70s,who at that time were able to believe the purist pacifist theories of the earlier Peace Movement,there will be posed the crucial question....DO WE FIGHT ON?DO WE FIGHT ON OR DO WE SUBMIT TO THE INEVITABLE BARBARITY WITH WHICH THE STATE WILL REACT TO A REVOLUTIONARY SITUATION?If the Peace Movement is truly a Peace Movement it CAN NOT AND WILL NOT TOLERATE THE EXISTENCE OF THE STATE IN ANY FORM WHAT-EVER BECAUSE TO DO SO WOULD BE TO ACCEPT THAT IT IS NOT ACTUALLY PEACE THAT WE SEEK,BUT A MERE SENSE OF SECURITY,A SENSE OF SECURITY CONTROLLED BY THE STATE.By seeking REAL peace,just as by seeking an end to sexual role play,we are seeking REVOLUTION because BY NO OTHER MEANS WILL OUR DEMANDS BE MET.

I believe that there will come a time when we are no longer confronted by the 'thin blue line',but by the fat khaki one,that is,I believe that the Peace Movement is by its demands creating a climate that will inevitably blossom into CIVIL WAR.I believe that ALL members of the Peace Movement,be they leftist,rightist,feminist,pacifist,militant etc. are contributing to a situation THAT WILL LEAD TO BLOODSHED,AND THAT IF THAT MOVEMENT IS TO SUCCEED IN ITS STATED AIMS,IT WILL LEAD TO MORE AND MORE BLOODSHED.It is no good pretending that this isn't the case,IT ALWAYS HAS BEEN THE CASE,AND ALWAYS WILL BE.So,as a pacifist I am actually directly contributing to a situation that essentially contradicts everything that I believe.Catch 22.

As a pacifist WILL I BE PREPARED TO PASSIVELY STAND BY AND WATCH OUR LONG STRUGGLE DESTROYED BY THE UNCARING CYNICISM OF THE STATE?Isn't our years of hard work TOO PRECIOUS to be given away without a fight?By the acts that I have thus far involved myself in I HAVE ALREADY DETERMINED THAT ONE DAY IN THE FUTURE I HAVE PLACED SOMEONE'S FINGER ON THE TRIGGER,WILL IT BE MINE?When the time comes,pacifist or not,I believe that I SHALL BE RESPONSIBLE,AS SHALL WE ALL,FOR THE INEVITABLE SITUATION OF WAR IN WHICH WE FIND OURSELVES.We will be faced with the dilemma of whether or not we fight beside those who believe that it is their moral responsibility to do so.IS IT NOT THE CASE THAT IF WE ARE CONTRIBUTING TO THAT POSSIBILITY,WHICH WE INDISPUTABLY ARE,WE WILL BE MORALLY RESPONSIBLE TO SEE IT THROUGH?PERHAPS THIS CONFRONTATION WON'T HAPPEN IN MY LIFETIME,BUT THAT DOESN'T ALTER MY RESPONSIBILITY IN HAVING CREATED IT.MY FINGER OR YOUR FINGER?WHAT'S THE DIFFERENCE?IT IS OUR SHARED STRUGGLE AND WE ARE ALL MUTUALLY RESPONSIBLE FOR ITS OUTCOME.So,when the time comes,I accept that I will have played a part in creating a situation of armed confrontation.IF I FIND MY FINGER ON THE TRIGGER,WILL I PULL IT?THAT IS A QUESTION THAT I CAN NOT AND WILL NOT ANSWER.I categorically KNOW that if the world isn't destroyed by the State,THERE WILL COME A TIME OF REVOLUTION,I CATEGORICALLY KNOW THAT ALL OF US IN THE PEACE MOVEMENT WILL HAVE CONTRIBUTED TO THAT REVOLUTION.I CATEGORICALLY DO NOT KNOW WHETHER OR NOT I WOULD BE PREPARED TO PULL THE TRIGGER AND IN THAT,AND THAT ALONE THERE IS A SPARK OF LIGHT THAT RISES FAR BEYOND ANYTHING THAT THIS ARTICLE HAS TOUCHED UPON.BECAUSE I DO NOT KNOW WHETHER OR NOT I WOULD PULL THAT TRIGGER I HAVE,I BELIEVE,MAINTAINED INTACT OUR MOST HUMAN AND ESSENTIAL ELEMENTS.... CHOICE AND HOPE.I hope that one day I might be able to create a philosophy that does not include suffering and pain,that gives us ALL dignity and integrity and I hope that we will all choose to take that option.For the while,my sense of reality precludes such possibilities,but I shall continue to look elsewhere,IN HOPE.

How very far removed from what I KNOW is right and decent and life-loving this all seems,yet now,apart from ignoring that sense of life,can I honestly perceive the outcome of our struggle in another light?

In love,peace and hope,a member of CHAOS.

Red leb. Black leb. Sticky black.

Greg Bull

At some point somebody we knew must have introduced us to the delights of smoking. Anarchy wasn't all about being miserable and trying to smash the system. There were almost moments of pure unabated joy and laughter relaxation. Fun. A laugh.

Its probably one of the reasons why we never actually got round to smashing the system. Or introducing a fair and free society. A lot of the time the anarchists I tried to engage with were just so dour and so.

Oppressed.

You know? All the time.

But there were those who would have a laugh on the quiet. And those who were quite happy to take drugs. Relax and smoke some hash.

Not smoking fags.

Weed. Hash. Gear. Stuff. Resin. Oil.

For me it was in the park with J.

She was the first person who did this. She was older than me. Nice. Kind. Took me under her wing. Gentle. We must have sat and she must have rolled the joint. Must have been happening to us all around the same time. Independent of each other.

She sat rolling.

Me watching.

Taking the tobacco from a cigarette. Later a male J taught me you need to roast the tobacco first by running a Clipper along under the cigarette and gently burn the paper. You then had to put the cigarette in your mouth and blow through it.

Apparently this technically removed all the harmful shit that they had put in cigarettes to kill the poor. It was all a conspiracy to kill the poor. Everything was aimed at killing the poor.

Us down in Happy Valley on the Racecourse. Away from prying eyes.

In the sunshine. In the sun. Sun hung golden globe suspended in the blue. Shining. Beautiful azure blue sky like sea. Us chatting and talking. How we discovered the smoke. The cannabis. And I peered closer as she sprinkled in some stuff she had heated with a lighter and then crumbled it like Oxo cubes onto the tobacco. Whatever it was gave off a strong smell and a wisp of smoke which she chased into her mouth smiling. Offered to blow the smoke into my lungs but I shook my head no. She was careful to evenly spread the crumbled Oxo up and down the full length of the tobacco which was carefully laid out on three Rizlas all stuck together.

Blue Rizlas. Thinnest skins she had confided in me earlier in the tobacconists on St Giles Street. Blue papers are thinner. More smoke from the hash and less from the paper. So she sprinkles the Oxo cube in and spreads it out carefully with a finger. Taking great care. Red leb? No idea. The names were probably made up I think. By dealers. To make it sound more exotic. Like it needed that frisson of added glamour when there was the whole danger associated with breaking the law in public. Red leb. Red processed cannabis resin in a block from the Lebanon. Afghan black. And the rest. All shipped over. Smuggled. Travelled thousands of miles in soaps. Blocks. A block of cannabis resin was called a soap. Or its what I was told. Once saw eight soaps in a dealer's house. Worth about eight grand. Bricks of cannabis. When eight grand could buy you a house. Sometimes the soaps had a kind of stamp or seal on them. Quality control? Or proof of production? Advertising?

So J is rolling the joint and she fashions a roach out of the top right hand corner of the inside of her Marlboro packet. We all smoked Marlboro in those days. Made you cough. Stink. Strong. Made up rough joints. Harsh throat burners. Naive I guess. So she looks up from her work and smiles that warm crushing smile at me. Happy. She has finished her work and made the joint in a slow and methodical process. A ritual. Always rituals. She lights the end and inhales the smoke drawing deeply the red lit end flaring and the paper burning and crackling the tobacco. She draws deep and long. I rock on my heels a little. Excitement. Nervous. But no. Not nervous. Never was nervous in those days. Before. Never felt much fear then. Indestructible. So she inhales. Takes long puffs. The end glows brighter.

Glowing. And she passes it to me exhaling telling me not to hog it or waste any or let it burn down as that's just plain bad manners. Etiquette.

I inhale thinking the world was about to become Day-Glo and psychedelic and that everything would be changed and I would be on some mind-bending acid trip seeing colours and lights and hearing sounds and seeing visions. But nothing happens. I mean very little. Close to nothing. Normal tobacco rush as we hadn't learnt then how to burn out the tobacco to remove whatever we started to remove in bongs or joints later on. The rush hits the back of my head just like normal. Smoke rushes into my lungs. Burns my throat. Eyes water. A bit. Strong choking smoke. Hits my throat again. Hard.

J is a punk. Not just a normal spiky haired type of punk. An anarchist punk. Vegan. Dressed in black. Before the hair style became dreadlocked and backcombed. Black spiky hair. Layers of black clothes hiding her body shape. Probably a statement I was missing. A set of signifiers. Floating chain of meanings.

She goes on hunt sabs. Stops hunters chasing foxes. She's brave. Braver than I will ever be. No animal products and no makeup tested on animals. Mostly stolen from The Body Shop.

J doesn't live at home. She roughs it on sofas in between bedsits and signing on. We are all signing on one way or another. Most of us. Some turning down the government's blood money and begging. I cant see the difference. But then that's me. Everyone's on the dole. Signing on. Income support or whatever it was called. Tuesday morning at the Dole Office was like a party. See the punks down there passed out sometimes. Sometimes we go there first thing on a Tuesday morning after Monday Night's party at the Regent having stayed up all night. Old men. Middle aged men. Well dressed women. All signing on the line to claim their two weeks' benefits. Some arguments. Some hope. Mostly despair. But for us young it's more money to go to gigs. Drink at parties. Go to the pub. Buy the latest albums. Maybe some old clothes from a charity shop. Its life. And we live it. Free money from the State. Taking their handouts and pretending to stick two fingers up to them behind their back.

But J is an anarchist punk. She listens to Crass. Sometimes Siouxsie. Sometimes Discharge. Sometimes Flux. Has a Flux symbol stencilled onto the back of her black heavy cotton jacket. And she isn't scared of anyone or anything. She's a punk through and through. She dyes her hair. Now it's half red half green. Now it's blue. Now it's black. Sometimes it blonde and sometimes we cuddle. Nothing rude or sexual. When we part she always gives me a huge kiss on the cheek leaving a large kiss mark in bright red/orange/black/brown/white or whatever colour she's wearing that day to match her hair and her mood. She does this so my mum can see it. It amuses J every time. She gets on ok with my mum. My mum gets on ok with everyone. Shiny spiky punk rockers, hard faced skinheads, long haired hippy types, mock-bikers, and all the rest of the tribes who pass through our house on a regular basis. My parents are pretty alright really. On the balance of it. They put up with the endless trail of us coming and going. They even make tea for me mates when I'm not there. Its a big roundhouse on the corner of Abington Avenue and Holly Road. Still there. Beautiful place.

J laughs when I blush. She teases me when I look sheepish after a kiss and sometimes kisses me again. Throws her head back laughing so full of life. Her face and head silhouetted against the blue sky. Framed. And she exhales passing me the joint telling me to inhale hard as I can and hold the smoke there for as long as I can. At least to count to ten. The first time I do this I hold my breath for a second or two before I have to let it out.

Throat burned.

And she smiles and laughs at me gently teasing. Puts her hand on my leg. Strokes it in a friendly way and encourages me to do it again. I manage a bit more successfully the second and third times feeling proud of myself. And I hand her back the joint happy that I am in control and that no drugs is going to interfere with my control.

Must have control.

We lie down next to each other and stare up at the clouds in the sky. This is warm. This is nice. We are safe here together. Lying next to each other like children playing sardines. Its sweet. Someone would say. One day long time away from now. Like two lovers the joint is gone and we lie down each deep in our own thoughts. Must think. Must think. Stay in

control. She's. We aren't and never were. Should hold her now? Is this? Anyhow. No. Not now. Not right. And I find myself wearing a huge grin.
So we lie there silent and stare at the clouds scudding across the sky. Listening to the occasional hover fly or other insect. Feeling the warm grass across the back of my neck. I am happy then. Warm and alive. She is so close I can smell her body and her hair slightly sweaty. Not dirty. Just not clean. But a warm animal musky sensual human smell inviting me to. No. Like a leather. You know?

We go to punk gigs together on the bus sometimes or on a train or just walk there. And I spike up my hair for these. And it's not long before I will bleach it myself but just not quite yet. Still need mum's approval. Still need her love. Nowtime. When we go to London J looks after me. We wandered up the Kings Road and watched the other punks visually busking. Lost generation again. Not war this time though. Some punks. Discharge punks leather jackets. Exploited punks with huge Mohicans and plastic punk trousers on and ready made t-shirts and bondage trousers. So what. Saw Aaron there bleached blonde hair. Leather jacket. Shrugging. Indifferent. Posing for the tourists. Earning a few quid. Lost and alone. Or liberated and free depending on your point of view. Teenage runaways sleeping rough. Anarchy. Becoming black and white histories years later. Photos of a lost youth now in a book. Leaves of paper turned over page by page as the faces of the not quite blank generation peer out or across. Indifferent. Some angry. Some smiling. Some anxious. Some scared. The photographers knew. Some more than others. They knew this was to be history one day whilst the punks pranced and preened. Some leering for the tourists. Giving them a good shot. Whilst others stood staring vacantly into space. Their own pose. J and I wandered through them all. Occasionally getting a nod of recognition for being a part of their tribe. J was mostly oblivious to it all.

So this is stoned I thought. Whats it like? Warm happy. Like tipsy. Like slightly drunk. But without that bloated beer feeling. J does speed sometimes. The punks like speed. J does downers sometimes. Slurring her words. Like shes going to die. And we half carry her to the BHS cafe and pump her full of their cheap tea and walk her around. The old ladies often share their tea with us or give us half a cake or a sandwich. The old ladies know J is on something but shes so infectious they don't care. More worried for these waifs and strays.

Maybe they remember being young? Maybe they are jealous? SO we sit with them and drink tea. And most of the punks are kind and caring and thoughtful. Animal rights/Human rights. One struggle one fight. We aren't the monsters from off the telly. We are the real young people thinking we can change the world. Its going to happen. Like next month or something. Not like the caricatures they show on the telly. The plastic punks all gobbing and spitting. I never spat at a gig in my life. Never spat at a person. Only ever saw much spitting at a Damned concert in Brixton. Punk kit bought from Acme. Nothing wrong with it. Expression. Seeing adverts of Leo and Wilf looking so fucking cool you would die to be their friends. SO J is on downers and slurring her words and I really think shes going to die. Its nearly five oclock and its just her and me now and i get her to drink about four cups of tea. And then I take her arm and help her up and we walk around the Grosvenor Centre looking for help. And I see a friendly face and borrow 50p from it to by J some real orange juice. I read real orange juice can bring you down off drugs. But I'm not sure which ones. Acid I think. But she hasn't taken acid. Anyhow. Cant do any harm. Maybe it will help get rid of the poisons in her veins from the downers. So I hope.

Why the fuck has she done this? Does she want to die? It isn't for attention I realised years later. She was way too happy. Or was that just a veneer? She acts like shes going to shut down now. Eyes are closing heavy-lidded. And we lay next to each other on the Racecourse and look up into the blue just drifting along on a spinning blue planet filled with wonder and awe. And the beetles crawl through the grass and I feel so connected to the planet. Like I am a part of it and the warm happy feeling swells up in my stomach and my groin. Just feeling myself gently slipping into what Alan Moore will call The Green in a few years. And when I close my eyes it feels like I am moving slightly. Just gently floating. Just ever so slightly. Not really but there is a definite feeling of movement.

But before back then before J was going to die. I felt sure of that. And not knowing what to do my balls clenched up and tight with fear. Real fear. I wanted to shit myself badly. Let that out. Scared. Real fear.
We had walked to the graveyard together me dragging her now she barely able to stand. And I have tears in my eyes. Panicking. I don't know what to do. Tell the police? Take her to hospital? Its only a five minute walk to the hospital but they will bust her for sure there wont

they? I don't want to search her for drugs. I don't want anything to do with drugs. They fuck you up.

So I sit her down in the graveyard on a gravestone and begin to implore her. Plead with her not to give up. Not now. Not here. We need to be fighting J. We need to do this. Dont give up on me. Dont fucking run away. Theres too much left to do. Too much fight left in us. In you. In all of us. Come on. Whos the enemy J? No really who is the enemy? Thatcher? Reagan. The police? Carter? Doesnt matter who was president then. We were fighting them. Or we thought we were. Peace camps. Real people like us fighting them. Real anarchists living in their tents promoting peace J whilst you are here dying. Not in my arms yet. Just sitting there. Life slipping away. How are we going to smash this system if you aren't here with me. By my side. Helping me. Teaching me. Showing me those black and white record sleeves covered with densely packed and tiny writing telling me whats wrong with it all and how to change it and what to believe.

Fight war not wars.

Destroy power not people.

Endless slogans and rhymes meaning everything and nothing. There is no authority but yourself. And the police. And the state. And your parents. And your lover. And everything and everywhere. We are all being ruled J and we need freedom. Come back to me.

J is an anarchist punk rocker. She's taking the out option and pressing the off button. But the reality was that she wasn't. Her breathing steadied and she smiled at me and managed to stumble and blurt out some words to the effect of you silly silly boy I'm just tired. And she stroked my cheek with her hand and held it and cradled it looking deep into my eyes. And she sheds a tear or two herself and tells me that its all going to be alright and that shes going to take me on a hunt sab next weekend out at Oundle and we can take a picnic. And she asks me to watch her whilst she takes a short sleep and that when she wakes up it will all be ok. And she smiles that smile at me again and I blush. Feeling a bit stupid. Awkward. And so innocent. And as she drifts off into a snooze she tells me we will always keep fighting as long as there is breath in our lungs.

And I never did enough fighting. And then I am back on the Racecourse lying next to J and we are stoned. Well. I am pretty stoned. Everything just seems so more friendly and comfortable. Like I haven't lost all my worries but that they don't matter now. And that Now is all that matters and that Now will be for ever. Because Now must be forever. And that it will all be alright. Everything is just fine. And that the revolution will come soon. And the people will throw off their shackles and we will march on London peacefully and soldiers will put down their weapons and the police will join us and we will all hold hands like black clad hippies and surround parliament who will come out and greet us joyously and embrace us and a new day will dawn filled with hope and optimism. And I smile and turn my head to look at J and she is beautiful. And I look at the patches on her arm. Conflict. Crass. Discharge. Part 1. Rudimentary Peni. And they look beautiful as well. Its all beautiful and warm and cosy. And there isn't a breath of wind down here in the Happy Valley. A dog barks far away. Children's voices drift to us from the playground and she turns to face me. A look of.

What?

On her face.

We talk occasionally about things now. Half conversations which lead nowhere and mean very little. Just feeling right for the first time. Like it all makes sense. Like I am warm on the inside and cool to the touch. Just right. Its a bit hard to stand up. A bit wobbly at the knees. Weak knees. Ordinary things and thoughts seem funny and I giggle a little. A bit like an idiot. We must have looked a picture of modern love. We both crack up at stupid things. Just me and J together kind of half stumbling across the park looking at the sad faces of the sad people with their sad lives knowing we will never become robots like them. And we manage to get closer to my house and sit down again smiling and laughing watching the children in the playground. No mums. No dads. Children living their life with true freedom. With danger. With excitement. Falling over. Falling off. Like us. Like the hippies who now wear black. Living with danger and freedom. Freedom to do what though? But that doesn't matter.

And we chase down the joint with a fag to get that nicotine rush to enhance the cannabis glow. We share it. Going twos. We take off the filter to maximise the rush. Precarious. And the children all go home for tea. To their meat and two veg. And a part of us despairs for the poor dead animals. But its alright we don't eat them.

So we sit on the swings and come down gradually after an hour or so. And I feel ok to walk home and communicate. We chat and make our goodbyes and say our farewells to this glorious afternoon and we hug and she kisses me on the cheek as we embrace. And I can smell her body and her hair and its warm and fuzzy. A slight animal smell. I will see her later down The Slipper in Jimmys End. There's a punk band on tonight and the punks will be there.

And I walk home.

And I open the door and walk in.

And I say hello to my mum and give her a big hug.

And she looks at me and spits on a hanky and wipes the lipstick from my cheek.

And I act normal.

And I go for a lie down on my bed and fall fast asleep in an instant.

Am I an Anarchist? A Tale of Anarcho Curiosity

Russ Bestley

My first encounters with punk were similar to many others of my generation. Growing up in a small town in the middle of Kent, exposure to the revolutionary new phenomenon that was apparently all the rage in London in the summer of 1976 was limited to reading the shocking reports in my Mum and Dad's News Of The World. That, and the dramatic stories passed around like secret codes by a couple of the slightly older kids at school who read the Melody Maker and New Musical Express and therefore considered themselves pretty up there with the latest musical developments that were apparently largely passing us by thirty miles away in the capital. As a fourteen year old, such snippets of information were certainly intriguing, especially combined with my Mum's outrage at what was happening to the youth of the country, but it was still something of a distant phenomenon. Obviously, some of that was set to change by the end of the year – the Ramones, Sex Pistols and the Damned released records for a start, and it became possible (though still a little difficult) to actually hear some of this stuff on the radio if you searched hard enough. Stuart Henry's Street Heat on Radio Luxembourg was something of a clandestine newsreel for me, though I wasn't to discover John Peel until a little later. It's strange to think, with the benefit of hindsight and a modicum of maturity, that in fact our town was playing at least a small part in the birth of punk in the years and months leading up to the long hot summer of 1976 – Sid Vicious had lived two streets away from where I grew up, Joe Strummer visited friends in the town regularly during his 101ers days, at least one member of 999 lived locally, as did one of the Mark Perry's early collaborators on Sniffin' Glue, Rick Brown – credited in SG#1 as "Rick Brown from Tunbridge Wells (Kent's answer to Detroit)." Even punk face Shane MacGowan, of Nipple Erectors and later Pogues fame, was born in the same hospital as me in the late 1950s – who knew our humble little town was so, well, rock 'n' roll?

Records were passed around our group of friends with an increasingly anorakish approach to subcultural style (and I don't just mean the future Undertones fans), though for many that still meant Genesis, Deep Purple, Queen, ELP or (God forbid) Yes would be doing the rounds rather than this exciting sounding but still rather distant 'punk' stuff. Chart success for punk artists during 1977 changed all that – the Stranglers were to become my own main attraction and I pursued their releases with some vigour, and it soon became possible to see and hear other punk and new wave bands on Top Of The Pops (step forward X Ray Spex, Adverts, Saints, the Jam, the Stranglers, Generation X, Boomtown Rats, Skids, Elvis Costello, UK Subs, Siouxsie & the Banshees, Damned, Members, Eddie & the Hot Rods). Our local record shops were limited to the Rediffusion television rental and repair shop (which stocked a few chart singles), Boots the Chemist and a couple of established independents that were more concerned with prog rock than is strictly healthy and didn't exactly jump onto the punk bandwagon too quickly, despite the business potential. Luckily, at least the punk albums that had started making inroads into the charts were available in my Mum's Freemans mail order catalogue and I could pay in weekly installments, so that became a source of vinyl news and information.

Anyway, I digress. What I'm driving at, I think, is the process by which I, and many others like me in small towns, villages (and, I would guess, cities) adopted the punk subculture and began to establish our own take on the complex system of codes and conventions within it. That meant making a lot of mistakes, being 'uncool' from time to time when we misread the rules and (anti)social etiquette, buying records (and shirts, and trousers, and shoes...) that we would later regret and try to pretend had never existed, stumbling forward and growing up with a 'punk' identity. We weren't exactly sure whether we were supposed to swear and spit all the time, or just at punk gigs, or maybe in the park when we were hanging around being, you know, punks. Were we supposed to wear bondage trousers, leather jackets or swastikas? Was one local lad's predilection for dressing up in an original German SS officer's uniform a good idea (probably not)? There didn't seem to be anyone around to tell us the rules, and we were making them up as we went along. Pretending to be bored, 'rejecting authority' whatever that meant, a bit of petty vandalism, trying to find out the latest punk news and punk trends, nicking ethanol and chloroform from the school chemistry labs (for the purpose of drinking, sniffing and/or playing 'hilarious' tricks on others that would count as violent assault in any other context), it was all part of our regular day to day existence. Along with, in my case, going to school, working part time as a cleaner in the local hospital and delivering the football pools with my Dad and my brother (which at least covered the weekly installments on my growing punk rock record collection).

And then came anarcho punk. Obviously it wasn't actually called that at the time – it was just one of the many developments and fragmented spin-offs from the same root cause. New wave, post punk, hardcore, anarcho punk, new punk, real punk, oi!, progressive punk – whatever the journalists were trying to call these new genres, to all intents and purposes we all saw them as beneath the same broad umbrella that was 'punk'. I bought a few anarcho punk records – partly encouraged by the low prices I would think as much as the contents, since money was limited and I couldn't afford to buy too many each week. They weren't on coloured vinyl, which was a shame, so sometimes the latest release from X Ray Spex, UK Subs, the Lurkers, Generation X, the Dickies or whoever would take precedent for obvious reasons, but I had a few future anarcho 'classics' in the collection, some of which I even quite liked – Bloody Revolutions (and particularly Persons Unknown), Big A Little A... not as good as the Stranglers, or Dead Kennedys, or PiL, or Gang of Four, or Mekons, or Killing Joke, but not bad nonetheless. I left school in 1981 and moved to Portsmouth – supposedly to go to Polytechnic, having secured a last minute clearing place on a Mechanical Engineering course. It was an excuse to get away from home, my twin brother had already got a place on his course (coincidentally also in Portsmouth), and we both got full maintenance grants from the government. Free money. I lasted less than two months at college. My excuse has always been that I didn't get on, and being taken to one side by one of the tutors to be told that my green hair and painted leather jacket was influencing other students to take drugs didn't really enamour me to the place. All true (the tutor's comments, not the drug dealing), but on reflection and with the benefit of hindsight, I was an awkward sod with an attitude problem and if I was in their shoes I wouldn't have been too happy either. Still, I got to blow my entire student grant on records, which was great until I ran out of food.

The transition to becoming an anarcho punk (in all but name) was, then, a subtle one. I had drifted into buying a few anarcho records, and I got to see a few of the bands who were beginning to make up this new strand of punk, but at the same time a lack of money, a slowly developing sense of personal politics and an increasing awareness of the wider world around me were shaping my identity. Certainly my engagement with the local Student Union in Portsmouth was a bit of an eye-opener. I got a 'job' as a humper for visiting bands (a bit like a roadie but far less glamorous), at the Poly and the bigger local venues – the Guildhall and Locarno; carrying amps, speakers and lighting rigs into the venue first thing in the morning then carrying it all back out again in the early hours of the next morning. I also learnt to DJ, becoming a regular fixture at the Friday night Alternative Disco that attracted many local (non-student) punks. The politics of the Student Union itself provided a steep learning curve – being publicly reprimanded for calling my brother a cunt provided an introduction to 'feminism', and the difficulties the SU management had with local National Front supporters provided a lesson in both the left and right of the political spectrum (and, to an extent, the problems therein on both sides of that great divide).

Portsmouth itself was also undergoing some radical changes. The city suffered from increasingly high levels of unemployment as Thatcher's economic policies hardened up, and the build-up and execution of the Falklands conflict was felt very, very close to home, since this was the home port for the Task Force and many families in the area were linked to the military. It was all very well taking a stand against this unjust war from the safety of your home town in the suburbs or out in the sticks in the west country, it was another thing to face it in public in a city where it felt like 99% of the population had strong personal and political views in support of government action and where thousands would turn out at the harbour entrance to send the ships off and (hopefully) welcome them home. Local protest, then, was slightly muted by a fear for personal safety and the desire to avoid a good kicking.

Amidst all this, and following my 'leaving' college, I moved across the harbour to Gosport (which, for anyone who doesn't know it, is kind of like a downmarket version of Portsmouth, if that doesn't stretch the imagination too far) with my girlfriend, Cherry – who had dropped out from Art College around the same time. We set up house in a rundown rented terrace, complete with one single hot water tap from an electric heater in the kitchen and an outside toilet at the end of the garden. Now officially 'unemployed', we signed on – though we both continued to work at venues in Portsmouth humping equipment for cash in hand, and I carried on with my DJ stint at the Poly. Now justifiably (in our own minds, at least) part of the vast unemployed scrapheap caused directly by Thatcher and her nazi government (rather than through our own choice or stupidity, naturally), we could begin to legitimately take part in the anarchist punk scene on our own terms and our own merit. I became vegetarian, then vegan. I dyed all my clothes black. I got a puppy, a lunatic mongrel called Merlin, who proceeded to shit all over the house and eat anything that wasn't nailed down or locked behind closed doors – carrier bags, loaves of bread, bags of sugar, socks, carpets, furniture. I would cynically go to sign on every two weeks knowing that hundreds of others just like me were doing exactly the same thing, all innocent victims of the oppressive capitalist state. Do they owe us a living? Of course they fucking do!

I went to loads of gigs – working at the local venues ensured a free pass to pretty much anything of interest, and knowing some of the road crews meant I could sometimes sneak in backstage after bunking the train up to London and hanging around in the pissing rain outside the Lyceum or wherever, knocking the door and insisting for the seventeenth time that Monty or Baz or whoever had promised to put me on the guest list when they played Portsmouth two weeks earlier. I followed Poison Girls around for a while, and saw the Mob, Zounds, Subhumans and others on the circuit, though my tastes were catholic – one week an anarcho gig in a local community centre, the next the Stranglers at the Rainbow, Killing Joke at the Lyceum or Vice Squad at the Poly. And, still working on the local gig circuit, Motörhead, Saxon, Iron Maiden, Stiff Little Fingers, the Clash, Thin Lizzy, David Essex, Dr Hook, Chris De Burgh or the Nolans at the Guildhall. Some of those not strictly through choice, naturally.

My political 'awakening' happened slowly and erratically. I bought and listened to some of the new Crass Records releases, though some I enjoyed far more than others to be honest. I read the lengthy texts on some of the sleeves, along with fanzines picked up at gigs or sent with mail order records and tapes. I was interested enough to want to find out more, so I bought a copy of George Woodcock's The Anarchist Reader to try to get my head around it all. Like the anarcho punk music itself, I found some of the essays intriguing and some entertaining, while others were dense, boring and unreadable. I'd grown up, in punk terms, with the Stranglers, X Ray Spex, Damned, Sex Pistols, Rezillos, Skids, Undertones, Wire and dozens of others who could construct a simple message and carry it across with a catchy tune. The anarcho punk bands that I liked carried on in that manner, marrying a bit of politics to a decent melody, and the anarchist or libertarian texts that I engaged with and understood were probably more in the tradition of the great writers and satirists (from Wilde to Orwell) than the turgid theory of Marx and his mates. My dalliance with anarchism was perhaps more tentative than others – less anarcho punk stalwart, more 'anarcho curious'. That doesn't mean that many of the core principles of this new form of popular/populist anarchism didn't strike a chord – a sense of fairness and equality, respect toward other human beings, pacifism, a questioning of authority, direct action and self-assertion all seemed like pretty good ideas to me. In retrospect, I also recognise that those 'values' are pretty widespread beyond any kind of 'anarchist' identity – I remember having a long conversation with a nun on the London/Portsmouth train, after she asked about my views (presumably as a self-identifying 'punk rocker') and tried to persuade me that I was, in fact, a Christian, even if I didn't know it.

I guess from the outside the next few years of my life may have seemed pretty anarchic, if not anarchistic. I lived in a couple of squats, until I was evicted by the owner's (fresh out of prison) 'security' team – one of those old fashioned evictions that didn't bother with bailiffs or the police, just a small gang of men with baseball bats in the middle of the night – and I ended up living on an old fishing boat out in the middle of the harbour. The boat was owned by a local family of travellers who lived on a disused ammunition barge moored behind a chemical plant. Interestingly, this led to a few encounters with the Harbour Police: being boarded by the boys in blue was a whole new experience for me – sun, sea and piracy and all that. Eventually, after a long, cold and uncomfortable few months, that situation became impossible and I ended up living in a housing co-operative, in a condemned property scheduled for demolition to make way for a new supermarket. The supposed political ideals of an early 80s band of ex-squatters who had managed to set up a co-operative that was officially sanctioned by the City Council proved quite an eye-opener in the long run, and my cynicism toward middle class liberals masquerading as 'socialists' deepened. My frustration grew in direct correlation to the aspirations of certain co-op members to ingratiate themselves with senior figures in the local Labour party while at the same time maintaining something of an unspoken exclusion zone for genuinely desperate homeless locals to gain entry to their empty houses – apparently they weren't the 'right sort' of people to be part of a housing co-operative, and a variety of rather well-to-do student friends of the 'committee' were a far better proposition.

Of course, life moves on and things change over time. Following an acrimonious split from the housing co-op and a shambolic period living in very short-stay temporary accommodation, on floors and sofas, I ended up working in a record shop, having a family and being rehoused by the City Council on the Leigh Park estate outside the city. It's a long story with many ups and downs, and it doesn't need expanding on here – the key thing at this point I think is to look back at my 1980s experience and to consider what (if anything) it meant, and how, or whether, my engagement with anarcho punk (or anarchism) affected me subsequently. Certainly my views remained – and remain – broadly libertarian, and my mistrust of both Left and Right is still deep-seated, though I would probably identify more closely with the old Left nowadays (when it had principles and championed the rights of workers, rather that the Labour party's post-1990s model of neoliberal capitalism).

So where does that leave my 'anarcho punk' experience? Was it a brief flirtation with a 'political' movement, a natural diversion for an ongoing punk participant, or just a part of growing up and discovering new and 'radical' ideas, much as generations did before and after? Perhaps it's all of those things in some way or another – and I'm guessing it's not too dissimilar from many other stories from many other people who lived through the same period. It's been interesting in recent years to observe punk growing old(er) and reflecting upon itself, through books, magazines, exhibitions, television programmes, countless anniversaries and landmark events.

The 80s punk generation seem to be having their turn now, in the same way that the 70s punks held the limelight a decade ago – that re-evaluation of punk's evolution is welcome and long overdue, though I have to say (as a first wave/second wave punk fence-sitter) that the subsequent and increasingly dogmatic punk 'rule book' approach to authenticity sits uneasily with my passion for the original subculture in all its messy variety (and its lack of bloody rules – for me, one of the main attractions in the first place).

I think we are all a product of our history, our locality and our culture, and certainly punk – and anarcho punk – provided me with an awful lot of character-building experiences: though perhaps it is a broader sense of direct action, independence, critical awareness and self-reliance that has held sway far more than an allegiance to any particular political or ideological doctrine. Equally, I am still no fan of social etiquette, particularly when it strays into the realm of what constitute 'acceptable' beliefs and opinions, and I continue to take something of an oppositional view when I'm told that there are things that I am not allowed to do (or say, or think). That, to me, embraces all aspects of whatever 'punk' was, or is, in my terms. To paraphrase Johnny, "Am I an antichrist? Am I an anarchist?" – well, I'm still not sure, though I am certain that as I get older, I don't really get too hung up about it any longer.

Mindful Token Tantrums/Anarcho in Action

Darren Johns

"At 18 our convictions are hills from which we look, at 45 they are caves in which we hide"

F Scott Fitzgerald

It may be a '60s hippy conceit, but we are all connected: by ideas, words, music, culture, other people and otherness. Like thousands before and after me, my very first experience of connecting with anarcho-punk was through Crass.

The year would have been 1981, I was about 13 years old and had been into punk rock since I'd reached double figures. The Undertones, The Skids, SLF and Sex Pistols were my favourites. Lurking somewhere over there, in the half-light, away from all the leather, bristles, studs and acne, were Crass. A mysterious, cloaked entity that was catnip to young, impressionable punks who were drawn to the dark side like me. The more I read about Crass, the less I seemed to know, and the more I yearned to hear them (no internet insta-click'n'listen in those days).

I asked my dad if he would buy me the 'Stations Of The Crass' album because you had to be over 18 to purchase it in the Virgin record shop on Armada Way in Plymouth town centre. He refused. I cried. He relented. I listened. I didn't quite understand it, I was a little afraid of it, but I fucking loved it. From that moment (to this moment) I was a bona-fide anarcho-punk. Albeit one with terrible, terrible hair.

Despite loving the music from the get-go, I only began to understand the concept of free-thinking, anarchist philosophy, radical feminism and animal liberation a couple years later, fuelled chiefly by A Flux Of Pink Indians, Rudimentary Peni and Conflict, who seemed to clarify the parts of Crass that I couldn't quite grasp. Simultaneously, the Subhumans, Poison Girls and the Dead Kennedys were giving voice to my sense of personal growth with their more considered, yet no less revolutionary, approach.

I began reading up on all the influential anarchists of the past two hundred years: Peter Kropotkin, Pierre-Joseph Proudhon, Mikhail Bakunin, Errico Malatesta, Emma Goldman, Noam Chomsky. All the while, the magnitude of global cruelty, suffering and injustice that I was being exposed to was something that I found increasingly hard to cope with. Very few, if any, teenagers I knew were going through the same apocalyptic epiphany.

I started to suffer from depression when I was about 15 (although I wouldn't know it as depression until ten years later, and wouldn't be diagnosed for another three years after that). I'd surrounded myself, figuratively and literally, with harrowing images from record sleeves like MDC's 'Multi Death Corporations' and Conflict's 'To A Nation Of Animal Lovers'; immersed myself in the none-more-bleak existentialism of Rudimentary Peni's bitter ravings and The Mob's rampant pessimism; delved further into the unsettling yet still seemingly impenetrable psyche of Crass; joined animal rights groups; studied the invasion of Nicaragua; got fired up by Class War's distinct battle lines; had my male supremacy floored by strong women; had hunger myths debunked by Chumbawamba.

Essentially, my childhood innocence was deflowered by anarcho-punk. (Of course, all that overwhelming information and nihilist noise was enough to turn the most carefree of adolescent into a sullen, perma-frowning wreck, but I believe that my state of melancholy was destined to be, whether I was listening to Nick Blinko or Nik Kershaw.)

Mum was very worried. She was quite upset that I had a cut-out of Princess Diana hanging from a paper noose above my bed and that I would wear the shabbiest of black clothes ("We are the coffin-bearers of society," an anarcho buddy once said without a hint of jest) but was more concerned that I was so goddamn miserable. So, while my older, heavy metal-loving brother was aspiring to be a financial success and own a Porsche, I was suffocating under a crushing sense of helplessness.

(Footnote: I threw a pocket dictionary at my brother's head once for making a casual racist comment and tried to make him understand animal rights by reading him liner notes from a Flux single, to no avail. We both liked The Smiths and Spear Of Destiny though, so we had common ground. I think he even liked Chumbawamba's first album, probably because it had hummable tunes and nobody was telling him to turn vegetarian or throw dictionaries at his head.)

I think the reason I was as into Adam & The Ants and Tubeway Army as much as I was into Crass was a need for balance and pure escapism: be it the swashbuckling, Apache-appropriating Adam Ant (imagine the culture-theft uproar now!) or the dystopian android fetishism of Gary Numan. Worlds apart from Steve Ignorant, although Ignorant's love of David Bowie ties in nicely here.

Crass split up in 1984. I was 15. I know how fans of The Beatles and Take That must have felt when they split up because I felt like the bottom of my world had fallen out. I wrote a letter to Crass telling them how lost I felt without them. Joy de Vivre wrote a very sweet letter back, telling me that they would all still be active in their own ways, still making a difference, and that I should look to myself for answers. I still have the letter. It's all a little embarrassing looking back on it but I certainly wasn't the only one who felt that Crass were the glue holding my so-called life together.

But Joy was right. And, anyway, my sadness was rooted in something that I was too young to detect and that would become as much a part of me as my eye colour. It was during this time of despair that I met a kindred spirit at a record stall in Plymouth's open air market. He noticed The Mob in thick white lettering on the sleeve of my leather jacket (one step at a time!) and commented positively on it. A friendship was forged which led to four firsts: the first time I could open up to someone about how I was feeling; the first proper punk band that I'd be in; the first time I'd take part in direct action; and the first time I'd let someone down. Tim was my saviour. We formed a band called The Adult Crash (from the lyric to a Minor Threat song) with me on guitar/vocals and him on drums. No bass. Even though the Dead Kennedys were our blueprint, we ended up sounding like an amalgam of Antisect, Icons Of Filth and Rudimentary Peni. We put together about ten songs, taped a couple practices, never found a bassist, and never played a show. Still, it was the emotional release I needed.

Tim was a bit older than me, and a bit of a rebel too, and inevitably I was introduced to the concept of direct action, specifically criminal damage, and mainly in the furtherance of animal liberation/rights. We glued up butchers' locks, catapulted stones through abattoir truck windows, vandalised Rolls Royces, went on demos looking for trouble, sabotaged fox hunts, spray-painted the walls of anyone we deemed our enemies... It was thrilling, scary and the kind of political vent that I needed to cope with that crushing sense of helplessness.

In fact, I no longer felt helpless. I felt like someone fighting back and making a difference, however small. When we weren't conspiring to bring the state to its knees with Superglue and Black Widow catapults, Tim and I would go for drives or long walks or mushroom chow mein and he'd try and make sense of my

embryonic depression (not that he knew it was depression either), of my inability to rationalise or create some personal, mental place that didn't feel corrupted by world events. It didn't help when half the people who were writing the lyrics and liner notes to all my favourite anarcho records were equally as angsty, gloomy, neurotic, paranoid and confused as me. Thanks, Peni, Mob, Amebix – not quite the PMA [Positive Mental Attitude] that Bad Brains were singing about.

Still, me and Tim soldiered on, learning from each other, helping each other to grow, me the anarcho-apprentice (as he once jokingly referred to me) and him the anarcho-boss (ipso facto). Despite that ill-fated dynamic, he had a gentle way of explaining things that didn't leave me feeling empty or more confused.

One afternoon, my mum asked me if I was involved in the glueing up of butchers' locks in town. There had been a piece in the local paper about it. I said no, of course. She said that if she knew I'd been involved she'd shop me to the police. I think this was the moment when I knew that my lifestyle, my politics, my music and my activities were something never to share with my parents, or anyone's parents, ever again.

On a similar note, I remember the CID came to see me at our house once in 1986 because I'd written a little booklet called 'Beneath The Counter' which was a conscientious consumer's guide to vegan, anti-Tory, anti-apartheid, anti-vivisection living. It was inspired by Chumbawamba's literary output at the time. (More about them later.) A local Tory MP's wife had bought the booklet – pay no more than 5p – from an independent health food shop and complained to the police. As well as baiting the Tories, there was a line in the introduction that read: 'If it's dark and there's a brick, find a convenient home for it', which was tantamount to incitement, apparently, so the Director of Public Prosecutions became interested. Oh, and I'd put my address in the booklet. Now that was stupid. (The second pressing of the booklet contained the immortally overwrought line: 'Veganism is not a guessing game', much to my friends' mocking bemusement.) So this CID chap came round and interviewed me at home. He was very polite. Asked me what vegan meant. Asked me if I'd be doing anything like this again. Gently reprimanded me. Goodbye. I taped the conversation on a tape recorder hidden behind the settee. I was worried that the interview would go on longer than 45 minutes and he'd hear the tape click to a stop. The headline in the paper was 'Police probe 'Throw a brick' booklet'. I was very proud.

I had turned vegetarian and stopped drinking alcohol when I was 17, left home due to my dad's disapproving and defeatist attitude and went vegan at 18, and got arrested for the first time, five months after moving out. I was spraying anti-fur slogans on the walls of Dingles and got caught red-handed, quite literally. A year or so later, in December 1988, Dingles was ablaze from an incendiary device left in the fur department. The top floor was in flames, which could be seen in all its glory from the roof terrace of my house. It caused over £13 millon worth of damage. Naturally, I was questioned by the CID again but they knew, and stated, that it was very unlikely the suspect/s would be from Plymouth.

To this day I don't know who did it, which is the way it should be. And Dingles discontinued their line in fur coats.

Job done.

In the meantime, mum was devastated. She hated my dad for driving me out of the family home, and would cry herself to sleep, wracked with worry, bless her. She had irrational fears that I'd be sleeping in the streets or getting into drugs, despite the fact I was straight-edge (or teetotal as I like to call it) when I left home and had a positive hatred towards smoking (still do). Four years later she had a brain haemorrhage due, in part, to smoking since her youth. Another 20 or more years later and she developed lung cancer due also to smoking, despite stopping in her mid/late-40s due to the haemorrhage. Although she's now in remission, the

---

Police probe 'Throw a brick' booklet

by ANDY SMITH

PLYMOUTH police are considering action over a militant leaflet which urges violence against firms liked to South Africa, animal experiments and the Tory party.

The 5p booklet – Beneath The Counter – has been on sale in at least one city store. It lists companies with "shady dealings," including firms with branches in Plymouth. Readers are urged to "keep pushing and spreading the truth and if it's dark and there's a brick, find a convenient home for it."

Plymouth police say the phrase could lay the writers or publishers open to prosecution for inciting crime.

Detectives are investigating the leaflet – published at a Southway council house – but the Director of Public Prosecutions will have to decide whether to prosecute.

Tory candidate for Devonport, Tom Jones, is demanding the authors withdraw the leaflet and publicly renounce violence. "Here we are in the city with problems of unruliness in the street and trying to do our best to tackle it," he said.

"What help will this be? There is no excuse for advising people to start picking up bricks."

Mr Jones has tipped off the police and they have promised to investigate.

19th September 1986

Dear D. Johns,

Don't be confused, nothing's missing. Everything is here, just as it is. And we're still working, each in our own way, whether with words or our fingers in the soil or our heads in the clouds, to be together, to learn and love eachother. It isn't that words have no meaning for us — we've just come to a point of change and none of us are interested in endless repetition of the anguished rant. Our work has raised a lot of questions (we're still looking for the answers/explanations), opened a lot of eyes, been useful and successful in some ways and failed in others. We've spent the past year and a half deciding what we each feel and want to do. The band no longer exists as it did but none of us has 'stopped', we're all moving on. It has been especially good to be without the constant demands of the band, we've had time to find eachother, to get to know eachother again. So many problems were put aside in favour of 'getting on with "it"', whatever 'it' was/is. Our feelings about 'the system' are not suddenly different but I think that in the last year, after the Falklands, our work was very bitter, very aggressive and reactionary — and, in a way, we had become immersed in so much ugliness and brutality that we had little to offer that was positive, except in terms of what I hope kept coming through... that message about love, about being one's own authority, about responsibility and openness. 'Acts of Love' was made to bring that awareness into sharp focus because it is the inspiration of of our anger — not a sense of the ugliness in the world but a sense of beauty. Which is to say that there is no revolution without love. So, we haven't cut ourselves off or gone away, maybe just rephrasing our ideas.

We're working on a 12" single and still making a few recordings of other bands — and getting on with gardening, writing, talking, dealing with life.... etc...

The answer-phone message has changed but I should think the one before sounded angry because there was such a lot crammed into a small space. But that was the style.... forthright and full of info.

As for Class War. It's not my way. I don't feel interested in most of what they have to say. ~~their humour, their cheapness~~ To me the problems aren't all so one sided, so black and white simple. I find a lot of the humour hideous and the outlook negative. But I know some of the people and although I don't like Class War I don't dislike them.

Every larger problem is a reflection of thousands of other problems. If you only deal with what seems to be at fault outside you, then you are ignoring your internal reactions — and most likely reacting to the 'external' problems in the same way as they affect you... and they, in turn, affect you depending on how you see them.

Anyway, thanks for writing.

love. peace. Joy de Vivre.

treatment has ravaged her body and, to a certain extent, her mind. Tragic and harrowing. I don't think the cruel irony of all this is lost on her.

The activism expanded and continued throughout my late teens and early twenties, with depression tagging along for the ride, taking in anti-war, anti-apartheid, anti-Poll Tax and Troops Out of Ireland marches; membership of Direct Action Movement, Class War and Anti-Fascist Action, alongside forming our own Plymouth anarchist chapter; collecting funds for Anarchist Black Cross prisoners and hunt saboteurs; supporting new age travellers and fighting alongside striking News International print workers. We'd make rabble-rousing leaflets and hand them out on the streets, regardless of whether the content could get us into trouble. A lot of it was painfully affected and gauche but we stood by every word.

It was a time when your politics and lifestyle were inextricable linked, despite the usual in-fighting that prevailed, with all contradictions gleefully embraced. Throwing lumps of turf at the cops at Stonehenge or lumps of pavement at the cops in Wapping was the same battle. Drawing comparisons between the Angry Brigade, Red Army Faction, the Sandinistas, the ANC and the IRA (self-determination for all!) seemed like the most natural thing to do. The criminal convictions were growing too. Eight charges for Breach of the Peace, Criminal Damage, Disorderly Conduct and Obstruction. I'd really had enough of paying fines. I was always getting caught. Well, me or my friend, Steve T. If we were both on a demo or hunt sab together, we'd speculate as to which one of us would get arrested. (He once got arrested for smashing a mosaic of William Of Orange in a Plymouth subway, but not before I was almost arrested for the crime as I was with him and carrying a small branch at the time.)

Alas, around this period I began drifting apart from Tim. I had found new friends, new political outlets and new musical projects, and felt that I needed to escape from what I saw as a suffocating relationship and experience the world for myself. I didn't handle it well. But I guess I had passed my apprenticeship.

By now, the most popular anarcho-punk gangs in town were Chumbawamba and Conflict, and I, along with everyone I knew, was hooked on both. Chumbawamba were a troupe of young, lovingly righteous, Leeds anarchists who took the tender politics of Crass and turned them into performance cabaret. They were very smart, very imaginative, very witty, very angry, slightly po-faced and able to combine rabid punk proselytising with folksy charm. As far as band crushes go, this was the big one for me. I never got to see Crass play live so made up for it by seeing Chumbas about 40 times, getting to know, travel with and annoy (some of) them, and defending them throughout the years of 'bare faced hypocrisy' (*Google it*). I even put them on in Plymouth once, at the now-crumbling Dance Academy. 800 people turned up. Amazing show. Boff and Mave from the band have been friends ever since.

Conflict, on the other hand, were tooled-up, spiked-up, London working class warriors who took the tough politics of Crass and turned them into a bloody battlefield. Not so smart but bristling with anger and hate, Conflict's brand of one-dimensional punk rock combined with uncontrollable Tourette's-like outbursts was the perfect yin to Chumba's yang, despite the troubling aura of machismo. I got to know and travel with (and annoy some of) them too, and managed to see them about 20 times. When the two bands played the same stage, it was anarcho-nirvana. In Leeds University, October 1986, the combination resulted in a riot, with cops and punks engaged in pitched battles outside. This was commonplace at Conflict shows. I remember getting hit on the head with a truncheon by police in May 1985 when we chased neo-Nazis out onto the streets of Exeter with Conflict frontman, Colin Jerwood, leading the battle cry; and rioting flared up again in 1987 in Brixton after Conflict's infamous Gathering Of The 5000 event with Steve Ignorant. But I don't think Chumbawamba were so keen on this kind of confrontational approach during gigs. They were more considered, progressive and educational. I straddled the line between the two, like an Old Testament preacher with my moralistic Chumbawamba booklets in one hand and a (usually metaphorical) baseball bat in the other.

Another much loved, and seen, band at the time were Culture Shock, formed by Dick Lucas from the Subhumans, who were equally as popular but their more philosophical approach set them apart. Wry observations and ska/punk tropes meant that they appealed more to the festival-loving crusties than streetsmart anarchos. Me and my pals had feet in all camps so we took to the band instantly. Par for the anarcho-hippy course, and in the spirit of Penny Rimbaud and Wally Hope, I fell in love with free festivals. We'd travel to far flung corners of the country (but mainly south of Worcestershire) to sit in fields and watch frazzled bands that filled the gap between Hawkwind and Discharge. And Culture Shock would always be there. I even managed to get them to play a pre-summer solstice gathering near Stonehenge in 1987, at a place called Collingbourne Wood, after calling Dick's house from a nearby phonebox. No drink or drugs for us at these festivals however, just the excitement of the spectacle itself. Although when that spectacle was watching Ozric Tentacles play for seven hours straight, it did wear a bit thin.

We even organised our own mini-festival for a few years at a Dartmoor beauty spot called Denham Bridge. We'd drag a generator down the meandering path to the riverside clearing, set up our tents and indulge in our self-sufficient freedom for three days, or until the police came and moved us on.

By this time I had created my first band proper, called Good Grief. We were a clattering, joyful, anarcho-folk/punk mess with guitars, mandolin, penny whistle, dulcimer, bodhran and voices jostling for attention. We'd hand out lyric sheets and self-written political leaflets at our shows and wallow in second wave self-righteousness. Songs like 'Let's Firebomb The Sex Shop' and 'Superpowers At The Superbowl' will always remain a (slightly cringeworthy) part of me.

For those of us wanting to self-identify as a pacifist punk (or peace punk for Stateside readers), the physical reality of hunt sabotage put paid to that. Every Saturday morning for a few years, I would jump in a transit van with other skinny punks and go running around the countryside distracting hounds, getting wet and cold, getting arrested and/or getting into fights with men on horses or in Land Rovers. It got nasty pretty much every time, especially if we had succeeded in distracting the hounds. I had friends bloodied, hospitalised and/or arrested week in, week out. And if it was an uneventful day, I'd still get home with my painful bunions throbbing in my drenched Rucanor basketball boots (all the rage among those with all the rage). As learning curves go, it was a very sharp one that taught me more about solidarity and class warfare than anything by Kropotkin, Goldman or Bakunin.

Among our numbers was Harry Cross, a charismatic man who could single-handedly sabotage a hunt due to being as fit as an athlete despite being at least a decade older than most of us, as good with a hunting horn as any seasoned redcoat, as knowledgeable of hunting grounds as any local farmer, and as single-minded as a neuro-scientist. He was my hero. We once got arrested together when we were on bail conditions, and were both taken to the same police station for a couple days. I felt like Jimmy in Quadrophenia when he gets to share a police van with the Ace. Tragically, Harry received life-changing injuries in 1992 when he was hit over the head with a baseball bat, receiving a fractured skull. The hunt supporter who hit him escaped punishment as it was upheld on appeal that he'd wrested the weapon away from Harry and used it in self-defence. Either way, the wrong man got fucked up. (*Footnote: my first comical foray into hunt sabotage, aged 17, was when I observed a man walking down into the woods behind our back garden with a rifle slung over his back. I decided to follow him with a little rounders bat hidden in my jacket, hoping to catch him in the act of shooting rabbits and subsequently bosh him one. I lost him immediately.*)

From 1986 onwards, certain sections of the anarcho-punk music community were beginning to morph into new entities, and I welcomed it. A Flux Of Pink Indians shed most of their moniker and released the beautiful Taoist mantra 'The Uncarved Block'; Bjork had transcended from leftfield kid-punk to crypto-pop pioneer; Poison Girls were developing indie-pop sensibilities; Blyth Power were proffering a poetically seething post-anarcho critique; unique post-Crass bands like Fugazi, Disposable Heroes Of Hiphoprisy, Consolidated and The Levellers (and later, Rage Against The Machine, Atari Teenage Riot, Against Me!, Refused, Propagandhi, Ted Leo...) were pushing the envelope sonically as well as socio-politically; and Chumbawamba began to wholly embrace dance and pop culture oblivious to where this new direction would eventually lead them.

Of course, some bands were firmly holding onto the past but their days were numbered. As if to ring the changes, I formed a rap'n'roll band called Spleen in the mid-90s, combining Beastie Boys / Public Enemy-style looped beats and samples with punk guitars, funk drums and lyrical rants straight from the Crass camp. We got nowhere but our hometown loved us and we created a bit of a stir, including one local newspaper front page story after I'd sent out a gig press release questioning how our local Tory MP, Gary Streeter, was able to walk around the streets unscathed. The headline this time was: 'Anarchists Target City MP'. I was very proud, once again.

In 1992 I did the unthinkable. I turned my back on straight-edge, or 'broke edge' as scenesters are known to say. The discovery of recreational powders'n'pills, magic mushrooms and a reacquaintance with cider was something that, in hindsight, I consider a very bad move, especially as the comedowns and hangovers played havoc with my unstable mental health. And playing on stage under the influence of pills is shamefully self-indulgent. I guess my mum might have had good reason to worry at this point, if she ever knew.

Still, the festivals were now a lot more fun. I also 'broke veganism' the same year and returned to being a vegetarian. (This to-and-froing would continue up to this very day, however the drugs are long gone, bar the cider.)

And then, in 1997 Chumbawamba did the unthinkable. They signed to EMI (whom they had previously targetted for their involvement in weapons manufacturing), ventured into the mainstream and pissed off ALL the punks. I took the band's side because, well, why the hell not? It seemed more relevant and more exciting than shouting from the sidelines, and I much preferred the anthemic pop tones of 'Shhh' to the humourless Britcore of most of the second-wave anarcho brigade, especially when the pills were kicking in. Frankly, I'd had enough of staring at pictures of acid-maimed corpses and tortured animals on my bedroom wall – it was time to celebrate our victories. And I'd had enough of the old school crusties and their immutable self-righteousness (mine was becoming less rigid). To hell with the cries of sell-out! Chumbawamba took the bait, took the cash, took the flack, rode the storm and donated a lot of money to grass-roots campaign groups worldwide in the process. Whatever else you think about them, the latter is pretty damn decent.

During this time I had been writing for a free regional music/arts magazine called The Scene. After ten years of contributing and learning the ropes, I took over the editorship from 1998 until its demise in 2001. Fuelled by my political upbringing and by all the zines and pamphlets that would always be readily available at punk shows, I littered the magazine with commissioned and self-penned articles ranging from police brutality to the anarchist anti-G8 demonstrations in Genoa, to a fantasy piece outlining my imagined assassination of Margaret Thatcher after she visited our town – a good 13 years before Hilary Mantel's similarly inspired tale. (I guess that CID officer back in 1986 didn't reprimand me enough.) I was eternally frustrated that we never received any criticism or chastisement from the local council or local authorites. I just had one measly death threat (on the office answer-phone, in an American accent) after I wrote an article on the Twin Towers attack, titled 'America's Wake-Up Call'. These days, we would probably have been firebombed in our sleep. The magazine bowed out in November 2001 with an issue that had 'No To War In Afghanistan' on the front cover. A great parting shot. Within those three years that I ran the magazine we lost about 90% of our advertisers. No-one would touch us with a barge-pole. I call that an achievement. (*Footnote: I also contributed album reviews to the NME for a few years – what a bunch of self-serving, arrogant, middle class chumps most of them were.*)

Between then and now my crowning achievement has been managing to stay alive after years of still unresolved soul-searching, terrible lows and hundreds of anti-depressants. (People sometimes ask me if I'm glad that I survived my one suicide attempt in 1994. My answer is always the same: half the time.)

There are, of course, many more stories to tell in those intervening years but they're not that relevant to this book, except the one when I formed a band who started out with the name Chomsky.

So fast-forward to January 2015 (a time of unfathomable violence, intolerance, confusion and hypocrisy) and we find ourselves in a bizarre situation where every other original anarcho band is either reforming or being reconfigured for a new generation. I'm not sure how I feel about it.

On the one hand, I think that it cheapens the original ideas and turns the whole thing into nostalgia; on the other hand, watching Zounds or The Mob play their awesome anarcho-punk ditties 30 years later is rather thrilling. And the proliferation of anarcho-teens with Crass patches on their battle jackets is testament to the longevity of the genre.

And what of the Crassical Collection remixes?

Sure, the guitars are clearer but at the expense of soul, it seems. Or maybe it's more important that the music is given a modern overhaul to appeal to the young revolutionaries who might not warm to the harshness of the originals?

I guess we shouldn't be so precious about something that has already served its purpose. And my depression is always here, looming like a dark shadow, much like John Forbes Nash Jr's imaginary apparitions in *A Beautiful Mind*, but I've got a handle on it. I do feel that I'm getting worse but I think it's just getting older that makes it seem worse: more self-awareness, a more acute sense of mortality, more heartbreak, more regret, more tired, more cynical, less hair and so on. I now consider most political demonstrations as self-empowering yet ultimately futile (except anti-fascist confrontations) but still go on them, in much the same way that I still use energy efficient light bulbs and fill my recycling bin despite the fact that I know we're all doomed.

Old habits die hard.

For the past ten years I have been singing and playing guitar (and sometimes banjo) in a band called Crazy Arm. As I write, we're working on songs for our fourth album alongside more tours of UK, Europe and, fingers crossed, South Korea for the first time. Suffice to say, the spirit of anarcho-punk looms large within the ethos of the band and in my lyrics. How can it not do when the most formative years of my life were spent learning about atrocities and attitudes that have burnt themselves into my memory like nothing else before or since?

We even dress in black, although a little smarter than our Epping forebears. I also write songs about my struggles with depression alongside other neurotic manifestations. Mental health issues are a lot more understood now (although we have a long way to go) and I don't feel like I need to keep this kind of stuff hidden any more. It's now very rewarding to talk with people around the world who are moved, informed or inspired by the words and music that I write. That's how the chain works and I'm grateful to be able to give back to an underground music community that gave me so much.

Tim is a fan, and a friend again. He lives in the wilds of Scotland with his family but keeps in touch and comes to see us on the very rare occasions that we venture north of Carlisle. And Boff now reviews some of our records for R2, a nationally acclaimed folk/roots magazine run by Sean McGhee. Sean was the singer for first-wave anarcho-punks, Psycho Faction. As I said, we're all connected.

The legacy of this incendiary period in music and (sub)culture is something that shouldn't be underestimated. It has spread its tentacles far and wide, affecting modes of activism, of music, of literature, of expression, of love and of friendship worldwide, surpassing any expectations that we might have held at the time. A new generation of young radicals are keeping those ideas alive, forming and following new bands, writing/publishing new words, engaging in protest politics with a whole new set of global concerns, forging their own identity and asserting their own autonomy.

And when people like Russell Brand and Charlie Brooker are nudging the very same concepts into the mainstream using language that we melodramatically deployed 30 years ago, you can't help but feel that the wheel has come full circle.

Anarcho-punk was our Age of Enlightenment, despite the fact that we were in a constant state of fear and loathing.

It may be an '80s existentialist conceit but if you remember it, you were almost certainly there.

Andy Palmer [Crass]

Irene Frizzera

Rudimentary Peni Booklet

Courtesy Greg Bull Collection

EVALUATION SHEET

To be used in conjunction with Evaluation Chart

NAME OF CANDIDATE: **JESUS CHRIST**
POSITION APPLIED FOR **WORLD SAVIOUR**
NAME OF INTERVIEWER **P. PILOT** DATE **O.B.C.**

Tick Where Applicable

CHECK LIST TO HELP DETERMINE PERSONALITY

MATURITY — Does he show a responsible attitude towards his family?

Does he appear to have sound financial stability?

EMOTIONAL STABILITY AND EVEN TEMPER — Can he maintain composure in the face of frustration and set-backs?

ADAPTABILITY — Did he adjust himself to service life?
Is he able to change location easily?
Without being a 'rolling-stone', has he fitted into different jobs readily?

Polite questioning to elicit this sort of information should be put to applicants until you, the interviewer, are satisfied that you have secured enough information to grade candidates according to how they fit the 'man profile' required for a particular job.

APPEARANCE: Physical characteristics, carriage, posture, personal grooming, dress, features

A	B	C
Outstanding presence, clearly recalled, very distinctive.	Creates good impression, attractive presence, well and neatly dressed, energetic.	Adequate, but undistinguishable, in most respects.

D	E
Lax, careless or over-dressed, room for improvement, lacks energy.	Decidedly odd, unacceptable, well below standard.

The "EVALUATION SHEET" IS AN EXTRACT FROM A 4--PAGE FORM GIVEN TO AN INTERVIEWER SO THAT HE/SHE CAN ASSESS WHETHER YOU ARE THE "RIGHT PERSON" FOR THE JOB OR NOT.

WHAT IS "MATURITY" TO AN INTERVIEWER'S MIND? IS IT INDICATED BY A PERSON'S ABILITY TO THINK FOR HIS OR HERSELF? BOLLOCKS. TO THE MIND OF THE POXY, BRAIN--WASHED INTERVIEWER IT IS MEASURED BY WHETHER YOUR VIEWS COMPLY WITH THE "NORM" IE A SHORT--SIGHTED, HUMBLE, UNQUESTIONING, "I'LL BETRAY WHAT I BELIEVE IN 'COS I WANT THE MONEY" ATTITUDE. WHICH MAKES YOU A SMOOTH-RUNNING WORK UNIT WHICH CAN BE EASILY MANIPULATED. WHAT RIGHT HAS THE INTERVIEWER TO JUDGE YOUR "MATURITY" WHEN HIS IDEA OF MATURITY IS NO MORE THAN A LOAD OF DISTORTED SHIT?

THE "APPEARANCE" SECTION OF THE CHART IS JUST ONE OF 12 ASPECTS OF YOUR "PERSONALITY" THAT ARE GRADED FROM "A" DOWN TO "E." THE OTHERS ARE: "MANNER, VOICE & DICTION, SELF EXPRESSION, PARTICIPATION, DOMESTIC/FAMILY STABILITY, MATURITY, VIGOUR & ENTHUSIASM, ATTITUDE, GROUP BEHAVIOUR/ SOCIAL SKILLS & SERVICE RECORD (IF ANY)."

THIS SCALE IS A LOAD OF BIGOTED, STEREOTYPED SHIT.

"DECIDEDLY ODD" – IN COMPARISON TO WHAT? IN COMPARISON TO THE INTERVIEWER'S OWN APPEARANCE I'VE NO DOUBT.

"UNACCEPTABLE" – WHO CAN'T ACCEPT SOMEONE ELSE'S APPEARANCE? ONCE AGAIN IT'S THE BRAINWASHED & CONDITIONED INTERVIEWER & OTHER INTOLERANT PEOPLE LIKE HIM/HER.

"WELL BELOW STANDARD" – WHOSE STANDARD? WHAT STANDARD? THE IMPOSED STANDARD OF THE INTER-

—VIEWER ?? & OTHER SUCH "SHEEP"!

IMAGINE FOR A MOMENT A SITUATION WHERE A WOMAN GOES FOR AN INTERVIEW BUT DOES NOT FEEL THAT SHE SHOULD HAVE TO EXPLOIT HER SEX BY WEARING MAKE--UP, SHAVING HER LEGS OR WEARING TIGHTS OR WHATE--VER. THE INTERVIEWER CAN REJECT HER ON THE GROUNDS THAT SHE IS "DECIDEDLY ODD, UNACCEPTABLE, WELL BELOW STANDARD" PURELY BECAUSE THE INTER--VIEWER HAS A STEREOTYPED IMAGE OF "WHAT A WOMAN SHOULD LOOK LIKE" IE; PAINTED & GLOSSILY PACKAGED. SO IT COMES ABOUT THAT THE APPLICANT IS VIEWED AS A FAULTY PRODUCT AND THE INTERVIEWER THINKS, "THIS WOMAN DOES NOT COMPLY WITH MY IMAGE OF HOW A FEMALE WORK UNIT SHOULD PRESENT ITSELF, THEREFORE I SHALL USE MY POWERS TO RETRIBUTE HER — I SHALL REFUSE HER THE JOB."

FROM THIS SITUATION IT CAN BE SEEN THAT INDUSTRY DOES NOT RUN IN A FAIR WAY, BENEFICIAL TO ALL. IT RUNS FOR THE GOOD OF PROFIT-SEEKING CUNTS WHO WISH TO PROTECT THEIR MONEY/POWER BY ONLY EMPLOYING "SAFE" NON-INDIVIDUALS WHO WILL DO WHAT THEY ARE TOLD.

NB.
THE "A" TO "E" SCALES ARE THE FILES WE ARE INFORM--ED ABOUT. HOWEVER, SCHOOLS KEEP "CONFIDENTIAL" FILES THAT NEITHER YOU OR YOUR PARENTS HAVE LEGAL ACCESS TO. I HATE TO THINK WHAT ABSURDITIES AND SHIT THEY CONTAIN.

THIS IS A SHITTY SITUATION, WHAT WILL WE DO ABOUT IT?

(PATRONISING, AREN'T IT?)

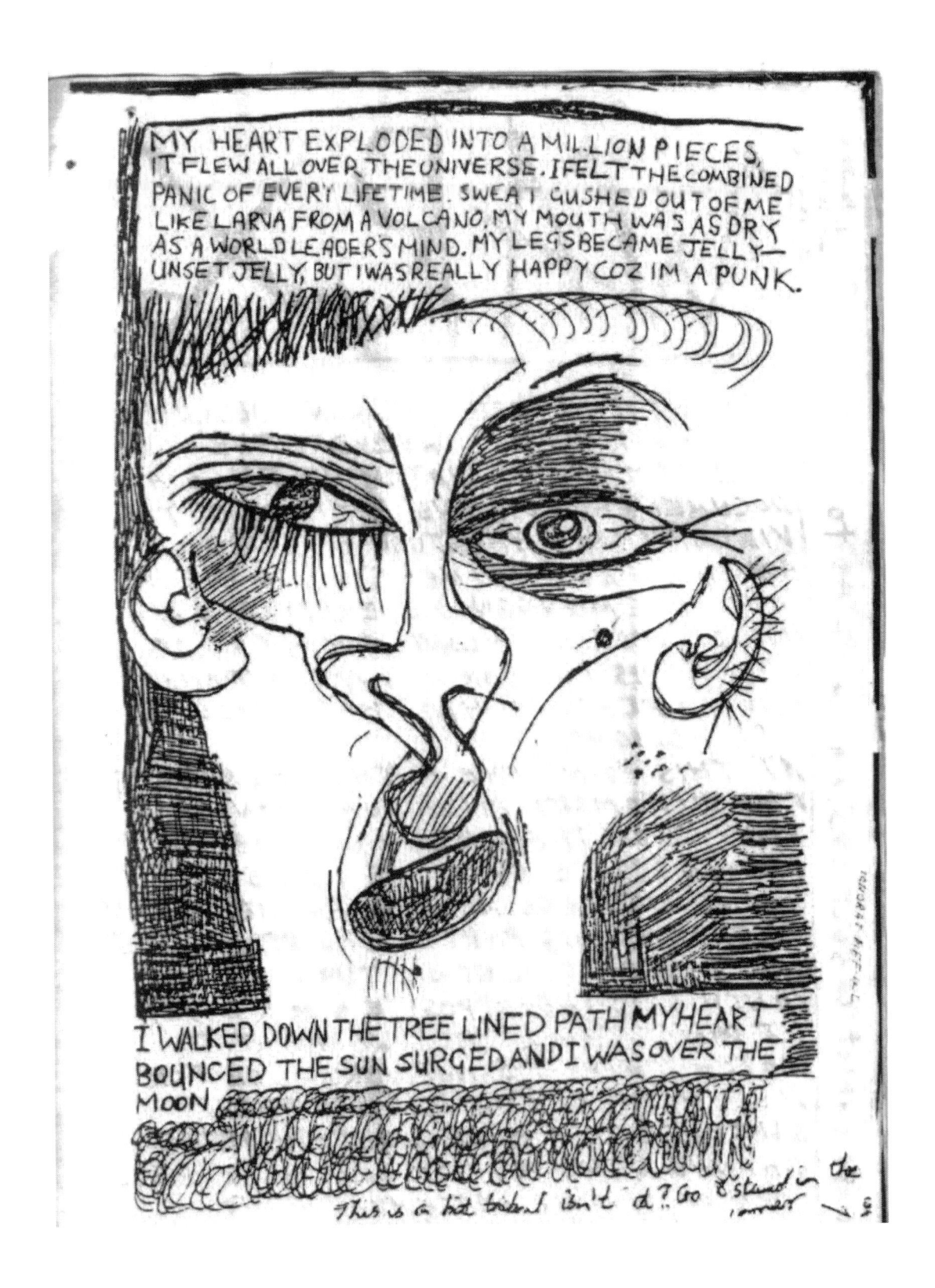

MY HEART EXPLODED INTO A MILLION PIECES, IT FLEW ALL OVER THE UNIVERSE. I FELT THE COMBINED PANIC OF EVERY LIFETIME. SWEAT GUSHED OUT OF ME LIKE LARVA FROM A VOLCANO. MY MOUTH WAS AS DRY AS A WORLD LEADER'S MIND. MY LEGS BECAME JELLY— UNSET JELLY, BUT I WAS REALLY HAPPY COZ IM A PUNK.

I WALKED DOWN THE TREE LINED PATH MY HEART BOUNCED THE SUN SURGED AND I WAS OVER THE MOON

WAR X

Imagine the scene; a non-descript sitting room one weekday evening. The family are watching T.V. & a documentary on the futility of the Vietnam war has just started. An injured marine is being taken into an emergency operating room. He is uttering a continuous cry of pain & his companions are attempting to reassure him that he'll "be alright."

At this point the mother performs the customary ritual of turning away from the screen in order to demonstrate that she finds the scene distressing. The father then performs his part of the ritual. He expresses concern & turns to the youth sitting opposite him & says, "I don't think that we ought to watch this. It's not very nice for your mother." The father then switches to a more light-hearted channel. The youth pulls an expression of annoyed amazement at this sudden censorship and leaves the

ROOM.

> NOTHING'S WORTH DYING FOR 'COS YOU WON'T BE AROUND TO ~~FEEL~~ PLEASED WITH YOUR-SELF. (MORONIC SHITHEADS!)

A FEW MONTHS LATER, THE SCENE IS THE SAME BUT THE PROGRAMME IS A FILM ABOUT THE 2ND WORLD WAR STARRING STEVE McQUEEN. IN THIS FILM 50 MEN ARE MASSACRED; A GERMAN IS KICKED INTO AN UNCONSCIOUS STATE & THE BODY OF A DEAD MAN HANGS FROM THE BARBED WIRE OF A P.O.W. CAMP. HE HAS JUST BEEN GUNNED DOWN AS THE RESULT OF A DESPAR-ATE ATTEMPT TO ESCAPE. HOWEVER, THIS EVENING THE MOTHER SHOWS NO DISTRESS, THE FATHER SHOWS NO CONCERN & THE FAMILY ARE MILDLY ENTERTAINED BY THE FILM.

THESE ARE ACCOUNTS OF SITUATIONS I HAVE EXPERIENCED. DO THEY SOUND FAMILIAR? WHEN VIEWED COLLECTIVELY THEY STINK OF A COMM-ON HYPOCRISY — PEOPLE ONLY WISH TO ACC-EPT THE GLAMOROUS & EXCITING PRESENTAT-ION OF WAR — THEY DO NOT WISH TO KNOW THE TRUTH EVEN IF CONFRONTED WITH IT. YET TH-ESE SAME PEOPLE ARE QUITE PREPARED TO SANCTION THE MANUFACTURE OF BOMBS CAPABLE OF WIDESPREAD DESTRUCTION AND CONTAMINATION OF COUNTRIES AND POPULATIO-NS, INCLUDING YOUNG CHILDREN WHO MAY NOT EVEN BE AWARE OF ANY CONFLICT & ARE CERTAINLY NOT RESPONSIBLE FOR IT.

SOMETIMES CENSORSHIP IS NOT EVEN VOLUNTARY. EVEN NOW, "THE WAR GAME" A FILM MADE IN 1964 ABOUT THE EFFECTS OF A NUCLEAR ATTACK ON A VILLAGE IN KENT IS NOT CONSIDERED ELIGIBLE FOR T.V. TRANSM-ISSION TO THE MASSES AS IT MIGHT CAUSE WIDESPREAD ANXIETY. HOW FUCKING STUPID. IF PEOPLE ARE PAYING A PERCENTAGE OF THEIR WAGES FOR THE MANUFACTURE & UPKEEP OF MISSILES THEN THEY MUST BE MADE AWARE OF THE CONSEQUENCES IE/ BY HAVING MISSILES WE ARE A PRIME TARGET FOR SO-CALLED "ENEMY" MISSILES AND "OUR" MISSILES WILL BE USED TO SLAUGHTER PEOPLE WE HAVE NEVER EVEN MET. WHEN THE BOMBS DROP PEOPLE WILL NOT BE ABLE TO EVADE THEM AS EASILY AS THEY SEEM TO BE ABLE TO EVADE CONSIDERING THE CONSEQUENCES OF WAR.

VIOLENCE

STRANGLERS "SOMETIMES" → WATCH OUT FOR SHIT → LIKE THIS, → IT APPEARS → EVERYWHERE.

IF SOMEONE FEELS THAT IT IS WORTHWHILE TO ATTACK YOU AND DOES JUST THAT THE CHANCES ARE THAT YOU WILL EXPERIENCE SOME FORM OF PAIN, OBVIOUSLY. WHAT IS YOUR REACTION? CHANCES ARE YOU WILL ATTEMPT TO INJURE YOUR ASSAILANT IN RETURN. IF LOGIC IS APPLIED TO THIS SITUATION IT BECOMES CLEAR HOW ABSURD IT IS; WHEN SOMEONE HURTS YOU THE PAIN IS

"YOU'RE UH/ PAST YOUR STATION... BEAT YOU HONEY 'TILL YOU DROP"

ABHORRENT & UNPLEASANT. HAVING ESTABLISHED THAT PAIN IS UNDESIRABLE (TO MOST PEOPLE ANYWAY!), WHAT CAN POSSIBLY BE GAINED BY INFLICTING MORE PAIN ON SOMEONE ELSE? PERSONAL SATISFACTION IN HAVING GAINED REVENGE IS WHAT YOU MIGHT SAY, BUT THE FACT IS THAT NO MATTER HOW VIOLENT YOU MAY BE, IT WILL NOT ERASE THE UNPLEASANTNESS OF YOUR OWN EXPERIENCE. IT ONLY SERVES TO CAUSE MORE PAIN & UNPLEASANTNESS. VIOLENCE PROVIDES NO LONGTERM SOLUTION (TAKE A LOOK AT N. IRELAND FOR PROOF OF THAT). THE PLEA THAT REVENGE BRINGS TRUE SATISFACTION IS SHIT BECAUSE IF YOU FEEL THAT YOU ARE ACHIEVING SOMETHING THROUGH CAUSING PHYSICAL PAIN OR TERROR ON OTHERS YOUR INTELLIGENCE HAS GOT LOST SOMEWHERE. VIOLENCE IS NO SUBSTITUTE FOR RATIONAL & POSITIVE THOUGHT.

"EVERY FIST THAT YOU RAISE IS A CORPSE AT YOUR FEET"

IF EVERYONE ACTUALLY CONSIDERED THE FUTILITY OF VIOLENCE & WAR THEN PERHAPS IT WOULDN'T HAPPEN.

WAR IS INEVITABLE. I MUST SHOOT.

I'M VERY CONCERNED ABOUT MY CHILD. THIS IS THE BEST WAY TO DEFEND HIM.

BANG

The Government, who repeatedly tell us that we must live within our means, seem determined that we shall die beyond them.

AT LEAST £5,000 MILLION is the amount they propose to spend on a terrible new weapons system.

4 TRIDENT SUBMARINES, each of which will carry 16 MISSILES individually armed with 8 NUCLEAR WARHEADS.

A total of 512 WARHEADS each with an explosive power equal to 100000 TONS OF TNT. Each warhead can be directed to a different target which can be altered during flight. This sophistication represents a FURTHER ESCALATION OF THE ARMS RACE.

It is inconceivable that Britain could ever use nuclear weapons independently. Trident could only be used to retaliate on behalf of an already devastated Britain.

WHICH WOULD YOU CHOOSE ?
DECENT HOSPITALS, SCHOOLS, HOUSING AND SOCIAL SERVICES, or TRIDENT, THE ONLY PURPOSE OF WHICH IS RETALIATION FROM THE GRAVE ?

CND 11 Goodwin Street, London N4 3HQ
CND 11 GOODWIN ST.
LONDON N4 3HQ

YOUR HOME IS A NUCLEAR TARGET BECAUSE:
- American and British missiles, bombers and submarines are based in this country
- Britain belongs to NATO
- The government has enthusiastically accepted the stationing of 160 cruise missiles here, which can only be used for nuclear attack and will be solely controlled by the U.S.
- Strategists think of fighting a "limited" nuclear war. In any nuclear war, Britain is bound to be destroyed.

A 4 MEGATON BOMB WOULD:
- Give off a flash bright enough to blind temporarily and probably burn the eyes of people looking at it up to 300 miles away
- Grow into a blindingly bright fireball 3 miles across — and as hot as the inside of the sun
- Burn people fatally up to 22 miles away
- Completely smash brick buildings up to 7 miles away and block up streets 15 miles away
- Instantly kill or fatally injure up to 1,000,000 people.

WHAT BRITAIN CAN DO:
- Scrap nuclear weapons and bases
- Leave NATO and stimulate world disarmament
- Transfer the skills and resources used in arms production to solving our social and economic problems.

'They'll never use it'

↑   ↑   ↑
BUT THEY ALREADY HAVE.

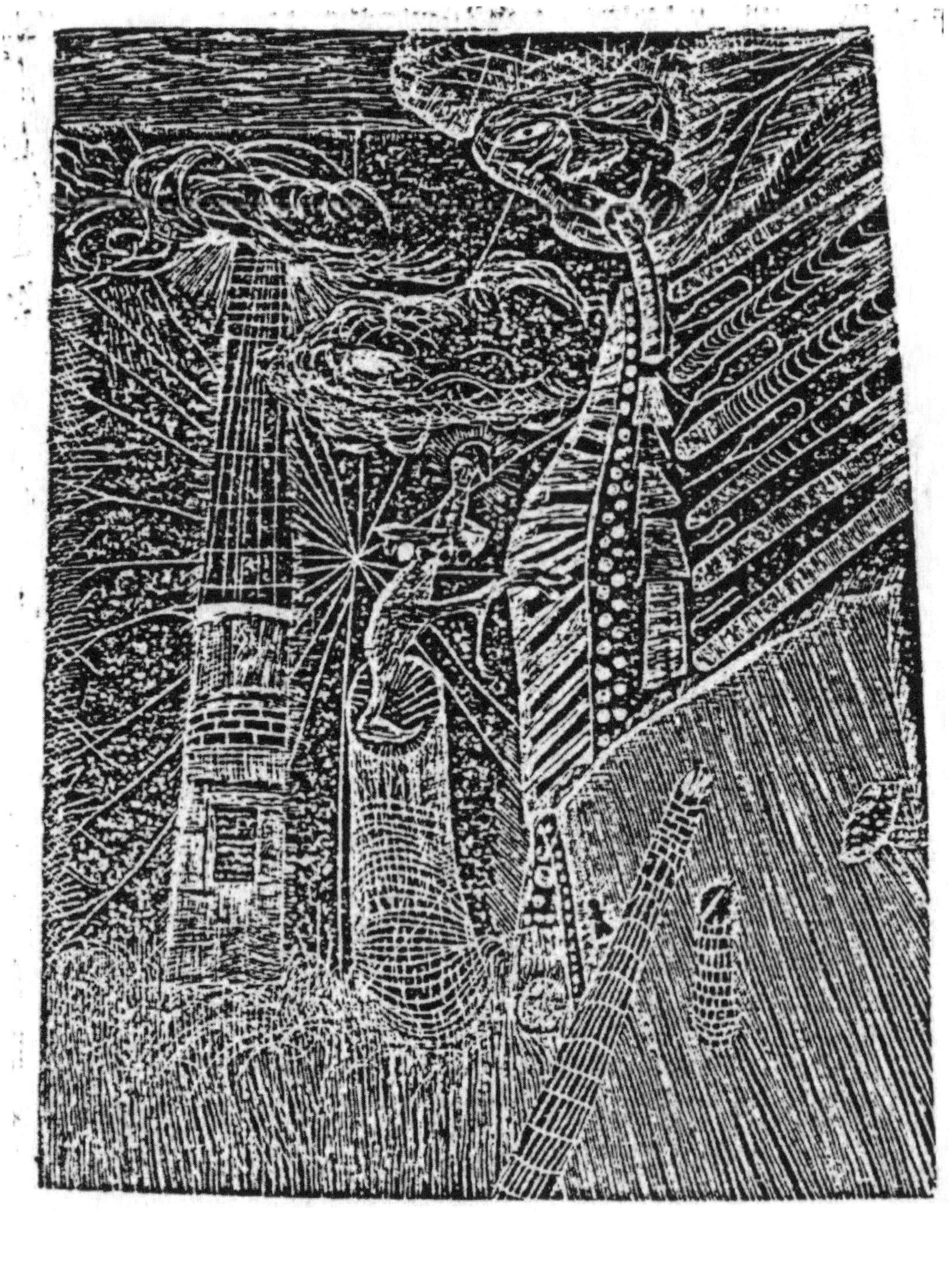

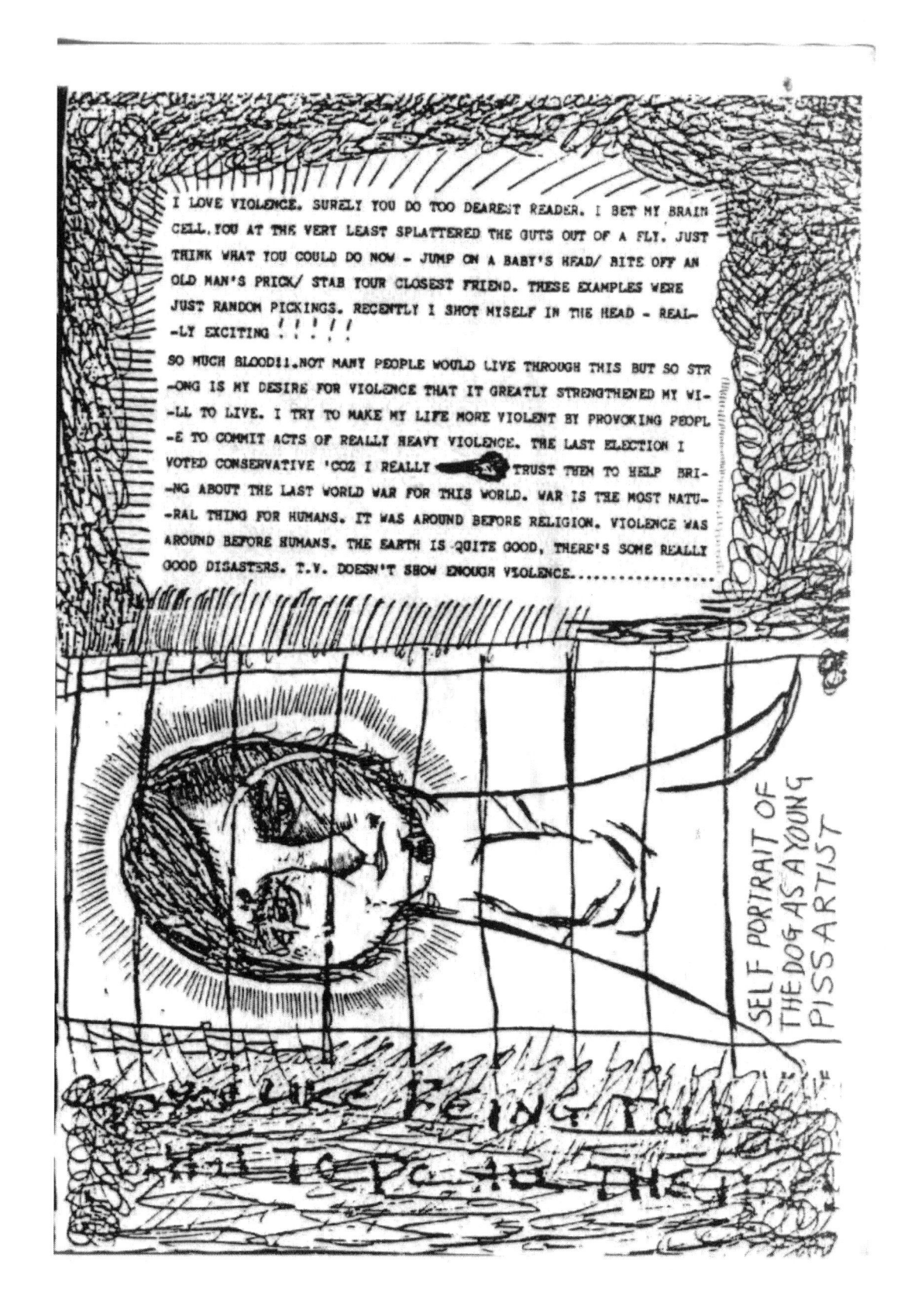

I LOVE VIOLENCE. SURELY YOU DO TOO DEAREST READER. I BET MY BRAIN CELL, YOU AT THE VERY LEAST SPLATTERED THE GUTS OUT OF A FLY. JUST THINK WHAT YOU COULD DO NOW - JUMP ON A BABY'S HEAD/ BITE OFF AN OLD MAN'S PRICK/ STAB YOUR CLOSEST FRIEND. THESE EXAMPLES WERE JUST RANDOM PICKINGS. RECENTLY I SHOT MYSELF IN THE HEAD - REAL--LY EXCITING !!!!!

SO MUCH BLOOD!!.NOT MANY PEOPLE WOULD LIVE THROUGH THIS BUT SO STR-ONG IS MY DESIRE FOR VIOLENCE THAT IT GREATLY STRENGTHENED MY WI--LL TO LIVE. I TRY TO MAKE MY LIFE MORE VIOLENT BY PROVOKING PEOPL-E TO COMMIT ACTS OF REALLY HEAVY VIOLENCE. THE LAST ELECTION I VOTED CONSERVATIVE 'COZ I REALLY TRUST THEM TO HELP BRI--NG ABOUT THE LAST WORLD WAR FOR THIS WORLD. WAR IS THE MOST NATU--RAL THING FOR HUMANS. IT WAS AROUND BEFORE RELIGION. VIOLENCE WAS AROUND BEFORE HUMANS. THE EARTH IS QUITE GOOD, THERE'S SOME REALLY GOOD DISASTERS. T.V. DOESN'T SHOW ENOUGH VIOLENCE....................

SELF PORTRAIT OF THE DOG AS A YOUNG PISS ARTIST

SO WHAT ABOUT THE FUCKER...

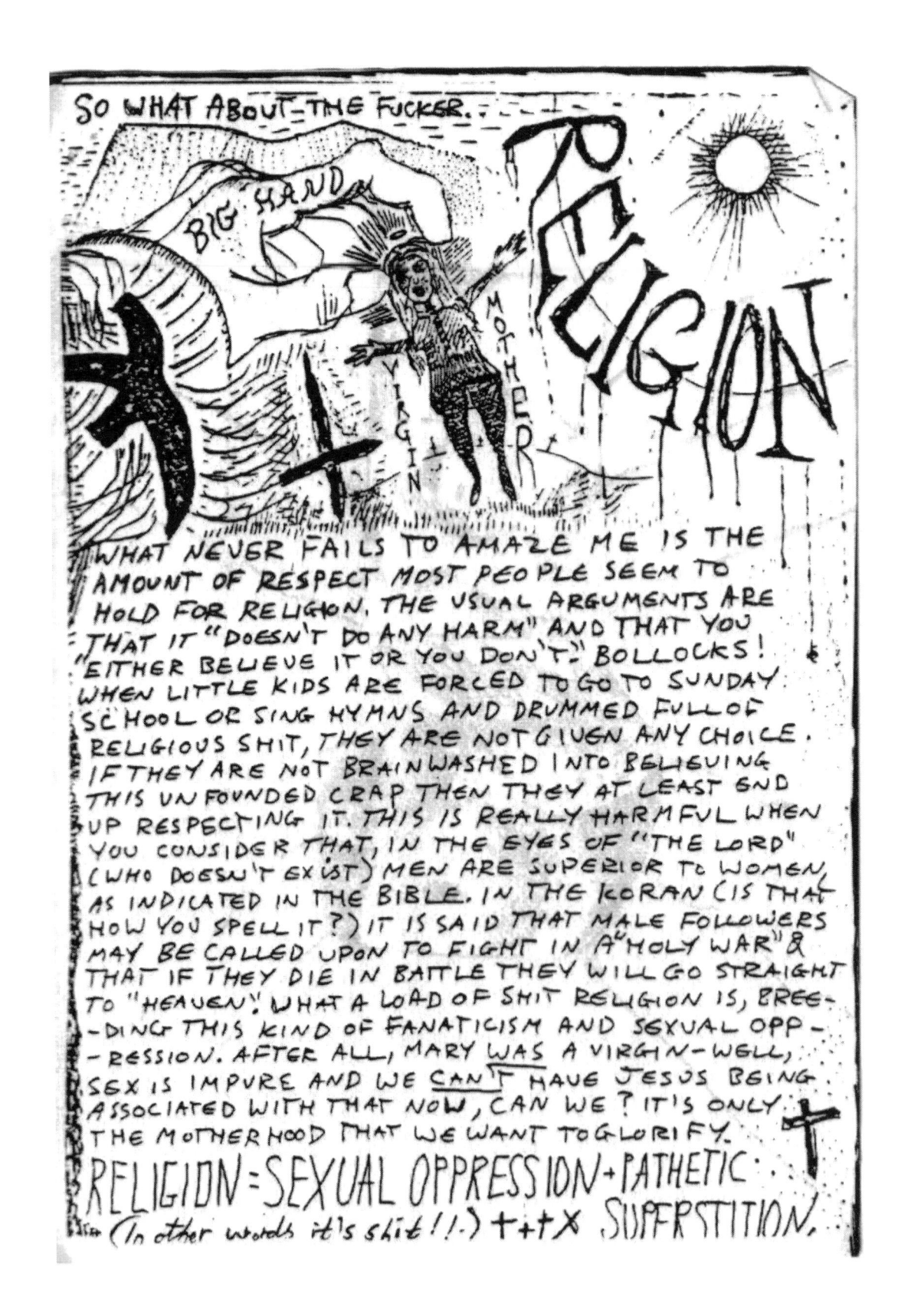

RELIGION

BIG HAND / VIRGIN / MOTHER

WHAT NEVER FAILS TO AMAZE ME IS THE AMOUNT OF RESPECT MOST PEOPLE SEEM TO HOLD FOR RELIGION. THE USUAL ARGUMENTS ARE THAT IT "DOESN'T DO ANY HARM" AND THAT YOU "EITHER BELIEVE IT OR YOU DON'T." BOLLOCKS! WHEN LITTLE KIDS ARE FORCED TO GO TO SUNDAY SCHOOL OR SING HYMNS AND DRUMMED FULL OF RELIGIOUS SHIT, THEY ARE NOT GIVEN ANY CHOICE. IF THEY ARE NOT BRAINWASHED INTO BELIEVING THIS UNFOUNDED CRAP THEN THEY AT LEAST END UP RESPECTING IT. THIS IS REALLY HARMFUL WHEN YOU CONSIDER THAT, IN THE EYES OF "THE LORD" (WHO DOESN'T EXIST) MEN ARE SUPERIOR TO WOMEN, AS INDICATED IN THE BIBLE. IN THE KORAN (IS THAT HOW YOU SPELL IT?) IT IS SAID THAT MALE FOLLOWERS MAY BE CALLED UPON TO FIGHT IN A "HOLY WAR" & THAT IF THEY DIE IN BATTLE THEY WILL GO STRAIGHT TO "HEAVEN". WHAT A LOAD OF SHIT RELIGION IS, BREE-
-DING THIS KIND OF FANATICISM AND SEXUAL OPP-
-RESSION. AFTER ALL, MARY WAS A VIRGIN - WELL, SEX IS IMPURE AND WE CAN'T HAVE JESUS BEING ASSOCIATED WITH THAT NOW, CAN WE? IT'S ONLY THE MOTHERHOOD THAT WE WANT TO GLORIFY.

RELIGION = SEXUAL OPPRESSION + PATHETIC SUPERSTITION.
(In other words it's shit!!)

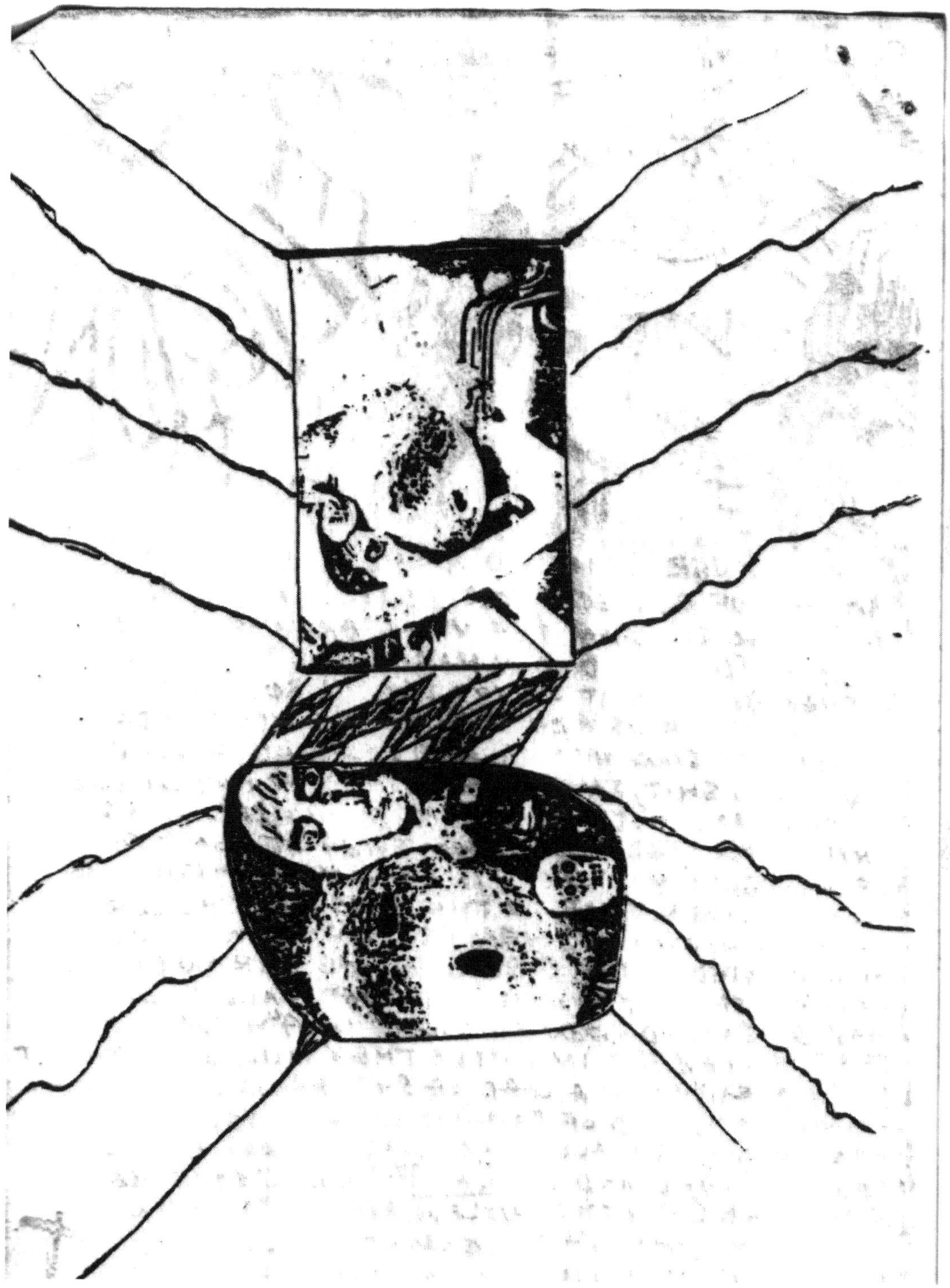

SEXUAL CONDITIONING

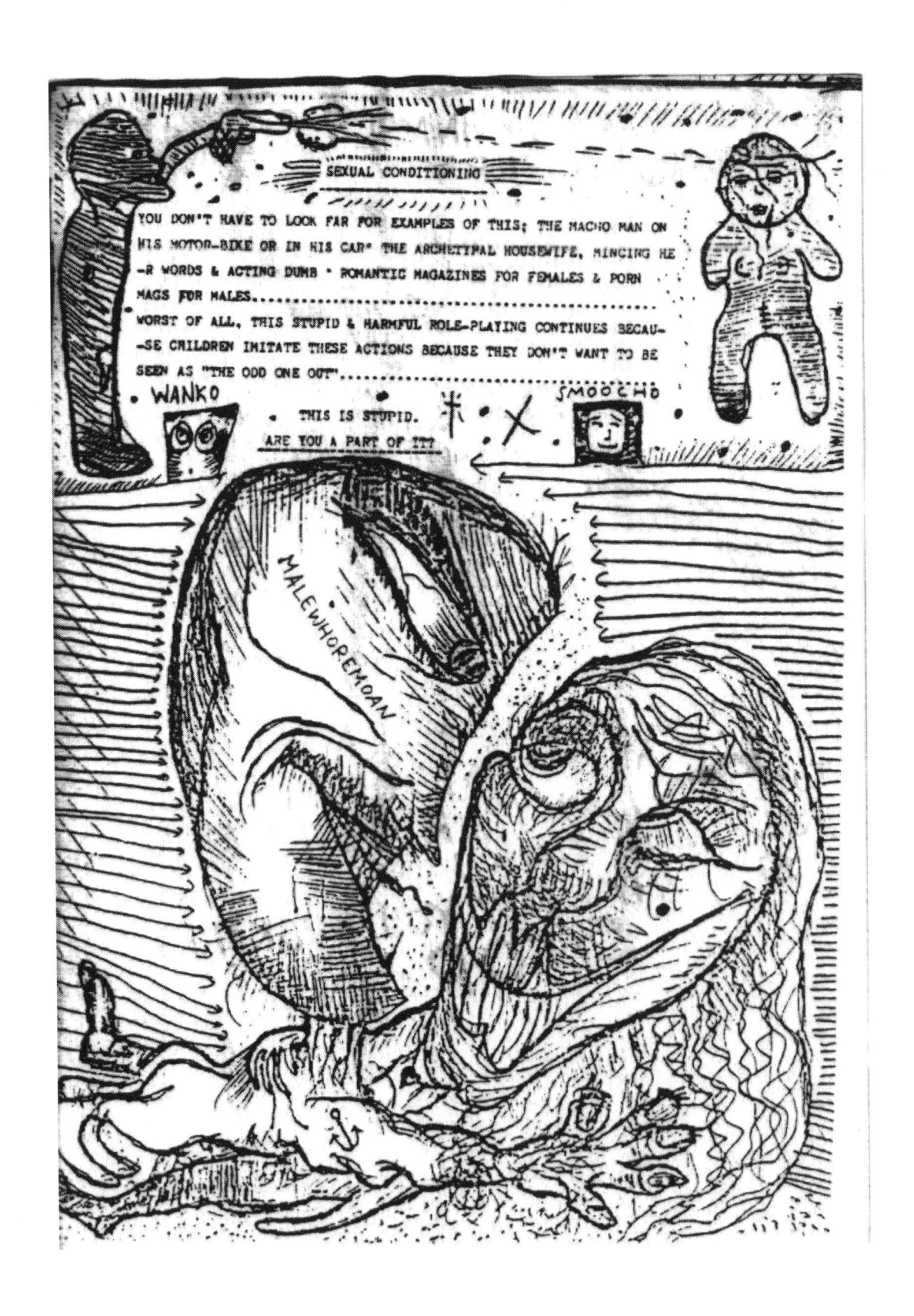

YOU DON'T HAVE TO LOOK FAR FOR EXAMPLES OF THIS; THE MACHO MAN ON HIS MOTOR-BIKE OR IN HIS CAR* THE ARCHETYPAL HOUSEWIFE, MINCING HER WORDS & ACTING DUMB * ROMANTIC MAGAZINES FOR FEMALES & PORN MAGS FOR MALES..

WORST OF ALL, THIS STUPID & HARMFUL ROLE-PLAYING CONTINUES BECAUSE CHILDREN IMITATE THESE ACTIONS BECAUSE THEY DON'T WANT TO BE SEEN AS "THE ODD ONE OUT".................................

• WANKO

• THIS IS STUPID.   SMOOCHO
ARE YOU A PART OF IT?

MURDERING ANIMALS for LUXURY

WHEN TALKING TO PEOPLE ABOUT WHY THEY FEEL THAT ITS OK TO HAVE ANIMALS KILLED FOR THE "BENEFIT" OF HUMANS THEY USUALLY COME UP WITH THE FOLLOWING ARGUMENTS. 1. "HUMANS HAVE TO EAT MEAT TO HAVE A HEALTHY DIET" **SHIT** IF THIS WAS TRUE I AND MANY OTHERS WOULD NOT REMAIN ALIVE AND "HEALTHY" IF YOU DRINK ALCOHOL OR SMOKE YOU'RE A PRAT TO TRY & USE THIS ARGUMENT 'COS ITS OBVIOUS YOU'RE NOT REALLY CONCERNED ABOUT BEING HEALTHY ARE YOU? 2. "HUMANS ARE NATURALLY CARNIVORES". THIS ONE'S **PATHETIC** IT'S "NATURAL" FOR PEOPLE TO DIE FROM SMALL POX ETC BUT THEY ARE PREVENTED FROM DOING SO BY MODERN MEDICINE. THIS SEEMS QUITE LOGICAL SO SIMILARLY ITS LOGICAL FOR HUMANS TO MANIPULATE "NATURE" BY NOT EATING ANIMAL FLESH... 3. "IF I DON'T EAT MEAT IT WON'T DO ANY GOOD 'COS EVERYONE ELSE WILL CARRY ON EATING MEAT ANYWAY" IF YOU WERE IN NAZI GERMANY & YOU SAW A CROWD OF PEOPLE KICKING A JEW WOULD YOU JOIN IN JUST BECAUSE YOU WEREN'T ABLE TO STOP THE REST OF THE CROWD DOING IT? 4. "ISN'T IT JUST AS BAD TO KILL PLANTS?" THIS ONE'S SO STUPID I'M NOT GOING TO WASTE ANY TIME WITH IT.

THERE IS NO WAY "MORALLY" OR PRACTICALLY THAT YOU ARE JUSTIFIED IN MURDERING ANIMALS FOR YOUR LUXURY

SO WHY DON'T YOU FUCKING STOP?????

BASICALLY, LIFE IS SHIT...... DAY IN, DAY OUT, THE SAME OLD POXY ROUTINES OF SHORTSIGHTED- -NESS & IGNORANCE..... THE RESULTS OF CONDIT- -ONING FROM BIRTH...... PEOPLE SHITTING ON OTHERS & BEING SHAT UPON THEMSELVES..... AN ENDLESS STREAM OF PETTY RESTRICTIONS ALL SERVING TO MAKE MY DAY TO DAY EXISTANCE SHITTY.... THE RESULT? I (YOU?) JUST SWITCH OFF FOR MUCH OF THE TIME..... ARE YOU KIDD- -ING YOURSELF THAT YOU ENJOY YOUR WORK? IS IT REALLY WORTH SUFFERING ALL THIS SHIT BECAUSE THE PEOPLE WITH THE MONEY THINK THAT THEIR WEALTH & YOUR POSITION OF DEPE- -NDENCY GIVES THEM THE RIGHT TO TREAT YOU LIKE A SHITHEAD?... ARE YOU A SHIT- -HEAD? (I KNOW I'M NOT.) SO WHY DO WE LET PEOPLE TREAT US LIKE SHITHEADS? THERE MUST BE ANOTHER WAY........ A LIFE OF SHIT IS NOT GOOD ENOUGH.

"FUCKED UP REALITY BASED ON FEAR"

"IF YOU'VE GOT ANYTHING TO SAY WRITE TO :- RUDIMENTARY PENI

OR RUDIMENTARY PENI

SEND S.A.E PLEASE

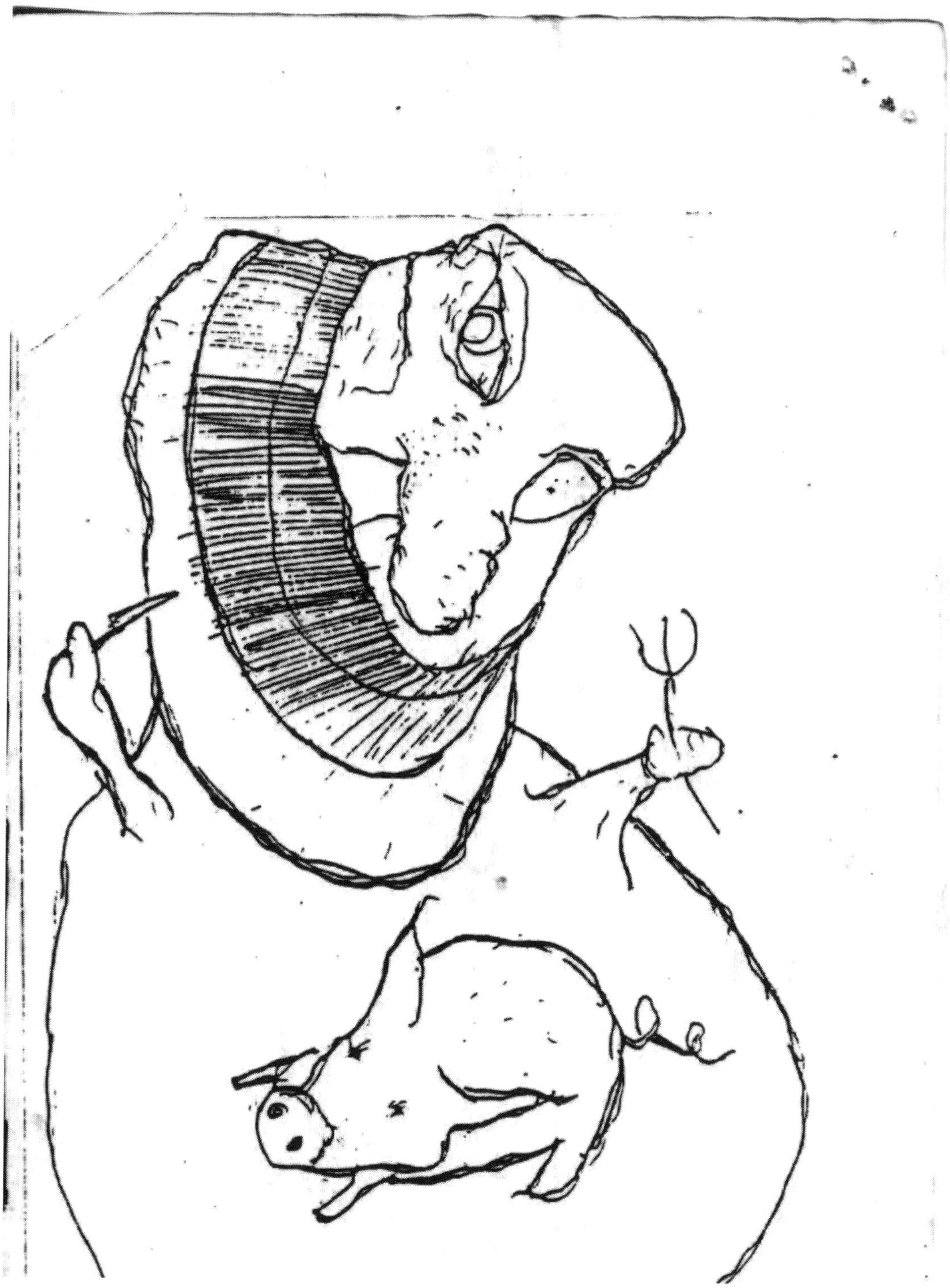

From Crass to Thrash, to Squeakers: The Suspicious Turn to Metal in UK Punk and Hardcore post '85.

Otto Sompank

I always loved the simplicity and visceral feel of all forms of punk. From the Pistols take on the New York Dolls rock or the UK Subs aggressive punk take on rhythm and blues. The stark reality Crass and the anarchist punk scene were informed with aspects of obscure seventies rock too. Granted. Perhaps the most famous and intense link to rock and punk was Motorhead. While their early output and LP's definitely had a clear nod to punk (Lemmy playing for the Damned), the t appealed to most if us back then with the sheer aggression and intensity. It's clear Motorhead and Black Sabbath influenced a lot of streetpunk and the ferocious tones of Discharge and their Scandinavian counterparts such as Riistetyt, Kaaos and Anti Cimex.

The early links were there but the influence of NWOBM (New Wave of British Heavy Metal) in turn influenced Metallica, Anthrax and Exodus in the early eighties. Most of them can be seen sporting Discharge, Broken Bones and GBH shirts on their early records. Not only that, Newcastle band Venom were equally influential in the mix of new genre forms germinating in the early 1980s. One of the early examples of the incorporation of rock and metal into the UK punk scene came from Discharge. After guitarist Bones left the band in 1982 leaving the *Hear Nothing, See, Nothing, Say Nothing* LP and the *State Violence, State Control* 7" as his intense legacy, the replacement of him with Pete 'Pooch' Pyrtle shifted the bands direction. Records such as 1983's *The Price of Silence, The More I See* and *Her Majesties Government* 12" ep clearly marked a shift in playing style with heavy nods to Ozzy Osbourne's vocal style and more rock style guitar and solos. Don't get me wrong, these records were killer, but still the importation and dare I say taming of the early, visceral and groundbreaking style was lost on these records. More on later Discharge in a bit. The circularity of influences in UK punk thus began to show themselves around 1983.

Around 1984/5 I spent a lot of my time hanging around with Victim in Nottingham. Guitar player with Concrete Sox, he turned me onto a lot of bands like Metallica, Anthrax and also the mighty Japanese band Gism who were pioneering a heavy mix of metal and aggressive punk into their innovative sound on the first (1984) LP, *Detestation*. All were ace records and marked a widening of my musical taste. My only flirtation with British heavy metal up to that point was buying Iron Maiden's *The Number of the Beast* 1982 LP. I was intrigued by the flirtation of demonic subject matter and now admit the clear punk influence on their earlier Paul DiAnno period LP's but that was my total experience of metal in that period. Really it did nothing for me. The Metallica and Anthrax LPs were different. Metallica were clearly drawing on the harsher aspects of UK punk and throwing the Danzig period (1982) *Earth AD* misfits records into the mix. The power they displayed had me hooked in late '84.

I'd met Victim hanging around the infamous Foresters Tavern Saturday afternoon punk drinking and gig sessions mid '84. We used to get pissed and watch the Seats of Piss with Hendrix Dead Boy singing into a traffic cone and pissing into pint glasses (another story). Other Notts bands playing these sessions were the Bloodsuckers and Concrete Evidence, Vic's band. Concrete evidence morphed into Concrete Sox shortly afterwards and Vic invited me down to their rehearsal sessions at the Nottingham Queens Walk Community Centre. This was a venue for loads of punk and anarcho-punk gigs alongside the Narrow Boat after the Union and Boat Clubs had ceased putting punk gigs on. Vic (guitar) and Les (bass) were clearly into all things thrash metal and through a few rehearsals I witnessed this influence appear in their sound. The rest is history and they were one of the UK bands at the beginning of a sea-change in the UK punk music sound. The other bands rehearsing there during this time was the early Heresy. They were an example of the faster versions of US hardcore such as DRI and Scandinavian Mob47 and also a peppering of the occasional metal riffs. Nottingham wasn't the only city to be feeling the shift in musical influence. Lots of other bands around the country were following suit. The other significant figure who used to sit in at these rehearsals was Digby Pearson, later of Earache Records, a dodgy lynchpin of the later shifts of underground punk music into the realm of the extreme metal.

Gradually, throughout 1985, the shift towards a metal crossover became increasingly evident in the UK punk scene at gigs. Key examples for me would be Sacrilege shifting from a classic Varukers sound to later metal; Onslaught becoming increasingly distant from their anarcho roots from their *Power from Hell* LP onwards and most notable would be Antisect's *Out from the Void* 7" demonstrating alongside the early germs of the later crust genre. Concrete Sox's first LP (1985), *Your Turn Next* equally captured the early spirit of metal influence in punk. On the other side of the coin, the influence of US hardcore sped things up musically. The Necros, Articles of Faith, Poison Idea, Negative Approach, Bad Brains, DRI, Septic Death, Minor Threat and the mighty Crucifix and MDC all helped shape up the increasingly diverse UK punk canon (and vice versa). A lot of bands began experimenting with both metal and faster playing double kick-drum styles such as English Dogs, Sacrilege & Onslaught, Cerebral Fix, Acid Reign etc. while Napalm Death, Generic, Electro Hippies, Heresy, Extreme Noise Terror and the Stupids experimented with international and US hardcore influences alongside new vocal and drum playing styles -the 'blast-beat- and song length. Things were clearly on the change.

Through 1986 things got more obvious. As with the first wave of punk the record labels came sniffing and a number of anarcho punk bands signed themselves into contracts and submitted to glossy pics in the metal press. The shouts of 'sell-out' soon filled the scene air. One of the key examples of this was the *Kerrang!* magazine, 1985-6 spin-off production, *Mega Metal Kerrang!* contained pictures of these once punk bands. Among the photos of Metallica, Anthrax, Coroner, Judas Priest were Sacrilege and the English Dogs, whose (1984) 12" *To the Ends of the Earth* contained some of the most intense punk/metal playing and song writing of that period.

Hair began to grow out too. Punk style was hybridised were with white basket ball boots, metal shirts, cut offs, long hair, colourful patches mixed in with all pre-existing styles. The world punk worked had clearly changed in a real short period. Eventually a lot of that long hair would revert to dreadlocks..., another bloody story.

The afore mentioned Discharge had encountered more line-up changes and the (1985) *Ignorance* 7" reflected this with a much more metal and rock approach to singing about traditional, political subjects. However by 1986, the band style had radically altered as had the singing style. This remains a divisive punk discussion to this day. Alongside Amebix's *Monolith* (1987) the merits of such 'albums' are endlessly and heatedly discussed. The record in question was Discharge's *Grave New World* (1986). Retaining the *Hear Nothing* record members Rainy, Cal and Garry Maloney and recruiting Skeptix guitarist Fish, the band released the first album since 1982. Let's just say it didn't go down well. Gone was the ferocity of the earlier records and instead a music more akin to hair metal bands such as Motley Crue etc. replaced it. Bad enough but this was topped by Cal's bizarre *squeaker* approach to the vocals. I clearly remember the utter disgust I felt after rushing home and playing it. Fucking hell, the band had lost it. This band were a massive influence on myself and peers back then and it seemed as if they'd become everything I hated. Poodle rock for fuck sake! I'll grant that some of the playing on that record is killer and the lyrics retained much of the harsh Cal style subject matter. That was it for me. Shite!

Discharge announced a UK and US tour mid 1986 to promote the new record: Nottingham was on the schedule. We blasted over to the Mardis Gras venue in Nottingham and got advance tickets. We all were pissed the new record sucked but held out that they'd at least play the old stuff......

A week or so earlier the Swedish powerhouse band roared through the Notts Mardis Gras venue. That was an amazing gig. Alongside killer sets from Agoni, Napalm Death and Heresy the show was a massive buzz. There's a YouTube video of me in the crowd dancing and headbanging like a maniac down the front; that was until some of the tough-guy wanker punks shoved everyone about and pissed me off. Still hated: wankers. Suffice to say the show was one of the best gig experiences of my life. The same could be said of the next Discharge gig albeit for entirely different reasons. Predictably the place was rammed. Skeptix opened and everything seemed as usual, good atmosphere, all the usual faces etc. Good times. Discharge were late on stage. Anticipation was high and good natured. Finally the band took to the stage. If I remember correctly Cal fell over on short stairs to the stage-side. Composure regained, the band burst into the first track off the new LP, *Sleep in Hope*. Bloody hell it was shit. Cal sounded like a drowned cat, and the metal stuff was not going down well. I noticed the bass player wasn't the mighty Rainy, who'd clearly had the good sense to see the writing on the wall. Another couple of 'squeaker number's later and Cal addressed the crowd in a corny American accent. "Whoa, we've been gone for a couple of years but now we're back and gonna shake you down!" he said wiping stage sweat from his eyes, wearing a white vest blue jeans and a long, bouffant haircut to match the other band members. The first 'boo, get off you're shit' rang out from the increasingly unhappy crowd of punks. We were all still angry about the world and this stuff wasn't resonating with us at all. Still we could wait in hope for them to do some of the old stuff. No chance....on went the squeaker with more of this metal dross., 'The crowd continued to shout for old stuff..... "'Fight Back', ahhh' 'Decontrol' and 'State Violence'". The band was deaf to this. Another couple of songs and the crowd was livid. The gap between band and audience widened and the beer and other 'stuff' began to rain down on them. They did another song but half way through one of the long benches in the venue was launched at the band followed by a few bar-stools. Off the band went to the dressing room which was subsequently surrounded by crossed-arm bouncers. Show over. Fuck sake, I was gutted.

The tour continued with similar reactions across the UK and US with HR, singer of the Bad Brains dousing the ill-fated Cal with a bucket of water mid-set. The tour ended and the band headed back to the UK with a seriously smacked arse.

The Discharge brand of metal was not of the thrash variety which, alongside Hardcore, took an increasing slice of the UK punk scene. Lots of bands grew their hair out, chugged the chords and learned guitar solos and double kick pedals. Don't get me wrong this was a significant yet not a totalising shift in the British scene. As Ian Glasper in *Trapped in a Scene* (2009) has noted in considerable detail in his collection of interviews with 1980s UK punk and hardcore bands there was still much to celebrate in innovative musical terms. Granted some bands like the Varukers grew their hair and played thrash metal in this case as Arbitrator, but at least changed their name to establish critical distance from previous outputs. That said the decade of 80s punk was marked by a clear merging of musical boundaries and in some cases a defence of existing ones.

Such innovations also had casualties stateside with bands such as SSD Control adopting hair and poodle-metal styles before exploding. The germs had been set free though. Underground punk genres began to explode into a bewildering amount of sub-categories all replete with individual takes on pre-existing punk, metal and rock influences, in addition to a host of other styles. Crust, stenchcore, Britcore, thrash, pop-punk, skate-rock, power violence, grindcore, epic crust, burning spirits, drunk punk, UK82, Nardcore, Horror Punk classic anarcho, NYHC, D-Beat, raw punk, scandi-thrash, straight edge, metal core, noise-punk, hardline, Boston style, Swedish mangel are a small off the top of the head example of the hundreds of international punk styles, communities of taste, now existing. Even the Discharge Pyrtle period and *Grave New World* record has admirers and those influenced by it for example. Japan's Final Bombs do an excellent take on the Pyrtle years in their 2011 *There Is No Turning Back* LP replete with silver *Grave New World* style art, while Scotland's Thisclose reinterpret the *Grave New World* LP in numerous records with Cal style 'squeaking' for a more accepting and open-minded punk generation. The discussion of style influence is endless and unsolvable regarding the merits, intricacies and failures or futures of it all: who sold out who ripped who off....yawn. All I've offered here is a very partial and personal take on it all. It is safe to say, however, that, thankfully, punk never stays still and is always producing new cutting edges: that's what keeps it strong in the 2010s.

There's more to be said on this, but that's for later

Chumbawamba. A retrospective.

Chris Butler

After 30 years of making music and mischief, Chumbawamba announced in 2012 that there would be no more recordings or concerts. So what? I don't hear you ask. No one died. And anyway, they were just a band! But for anyone who enjoyed and followed their work, it was a loss to the world of music and for those that found inspiration from them to channel into their own creative ways.

Anyone interested in them will have their own fond memories of times they've seen the band live and there's always a great back catalogue for people to discover in the future and some historians could do worse than see what some of us have been up to for the last couple of decades as those in power try to sex up, dumb down and whitewash over our recent radical and political history…

Since discovering music and beginning a life-long love and obsession with it, I now don't recall much of a time when I wasn't aware of Chumbawamba, or the times before I listened to them or awaited their next piece of work with interest.

My earliest recollections of them are during the early 1980's. I'd be around 11 or 12 years old and had already moved on from my mum's Elvis Presley records to my brother's punk rock records. With a bit of my own Adam and the Ants thrown in also. I'd sit with my brother in our shared bedroom and listen to his collection of mainly anarcho punk vinyl records. I didn't always understand everything I heard or read but was captivated none the less.

Those fabulous fold-out record sleeves which once unfolded became posters. I read every word and song lyric and slowly began to understand some of the ideas from some of the bands. One such record that I listened to was a double vinyl compilation album and this is where I first encountered Chumbawamba…

They stood out because they didn't sound like a lot of the other bands on the record or like anything else I'd ever heard. I remember writing to lots of bands around this time. I was inquisitive, enthusiastic and knew I wanted to be a part of this political and punk movement somehow. I just didn't know how yet. I'd write letters to bands asking for more information, sending them a S.A.E (at their request) and was always so excited when I'd get a reply - from an actual band member! You didn't get that sort of response from joining the Adam and the Ants fan club!

So, anyway, I'd written to Crass and Flux of Pink Indians and a whole load of others - and one of which was Chumbawamba. I remember coming home from school to find a package waiting for me from the postman which I tore open to find leaflets and flyers, a booklet and a lovely letter from a man called Dunstan. He thanked me for writing and for taking an interest and more importantly he didn't just send me a list of merchandise the band had for sale (which was so often the replies I'd received). He also enclosed a compilation cassette (which came with the accompanying booklet) called The Animals Packet. This featured Chumbawamba and a host of other artists all contributing songs in defence of animal rights. This also set me off on another trail of discovering and writing to yet more bands but that's another story!

And that was my first encounter with Chumbawamba. Then came more demo cassettes from them and me reaching my 14th birthday and now able to attend gigs and so by the mid-1980's I was able to see them live for the first time. They were my favourite band. They were humorous, inspiring, informative, clever, interesting, inclusive (I didn't look like a punk as I didn't wear a leather jacket and had a self-cut skinhead haircut but then neither did they - and yet, I was sure they were still punks!) and above all, they were listenable! Not only did some of their recordings sound totally different from each other but some songs on each recording sounded different from the one before!

Like my brother had done with Crass, I found myself attending any gigs I could get to when they (and others) played a town within reach. And before too long we were travelling all over the UK to watch Chumbawamba and other bands. And that's why they made such a big impact on me. For me, they've been an inspiration since not only when I became interested in music but from when I became politicised also. And that's two things that have stayed with me to this day.

The amount of time and money spent travelling around the UK to watch them live does really not bare thinking about. Was it time well spent? Well, I enjoyed it and I've got some incredible memories from those times and travels that will stay with me forever. Much in the same way that you will have your own fond memories of good times you've shared also.

There's been so many fantastic, strange, unique, funny, exhilarating and moving experiences over the last 20 odd years that I've been lucky to have enjoyed because of hearing that band called Chumbawamba: The recorded output which covered folk, pop, punk and even dance music. The pranks. The Brit Awards. Pantomimes and plays. The pop chart success (which I remember fondly as one of the few times I had a day job where my work colleagues had heard of any of the bands I went to see live) which saw politics and anarchism being talked and sang about intelligently on daytime national TV.

The other bands I discovered through watching Chumbawamba such as Tottenham AK47's, Back To The Planet, O'Hooley & Tidow and Credit To The Nation. The stripped down acoustic band. Dubiously convicted Armed robber Martin Foran while on the run from police custody coming on stage at one of their London gigs. Ambulance workers while on strike joining them on stage. Concerts that involved as much theatre and dressing up as they did music. Watching Chumbawamba in very diverse surroundings from community centres, arts centres and clubs to salubrious concert halls and outdoor festivals. Sleeping on railway stations after gigs when we couldn't get anywhere to stay - There was snow on the ground in Oxford and I didn't think I'd survive the night, we were locked in a railway workers shed overnight in Blackburn (for security purposes of the railway workers out working on the railway track on the night shift. They said we wouldn't last the night out in the cold so we lay in pitch-black darkness with rats or mice running over us all night and the railway workers unlocked the shed the next morning and gave us the most welcome cups of tea I've ever had) and then there was the time I was offered somewhere to stay after a gig in Leeds until the strange man noticed I wasn't on my own and so got back in his car and drove off...

And later when I became active in music myself (albeit on a smaller scale than Chumbawamba of course), they continued to be an inspiration which whether consciously or subconsciously has ranged from me having an idea and an enthusiasm to just 'go for it' to some very near plagiarising at times! The odd song idea, tune, title or melody sometimes has owed a nod to them while learning about song writing myself and on some of my recordings there are a couple of very obvious Chumbawamba references if you look carefully.

Most recently, I even covered one of their early songs on my latest CD. The song is a fabulous folk song despite being written by the band when they certainly weren't considered to be a folk band. And since their stripped down acoustic formation in recent years I was able to share a stage with them on a couple of occasions which for me was like travelling full circle and was a unique and enjoyable experience to play to their audience - of which I'd so long been one. Somehow though, I felt like an impostor. They were a proper band with great musicians and wonderful singing voices, all harmony vocals and a wealth of fabulous songs. I was just this bloke with a guitar who somehow had (almost like an Eric Morecambe sketch) took a wrong turn and walked out onto the stage by accident to find an audience facing me and waiting to be entertained…

But it was great fun to be a small part of their gigs and an education in watching proper musicians at work! I even learnt so much just watching their sound check! The Beatles song Help! springs to mind on one occasion and such was the version that it demonstrated their abilities as musicians which often got overlooked amongst everything else they were known for or labelled as.

The last 30 odd years of popular music was all the more interesting because of them. so, rather than lamenting the demise of one of the truly unique bands in my lifetime (and after seeing some of the diverse range of work the band members have already gone on to produce: Alice Nutter writing compelling works of drama for the BBC and Dunstan Bruce's latest band Interrobang?! being talked about in the same breath as Sleaford Mods and Eight Rounds Rapid as a band to look out for), I'm more intrigued to see what creative works happen in the future now this band of individuals are all doing their own thing!

Now that's got to be worth a look…

A KING ARTHUR FILM ON T.V.—

TWO MILITARY FORCES POISED — ALL IS SILENT NOW AS BOTH ARMIES WAIT. A SNAKE SLITHERS THROUGH THE GRASS, AND A SOLDIER DRAWS HIS SWORD FEARING THAT IT WILL BITE HIS LEG. SOMEBODY ON THE OTHER SIDE ONLY SEES A RAISED SWORD, AND INTERPRETS THIS TO BE A SIGNAL THAT THE OTHER SIDE IS ABOUT TO CHARGE.

THUS HE DRAWS HIS OWN SWORD, WHICH IN TURN IS INTERPRETED BY SOMEONE ON THE OTHER SIDE AS A SIGNAL THAT THE OTHER SIDE IS ABOUT TO CHARGE.

escalation → escalation → escalation →

EACH OF THE SOLDIERS, SEEING HIS OPPOSITE NUMBER DRAW FIRST, FIGHTS A WAR AGAINST THE AGGRESSOR, TO "UPHOLD THE PEACE"... AND YET

NOBODY QUESTIONS THE PRESENCE OF MILITARY FORCES AS ACTUALLY CAUSING THE WAR... AS THEY ADVERTISE IT'S WORTH AS "A THREAT WHOSE PURPOSE IS TO AVERT A WAR..."

CHUMBAWAMBA

CONFLICT!

Chris Butler

The date: Thursday 9th May 1985.

I was 14 years old and whilst already familiar with punk rock - the bands, the music and the whole punk rock movement, it was on this date that I saw Conflict for the first time.

I'd already started attending gigs after making the progression from becoming interested in music a few years earlier (around the ages of 9 or 10 when I'd avidly listened to any music I was exposed to - soaking up all genres and styles, listening to the differences in all the music I could get hold of which ranged from my mum's Elvis Presley records to my brother's punk rock records and anything in-between) to then listening, buying and swapping with friends my own collection of vinyl records.

By this time, I'd moved on from the Showaddywaddy single I'd bought from the music department in the local Co-Op store. I had even moved on from Adam & The Ants whose posters and pictures had replaced the Everton FC team poster on my bedroom wall. By the time I was in my early teens, I'd fell in love with punk rock.
[A footnote to this piece could add that I did eventually see both Showaddywaddy and Adam Ant live (in 2004 in Derby and at the Bearded Theory Festival, Derbyshire in 2012 respectively) and a great night out and festival they were too. However, those are other stories for another day...]

By 1985, my bedroom walls were draped in political slogans and foldout record sleeves from bands on the Crass Records label. I'd become politicised (of sorts) in that I was taking an interest in the world around me. I had been on a few demonstrations and marches regarding anti war and animal rights issues as well as raising money for the striking miners. I hung around alternative bookshops in the same way that today's teenagers hang around video game shops or fast food outlets. I developed a fascination with politics, the news and in history of all sorts - British, world, political, social - after deciding that I needed to know about things that had happened in the past if I wanted to make things better for the future.

In short, I maybe wasn't your typical kid. Though I was finding friendships with likeminded souls, from the kids at school whom I was joining anti-war and Amnesty International groups with to those I had met through punk music and was hanging out with, swapping and sharing records with and now going to concerts with.

My brother had followed such bands as Crass and Conflict around the UK and I will forever be in debt to him for that introduction to punk music and radical politics he gave (as well as Everton FC too but I digress...) and after taking me to a couple of gigs already, I finished school one day to find there was a place in the car for me for the trek to Surbiton in Surrey for that night's Conflict gig. With Mick (who later became the bass player of City Indians, Derby based anarcho punk band who regularly gigged with Conflict in the mid to late 1980's) driving his dad's car, my brother Kev, their mates Ed and Saul and I filled the last available seat in the back of the car as we set off straight after the school bell from Derbyshire to Surrey.

Keeping in mind this was long before words like 'sat-nav' were used and I'm sure none of the others despite their 5 years advantage over me had heard of the town of Surbiton either unless it was from episodes of the TV series The Good Life. I remember us being far too deep into London itself than we needed to be before then getting lost within the county of Surrey for some time.

How we eventually found the Assembly Rooms is anyone's guess but we did. I was a trainspotter, keen railway traveller and at 14 years of age - a non-driver of course, so you would be correct in thinking my input was nil. I wasn't any help at all but thanks to the others, after 4 or 5 hours travelling we somehow eventually arrived in Surbiton. Music was already blaring out of the Assembly Rooms. We had certainly missed a band or two for sure but had now arrived. And the last hurdle for me (and especially after such a long distance to travel) was the possibility of being turned away at the door for being too young to gain entry! Left to sit in the car all night knowing that Conflict, yes, Conflict! were on stage inside that concert hall across the street!

I'm not sure how I would have taken such news to be honest. However, I needn't have worried. We made our way through the entrance of the town's Assembly Rooms and I paid my £1.50 to the female punk sitting on the door. Holding out my soft, never-done-a day's-work hand whilst trying to look old enough to be admitted into the venue, I received the stamp of confirmation on the back of my hand and the assurance that I was in, accepted and welcome to be part of this radical tribe inside. The punk girl on the door held out a plastic tub full of pin-badges and asked if I'd like a few. I picked a few out, put a couple in my pocket and pinned one onto my self-dyed black ex-army shirt.

(I went through a phase of dying various garments black. Some results were better than others though the inside of the saucepan I used to mix the dye and the water in wasn't fit to be used for cooking food ever again.)

The badge featuring a picture of then Prime Minister Margaret Thatcher with a gun-sight over her head gave no room for doubt to where this concert's allegiances lay. As an aside, I've still got one of the badges, thirty years on it's pinned to my guitar strap.

The room inside was busy with people talking, laughing, drinking, dancing, staggering or jumping about. Whatever took their fancy I suppose as the band played from upon the stage. A nice high stage too in order for a young kid like myself to get a good view of the bands. I had recognised the unmistakeable sound of vocalist Stig of Icons Of Filth as I walked into the hall and almost hypnotically, felt myself pulled to the stage hoping that it wasn't their last song we'd just arrived in time to see. Luckily, they had only taken to the stage a few minutes earlier and I was able to enjoy my first Icons Of Filth gig and the passion and raw emotion that Stig and the band provided from the stage in front of me. I was lucky enough to see Icons Of filth again on occasion and they became a firm favourite of mine - not least because of their brilliant performance on this first night that I saw them.

I met up with my own crowd and got talking to others - strangers I had never met before who treated me kindly and didn't dismiss or ignore me for being a kid. I felt included and a part of what was happening. I had found somewhere that I felt I wanted to be a part of in such a way that I hadn't felt previously.

I met Colin, the singer of Conflict. He seemed huge with his hair in long rigid spikes and seemed to tower over me as he shook my hand and asked if I was alright before thanking me for coming. I stood there probably looking a bit of an odd kid with my toothy grin beaming from ear to ear, nervously shuffling from one foot to the other and not really formulating much of an answer in response. I remember some years later thinking that this particular memory must have been exaggerated over the years and he wasn't really that large a character - It was just that I was young at the time. And you can take a few inches off him for that hairstyle he had!

But then I stood chatting to him at the Rebellion Festival in 2012 (and I'm in my forties now so not expecting to grow any taller) and I realised he really is a good few inches taller than me - and without his spikes! I found that we had already missed a few bands due to our late arrival into Surbiton, namely AYS, State Hate and Stigma but luckily we hadn't missed Lost Cherrees who took to the stage next. They, like Icons Of Filth were a band I was already aware of and enjoyed but hadn't seen live until this night.

This gig was getting better all the time! With their thoughtful lyrics wrapped up in melodic tunes, distinctive keyboards and harmonious singing from the two female singers, the Lost Cherrees stood out from other punk rock bands both at this gig and on the punk scene throughout. They were on excellent form with a mix of their album and earlier recordings along with newer songs that became the Unwanted Children 12".

Following their set was Legion Of Parasites. I'd not heard them previously so this live set was my first introduction to them. Their hardcore thrash punk sound was different again to the bands already played and I enjoyed their energetic and noisy set despite being unfamiliar with the songs.

Eventually, it was time for Conflict. Anticipation filled the room and with an introduction to get the audience fired up and ready for a blatant assault on the ears, the band launched into a ferocious set of some of the best punk rock songs you are ever likely to hear. Even back in the 1980's, the band had already in their short lifespan notched up a terrific back catalogue of anarcho-punk songs. Their albums (which still hold up to a listen today) were benchmarks for other politically charged punk bands to aim for. Their use of artwork, colour sleeves (amongst the generic black and white foldout poster sleeves within the anarchist bands and labels), clever song writing, listenable tunes within their fast hardcore punk sound and subjects covered that left you under no illusion what this band's opinion was on any given subject.

I watched them from start to finish, a 14 year old lad half mesmerised and rooted to the spot, never wanting their set to end and half set to leave the venue with a belief that we can change the world for the better. It was one of those eureka moments. Like a light bulb being switched on. Sure, I'd already been reading up on politics and history, had decided that this world wasn't always just or fair and had already been turned on to punk music but this night and this band was a revelation. A change is needed I thought and I wanted to form a band or write a fanzine or organise concerts and basically throw myself into this punk rock movement to help make those dreams of peace and equality a reality... If you're going to have ideas, then have big ones I thought.

What happened at the end of this gig is now part of punk folklore and history.

Possibly one of the earliest Conflict concerts to attract a major police presence?

The police were waiting outside the venue at the end of the gig. Not just a couple of 'bobbies' walking the beat either. But to my thinking, it looked like half the Met. had been placed on duty. SPG (the infamous Special Patrol Group) were on standby with vans usually on hand for riots and football hooligans. As I recall, we were heading out of the venue when the police blocked the entrance in the hallway.

I was penned in and unable to see what was ahead and unable to move out of the throng. It was frightening but all happening so quick that I wasn't sure what to do except to keep my eyes on my friends and my brother as I didn't wish to be separated from them.

I saw a few objects fly overhead in the direction of the police and as I'm sometimes reminded, I was heard to shout the least threatening call ever at any punk gig in "Come on, let us out - I've got school in the morning!" We headed back into the venue as some of the punks started to move away. A fire-door was now open and so we walked out into the street.

Within a couple of minutes we had re-grouped, were in the safety of our car and driving away from the surreal images of a leafy middle class suburb with more police vehicles than I'd ever seen outside of Saturday match days.

I've since seen press cuttings and media reports about the trouble that happened that night. Arrests were made, some people went away with sore heads and I believe Colin of Conflict was kept in custody overnight and in the courts the following morning charged with ABH (aggressive bodily harm) on a police officer...

Me? I was back at school the following morning with a swagger that only an anti-Margaret Thatcher badge on your school blazer can give you.

No Defences Booklet Worried

Courtesy Nigel Crouch and Darren John's Collections

this booklet was written and put together by the
people in NO DEFENCES in april 1984.
the way some of it is written may make you think
it's propaganda,(which it is like everything else)
but at least it's blatant and you can put it in
the bin if you don't like it. the subtler propaganda
of school,home,work and society in general is much
more diffucult to throw away.

NO DEFENCES - there appear to be barriers which
prevent communication between people. these defences,
purely mental attitudes,have to be broken if we
are to attain any level of unity sufficient to
effect real change.

you can write to us if you like via:

We live in a society governed by money, the relentless, ruthless search and protection of wealth - where 'to have' is more important than 'to be.' The population's worth is decided by each person's ability to make money - sometimes vast amounts of it, money so abundant that its only use is making more money.

Big men, big houses, big cars - not forgetting the other little possession, a must for every businessman, the wife. 'Oh let's buy little Andrew a BMW for his birthday, he might pass his driving test soon.' The wealth of the country and all its merry tycoons is evident all around.

But at the same time there are people in less well off neighbourhoods who find it almost impossible to afford basic human neccessities like food, clothing and housing. We are led to believe that poverty does not exist in this country, and that the welfare state will take care of anyone who believes otherwise, but every Christmas hundreds of people die in Britain because they cannot afford to both heat their homes and eat. The Church is one of the wealthiest landowners in Britain today and, ironically, it is often most popular in poor areas. Yet the Church won't hesitate to evict the poor who cannot pay their rents, as it furnishes its palaces with gold, silk and priceless treasures.

Meanwhile, back in the City, the company director earning £25,000 every year has his two company cars, his cheap mortgage, his expenses paid holiday abroad and a pension plan designed to give him a large income from when he retires to the day he dies. A recent article in the Daily Mail attacked those who would raise their voices in protest at this obscene wealth. It stated that the only reason for these atacks was ENVY. Can you believe their arrogance? Envy. every week millions of people are forced to accept insultingly low wages or are slapped in the face with a Girocheque worth a few quid. Is it so wrong for those people to look at the company executive and wish for just a little of that man's wealth? Is that what the rich would call envy? The Daily Mail article goes on to imply that this poverty need not exist, that poverty is the fault of the individual due to lack of ambition. The social do-gooders, states the article, should not look to reducing the wealth of the rich, but to increasing the wealth of the poor. Oh yeah, who do they think they're fooling? Without those poorly paid workers the rich bloodsuckers could make little of their

money,while the socialist elite
exploit the votes of the poor to
maintain their popularity.

By aspiring to their money
orientated way of life we are playing
right into the hands of the parasites
who exploit our labours.But if we
realise that large sums of money
are not neccessary to sustain
ourselves,both physically and also
spiritually,the parasites begin to
lose control.

The wealthy appease their consciences
in the face of poverty by donating
piddling little sums to charities.
They send money to the starving
in Africa,the diseased in India
and to the orphans and homeless
in war-torn Asia - places
sufficiently remote that they never
truly confront the problems.

Harrods' largest egg is called Big Bertha, weighs 22 lb and costs £185. This year one was

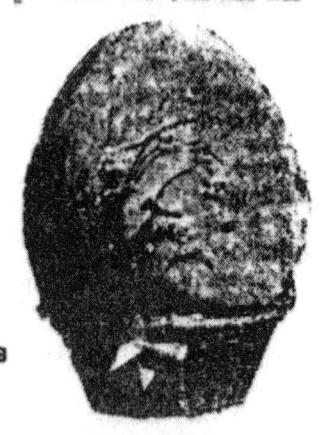

**Pride of Harrods :
An egg costing over £100**

bought by a gentleman who had accidentally crashed his helicopter on a lady's lawn and wanted to give her a present as an apology.

> 'You're the first with food parcels
>   to the starving in Afghanistan
> India or Kenya or anywhere really.
> And when the war was over in Vietnam
> You had three adopted boys and five adopted girls.
> You're too busy fighting your   irrelevant battles
> To see what's going on in your   own back yard.'
>
>   Patrik Fitzgerald -'Irrelevant Battles'

In the press every week we are confronted by pathetic
appeals for help from countries stricken by drought,famine,
war and disease.An old woman is freezing to death in her
East London home because she cannot afford coal - the
agony is the same,yet no one holds out the collecting
plate for her.

While there is a tremendous difference in the scale of
poverty between the 'Third World' (patronisingly termed
'underdeveloped' by the wealthy nations) and Britain,the
reasons for their continuance are very much the same:the

rich and people who support the concept of wealth are loath to see any of their money go to those less well off than themselves.It's in their interests to see that the less fortunate stay that way.Notice the delight with which the media report any 'rags to riches' tales and the popularity of the 'working class hero.'They are well publicised, creating the impression that real wealth can be earned by starting at the bottom and working up,giving the poor a false sense of hope.If they allow a few to get rich,the rest will be happy thinking they could do the same.

Our worth is decided by our ability to buy.Everyday,at school,at work,in the street,at home,on t.v. we are bombarded by the notion that happiness can be bought.Not content with exploiting our labour making cheap crap,they sell it back to us at a huge profit.They invent products, commodities,useless little toys and then convince us that we need them.Like children in a sweet shop we reach out and grab all we can.

Well we don't need their toys.We can do without their three-speed ovens and luxury cars with detatchable swimming pools.There IS more to life than money and possessions.

Perhaps some of what I've written is verging on 'Class War' politics.But I know that where a THEM vs. US situation exists no change will ever come.The authorities make sure that the 'US' remains,in the eyes of the public,a very small reactionary minority whose only aim is to create social chaos and moral decline.This was demonstrated during the 1960s,especially in the USA,to a lesser extent in Britain.The 'Them vs. Us' ethic is manipulated,or rather invented,by the government and its media to set up a barrier to effective scial change.We must allow as few barriers as possible to exist between people,drop our own defences to eachother and realise that the only way to true freedom, and quality of life,is to rid society of the creeps who seek to rule us.

> The rich would have to eat money,but luckily the poor provide food.
> Russian proverb.

WE LOSE PEOPLE - absorbed when they leave school or home and have to fend for themselves. Forced into compromise to 'look after number one'- an excuse to sell out. Looking after yourself doesn't need to be an excuse for doing something you hate - it's like eating meat, we know that we can survive without it, so why cause suffering?

In the same way we must become aware that our visions of of how it could be are liveable alternatives NOW. Certainly there are restrictions, but the biggest appear to be our fear and lack of imagination. So why do a job that exploits others and in which you are exploited? Can't we earn money without causing suffering?

I don't believe that most of the British public will have decided to oppose all power by the end of my life. Yet why should this be an excuse for not bothering to act? It doesn't affect my desire for total change at all.

Co-operation and understanding is the best way to exist with the people whom we love and trust, that is something to aim for now, not in the future.

Ifeel it necessary to express my hatred for control, even iftis having no effect (and who can guage that?). Otherwise I would feel Iwas betraying myself and future generations. People have different reasons for their need to remove this corrupt system which virtually swamps us, yet surely a lifestyle which is closer to the life we would like to lead IDEALLY must be better than a compromised existance for which we continually feel guilty and only do because it brings home a few extra quid.

AT PRESENT THIS WORLD HANGS AT THE BRINK OF NUCLEAR DESTUCTION.YET EVEN IF IT DOES ESCAPE THIS,THE WORLD IS STILL FACED WITH THE PROBLEM OF THE PROFIT-SEEKING, INDIFFERENT ATTITUDES THAT GOVERN AND DESTROY OUR EARTH.

Each day as the population increases,fertile land becomes more scarce,either turned over to housing development or agriculture to feed and house this growing population.Our countryside and even vast forests such as those in Brazil are rapidly being destroyed,which in turn threatens the balance of nature which has existed and prospered for millions of years.The earth's resources are rapidly being exhausted whilst nothing is returned,leaving the mere skeleton of a planet.Factories and carspump out deadly carbon monoxide and other gases into the air we breath whilst acid rain threatens the remaining European forests and wildlife.Radioactive waste is carelessly pumped by Sellafield (Windscale) into the Irish Sea only to be swept back by the tides to polute the coastline and its population. And now the government,despite repeated leakages at Sizewell and Windscale,considers nuclear power stations safe enough to be built in large conurbations such as Hartlepool.

While millions die in poverty in the third world the western world indulges in gluttony,feeding on unhealthy processed foods,its consumerist society creating excessive waste out of indifference and greed.Butter and other food mountains are kept merely to preserve economic order and are eventually destroyed rather than supplying them to the underfed.70% of Americas most fertile land is devoted to grazing or crops for cattle,which are slaughtered to satisfy western diets,when it could be used more efficiently and humanely to grow crops for human consumtion.I could go on but it's clear that the economy of the western world is based on greed and waste.Such a society will surely destroy both itself and the world it inhabits.

Yet any protest seems futile,lost like a voice in the wind. It's situations like these that test and expose the sham of democracy,for we seem powerless against the deaf ears and layers of bureaucracy that fill Westminster,and any change is so compromised that it becomes worthless,for government always seeks to maintain those with power already i.e. themselves and wealthy industrialists.

But it's not merely enough to demonstrate in CND rallies

even though it's easier not to bother at all. For this is a universal problem not a petty side issue for even our remaining freedoms are being eroded. Cameras survey on marches and on motorways. The authorities have access to a wide range of personal computerised information and even now in the bill to control video nasties, the government has introduced a measure which could place all films at the hands of the government censor, and so control political information should the government see fit to do so.

Furthermore, a new police bill is being introduced giving the police the right to hold people for over 96 hours, whilst the basic freedom of movement that was once taken for granted is now being eroded, as the miners strike has shown. On their own these facts mean little, but together they show the gradual slide towards a highly centralised police state in which we will become even more powerless.

It's so easy, therefore, just to sink into an existance of apathy and fall into the trap of vegitating in front of the t.v. or escaping this world at the disco or pub every night. But this apathy offers no hope. At least protest does, for although as individuals we may be powerless, co-operating together there is still a chance to defeat the life-destroying madness that governs our existance and our earth. Those that govern us are lifeless, burnt out corpses feeding off those they rule. We, however, are young and given the chance have the rest of our lives to live. It's up to us not to let them steal it from us.

there is a scream behind a door,an agonised cry of terror.
the animals die in secret.joe public thinks that if it
happens at all,it must be for the best,to protect him against
thalidomide and tell him bleach burns.he thinks they must
treat the animals kindly while they live and kill them
quickly and painlessly,he thinks lots pf people would
suffer if a few animals didn't.he loves animals,his kids have
a rabbit,he has two dogs.he hasn't seen the rows of drugged,
dying rabbits in the labs,the corpses thrown in a heap,dogs,
rats,cats,mice,hamsters,monkeys,he sees only anti-freeze,
aftershave and phensic.
   jane public loves animals too.she imagines foxes are
lovely because her fox-fur stole is so nice.she thinks
revlon's factories must be full of beautiful people like in
their adverts,she dreams of modelling the new spring range
for revlon.she doesn't know revlon first test their
glamourous make-up before she buys it.they test in modern
scientific laboratories full of white coats and bags of
rotted fur and guts.
   the vivisectionists know what they are doing,they're
doing their job.maybe once they thought it was crazy that
the river of animals flooded through the lab,coming as pets
in crates and leaving in bin liners,soft and lifeless.now
they accept it,they say it's the bosses responsibility,
they're only following his orders,hoping for promotion.they
are cynical about the world,it stinks,always has done,
always will.
   mr. revlon has never seen the labs but he knows theycost
him a great deal of money.he couldn't care if his products
were safe or not,except that a scandal might wound his
sales,and as long as they are tested no one-can complain.
he is desperate to get the new range of lipsticks out before
the gimmick leaks to his competitors.his profits on this
one could be enormous.still that infuriating legislation
keeps the new range off the shelves for another week and a
week's a long time where competition is the name of the
game,where a new product every month keeps the fickle heart
of the consumer fluttering with excitement,tantalises them,
the purses open.every product advertised as'new' must go
through the l.d.50 test where a group of labradors or
alsations are force-fed increasing quantities of revlon's
new lipsticks until half of them die.the purpose of this is
to determine the quantity of revlon lipsticks an alsation

would have to eat before it poisoned itself.at the end of
the test all the living animals that remain are killed too.
mr.revlon couldn't give a monkeys about the animals.he
just wants to see the product in the shops and the profits
rolling in.
   the doctors are embarrassed,they've nearly lost the
confidence of the common people.some kwacks and misfits
almost managed to expose the shakey foundation of western
medicine.they made the doctors look like babies at play.
the doctors' careers rest on a system for human repair that
is only 80 years old.the doctors have the confidance of
alchemists who'd discovered the secret of eternal life.the
chinese laugh modestly at them,the chinese have a system
for human repair and maintenance that is 8000 years old.
the doctors are panicking as the geriatric wards are nearly
half-filled with victims of drugg abuse.drugs the doctors
prescribed.they knew the drugs were tested millions of times
on millions of animals,but in the end rats aren't the same
as people,nor even are monkeys.and nearly every time the
doctors prescribed to make people better they just get
worse or die.
   the anti-vivisectionists break into the labs and steal the
animals.they don't care what anyone thinks about it because
no-one except them cares what the animals think about it.
they speak for the animals who don't speak english.maybe
they think they'll have to keep stealing the animals until
there's a revolution in the way people think.the animals
will be free when profit,make-up and phensic mean nothing,
when life is more important than anything and humans learn
to be responsible for their actions,when there are no more
scapegoats,human or animal.

   it's true that the problems we face are easier to
perpetrate than solve.tradition fills the mind
like concrete - we all feel that - but these
barriers must be broken.we must learn to get
through.

we play,dance beats,funk,punk,
regular beats to dance,dance,dance,
like the pub acts,bars,booze and
cigarettes,a stage,an act,40
minutes of entertainment,not a
word gets through,macho dancing,
pushing,releasing aggressions,
teeth clenched.

pretty girls,pretty boys,too
loud to talk,just drunk and
pick up,the girl singers they
fantasise fucking,the boy singers
they wish they'd raise their
fists and incite them to rip it
up,not a word gets through,
all the abuses of the streets
and homes brought into the
gigs,one samey conventional
good time when there's a
million different ways.

something more - communication,
inspiration,information,music,
words and pictures,if you don't
participate this time,at least it
must be possible to hear,see and
understand so you can criticise
or use what is done.when we all
know what it is we're up against
and what to do about it,then
maybe it's solidarity we need,
ideas in the face of fear.

gigs are a chance for so much more
than following the conventions
to which we all say we are opposed.

'Money may not buy happiness, but it does buy good psychiatric help.

Fuck War.

Paul Davies

It was 1981 or maybe 1982 and I had just left home and I was a depressed teen. I moved into a shared bedsit with two punks listening to Crass, Adam and the Ants, Toyah and Damned.

I met James who lived downstairs with his brother who introduced me to TRB then suggested I get involved with Nottingham CND. While volunteering in the office, James invited me to a local anti-war demonstration outside of the army careers centre – a mixture of middle class pacifists and a few local anarchists.

When we turned up, the organisers asked for volunteers to climb up on top of the large flat canopy above the door. I never looked back. For the next couple of years, I continued volunteering at the office, mixing with the local anarchists, marching with CND, occupying grain stores, RAF bases and being held on remand for refusing to give my name. In 1983 / 1984 the underground grape vine called for a general blockade in London against war.

James and a few of us hitch-hiked down the M1 to the Ambulance Station and Bingo Hall squats for a bit of DIY. I recall Crass, Flux and No Defences playing at one or the other of the squats - it's all bit fuzzy.

We did manage to Stop the City (well, the police actually closed down the whole area for us) and right in the heart of financial London, but the cops used their horses to kettle us in and slowly began crushing us. Everyone wanted a toilet and no one was allowed to leave for several hours. People were scared and became more agitated. I saw a few smashed windows lots of angry punks with anarchist flags and logos screaming Poison Girls, Mob and Discharge.

We had become politically radical and that felt very good. We felt we were helping reveal the real social problems. We didn't always have an answer, but we were standing up and, very actively, shouting NO.

The punk era was so important because the music produced a youthful voice, energy and encouraged action. The political logic of groups such as Crass seemed unquestionable as they revealed the ways in which war and capitalism and the abuse of power served to benefit the few and disempowered the many.

We stood up and we stood out and sometimes I felt I was a lonely minority on one.

The problem of social isolation infers an inability to change the status quo, and the anarcho-punk scene simply embraced this isolation and helped us all scream our way through. In short, the sense of culture and community helped to offer a glimpse of hope, and the solution was you acting together as one 'multi-vocalised' voice.

It was all too much for society to comprehend – the politics – the music – the energy were beyond the capabilities of most and we all retreated into our select circles to discuss the politics of hope and dissent, smoke dope, party and dance at benefit gigs for the striking miners – Poison Girls or Toxic Shock and always Crass.

If I fancied a night dancing, I would go to see Siouxsie, The Stranglers or The Professionals. I rather enjoyed watching the Damned supporting Slade at the Palais. As Emma Goldman said, 'if I can't dance to it, it's not my revolution'. By 1984 all the anarchist travellers had taken to the road and the big party was Stonehenge Free festival. I joined the hippies and drop outs for a few days of pure Green Anarchism. There were so many great bands playing but I was too busy to dance - meditating with the burial mounds in the Kings Field, exploring the buses and trucks on site. The Hippy Convoy were saying that 1984 was to be the last festival and two travellers explained something about a by-law permitting a 11 year gathering to become formally legal.

They thought the police would stop the festival in 1985 and advised me not to attend.

Later in the summer of 1984 a contingent from Nottingham joined a group of hippies at Menwith Hill. James, my partner and me joined them and the party went on. We sang Beatles songs in the BB, Chumbawamba played (a great gig), a mad axe man disturbed our peace, and the larger louts from Harrogate stoned the Green Bus. We were a small camp essentially serving as a beacon for other peace groups and anarchist drop outs to focus on. We received visits from Quakers, and peace groups from Harrogate, York, Leeds, Hull and Sheffield. Menwith Hill is an American National Security Agency spy base connected to Fylingdales and part of the 'early warning system' against Soviet nuclear attack. It was leaked that the NSA were also involved in phone tapping and, more importantly, the development of the nuclear missile defence shield aka Star Wars. CND didn't much like that and the base became a target for some of the Snowball Protests (more popular around USAF Greenham, USAF Molesworth and USAF Alconbury) that helped rid Britain of US owned nuclear missiles.

Today, the NSA are famous for spying via the www and sharing info with GCHQ Cheltenham.

Pressure remains focused at Faslane.

After meeting several other peace campers from Europe in Florennes, Belgium, We moved away from Menwith Hill and camped around Glastonbury for a few months. I moved to Bath, protested over Iraq, visited the anarchists at USAF Fairford Peace Camp (from where the B52 bombers took off), lived on the Kennet and Avon canal for 7 years until evicted (on a technicality), worked on the Northampton Free Festivals and finally, moved to Norwich where I fell in love.

Today, over 30 years later, the pacifism and love I have for humanity and this Earth remains. I find myself still involved in peaceful protest at RAF Waddington, London and in Norwich. I can't quite believe what the NSA are up to… I now realise that the anarcho-punk rockers of the wild 80s were quite right to be angry with capitalism and its military and economic abuses – we were absolutely correct to Stop the City and we should all be very proud.

My greatest concern today is the false economy and, as the anarcho Zeitgeist Addendum on You Tube states, the 97% economic lie.

Antisect Handout

Courtesy Nigel Crouch Collection

HUMAN BEINGS...WE HAVE ALLOWED OURSELVES TO BELIEVE THAT WE ARE THE SINGLE,MOST INTELLIGENT SPECIES ON THIS PLANET.IN MANY INSTANCES THIS CANNOT BE DOUBTED,BUT IN MOST CASES IT SEEMS THAT OUR INTELLIGENCE HAS TAKEN US IN DIRECTIONS THAT HAVE NOT BEEN ALTOGETHER SUCCESSFUL.OUR MAIN 'ADVANCEMENT' IT SEEMS,HAS BEEN IN THE MATERIAL WORLD,RATHER THAN THAT OF SPIRITUAL,OR EMOTIONAL FULFILMENT.IT IS FACT THAT EVERY SINGLE, LIVING,PERSON IN THIS WORLD DESIRES THE MOST BASIC OF ALL FORTUNES...THAT IS,HAPPINESS.IT IS ALSO A SAD FACT THAT THE MAJORITY OF US DEVOTE MOST OF THEIR TIME TO COVERING UP FOR THEIR LACK OF HAPPINESS BY WAY OF SURROUNDING THEMSELVES WITH MATERIAL POSSESSIONS.

THE MAIN IRONY OF OUR EXISTANCE HAS BEEN THE INABILITY TO OVERCOME FUNDAMENTAL OBSTACLES,WHILST,NEVERTHELESS,POSSESSING THE ABILITY TO TAKE OURSELVES BEYOND THEM.IT SEEMS THROUGHOUT HISTORY WE HAVE UNDERSTOOD THAT COOPERATION IS BETTER THAN CONFLICT, BUT EVEN UP UNTIL THE PRESENT DAY WE HAVE FAILED TO GRASP THE FULL SIGNIFICANCE OF SUCH A PRINCIPAL.THE HUMAN RACE,IN ALL FORMS OF SOCIETY,HAS STRUGGLED TO CREATE COOPERATION BUT HAS FAILED IN EVERY MAJOR INSTANCE. THE REASON BEING,THAT IN ORDER TO ESTABLISH COOPERATION,WE HAVE THOUGHT IT NECCESARY TO DO SO VIA THE MEANS OF FORCE.MOST PEOPLE HAVE LED THEMSELVES TO BELIEVE THAT WITHOUT THE USE OF FORCE,WHEN A SITUATION SUCH AS THE CONFLICT OF OPINION WOULD ARISE,THE INEVITABLE OUTCOME WOULD BE CHAOS.THE MAIN PERPETRATOR OF THIS BELIEF IS THE FACT THAT MOST OF US ARE,IN SOME WAY,FRIGHTENED OF ONE ANOTHER,THEREFORE THEY FEEL THE NEED FOR THE PROTECTION GIVEN TO THEM,ALBEIT LIMITED,BY THE USE OF FORCE,OR IN THIS CASE, AUTHORITY.INSTEAD OF RESOLVING WHATEVER THE CONFLICT,THUS CREATING UNITY,THE USE OF FORCE/AUTHORITY MERELY GLOSSES OVER THE PROBLEM.THE METHOD OF AUTHORITY,ALTHOUGH REVISED AND MODERNISED OVER THOUSANDS OF YEARS, RATHER THAN GIVING US ORGANISATION,HAS YIELDED EXACTLY THE OPPOSITE,THAT IS TO SAY... CHAOS.INDIVIDUALS ARE FORCED IN MANY WAYS, MENTALLY,EMOTIONALLY,AND IN SOME CASES PHYSICALLY,TO PLAY OUT THEIR ROLES IN THE AUTHORITARIAN SOCIETY.WE FEEL THAT THIS IS THE MAJOR REASON WHY AUTHORITY ULTIMATELY LEADS TO CHAOS.BASICALLY,THE FAILING IS THAT AUTHORITY DEFINES A UNIVERSAL PATH OR GUIDELINE WHERE THERE IS NONE.IF THERE WAS A UNIVERSAL PATH,THERE COULD NOT BE SUCH A THING AS FREE THOUGHT.WHICH,TO US,IS A TOTAL ABSURDITY.AUTHORITY IS THE MANIPULATION OF FREE WILL,RATHER THAN THE NATURAL PROCESS OF INDIVIDUAL THOUGHT.

EXTERNALLY,WE ARE LIMITED BY OUR PHYSICAL CAPABILITIES,WHILST INTERNALLY THE USE OF FREE THOUGHT KNOWS NO BOUNDRIES.OUR TRUE 'SELF' IS INSIDE OUR MINDS,AS THE WAY WE THINK ULTIMATELY DETERMINES THE WAY WE LIVE. UNFORTUNATELY,IN TODAYS SOCIETY,THE THOUGHTS OF OUTSIDERS CAN ALSO DETERMINE THE WAY WE LIVE.

BECAUSE WE EXIST IN AN AUTHORITARIAN SOCIETY, IT IS AUTHORITY THAT SETS OUR BOUNDRIES, AND THESE BOUNDRIES, IN MOST CASES BECOME OUR PHYSICAL CAPABILITIES. THE USE OF FREE THOUGHT IS IMPORTANT, AS IT IS THE ONLY THING THAT GIVES US TRUE INDIVIDUALISM, AND ALTHOUGH ALL MAY POSSESS FREE THOUGHT, FEW OF US USE IT. THE REASON BEING THAT MOST ARE UNAWARE OF IT'S EXISTANCE, AND OF THOSE THAT ARE AWARE, SOME USE IT, AND OTHERS DON'T BECAUSE THEY FIND IT EASIER TO FIT IN WITH THE MAJORITY, OR, 'THE NORM'. HERE, ONCE AGAIN, AUTHORITY INTERVENES. MOST OF US ARE UNAWARE OF THE EXISTANCE OF FREE THOUGHT BECAUSE IT IS DESIRABLE FOR AUTHORITY THAT THIS SHOULD BE THE CASE. IF THE MAJORITY WERE TO USE FREE THOUGHT, THE RULE OF AUTHORITY WOULD BECOME ALMOST OBSOLETE. AUTHORITY HOWEVER, ONCE AGAIN LAYING DOWN THE STANDARD GUIDELINE, HAS GIVEN US A DEFINITION OF FREE THOUGHT THAT IS COMPLIMENTARY TO ITSELF. THIS IS WHY, WHEN ASKED, MOST WILL SAY THEY POSSESS IT, WHEN IN REALITY THEY DON'T. IF WE APPLY THE SAME LOGIC TO 'FREEDOM', WE WILL FIND THAT SIMILAR CIRCUMSTANCES PREVAIL. FREEDOM TO MOST OF US MEANS THE ABILITY TO DO WHATEVER WE DESIRE TO DO, WHENEVER WE WISH TO DO SO. IT IS TRUE, ALBEIT TO A LIMITED EXTENT, THAT MOST OF US ENJOY OUR FREEDOM, BUT THIS 'FREEDOM' EXISTS ONLY WITHIN THE BOUNDRIES CREATED BY OURSELVES AND DEFINED BY AUTHORITY. 'DEFINED BY AUTHORITY', BECAUSE AUTHORITY IS UNABLE TO GIVE US TRUE FREEDOM OR ALLEVIATE THE BOUNDRIES, BECAUSE TO DO SO WOULD BE TO DESTROY ITSELF. HENCE, IN EFFECT, THE 'FREEDOMS' WE ARE GIVEN BY AUTHORITY, ARE FALSE. 'CREATED BY OURSELVES', BECAUSE INEVITABLY WE MAKE OUR OWN DECISIONS, AND UP UNTIL NOW, AUTHORITY HAS BEEN OUR PRODUCT. (HOWEVER, AS STATED BEFORE, THE DECISIONS WE MAKE ARE AFFECTED BY OUR MODES OF THOUGHT, SO SHOULD WE NOT POSSESS TRUE FREEDOM OF THOUGHT, IT SO FOLLOWS THAT WE SHOULD NOT HAVE THE ABILITY TO MAKE FREE CHOICE.)

"LOOK INTO THE DEPTHS OF YOUR OWN BEINGS, SEEK OUT THE TRUTH, AND REALISE IT IN YOURSELVES. YOU WILL FIND IT NOWHERE ELSE".

AS HAS BEEN STATED BEFORE, MOST PEOPLE ARE, IN SOME WAY OR FORM, FRIGHTENED OF ONE ANOTHER. THE REASON FOR THIS, BEING ALIENATION, WHICH LEADS TO A FUNDAMENTAL LACK OF UNDERSTANDING BETWEEN INDIVIDUALS. PEOPLE HAVE BECOME RELUCTANT TO EXPOSE THEIR TRUE FEELINGS/THOUGHTS/SELVES FOR FEAR OF CONFLICTING WITH THE NORMS AND STANDARDS THAT OTHERS, AND IN MOST CASES, EVEN THEMSELVES, HAVE CREATED. AS ALSO STATED PREVIOUSLY, AUTHORITY ENDEAVOURS TO CREATE A STANDARD GUIDELINE. ONE OF THE FUNCTIONS OF WHICH IS TO IMPOSE A STANDARD NORMALITY, WHICH, IN REALITY, DOES NOT EXIST... A DICTIONARY DEFINITION OF THE WORD 'NORMAL' IS AS FOLLOWS..; 1/ACCORDING TO WHAT IS EXPECTED, USUAL, OR AVERAGE. 2/(OF A PERSON) DEVELOPING IN THE EXPECTED WAY; WITHOUT ANY DISORDER IN MIND OR BODY... INEVITABLY, AS PEOPLE AGREE WITH ONE ANOTHER OVER CERTAIN ISSUES, FOR EXAMPLE, THE CONCEPT OF RAIN BEING WET, CERTAIN IDEAS, IN SOME CASES CAN BECOME BONDED WITHIN THE MAJORITY. HOWEVER, THIS DOES NOT MAKE A RULE THAT SUCH CONCEPTS BECOME STANDARD, AS, SHOULD ANOTHER INDIVIDUAL ANNOUNCE A CLAIM THAT, ON THE CONTRARY, RAIN IS NOT WET BUT DRY, SUCH A CLAIM, ALTHOUGH CLEARLY IN THE MINORITY, SHOULD BE, IF NOT UNDERSTOOD, RESPECTED. IT IS BECAUSE OF THE MASS ACCEPTANCE OF AUTHORITY AND ITS GUIDELINES, STANDARDS AND NORMS, THAT MOST ARE FRIGHTENED TO PUBLICISE THEIR TRUE PERSONAL OPINIONS AS THEY BELIEVE THAT MAJORITY OPINION, (THE NORM) WILL GO AGAINST THEM. ALTHOUGH NORMALITY CANNOT PREVENT FREE THOUGHT, IT CAN LIMIT, TO SOME EXTENT, THE EXPRESSION OF FREE THOUGHT. WE MAY BELIEVE WHAT WE LIKE. WE MAY SPEAK WHAT WE BELIEVE, BUT BECAUSE OF THE BARRIER OF NORMALITY, OR ACCEPTED OPINION, OTHERS CANNOT ALWAYS UNDERSTAND OR EVEN GET TO HEAR OUR BELIEFS. FOR THIS, AN APPROPRIATE EXAMPLE WOULD BE THE EXTENT TO WHICH THE MESSAGE OF THIS RECORD AND ALL ITS ACCOMPANYING LITERATURE WILL BE HEARD. WE ACKNOWLEDGE THE FACT THAT THE PROPORTION OF PEOPLE THAT HEAR ITS MESSAGE WILL BE BUT A SMALL AMOUNT, COMPARED TO THOSE WHO DON'T. THE REASON WHY THIS WILL OCCUR, (ASIDE FROM DIFFERENCES IN MUSICAL TASTE) IS BECAUSE ITS CONTENT GOES CONTRARY TO ESTABLISHED OPINION. THEREFORE NORMALITY TAKES HOLD, AND IN ORDER TO UPHOLD ESTABLISHED OPINION, SEES THAT THE ALTERNATIVE ISN'T MADE KNOWN TO THE MASSES.

ON THE SURFACE, PEOPLE ARE UNABLE TO BREAK FROM PAST TRADITIONS AND PRESENT STRUCTURES, BECAUSE, FIRSTLY, NORMALITY, AND SECONDLY, PAST TRADITIONS ARE SO DEEPLY INGRAINED AND PRESENT STRUCTURES SO VAST THAT TO CREATE A RECOGNISABLE ALTERNATIVE IS NIGH ON IMPOSSIBLE. WE SAY, 'ON THE SURFACE', BECAUSE DEEP DOWN, PEOPLE ARE ABLE TO BREAK AWAY AND BUILD THEIR OWN ALTERNATIVES. THE BARRIERS, AT PRESENT, BEING THEIR MEANS. PEOPLES MEANS ARE, IN EFFECT, THEIR BARRIERS, AS IN MOST MAJOR INSTANCES THE WAY IN WHICH THEY SEARCH CAN BE CONTRARY TO THEIR AIMS. A MODERN EXAMPLE OF SUCH COULD BE OUR EVER GROWING DESIRE FOR WORLD DISARMAMENT AND PEACE. WHEN ASKED, MOST WOULD SAY THAT THEY POSSESSED THIS DESIRE FOR PEACE. WITHOUT DOUBTING THAT THIS IS SO, THE QUESTION THAT REMAINS UNANSWERED IS THIS,-"WHY THEN, DO THE PEOPLES OF THE WORLD NOT LIVE IN PEACE ?"-OUR ANSWER TO THIS IS THAT FOR FAR TOO LONG, HUMANITY HAS BEEN SEARCHING IN THE WRONG PLACES. IT SEEMS THAT IT IS THE ESTABLISHED OPINION THAT THE MOST SUCCESSFUL WAY TO PREVENT WAR IS VIA THE THREAT OF WAR. THIS RULE ALSO APPLIES TO THE ACKNOWLEDGED REASON FOR THE JUSTIFICATION OF NUCLEAR WEAPONS. THIS IS SO BECAUSE SOME HOLD THE BELIEF THAT TO POSSESS NUCLEAR WEAPONS WILL PROTECT THEM FROM ANY WOULD BE AGGRESSOR THAT SHOULD ALSO POSSESS NUCLEAR WEAPONS. THIS IS KNOWN AS DETERRENCE. BASICALLY DETERRENCE REVOLVES AROUND FEAR, AND IT IS THROUGH THIS FEAR THAT ON OCCASION GOVERNMENTS CONSULT ONE ANOTHER, WITH THE INTENTION OF REDUCING, OR ULTIMATELY REMOVING FROM THE WORLD, ALL NUCLEAR WEAPONS. IT IS VERY RARE THAT PERSONAL MORALITY PLAYS ANY PART IN THIS, AND IT SHOULD ALSO BE NOTED THAT THE REMOVAL OF NUCLEAR WEAPONS IS NOT, IN ITSELF, SUFFICIENT, AS THE MORE IMPORTANT ASPECT IS THE REMOVAL

OR YOU WILL NOT POSSESS THEM. IT IS SAD, EVEN WITH EXAMPLES SUCH AS THIS, THAT PEOPLE SHOULD STILL LAY THEIR FAITH IN AUTHORITY, RATHER THAN REALISING THE STRENGTHS THEY POSSESS WITHIN THEMSELVES, AND PUTTING THESE STRENGTHS TO USE IN THE ATTEMPTED SOLVING OF THE PROBLEM IN HAND. AGAIN, WE STATE THAT ALTHOUGH EVERY PERSON DESIRES THE SAME GOAL, WE BELIEVE THAT THEY ARE USING THE UNSUCCESSFUL METHOD BY SEARCHING FOR IT IN THE WRONG PLACES.

"THE HUMAN...WHAT CREATURE ELSE CONCEIVES THE CIRCLE, THEN WALKS THE SQUARE ?"

WE INCLUDE THIS QUESTION AT THIS POINT, AS WE FEEL IT TO BE AN APPROPRIATE WAY OF EXPRESSING OUR FEELINGS ON THE SUBJECT OF SCIENCE AND TECHNOLOGY. WE BELIEVE THAT SCIENCE IS OF GREAT CONSEQUENCE, AND DULY PLAYS AN IMPORTANT ROLE IN ORGANISED SOCIETY. WE ALSO BELIEVE THAT, ALTHOUGH IT HAS BESTOWED UPON US MANY USEFUL CREATIONS, SCIENCE IN ITS PATH, HAS, THROUGH THOUSANDS OF YEARS, LEFT A TRAIL OF MISERY AND DESTRUCTION. ALTHOUGH THE PURPOSE OF SCIENCE AND TECHNOLOGY IS TO USE WHATEVER RESOURCES THERE BE TO THEIR UTMOST LIMITATIONS IN SERVING THE HUMAN RACE, WE SEEM TO HAVE OVERLOOKED ALL ELSE. THIS BEING ALL OUR FELLOW CREATURES, WITH WHOM WE INHERIT THE EARTH, AND THE VERY ENVIRONMENT FROM WHICH WE GATHER THESE RESOURCES. WE APPEAR TO HAVE ACCEPTED IT AS RULE, THAT HUMANKIND IS THE MASTER RACE AND ANYTHING ELSE THAT MAY EXIST ALONG WITH US BELONGS TO US, AND THEREFORE WE MAY DO WITH IT AS WE WISH. WE TAKE FROM THE EARTH RATHER THAN COMPLEMENT IT, AND WE USE AND ABUSE THE OTHER CREATURES THAT IT HAS SPAWNED, RATHER THAN CO-EXISTING IN HARMONY WITH THEM. IN OUR TIME, WE HAVE TAKEN THE LIFE FROM MILLIONS UPON MILLIONS OF CREATURES, IN OUR ATTEMPTS TO MAKE OUR OWN LIVES MORE LUXURIOUS AND EXCITING. WE HAVE MANAGED NOT ONLY TO RECOGNISE ONE OF THE UTMOST SECRETS OF NATURE, IN SPLITTING THE ATOM, WE HAVE ALSO INCORPORATED IT INTO OUR OWN TECHNOLOGY, BUT, FOR ALL OUR EFFORTS, WE HAVE PRODUCED WHAT WE KNOW AS BEING THE SINGLE MOST DESTRUCTIVE FORCE ON EARTH...THE ATOMIC BOMB.

"WHAT IS THE TIME ?"

IT IS NOW THE YEAR ONE THOUSAND, NINE HUNDRED AND EIGHTY. FOUR. SLOWLY, AS WE BREATHE AND MORE CONSTITUTE _____ WAITING _____ AND ITS _____ WORSENS. WE HAVE, AT THE PRESENT, TWO THIRDS OF THE WORLDS HUMAN POPULATION LIVING IN STANDARDS BELOW THE ACCEPTED POVERTY LINES OF THEIR RESPECTIVE NATIONS. EACH AND EVERY DAY, WE SUBTRACT MORE AND MORE OF THE EARTHS VALUABLE RESOURCES, AND REPLACE THEM WITH LITTLE ELSE BUT WHAT WE SEE AS BEING POLUTION. WE HAVE ALSO, THE TWO MOST 'WEALTHY' NATIONS ENGAGED IN A PARANOID BATTLE OF WITS OVER ONE ANOTHERS ABILITY TO DESTROY ITS ADVERSARY. TAKING THESE EXAMPLES INTO ACCOUNT, THE CLOSER WE EXAMINE THE FACTS, THE MORE WE LEAN TOWARDS DRAWING THIS CONCLUSION.

--IF WE CONTINUE TO FOLLOW OUR PRESENT PATH, IN THE FUTURE, WE STAND TO FACE SEVERE ENVIRONMENTAL BREAKDOWN, OR, MORE IMMINENTLY, NUCLEAR OBLIVION.

UP UNTIL NOW, IN THIS PIECE, WE HAVE STATED WHAT WE BELIEVE TO BE OUR TRUTHS. WE HAVE ATTEMPTED TO PORTRAY TO YOU, THE READER, A BROAD MINDED VIEW OF WHAT WE SEE, IN THE HOPE THAT YOU, WILL REFLECT UPON IT. WE HAVE ENDEAVOURED TO BRING TO LIGHT BOTH WHAT WE SEE AS BEING THE MAJOR FAILINGS, AND, TO AN EXTENT, THE STRENGTHS OF INDIVIDUALS, IN THE PATH THAT THEY HAVE TAKEN. AT THIS POINT, WE WOULD LIKE TO EXPRESS OUR FEELINGS, (AS INDIVIDUALS AND AS A GROUP) AS TO HOW WE CAN CREATE A MORE JUST AND COMPASSIONATE WORLD, THAN THE ONE IN WHICH WE CURRENTLY EXIST. WHAT COMES NEXT IS NOT TO BE, IN ANY WAY, CONSTRUED AS THE GUIDELINE FOR ALL TO FOLLOW. IT IS BUT OUR OPINION OF SUCH.

WE BELIEVE THAT THE PATH TOWARDS SUCCESSFUL CHANGE BEGINS WITHIN OURSELVES. AS INDIVIDUALS, WE CAN WORK COLLECTIVELY TO MAKE CHANGE, BUT THE REASON, THE WILL, AND THE MEANS, MUST FIRST COME FROM OUR OWN MINDS. WE MUST LEARN TO REJECT THE ESTABLISHED BOUNDRIES OF THOUGHT I.E. NORMALITY, AND TO ACKNOWLEDGE THAT THERE ARE NO LIMITATIONS TO THOUGHT, BARRING THE LIMITATIONS OF PLACE ON OURSELVES. HAVING STATED THIS, IT SO FOLLOWS THAT THE ONLY TRUE LIMITATIONS ARE OUR PHYSICAL CAPABILITIES, WHICH, OBVIOUSLY, VARY FROM INDIVIDUAL TO INDIVIDUAL. HAVING SAID THAT WE MUST REJECT THE ESTABLISHED BOUNDRIES OF THOUGHT, WE MUST, AFTER FORMING OUR OWN PERSONAL STANDARDS, FOLLOW THEM. THIS MEANS THAT SHOULD ONE CONVEY THAT THEY POSSESS A CERTAIN BELIEF, IT WOULD BE IRONIC FOR ONE TO KNOWINGLY ACT CONTRARY TO THAT BELIEF, AS TO DO SO WOULD MAKE THE SAID BELIEF INVALID. FOR EXAMPLE, IF AN INDIVIDUAL WAS TO CLAIM TO UPHOLD THE VIRTUES OF PEACE, BUT TO DO SO VIA THE THREAT OF VIOLENCE, THIS DOUBLE STANDARD WOULD MAKE THE CLAIM HYPOCRITICAL AND/OR WORTHLESS. IT IS A VERY IMPORTANT FACT THAT ALL AUTHORITIVE SOCIETIES USE THIS DOUBLE STANDARD, AND REGARD IT AS ACCEPTABLE. THUS, THEY ATTEMPT TO REPRESS CONFLICT RATHER THAN CREATE TRUE CO-OPERATION. TRUE COOPERATION MAY ONLY BE ARRIVED AT _____ JUSTICE, WHICH, IN TURN, MAY ONLY BE ACHIEVED _____ AND OTHERS _____ REASON. (HOWEVER OBSCURE AT ___ SEEM).

SO FAR IN THIS PIECE, WE HAVE INCLUDED THE WORD 'AUTHORITY' IN THE CONTEXT OF ESTABLISHED OPINION. THAT IS TO SAY, A SUPERIOR OUTSIDE BODY OR INSTITUTION. IT SHOULD BE NOTED THAT AUTHORITY, FAR FROM BEING AN OUTSIDE BODY OR INSTITUTION, IS ACTUALLY, THE WILL OF PEOPLE. YOU, AND I. IT IS ONLY WHEN INDIVIDUALS BECOME MORE TRUTHFUL, INTERNALLY AND EXTERNALLY, THAT THE PERSONAL AUTHORITY THEY POSSESS WILL BE ALLOWED TO CO-EXIST WITH THE PERSONAL AUTHORITY OF OTHERS. WHEN THAT TIME COMES, WE MAY THEN TAKE THE STEP OUT OF OUR DARKNESS AND INTO THE LIGHT.

ANTISECT; FEBRUARY 1984

Antisect Live Gig Review and In Darkness... Album Review

Tony Drayton

ANTI SECT

The Ambulance Station, London

THE FUTURE is Peace,
The Future is Love,
The Future is Here,
The Future is You.

The fourfold frontstage banners stamp out ~~the~~ slogan~~eering~~ s in no nonsense black and white. Beneath and behind them the cluster of support bands have been busy constructing a cardboard flimsy facsimilie of the current anarcho-noise.

Sometimes the songs leant heavily on the drums, occasionally a guitarist would hitch the buzztone up another chord or so and almost all floundered in the sorry pits of imitation. Sitting clustered upon the floor, the audience acknowledge their indifference and await the shadowy spectre of Anti Sect.

~~The vogue for baggy black army surplus and shaggy black greasy dreadlocks is not lost on the Sect,~~

Do the shamble, brothers and sisters though let us not be misunderstood. Glaring in black 'naturally greasy' dreadlocks and shabbier, baggier equally monochrome army surplus uniforms; the fashion for twin vocalists is not lost on them. They plug in ~~then~~ as suddenly an aircraft appears to crash into the street outside this very hall. Another premature ending, but no, as the dust settles you peer through the wreckage to see Anti Sect preparing to ~~perform~~ let rip with their second number.

The Crass/Discharge detonation of anarchy as harsh and furious noise has come to this, whilst still under the shadow of influence their spawn is crawling from the manger making its own vociferous demands.

Their numbers don't stop but merge into one another through troughs of feedback; the severest damage done by the pneumatic-hairdryer guitarist firing live amunition as he slumps near his amps, appearing dead to the world. Or perhaps deaf, though the resultant volatile concoction has more effect than the sum of its parts.

A whirlwind picks you up bodily and hurls you senselessly around the hall - in darkness there is no choice being their rationale x and, somehow enjoyably, they give the appearance of believing in themselves. A solid rock jutting out of the murk, the future is ~~dxxnd~~ metaphorical.

Tony D

ANTISECT
'In Darkness There Is No Choice'.
(Spiderleg SDL 15 £3)

A long, insistent and angry buzzing assails the air, underladen with a gruffly argumentative voice. Its speeding whirl descends with a heaviness upon your shoulders like some large, unfriendly bison. Keeping things stable and driving in one hefty chunk are the drums, giving form and direction as they seek to pummell you to submission.

So this is Antisect - a name bounced and scribbled around upon the city walls with increasing vigour of late. Now we find out why. Also highlighting their subtler shade with an instrumentally atmospheric interlude, the album falls down in its desperately serious manifesto and lecturing style, coming accross as little more than self-righteous anguish.

This 'look mummy intellectuals' approach approach drags the proceedings irritably when things threaten (as they do) to get totally out to lunch in one almighty frenzied thrashout morass. A problem solved on the title track 'In Darkness' when it takes off halfway through as an instrumental and presses you forcibily against the wall. Heavy? Combined with surrounding two songs, 'Education' and 'Heresy' a churning up of the deepest black anarcho-punk sea Turning it into one murky, foaming whirlpool - a satisfying feeling spreads through the loins and we play the segment again in gratitude.

Craving the darkness of eventide they deliver the evidence of a new wave of heavy punk protest noise washing up upon these drought-addled shores.

What shores?

Why thats very kind, another of this fine vintage, Chateau Crass whine with a fine smattering of Pink Indian. Tasty!

Tony Puppy

Antisect

Caro Wallis

ANTISECT FORMED IN 1981, WE ALL KNEW ONE OTHER AND WERE INTO THE SAME THINGS, SO WE DECIDED TO GET TOGETHER AS A BAND BECAUSE WE FELT WE HAD SOMETHING VALID AND REAL TO SAY AND A GOOD WAY OF GETTING IT ACROSS TO A WIDER GROUP OF PEOPLE WAS TO JOIN TOGETHER AS A BAND. THE ORIGINAL LINE UP WAS FOUR,

PETE P........ DRUMS,
PETE B........ VOCALS,
PETE L........ GUITAR,
WINK.......... BASS,

THE MUSIC WAS LOUD AND FAST AND THE SONGS WERE SHORT AND TO THE POINT, AT THIS TIME WE DID SOME GIGS WITH DISCHARGE, PEOPLE STILL COMPARE US WITH THEM BUT WE ARE NOTHING LIKE THEM, PEOPLE ALSO STILL GIVE US LABLES WE ARE ALL INDIVIDUALS AND WILL STAY THAT WAY, WE THEN GOT ANOTHER VOCALIST RICH, AND THEN I JOINED, WE,VE PLAYED BETWEEN 30 AND 40 GIGS SO FAR PLAYING WITH LOTS OF BANDS EG FLUX, DIRT, AMEBIX, ETC WE WERE DOING GIGS WITH FLUX WHEN THEY ASKED US IF WE WANTED TO PUT OUT A RECORD WE SAID YES AND RECORDED OUR ONE AND ONLY RECORD TO DATE THE ALBUM IN DARKNESS THERE IS NO CHOICE ON SPIDER LEG RECORDS.

AFTER WE DID THE ALBUM WE DID A SHORT TOUR WITH AMERICAN BANDS, CRUCIFIX, AND DIRT, A SHORT TIME AFTER THE TOUR OUR BASSIST WINK LEFT THE BAND AND HAS SINCE JOINED ANOTHER BAND, WE THEN ACQUIRED A NEW BASSIST JOHN, THEN OUR VOCALIST RICH LEFT BECAUSE HE WASENT KEEN ON THE WAY THE MUSIC WAS GOING AND FOR OTHER REASONS TOO NUMEROUS TO MENTION, SO WE NOW HAVE A LINE UP OF 5 OUR MUSIC HAS CHANGED SLIGHTLY, ITS GOT A BIT HEAVIER AND IN PARTS A BIT SLOWER, AND THE SONGES ARE NOW LONGER, WE HAVE CHANGED BECAUSE WE WANTED TO PROGRESS AND WE FELT WE NEEDED A CHANGED FOR OURSELVES AND FOR OTHERS BECAUSE BEING IN A BAND PLAYING THE SAME SET MONOTONUS FOR US AND THE PEOPLE WHO COME TO OUR GIGS, HOWEVER OUR BELEIFS AND SENTIMENTS ARE THE SAME AND WHAT WE WRITE AND SING ABOUT IS FELT AND LIVED BY US ALL.
WE BELIVE IN PEACE AND FREEDOM FOR ALL HUMANS AND ANIMALS ALIKE WE BELIVE THAT CARING AND SHAREING TRUST AND UNDERSTANDING ARE THE MAINSTAY FOR US TO IMPROVE THE SOCITY WE LIVE IN, WE FEEL THAT WAR AND VOILANCE OF ANY KIND SHOULD BE CAST ASIDE BY US ALL BECAUSE IT BRINGS NOTHING BUT SUFFERING TO ALL LIVING BEINGS. WE ARE AGAINST VIVISECTION AND CRUELITY OF ANY KIND TO ANY LIFE, AS WE HAVE NO RIGHT TO DETERMINE THE FATE OF OTHERS, IT GOES WITHOUT SAYING THAT WE ARE AGAINST ALL FORMS OF OPPRESSION AS IT TAKES AWAY WHAT LITTLE WE HAVE, AND WE BELIVE IN TOTAL FREEDOM FOR ALL INDIVIDUALS WE DO NOT TELL PEOPLE HOW TO LIVE THIER LIVES BECAUSE IF WE DID THIS WOULD GIVE US POWER OVER OTHER PEOPLES LIVES AND WE ARE AGAINST POWER, ALL WE ASK IS THAT PEOPLE OPEN THIER EYES AND LOOK AROUND THEM AND SEE THE DESTRUCTION THAT IS GOING ON NOT ONLY TO OTHER HOMANS AND ANIMALS BUT ALSO TO THE EARTH THAT WE LIVE ON, AND TO RELIES THAT IT IS ONLY" MANS" GREED AND STRUGGLE FOR POWER THAT HAS LED TO THE DEVESTATION WE SEE AND FEEL AROUND US, AND TO KNOW THAT IT IS ONLY US WHO CAN CHANGE IT.

LOVE AND PEACE
CAROLINE (ANTISECT)

Antisect - The Buck Stops Here

Lance Hahn

The Buck Stops Here: The Story of Antisect
By Lance Hahn

Daventry, Northants is a little ways to the northwest of London past the architectural wasteland of Milton Keynes and on the way to Coventry and Birmingham. The virtually rural town would also be the birthplace of harbingers of doom, Antisect.

Formed in 1982 by Pete "Lippy" Lyons, guitars, the band's initial line-up would also include Pete "Polly" on drums, Renis "Wink" Rekiki on bass, and Pete "Little Pete" Boyce on vocals.

Said second bass player John Bryson, "Most of the boys new each other from school in Daventry UK. The Pete thing was always a pain to me. Pete Lyons was known as Lippy, Pete Polluscavitzc was known as Polly, and Pete Boyce as Boycie. All of a sudden they all decided that they wanted to be called Pete! Thank God I was (and still am) called John!"

They had mostly come with a bit of experience in punk bands though not of the political variety.

John, "If by more straightforward you mean more punky musically and with less of the morality trip, yes. Lippy and Polly (Maybe Boycie too, not sure) were in a band called Xylum, much in the Discharge vein, and I had FaceAche as I said before. My very first punk band was called Dross back in '77 and that was about as "straightforward" as you can get."

With Antisect, Lippy was determined to mine a new area of punk. The riff heavy, metal influenced hardcore was only starting to develop with groups like Discharge.

John, "Lippy was always very much the man behind Antisect from a musical point of view. He became interested in a lot of more complex and "progressive" or "metal" type rock quite early on, and this very much influenced the sound. Lippy, Polly and I, were very much going for a heavier than thou sound, drawing on influences such as early Metallica, Slayer, etc. I am still interested in finding the heaviest riff in the world. My all time favourite riff, and one which can clearly be heard influencing later Antisect, is from "Symptom of the Universe" by Black Sabbath. I still think its right up there with the heaviest 25 plus years on."

Of course, Discharge was a major influence. Aside from being inspiration for many of the heavier punk bands to come, Lippy had a standing relationship with them.

John, "Discharge really. Discharge and Antisect both started going down a more metal route musically kind of simultaneously. Antisect was partly born out of Lippy's connections with Discharge, as I understand. Xylum certainly supported them, as did Antisect early on."

By the years end, they would have played their first gig supporting the Varukers in Preston. From then, the band was constantly playing live and recording demos documenting their evolution. That November, a gig with Flux Of Pink Indians in Nottingham started a fruitful friendship. Dutifully impressed, a friendship was bonded with the two bands at one time influencing Flux to head in a heavier, more metallic direction. The lasting result was that Antisect would record their one and only studio LP for Spider Leg, the label run by Flux.

So, in 1983 the first line-up went to Southern Studios in London to record what would become one England's most respected (and copied) hardcore albums, In Darkness, There Is No Choice.

The record is a powerful statement fusing together the ferocity of hardcore bands like Discharge and GBH with the passionate monologues of Crass and Flux. Taking the sheer guitar sound of label mates Amebix, they escalated it to high speeds only to juxtapose it with slower gothic and industrial moments.

Lyrically the record is not the bleak, post-apocalyptic vision you would expect from such heavy and dark music not to mention the album title. Instead it's a mixture of anti-mass media, anti-war, and animal rights propagation and a sort of indictment.

"Eat your pet puppy? What a cruel thing to say."
But lead a lamb to its slaughter and of course that's okay
The blood soaked death-house to the well grilled meal
What right do you offer for the life that you steal?

The band's commitment to animal rights and other causes was more than just lyrics, as extracurricular band activities often resulted in visits from the law.

John, "Too much to detail, but mainly this came from Lippy and associated activities in connection with the Animal Liberation Front rather than anything specific to Antisect. Our house in Northampton UK was frequently visited by the Police, and Lippy often joined them at their place!"

Only on the song "Heresy" do the lyrics head into more cerebral existentialism.

> "What is your purpose
> Who is your god
> Who owns your mind
> What path do you follow
> For whom do you speak
> Which mask do you wear
> Who draws your line
> What is your weakness"

The cover art was also unique. While packaged like a Crass record with the foldout poster and all, the black and white art is in many ways different. The start imagery that at first glance appears to be more anarcho symbolism, is at closer look a frame of vines and leaves and is sort of naturalistic in a way. The foldout poster, on the other hand, is a grim drawing of different images depicting various anxieties from pollution to nuclear war. The artwork was credited to Fish.

John, "I think the artwork speaks for itself actually. What ever it means to you, that's what it means. Fish was a guy we knew from Nottingham in UK. (Had a girlfriend called Cat, comically)."

Produced by Colin from Flux, the band were also involved on the production end. But as is the case with most bands, that didn't guarantee total satisfaction with the results.

John, "I know Lippy was very involved at an executive level. Lippy is now a producer and engineer so that's his thing now.

"...Lippy was never 100% happy with it, but I always thought it was great. Yes one expected the success I do know that."

By the time of the records release in 1984, the band was changing. Wink left and was replaced with John Bryson.

John, "He left in 83/84 and I was his replacement. I am not sure of the ins and outs but I think he just wasn't really enjoying it anymore."

Coming from Northampton's Face Ache, he was from a similar punk-via-hard rock background as the rest of the guys.

John, "I heard a demo of New Rose by the Damned on John Peel's radio show in 1976 and that was that. A frantic and desperate scrabble to get hold of as much similar music as possible followed and soon I was listening to, and going to see such bands as, The Damned, Pistols, 999, The Drones, Lurkers, The Boys, Ramones, etc. My long hair got cut and dyed, my trousers got narrow and my attitude became questionable but suitable to a 15-year-old boy. (Prior to this I had been listening to such bands as Hawkwind and Black Sabbath, and incidentally I still do)."

He was a natural to join the band already being friends with Lippy.

John, "Lippy and I became friends through the small network of local punks in Northampton UK. We very much clicked straight away and were close friends for a long time. I think most of the band were a bit worried when I first came along because I was not a 'long haired veggie punk' like them, but it worked out well in the end."

Politically, Bryson came from a similar area, fascinated with Crass like many English punks at the time.

John, "Found Flux through hearing 'Tube Disasters' on John Peel's radio show. Actually not that keen on Flux myself. I found it rather contrived both musically and lyrically, however, I am sure they were sincere in their ideas.

"Lippy and co met Crass through other bands I think. I always loved the Crass message (less so now, actually), but musically it never did it for me really.

But it was through his involvement with Antisect that his interest in the anarcho scene became more profound.

"...The sheer genuine subversiveness of it all. The courage to attack the very pillars of society with intelligence and creativity. It felt dangerous and real.

"...Prior to meeting Lippy I had been very aware but hadn't really bought into the whole thing. Long nights of discussion with Antisect members slowly pulled me in that direction."

At one point, the band expanded to a six piece with Rich Hill and Caroline Wallis joining as vocalists.

John, "Caroline was Rich Hill's partner and a friend of mine from college too. She was a fully participative member of the band.

"...By the time I joined, we were shedding them (vocalists)!!"

In 1984, original singer Pete Boyce left, leaving the band to carry on without a lead vocalist. As a trio, the band set out on a relentless touring schedule. The band would tour at home and abroad.

John, "The gigs did get busier after the release of In Darkness. Some people never really take a band seriously until they have product even in the punk world. Funny really.

"We toured UK, Italy, Holland, Belgium etc. Great days, hundreds on funny stories, lots of fun."

Their anxiousness to hit the road led to a first UK tour that, while successful, they weren't entirely practiced for.

John, "I'll tell you a secret between you and I. On the first UK tour as a three-piece (Lippy, Polly and I), we hadn't learned the words because Boycie had left the band suddenly for personal reasons and he was the singer then! We tried to learn the lyrics in the back of the van on the way to our first gig in Leeds but it was hopeless. (Even Lippy who wrote most of them couldn't memorize them!) We then proceeded to play live singing names from England's 1966 World Cup Soccer squad to the Antisect tunes. No one noticed!!"

The band was constantly on tour playing with likeminded American bands like MDC and Crucifix on their European tours, as well as label mates Amebix and the Subhumans.

John, " We had a bit of a fallout with Subhumans which nearly came to blows at a festival in Portsmouth UK. Hilarious! I shan't go into the gory details. Myself, I love the Subhumans and Amebix. Last I heard of Rob from Amebix he was a member of a patch wearing motorbike club.

"...Different at the different eras of the band. In the In Darkness days it was all a bit politically aware and serious for me. A bit bloody miserable actually. Things jollied up a lot later on and the later tours were a hoot. Tours with Dirt were always brilliant fun with lost of practical joking and banter between bands.

"...Dirt, Crucifix, Flux, Amebix, and loads of others but it was a long time ago and my brain isn't good in recalling lots of what went on in those days!"

Tours abroad were especially enjoyable.

John, "Italy in '84 has to be at the top of the list for me. Based in Milan with the coolest people I have ever met. (Chris from Crucifix turned up out of the blue while we were there too!) Lippy and I kept getting arrested though!!"

Of course, all the touring made the band quite a musical force.

John, "As the years passed it got better and better musically. What a shame so little in the way of recordings survive!"

In 1985, the band recorded one last EP, this time for the Oxford based Endangered Musik.

John, "The only company who approached us to do a record! Fair play to him!"

By this time, the band had spent much time on the road but was still relative novices in the studio. The two aspects of the band never completely reconciled.

John, "We were a seriously tight and heavy three piece. Those tracks sounded so much better live than on vinyl."

The result was the Out From The Void EP. Taking off where the LP ended, the mood was darker and the sound even heavier. While maybe not totally obvious, their interest in industrial music as well as heavy rock had something to do with the band's sound while keeping them free of overt metal trappings.

John, "A lot to me but less to Lippy who as I have said really 'was' Antisect musically in my opinion. I loved Test Dept and the like very early on, before the word 'Industrial' was coined. I still like the genre but I'm often put off by the slightly ludicrous personas put across with the music.

"...Also I have always loved, Motörhead, Zeppelin etc. Lippy's record collection was always very varied but we both liked Hawkwind, and Bob Calvert's solo stuff."

It was clear that the band were heading farther and farther from the traditional punk sound mining new areas risking any commercial viability.

John, "Lippy is a perfectionist. If he is not happy with something he would rather ditch it than make do. I have never had a problem with a 'traditional punk style' but then so many other bands were, and are, doing that perfectly well so why duplicate?"

The record is lyrically darker and another scream into the existential void.

"Sucked in the by flow of the tide

Whatever the circles it's the easier
ride
But in doing so you sacrifice yourself
Fear of being out on your own
Fear of setting foot out in the great
unknown
Binds you to captivity you create your
chains
Freedom is not out of reach
But one must learn before one may
teach"

    Even the cover art showed a change. The black and white image was a horror landscape of skulls and demons. Drawn by Paul Garner, the cover is not unlike something you would expect from early Pushead or Mad Mark Rude.

John, "A friend of mine from art college, which incidentally I dropped out of. Paul is a very talented artist who now works a lot in the film industry doing set and creature designs and storyboards. He's worked on some very famous films including Hellraiser."

As was the case with the full length, the band was less than happy with the studio results. So disappointed with the first version, they recorded the EP twice.

John, "We actually recorded the whole thing twice in two different studios, as the first attempt was so poor We were kind of having 'too much of a good time' if you know what I mean as well. The final version was recorded in one day in a tiny studio in East London.

"We were never happy with it and still aren't. We simply didn't have the budget or the expertise to get the sound we wanted. Also there were some cracks in the band starting to appear even as we laid down the tracks."

Despite the bands reservations, the record was a success.

John, "Got to number 7 in the UK Indie chart. The fans loved it."

The following year, "skint, bored, tired" John left the band.

John, "When I left in '85, a guy called Lawrence took over for the last year or so. He was good." recordings, the band carried on for another two years. The band came to a crashing finish in 1988 due to robbery

John, "...all the gear was nicked out of the van one day and that was pretty well that."

While the various band members went on to other musical projects like Kulturo and Splitpigs, a sad note was the passing of original bassist, Renis "Wink" Rekiki in 2000.

John, "It is very sad that Wink took his life and what little I know of him I liked very much. He always appeared 100% genuine to me, and a real thinker. Perhaps that was part of the problem. Good man."

The band's legacy was clearly marked on the following generation of political hardcore and is reason for them still being cited as an influence today on bands worldwide.

John, "Oh yes. Look at Napalm Death and the bands that followed them. All started with us I'm afraid. ND took it to another level like we took Discharge influences to another level. So much black metal and associated genres remind me of what we were doing back in the mid-eighties.

"...I have strong beliefs and so do all of the band members but I still feel let down by many characters on the scene back then. Integrity and honesty is all, I'll say no more."

Antisect - Postal Interview 1

Persons Unknown

I met Pete and John from Antisect a little before their gig at Newcastle Station on 5.10.84. The interview took place in the back of their transit and it was very cold so if you want to add some realism, make teeth chattering and cough! cough! noises every two minutes.

Would you agree that you were very lucky to be able to have as your first release an l.p. on Spiderleg? Do you think that people bought the l.p. because it was you or because of the Flux connection?
Probably a bit of both...It could partly be that. There were probably a few people who had'nt heard of us who, when our record came out, went out and bought it just because it was on Spiderleg, the same as I did a couple of years ago with Crass records.. But, then again, people also bought the record cos they had seen and heard us.

Were you lucky?
Yeah, lucky to have a record out at all on any label. But it was good that it was out on something like Spiderleg... But it was the only one where we could do exactly what we wanted.

You've said in the past that you'd be willing to play with other bands to reach a wider audience. Surely the only people you could realistically play to are heavy metal people or Punks. Are you happy with this?
Not at all. We have to put up with it though....We have to play this sort of music cos we're not actually technically good enough to play anything else...so we might be able to play disco or something and get over to a totally different set of people but we'd lose the one we've got and like Pete says, I doubt if we'd be able to play that kind of music and I doubt if we'd enjoy it if we could.... But it's really difficult.

would you play with Heavy Metal bands?

...last six months we've been sorting ourselves out and we certainly have'nt been approaching anyone...You see, we'll play with any bands as long as we could agree on things like admission and also we'd like to know a little bit about the bands we'd be playing with. Even if they did'nt agree with anything we were saying (people enter and start rummaging around "where's my fucking fags gone?")- it'd be beneficial for us to play with someone like that.

Does it 'amuse' you that you see a lot of people walking around looking exactly like you?

...not really. I don't think about it that much. The way I see it, they're probably doing what they want to do in some sort of way...sometimes it's a bit funny cos I think 'hey, there's Pete our drummer or Pete our guitarist' but you know, so what?

Do you think your live performances are let-down by your recordings or vice-versa?

...don't think we've been really happy with either up until now. At first we liked the lp but the more we hear it the more we dislike it now. The album is definately different to the live performances. It was the best thing we could have done at the time and so we were pretty pleased with it. But a lot of the time at gigs we can't say we've had a really good sound. Sometimes we've played really well and enjoyed it but thought 'It could have been better'....I think a lot of bad gigs can be put down to our own disorganisation.

<u>You've been around for 4 years now and for half of that time you've been relatively famous and the other half quite unknown. Which do you think suits you best?</u>
We have'nt noticed that we've become famous or whatever...I don't think that we're particularly famous and even if we are I have'nt really noticed it. As a band we probably a lot more well-known than we were 3 or 4 years ago but things like that, they sort of creep up on you. It's not something that happens overnight.

<u>How far do you think you can go in your present format before you begin to get a bit tired and predictable?</u>
I don't think so but I don't know. I think bands can play more or less the same music for years and years and even though they lose one audience they'll find another....No doubt we'll change...It's so hard to say. In the last couple of years our ideas have changed, well, not so much changed as progressed.

What's the most important thing that people should get from your music, or if you like, what's your purpose?
Basically and obviously to get across what we are saying.

Which is?
Well for a start we don't regard ourselves as a punk band. We don't agree with any kind of label like that. Well it's very hard to say cos everyone in the band will have their own opinion but presonally I'd like to help people to become aware, not just like 'Oh, the bomb's gonna drop' but to help them as people. You've heard the same sort of thing going around for 4 or 5 years now and I suppose it's become a bit of a cliché.....

Just because people say something is a cliché doesn't mean it's not true
Oh no, I'm not knocking it. But lately we've been looking at it from a slightly different angle and instead of catagorising what we sing about, we broaden it out.

Omega Tribe have just used a pop producer to the 'poppy' sound they wanted. Would you use a producer from outside punk to create the sound you wanted?

Yeah, if we found a producer who could produce the sound that we wanted and if they were a person that we could get on with. But we would'nt bring someone in to produce our l.p. just to make a packet from it. Saying 'It'd be a sell-out' is just limiting yourself to Punk and that's something we don't want.

Since we're in Newcastle and it's just a new series, I suppose I'd better ask you about 'The Tube'. Would you play on it?

I don't really know that much about 'The Tube' but I watch it occaissionally, like if I'm in the house and the telly's on and 'The Tube' is on, then I'll sit down and watch it and sometimes I'll enjoy it. If we could find out a little bit more about it and how it worked and what goes on behind the scenes then I think we would... It would depend on the set-up. If it contradicted what we try to say, then I don't think we would....We'd find it strange playing on television but if it gives us the chance to get over to more people....

How do you think you'd come across?
I'm pretty sure a lot of people would say 'Ugh! Noise! I can't hear the lyrics' but it'd still be worth getting up and having a go though.

Would you ever get to the stage where you thought 'Fuck it. Nobody takes any notice of us' and give up?
Possibly we could get disillusioned with what goes on around us but, personally, I'd never get disillusioned with the way I feel.

Not so much that, but the feeling that you just are not getting through to people
Oh yeah, I get like that loads of times... I was going to say that. We all get like that sometimes but I could'nt see us or rather, myself, getting to the stage where I'd just pack everything in.

Renusze (Wink) Rokicki [Antisect]

Irene Frizzera

Antisect - Postal Interview 2

Persons Unknown

In the past, you've been portrayed as a band who have no sense of humour. Why do people choose you of all bands to say that? Do you think that they have surely nothing better to do than stir up shite?

AntiSect- To be honest we don't fucking care what we've been portrayed as. We know what we are, & what we're like, & that's enough for us. But for the record, we haven't got any sense of humour at all, we hate the entire world, & we eat baby tortoises.

I thought that the ep was very shoddily produced on record, but I heard a 1st mix of the ep & it was much clearer vocalwise & a much cleaner sound. Was the final mix a cock-up or something, & were you happy with the packaging of the ep, with Endangered Musik, & the sound?

AntiSect- Yeah, the ep was shoddily produced, mainly due to the lack of finance it had. We were considering re-recording it & putting it on the LP, but we decided that in the end we have to accept our mistakes & live with them.

The sleeve also left a lot to be desired, to be honest it was a rush job that we didn't do anywhere near well enough, & it has given us the kick up the arse that we probably needed.

"Endangered Musik"??? Well, they were a small label that, until they approached us, we hadn't even heard of. We have heard a few stories about the guy who runs it fucking people about, so at the moment we have mixed feelings about them.

I heard that you regret the demos you did early as a band. Even though they may seem irrelevent musically now, don't you think they did(& still do for listeners) serve a purpose in AntiSect?

AntiSect- No, we don't really regret the demos that we have done in the past. What they were, & still are, are statements of what we were like at the time. Listening to them now, they sound an appaling load of shite, but they're alright if you don't, or rather we don't, take them seriously. Okay for a cringe & a laugh, but that's about all they're worth to us really.

One thing that intrigues me is the way you can go straight through a set without stopping. How long did you take to master this, & do you have patience practising new material & fitting them into a set?

AntiSect- We used to do a set song by song, but we thought that when we watched other bands, the momentum was lost every time they stopped after a song, so we thought "Fuck it, let's try & go all the way through without stopping".

It seems to work okay for us, the problem really is when Polska(the drummist) gets knackered, or when bits of his kit come flying off.

What made you change your musical approach & how long ago did you consider changing it?

AntiSect- We haven't ever sat down, so to speak, & said to ourselves, "Right then, let's change our musical approach". It hasn't suddenly happened overnight. What we have sounded like has constantly changed ever since we have been going, although during the last couple of years or so we do seem to have gone a bit heavier. But even on the first LP there were a few hints at that anyway, looking back on it.

How come you never seem to have interviews in zines? Surely people write to you with interviews, or is it that I just haven't read the zines you're in?!?

AntiSect-We haven't had many interviews in fanzines because we fucking hate most of them. Usually the questions are a pile of cliched obvious, garbage; ie who's in the band? How long have you been going? What tattoos have you got? Are you anarchists? What colour Y-fronts do you wear?, etc, etc. A few here & there are alright, but most of the ones who send us questions like what I've mentioned just go straight in the bin. Sorry & all that but they just fucking wind us up.

Anyway, you must be a fucking brilliant bloke 'cos you've got a reply.

A lot of people have taken to your "raunchier" sound, though no doubt there are cynics who will say you've "turned heavy metal", assuming that you've taken in the "heavy metal conditioned lyrics". How can you persuade them that you haven't, or would you just allow them to think what they think?

AntiSect-People can think whatever the fuck they want, that's freedom ain't it maan. We haven't turned "heavy metal", we just play music, we don't call it anything else. We've never called ourselves a "punk band", nor are we about to start calling ourselves a "heavy metal band", or a "carribean steel band" for that matter.

We are not in the least bit influenced by so called "heavy metal lyrics", ie Satan, Two cocked demons fucking eight year old virgins, & other shite like that. Anybody who knows anything about us should know that by now anyway. We couldn't suddenly turn around & change our whole attitude overnight, & nor do we intend to.

Who(lyrically) do you admire, & why?

AntiSect-This would vary from member to member obviously, but on the whole we would say that we admire anybody who speaks his/her mind. As far as we're concerned it's far more important that people should do that, other than spouting off the words of others whom they would follow like sheep. If we're ever going to sort the world/ourselves out, then we've got to learn to communicate to each other. This involves complete honesty, whether or not at times it may seem to our disadvantage.

This is the only way we can begin to trust ourselves & each other, & until we begin doing this, we haven't got a fucking chance of saving anything.

You're meant to be having an LP released by Mortarhate soon, are you staying with Mortarhate & leaving Endangered Musik or do you see the idea of sticking to one label irrelevent?

AntiSect-Yes, we are having an LP released soon, at the moment it is undecided whether it will be released on Mortarhate or on our own label through their distribution. We've never really given much thought to whether or not we should stick to any particular label, it doesn't seem to matter, apart from whatever seems right at the time.

Someone told me that you used to wear "false hair". Where do you think these comments come from?!?

AntiSect-No, nobody used to wear false hair, although I've got a false leg, & our vocalist has arms & ears that are false.

We don't know where these comments came from, but between you & us, if you find out, drop us a line & we'll go round & give them a pair of false kneecaps.

Finally, you no doubt saw the picture of the record reviewer in "Kerrang!" burning the ep. Any comments on this?!? Does this mean he thought it was "hot wax" indeed?!?

AntiSect-Yeah, the "Kerrang!" thing was brilliant, it probably helped the sales of the ep a bit too. Lovely magazine, lovely singles reviewer, lovely girl in the picture, lovely world.....lovely everything.....lovely, lovely, lovely. (Pathetic word isn't it?).

I'd like to thank Lippy & AntiSect for taking some time to do thee interview for this. If you'd like to get in touch with them, then send an SAE/IRC(if abroad to ANTISECT
                                        alright????If you want to do an interview with them, then I suggest you write some good quezzies out for them, none of the questions that they've mentioned in the interview, okay???If you send in an interview, with the shitty questions that they mentioned, then you've only got yourself to blame when you don't get a reply, haven't you?

HEX

Darren Pike

Coming from Sunderland, and forming in 1984, Hex came together as a result of a thriving punk scene that was happening within the city. Having a musicians' collective and a totally independent venue, The Bunker at Green Terrace which later moved to a new venue at Stockton Road, there was no shortage of likeminded people wanting to form a band and become actively involved in something worthwhile.

We had a great local record shop and the lad who worked there had all the Crass label records on display and would let you listen to them, Zounds –Can't Cheat Karma -was the first one I bought and my passion and interest grew from there. Conflict was the first band I saw at Green Terrace and they totally blew me away. At this time you had the likes of GBH, Exploited etc. who were and still are great, but for me, and most of my mates at the time, the anarcho punk scene, if you like to call it that, was a community and to me that's what punk has always been about, people who have got the same ideals helping each other out, it may be putting on gigs, promoting each other's music, printing of t-shirts, putting a band up after a gig, like I said A COMMUNITY.

Golly had left LAMF and wanted to start a new band and so formed Hex who were Pikey (vocals) Golly (guitar and vocals) Lainy (bass) and Cubby (drums). Looking back we were really keen and enthusiastic and full of ideas living the band 24/7. Practising in a local youth club twice a week, we would store the gear in Lainy's mams and use an old shopping trolley to hump the gear backwards and forwards, it used to take ages then after practising reverse the process.

After a few months of practising we did a few gigs, went into Desert Sounds studio and recorded the first of 5 demos, made our own tapes with covers and put an ad in Sounds advertising the demo and sold quite a few.

One of the people who got hold of a copy was Karl who then formed his own label-Words of Warning- and in 1986 released You Are Not Alone 4 track E.P. which featured Hex (our track being Is this to be?), Oi Polloi, Stalag 17 and Symbol of Freedom, it sold well and got favourable reviews.

We did a few more gigs around the North East and enlisted 2 more members Sharon and Cas, both on vocals. We were proactive as a band (doing benefit gigs, turning up at protest demos etc.) as were most people involved in the scene. We played with Conflict in Newcastle and Steve (Conflict) asked us if we wanted to do a couple of gigs in London with both Conflict and Liberty. It was our first time playing in London, we were well looked after and both gigs were great, …..It was a different world down in London, it was all squatting, demos and direct action you could see people didn't mess about everything was planned and well organised.

Sharon and Cubby left the band and after recording our 4th demo with Lainy reverting to drums with Dickie Hammond joining on bass.

In 1987 Words of Warning released Nothing Ventured Nothing Gained split single with Feed Your Head, Hex contributing the tracks Corruption and Initiative, both bands did a short tour together to support the single. Around this time Hex started to promote and put on gigs at the Bunker, where everything from posters and fanzines to screen printing and practising was done in house. (In the past we had seen great gigs there, Antisect, Omega Tribe, Poison Girls, Flux, The System, Amebix, D and V, Conflict, Chumbawamba, Icons of Filth and KUKL to name but a few) so it was great to follow in the footsteps of people who we shared our ideals with, had looked up to and had done a lot of hard work to get it off the ground but over time had moved on…

My favourite gig I ever saw there, and there were a lot, was Conflict, it was around the time when rioting was taking place in Birmingham and Liverpool the atmosphere that night was electric, Colin had given a speech and when they started playing the whole place erupted and went fucking insane…

Unfortunately things came to a head when we were asked if we would put Conflict on at the Bunker (this was the first gig they were due to play after the Gathering of the 5000 at Brixton Academy a couple of months earlier) and because they had an unofficial ban we had to keep the gig a secret until a few days before. They were billed as Steve Ignorant and his Banned, unfortunately the news of the gig was leaked to someone from within the local council and we were told that if we went ahead with the gig on they could revoke our licence. I was incensed by this, so we contacted a local radio station, who interviewed us and later broadcast the interview. The gig went ahead and low and behold a little while later our licence was revoked... I recall some people giving us a stick for putting the gig on ...we were supposed to be a movement, all in it together as a community. I was left pissed off by some of the comments aimed at us ... Citizen Fish being the last gig we promoted and last band to play (I do remember they stayed at the house some of Hex shared and we had a right old session afterwards with them).

In early 1988 Lainy left and was replaced on drums by Anth Irwin from the Famous Imposters, we recorded our 5th and final demo in the spring of that year. We did a few more gigs then Golly decided to leave, we continued on for a while but finally called it a day in late 1988.

We have remained as friends to this day. Golly joined HDQ with Dickie and Lainy (both Dickie and Lainy later formed Leatherface).

I went on to work with Leatherface, HDQ, China Drum and S*M*A*S*H as well as setting up Truncheon Music with Dickie and releasing the Doctor Bison E.Ps

HDQ are still going strong and Lainy is now playing in the Cockney Rejects.

Hex contributed a track (Decide) from their final demo on the Anti-Capitalism vol.4 compilation on Overground records a couple of years back. The Bunker is still a musician's collective which does fantastic work in supporting local musicians and bands but gigs no longer take place there.

Did the scene leave a legacy?

Is the scene still important and relevant?

I would like to think so. Over the last few years we have seen groups set up on social media, books have been written and documentaries made. New bands starting up and bands re-forming, new record labels putting out new music and old records re-released.

What people have done and continue to do is important to our past, present and future, Hex were only a very small part of a movement that changed the way people thought and lived and for those who still live life by their rules and stand up for what they believe to be right and think for themselves ..Remain In Protest

On Tour With Crass

Vincent Learoyd

In the run down back streets of Lower Edmonton one grim poxy evening at Saint Peter's church hall, DIRT performed an exclusive gig in front of an audience of three people.

Yeah! Three bloody people!,

But to be fair these weren't your average punters. For a start they never gobbed at us once or paid a pound to get in, (which was customerary back then). No! Sitting in judicious observation were Penny Rimbaud, Steve Ignorant and Pete Wright. They had come along to see how we faired when performing under pressure and also I assume, to see how we would slot into the vacant space vacated by their anarchic cohorts the POISON GIRLS.

After a rather melodic rendition of MOTHER they were sold. I gathered that from the smirk on Steve Ignorant's face and his wry nod of approval in my direction when the song ended. Penny then stood up and asked us if we would be interested in gigging with them and handed us a list of dates. After some two seconds of deliberation we all agreed and the date was set.

We (DIRT) arrived at Dial house for our first tour bright and early one September morning in our old Bedford van. Everyone was milling around the house with boxes and amplifiers. The boxes contained tobacco mostly. For some reason back then, everyone in CRASS, bar Gee Vaucher and Pete Wright took their tobacco smoking seriously. It was always a Dutch Niemeyer tobacco mixed with Black beauty shag. I guess once you've fucked over commercialism and lived an abstinence based vegan existence what else have you got? Other than connoisseurship.

After all the equipment was loaded up (and the tobacco), we set off for Swansea in the vans. There were usually three vans in the convoy, a large Luton truck containing the P.A. This was supplied by 'Concert Systems P.A Hire'. CRASS always used 'Concert Systems', I guess they had known Paul Tandy and Ian (The sound engineers) for some time and knew they could rely on them getting the sound they wanted, either that or they were just bloody cheap.

CRASS also hired a van from Arlington's van hire. A nice bright orange Bedford van with the company name plastered right across the side of the vehicle. This was used for the transportation of amps and guitars. Pete Wright would usually drive the hired van with Annie anxiety and Fox for company. The rest of us piled into the back of a Navy blue Leyland Sherpa minibus.

One thing I must say about CRASS, they were always well organised, apart from the copious amounts of tobacco they always had a large wicker basket with homemade bread, cheese, butter and celery (not sure why it was always celery) on board for anyone to help themselves to. Gee would normally drive the Sherpa, in fact I don't recall anyone else driving the minibus but Gee. I guess she always drove because if she had sat in the back she would have had to contend with the thick bellowing tobacco fog emanating from our rather well crafted roll ups.

Travelling from town to town in the back of a van ain't as bad as it sounds. You undoubtedly end up in a deep discussion en route about some bollocks and before you know it you've arrived at the venue. Some of the places we turned up at looked like bloody ghost towns. honestly! There was no sign of life at all, apart from the odd pensioner walking his equally tired old mutt past our vans and looking at us as if we were from fucking Mordor.

Then I hear we are playing at the local community centre. "No one's ever gonna turn up here!" I convince myself, but we check out the facilities none the less. Normally we are greeted by a couple of punks who have organised the gig, and in the community hall kitchens they have laid on some veggie food. After woofing it down we begin to unload our gear and start setting up the stage area.

It's amazing to see the transformation in progress. One minute there's some empty dilapidated village hall that hasn't seen a lick of paint since the nineteen seventies. Paisley carpets and glittery curtains etc., the next minute it looks like a serious venue. TV screens and lights, huge banners with anarchy symbols blazoned across the walls, you can't help but be impressed.

I do have one criticism though. For some reason CRASS, whilst setting up the stage love nothing more than listening to music blasting out through the P.A. system (That's fine!). But it's always the same song, never anything different. Every single gig I did with them (and it's quite a few) they would play 'Birdland by Buddy Rich' over and over and over a bloody gain!

(I'm glad I got that off my chest).

As soon as it was time to open the doors the whole town was suddenly overrun with hundreds and hundreds of punks. It would appear that for the punks in surrounding towns this was an event not to be missed. So they would turn up out of nowhere like pissed up zombies walking along the motorways verges and across farmers fields on their way to the gig, such was the magnetism of CRASS.

CRASS never failed to deliver. By the end of the evening the whole place is going mental. Everyone is leaping through the air swigging cider shouting 'Fight war not wars!' Whilst gozzing at Steve (even me!). The atmosphere is charged with an energy that feels as if a riot is about to erupt any minute but never quite does.

It's hard to come back down afterwards, I scan the floor for badges and studs that departed their owners during the earlier fracas. So many finds and so many stories to tell. I recall one occasion when I spotted someone pogoing with a hot dog during a gig and dropping it on the floor. Later that evening after around five hundred punks had stomped on it I saw it again, covered in muddy boot cleats and as flat as a hedgehog on the M25. Then from nowhere a scruffy Mohican turns up holding a can of cheap cider! He also spots the planate morsel but instead of looking on in abhorrence he swiftly necks the flattened snack before trundling off again.

We begin breaking down the gear all sweaty and burnt out, then make our way to our sleeping bags. We usually end up sleeping on the floor in someone's house like a load of rough sleepers. I remember sleeping under a snooker table in someone's shed with Phil Free once.

The next morning Andy Palmer counts out the taking from the night before and we buy fuel and food for the next gig and off we go to do it all again.

Punk Was Once an Answer.......

Anth Palmer

The anarcho punk of the early to mid nineteen eighties that I grew up with wasn't all sensationalist idealism, bucking the system, buying every release on Crass records and creating something new. It had it's moments that seemingly collectivised a radical shift in the mindset of some, including myself, but it was a shit time in recent history that spawned it's creation.

I hated my life then because I didn't want that life. At the time I was just some thirteen year old kid locked into my own abject mental loneliness and the physical security and haven of my bedroom because the majority of my peers were intolerable assholes, my parents who were working class Conservatives held values that were the complete opposite of my own and they had no interest in trying to understand anything from my perspective or viewpoint.

Those formative years weren't part of some vibrant community that espoused similar or identical ideologies.

I had no 'movement' to feel a connection to, it was just myself and the minute corner of the world I happened to be in. In addition to the alienation that had engulfed my world, the enormity of the world around me appeared to be crumbling at a rate even I couldn't fathom as it seemed like a continual bombardment of bleak and successive obstacles that instilled further panic, fear and isolation.

Throughout that time we had Margaret Thatcher, Trident missiles, the Falklands War, the miners' strike not to mention the exasperating government information films explaining how we could Protect and Survive ourselves against the alleged continuing nuclear threat of the Cold War by building our own makeshift coffins (aka indoor fallout shelters) out of our own mattresses.

On reflection, my introduction to punk was perhaps just by pure chance but then my embracing of what became known as anarcho punk served as a major catalyst for the ethics and values that are still resonant today, thirty years on.

I guess if it hadn't have been for my best friend at the time playing me those two Discharge records my life may have become a whole different ball game and whether that life would have been better or worse is anyone's guess.

What follows are just recollections of those times that hold unforgettable memories and the sheer contrast of both the disillusionment and hope that were in absolute abundance during that period.

Tomorrow Belongs To Us

Sean had been my best friend for years, ever since that initial first meeting when he stuck his nine year old head over our back garden wall and was caught throwing stones at my five year old sister who was busy feeding her pet rabbits. My stepmother came to the open backdoor having heard my sister squeak with horror as one of the pebbles bounced off her head and hollered out to him to stop that nonsense. Sean's resilient response was to flick her the V sign before doing a runner. The fact that he'd managed to annoy both my sister and stepmother in the space of a minute was enough for me to do a runner myself and chase after him to congratulate him on his bravado.

The subsequent next few years saw our friendship bond to the extent that we became practically inseparable and we took full advantage of the new experiences we could indulge in together, from the skateboarding craze that seemingly engulfed the nation to consuming the music and ethics that the Two Tone movement had with it's massive impact. We strutted around Hebden Bridge wearing our pork pie hats, sta-press trousers and brogues looking like a right couple of sharp dressed Rude Boys.

Then The Specials released 'Ghost Town' and that it transpired, was the end of that.

It also coincided with the end of my parents marriage and on one dreary weekend in January I was sat riding shotgun in a battered Ford Transit van with my dog on the middle passenger seat being driven away by my father from my hometown, my friends and my identity to my grandparents house over in the next valley. None of this made any sense at the time nor did not having a say in the matter. It was just a further extension of the long worn "Shut up and do as you're told" adage that had been part of my upbringing.

At school the following Monday Sean excitedly insisted I had to go back to his house to listen to some new records he'd bought that weekend.

War's No Fairytale

He handed me both seven inch records, both had black and white sleeves and both instantly struck a chord before either had been played. I'd never heard of the band but the titles for each were succinct, direct and straight to the point – 'Fight Back' and 'Decontrol'.

It was January 1981 and that was the month and year Discharge entered my troubled early life.

The raw passion, energy and anger of the simplistic lyrics combined with the equal measure of aural brutality both those singles possessed led me to purchasing them both the following weekend with my weekly allowance. I played both records to death, one after the other, continually.

A few weeks later at school and following morning registration, another kid in my class came up to me with a cocky attitude and asked if I wanted to buy a record from him because he'd heard I was now a punk and the record he had wasn't his thing.

"You can have it for a quid", he said whilst holding out a copy of the Crass 'Nagasaki Nightmare / Big A Little A' 7". I handed over the cash without hesitation despite having never heard of the band nor realising he'd deliberately covered over the pay no more than 80p imprint on the sleeve. He laughed as the exchange was sealed, the oneupmanship of him making a meagre profit would prove to be irrelevant and meaningless given the impact this band would have on my life.

At home that evening I was completely consumed by the product, from the haunting A side to the relentless lyrical fury and barrage that Big A, Little A conveyed. The additional aesthetics, artwork and missives contained on that foldout sleeve went far beyond either of those two Discharge records.

"Who the fuck are Crass?", I probably pondered and pondered and quizzed furthermore only a week later having purchased 'Stations Of The Crass' whilst attempting to make sense of the massive breadth of issues the band were obviously none too happy about.

They've Got A Bomb

Thatcher had been elected in 1979 and by the following year the Conservative government announced its intention to replace the current nuclear deterrent with the Trident I C-4 missile. I knew practically nothing about nuclear missiles or bombs other than they were wrong, had the ability to kill a lot of people and that Crass and Discharge weren't particularly happy with them either. So I joined the Youth CND movement and attended meetings in one of the local community halls and soon found myself being bored as hell with liberal minded individuals who extolled peaceful demonstration marches so no doubt they could return home safe in one piece afterwards and have a comforting cup of nettle tea.

I attended my first CND rally and demonstration a few months later that marched through the liberal minded town that had once been my home. Other than the excitement of being part of a huge crowd all shouting slogans of peace and the fact that myself and Sean had made our own placards, the conclusion with more speakers droning on proved to be a legacy that peace abiding marches and demos were ineffective when a more direct action approach obtained better results.

Fight For Your Life

Nothing had changed in Hebden Bridge since leaving the town six months earlier. The dark, cold and foreboding mill behind my former childhood house still stood as a place where we as kids had played childhood games such as kick the can, hide and seek and sardines around it's many connected buildings and walkways.

One of the dilapidated garages we once broke into to use as our gang house for secretly smoking cigarettes still stood there, propped up on either side by an equally rickety piece of wooden garaged framework and corrugated iron roof. The local fire station, the outdoor market area used every day of the week as a car park except on Thursdays and the public conveniences built next to a mortuary building. They were all still intact.

Nothing had changed in that respect except for everything in my own life. I'd transformed from this naive thirteen year old who hated his new forced beginning in another town away from friends and my own personal security to a thirteen year old who had heard Discharge and Crass for the first time and reminisced of those occasions seeing older kids around the town with their bright blue mohicans and studded leather jackets.

I'd never had to use this particular public convenience as it was literally a twenty second dash to my own house but that's where we were that night, myself and my best friend Sean, swigging away on a bottle each of cider that we'd had a complete stranger buy for us. Using the sink's cold water to lather up the meagre bar of soap so we could drag it through our teenage hair into the spikes we associated with the anticipatory rebellion that was further fuelling our bravado.

I felt on top of the world, cider, soap and singing Charged GBH lyrics with my best mate in a public toilet on a Friday night and I was going to my first punk gig at the Trades Club. Hebden Bridge had spawned it's first punk band Crash who had released their own four track 7" complete with no cover and no labels and at 50p a time had long sold out. Crash were playing tonight and they were the ones who everyone looked up to.

"Do you want some of this?" asked Sean, showing me the palm of one hand with a small amount of white powdery substance barely visible upon it.

"What the fuck is that?", I quizzingly asked.

"It's speed, it's what all the punks do" he replied.

"What does it do?" I asked, having no idea what the hell he was talking about other than innocently assuming my own answer that the concept of speed related to a maths question.

"I dunno, but it'll be good I reckon" came his innocuous response and before waiting for a further response sprinkled an equal amount into both our bottles.

"Swirl it around and then have some".

This was my first experience of alcohol and having consumed half the bottle already and thought nothing of it yet the latter half proved fatal with its consequences as the meagre ten minute walk to the venue became a series of intermediary blackouts closely followed by epic proportions of my stomach rejecting it's contents en route.

I somehow managed to stumble up to the venue's doors without losing consciousness for a third time only to throw up again against the wall in plain view of everyone including the member of staff monitoring the melee of multi coloured haired punks and other local misfits.

It came as no surprise that he refused my admission as I swayed and staggered before him in all innocence declaring that I was fit for purpose. The words fell completely on deaf ears, those too of Sean's who glibly remarked that he would see me at school next week and walked right in.

I therefore missed my first ever punk gig and was unsurprisingly banned from my stepmother's house for a month after I'd somehow managed to make it back there, only to desecrate the hall carpet, my sister's bedroom and the bathroom with further copious amounts of froth, bile and vomit.

No Doves Fly Here

The month of March in 1982 was just another day that began with the constant bombardment of torrential rain backed by a vociferous wind that rattled my bedroom window.

I had begun to detest my now new home town by now, a town seemingly devoid of independent thought, a small town mentality awash with pubs where pissed up wankers fell out of their doors on a Friday night and my equally aged peers who's only interest was going to football matches and by their own admission in doing so "was to cause a ruck".

Being asked why I didn't eat meat was fucking tiresome, being asked why I dressed like a freak was equally tedious and often followed by the cliché of "Did you put your finger in the electric socket to make your hair stand up like that?" were all the usual remarks from one day to the next.

In response I cocooned myself in isolation. I made weekly pilgrimages to the only place of solace I knew and that was Groove records in Halifax and continued to hand over my meagre pocket money for any piece of vinyl that I could afford. I became absorbed if not obsessed with every release that appeared to echo the sentiments and thoughts that were continually swarming through my head. It was a never ending spending spree to indulge in due to the vast myriad of releases on Spiderleg, Crass, Bluurg, Fight Back, Mortarhate, Corpus Christi plus the countless others who all seemed to have a message that indicated similar individuals were coequally pissed off, angry and of wanting to make something good out of the bad.

The rain never abated that day whatsoever. I took the twenty minute bus ride and watched from the upper deck with despondency the public outside crawling under their umbrellas and raincoats, obviously going somewhere but seemingly going nowhere under the grey and miserable sky.

There seemed to be a similar sullen atmosphere at Groove records that day with little traffic of punters scouring through the records and it would seem I'd exhausted them myself as I departed with but just one item stuffed into the inside of my studded jacket.

Back home pissed wet through and thoroughly depressed I placed my purchase of the day onto the turntable and five minutes later had a somewhat epiphany that The Mob and their 'No Doves Fly Here' lament was the most captivating piece of music I'd heard yet and the most sombre and dismal soundtrack that echoed this bleak existence so far. The back panel of the sleeve picturing some disillusioned punk with his head bowed over a bottle of booze in his lap was neither an uplifting image that offered much in the way of possible hope.

Nurses

I was going out with my first girlfriend at the time who was the only distraction I had from the misery I felt with living in a town that was devoid of anything I shared an affinity with. I wasn't actually interested in girls but we were thrown together by mutual friends who probably figured that the only two misfits within a half mile radius should hook up.

The sexist comments from my peers regarding girls or women being either slags or birds were continual offensive slurs and banter that were just more tedious diatribes to listen to.

I'd just discovered the written works of Bakunin and picked up the first Rudimentary Peni 7" and two singles by Six Minute War and they seemed more important than a relationship.

I guess she wasn't really interested either. Despite my father's somewhat cajoling excitement having invited Janine to 'come over and listen to some records', my attempt to impress her with 'Teenage Time Killer' was met with clear disinterest and the anti anarchic polemic from Six Minute War with their brazen and lo-fi aural aesthetics didn't register any appreciation either. We broke up a few weeks later having finally realised through a mutual understanding that neither of us were interested in the other.

Sick Butchers

"If you're now a vegetarian, then you can start cooking your own meals".

That was my father's response after I informed him that I wouldn't be consuming anything that was once alive and I certainly wouldn't be sitting at the same table with anyone else who had a piece of meat on their plate. This by now was pretty much the belligerent response to virtually anything that I considered to be the norm or tradition.

I'd never once questioned the food I was eating or whether it had once been living. I knew cruelty to animals was abhorrent having once witnessed a gang of kids some years earlier put a cat in a sack and throw it on a bonfire. I ran home in tears, told my parents and those responsible received a police caution. Roast beef on a Sunday or Fish and Chips on a Friday were just something I'd accepted because that's just how it was but with every piece of vinyl I bought it appeared eating animals was completely unjustified and the lyrics and imagery only furthered the reasons why.

'Meat means dinner' was a badge someone at school wore on his blazer and who made a significant point to make sure I acknowledged it. Childish antics and from someone who a few months earlier had gleamed great amusement from the fact I wasn't aware of a band called Conflict. The rebellion of punk may have permeated this dullard of an individual into thinking the more studs one had embedded in his leather jacket was far more credulous than the lyrics of said band, particularly moreso given that he had also taken so much time and effort to paint the band's logo on his said leather jacket and the irony of it being absolutely lost.

Becoming vegetarian and then six months later adopting a vegan diet seemed another notch to mark up on the anarcho punk checklist. I had no culinary skills whatsoever but then that didn't matter, nor did the continual berating or humiliation others attempted to do with their sarcasm and belittling just because I'd chosen not to eat dead animals.

Now I held another firm conviction and one which I vowed to uphold and so forged ahead on my dietary journey of lentils, textured soya chunks, over priced vegan margarine and the then only available soya milk I could buy that tasted like it had been filtered with chalk dust.

As much as I wanted to throw a brick through the local butchers shop window I was aware enough to think that if I did, the mentality and the small closed environment and those who lived in it would be astute in assuming that I was the culprit and that would have the old bill knocking on my door. Instead I took other steps to support the animal rights cause by paying my grandmother £2 a month to send a cheque of the same amount to the ALF Supporters Group for which I received in return a monthly posted bulletin full of masked activists complete with photographs of themselves and liberated animals.

My initial involvement with the Hunt Sabs movement proved a horrendous experience with a meeting that was unwelcoming, clique ridden and led by ego driven boorish males. It would be a few years later and a move to Leeds before I finally began direct action against the tireless violence perpetrated by those involved in this blood sport and the ridiculous comments heard week in, week out with many of them asking how much the KGB were paying us communist scum for spoiling their Saturday morning fun.

The Buck Stops Here

It would be a year later after having started to attend gigs in Leeds and Bradford and then finally moving to Leeds when I finally began to experience the community I had sought to feel a part of and the like minded individuals who were the intrinsic make up that personified the same struggles, hopes, wishes and dreams that we all seemingly wanted to be a part of. Other than brief and ineffectual contact at the local record store, my only contact with others who shared similar beliefs had been attained through contacting bands, buying as many fanzines I could afford, sending away for demo tapes with a soaped stamped addressed envelope and eliciting as much information on direct action from various activist organisations.

I spent a sheer twelve months in self induced seclusion consumed just with writing letters to others, expressing my inner demons whilst sat at my bedroom desk watching the world go by in a desperate shroud of frustration. I may have developed a considerable record collection that contained lyrics I vehemently agreed with but this was no substitute for having the physical contact of others with which to share those feelings.

Sure, at fourteen years old and with a two bus journey each way to school I had managed to learn and recite the entire lyrics of the first Subhumans album and a year later had managed to overcome the absolute disappointment of the second Flux Of Pink Indians album but the solitary existence never abated.

By the mid nineteen eighties I'd endured countless spats, arguments, being lifted by the police, violence and intimidation from hunt supporters and brain dead fascists, being grounded, being labelled a communist (which I found completely offensive due to the absurd assumption that the opposite of being right wing meant left wing) and by now anarcho punk as it was once was, appeared to slowly yet readily disappear in some respects.

Then one evening whilst walking to a Disorder gig in Bradford I got talking to a kid who had spotted the Chumbawamba logo painted on my battered jacket and we struck up a conversation that a few months later became a telephone call asking if I was still moving to Leeds as there was a vacancy in the all vegan, anarchist shared house he lived at.

A few weeks later having sold a proportion of my vinyl collection to help secure the deposit I had moved in.

Finally, it all seemed to fall into place and the psychological mist lifted.

Crass may have broken up but the battles, the homebrewing, the endless cups of that foul Barleycup beverage, law breaking and overall general nuisance making continued.

The Snatcher (Remix)

Marcus Blakeston

At twelve years of age, Scar Gill knew he was too old for stories. He had responsibilities now that his father was dead. He guarded the village of Gold Thor's sheep from the scabbed ones who roamed the countryside, just as his father had done before him. It was an important job, and one that Scar Gill was proud to have. Gone were the carefree days of childhood. He was a man now, and soon it would be time for him to choose a wife and begin the task of creating a new generation.

But despite his age, Scar Gill still liked to hear the stories the village elder told in the evenings. Stories of the great Yarksher warrior of legend with the same name as him. Of The Snatcher, the Scar Gill of legend's arch nemesis, and the many battles they fought.

He knew they were only fanciful stories, that they couldn't possibly be true, but Scar Gill liked to imagine they were a real part of his family's history. That the Scar Gill of legend was a distant ancestor of his, and the warrior blood flowed through his body.

When the village elder called out to the children, Scar Gill crept closer to listen. He kept an eye on his sheep as he settled down behind an old oak tree, close enough to hear the stories, but far enough away not to be seen in the gathering dusk.

"Gather round, children," the elder said, "sit closer to the fire so The Snatcher's scabbed ones won't get you." Scar Gill heard gasps from the younger children. He shivered involuntarily when he heard the name of the evil one, though he would never admit it to anyone. The Snatcher wasn't real, he told himself. She was just a monster invented to frighten children. Nobody would ever be so evil, it was impossible.

"Long, long ago," the elder began, "long before The Great Gee Had laid waste to our country, there was a village called That Lunn Don. It wasn't a small village like our very own Gold Thor, not even one like the mighty Barn Slay of which we were once a part. That Lunn Don was a vast metropolis, populated with many hundreds of people. Within its walls lived an evil witch, known as The Snatcher, who liked nothing more than to steal the milk from new-born infants.

"One day, The Snatcher decided this wasn't evil enough for her, and set in place her plan to rule the country so that she may steal much more than a baby's milk. So The Snatcher tricked the people of That Lunn Don into making her their queen. She promised them riches beyond imagination, said they would own their own dwellings and places of work if only they would make her their queen. But the people of That Lunn Don did not know her true intentions, for The Snatcher was wise and cunning as well as wicked and evil. On the very day she was crowned queen, The Snatcher set her dastardly plan into motion.

"She passed new laws to set the money lenders free from their chains. She created an army of Lords of the Land who were free to charge the people of That Lunn Don rents far in excess of what they could afford, making them reliant on charity to survive. Many travelling minstrels of the time sang songs of protest, but these fell on deaf ears and The Snatcher ruled for many years with an iron fist.

"It was not long before The Snatcher turned her steel gaze to the land of Yarksher and the riches it contained. The Under-dwellers, who had been supplying the village of That Lunn Don with their magical black rocks for many years, were the first of her targets. This angered The Under-dwellers, and they sent forth their champion, Scar Gill, to do battle with The Snatcher. Scar Gill was a mighty warrior, with many scalps to his name, but he was also a man of great compassion. He attempted to reason with The Snatcher, but his words fell on deaf, uncaring ears."

Scar Gill felt an immense pride well up within him as he listened from behind the oak tree. He imagined his warrior ancestor dressed in battle armour, standing bravely before the evil Snatcher. How The Snatcher would have trembled before him if it were not for her guards and their impenetrable ring of steel around her. How he, if he were the real Scar Gill of legend, would have fought through the guards and chopped The Snatcher's head off, put an end to her years of torment forever. He sighed. The sad part of the story was coming up.

"In retaliation for Scar Gill's effrontery," the elder continued, "The Snatcher decreed that she would seal up the caves from which The Under-dwellers extracted their magical black rocks. Without the black rocks to trade for food, The Under-dwellers were left hungry and destitute. Some of The Under-dwellers were so destitute they developed scabs upon their bodies, and The Snatcher took advantage of this. She used her evil powers to control the scabbed ones, to turn them against their fellow Under-dwellers."

Scar Gill wanted to shout "Boooooo," along with the children. But he knew he was too old for such things. He contented himself with striking his fist into his palm, cursing the scabbed ones for their traitorous ways.

"But Scar Gill held strong. His loyal Under-dwellers fought ferocious battles with the scabbed ones, and cast them from the villages of Yarksher for all time."

Scar Gill nodded to himself. Even to this day, the scabbed ones were still banished from Yarksher, and lived their cursed lives in the wastelands to the south of Barn Slay, in the ruins of Notty Ham. Sometimes they would try to sneak back into Yarksher under cover of darkness and steal sheep, but they were always driven away because they were such a cowardly race.

The first time Scar Gill had seen a scabbed one he was just a small child. His father, Gold Thor's sheep watcher at the time, had caught a scabbed one on the fringes of the village one night, and paraded him through the village, bound in rope, the following morning. Scar Gill watched as the scabbed one was stoned to death by the whole village. He felt no pity. The scabbed ones deserved much worse than death for their betrayal in the times of The Snatcher.

"The Snatcher was not happy with the defeat of the scabbed ones," the elder continued. "She sent forth her Army of Blue Men from the village of That Lunn Don to lay siege against The Under-dwellers of Yarksher and their families. There was a great battle at the village of Org Reeve that took many lives on both sides of the conflict. But the Army of Blue Men had far superior weaponry to the sticks and stones of The Under-dwellers, and The Under-dwellers were defeated with mighty clubs and giant beasts.

"The caves of The Under-dwellers were sealed for all time. Entire villages who relied on trade from The Under-dwellers shrivelled and died. The Snatcher cackled in her castle while The Under-dwellers were forced to beg for scraps of food. All the riches of Yarksher were transferred to the village of That Lunn Don, while the people of Yarksher went hungry.

"But still The Snatcher was not satisfied. She created a new tax, one which everyone in Yarksher was forced to pay even if they were destitute and could not afford to do so. She used her Army of Blue Men to enforce the tax, throwing people into dungeons for the rest of their lives if they refused to pay.

"Scar Gill was angered by this. Although forced to live on the surface, The Under-dwellers had remained strong and formed communities together, so Scar Gill did not find it difficult to rally his army. They marched on the village of That Lunn Don, where they were joined by other armies. Armies from outside Yarksher. Armies from a land far away, where men wore skirts and spoke in a strange tongue."

A child giggled, and was hushed by the elder. Scar Gill smiled. He knew why the child had laughed. While the wives of The Under-dwellers themselves were fierce and strong, and fought alongside their men in the battles with The Snatcher's Army of Blue Men, the idea of men wearing skirts was preposterous. Somewhere down the ages, as the story was passed from generation to generation, this absurdity had entered the legend. Scar Gill vowed that if he lived long enough to become the village elder he would change this part of the story to make it more believable.

"Yes," the village elder said, "the men of this strange army wore skirts. For they were a mighty warrior tribe who didn't care what anyone thought of them. The Snatcher sent forth her Army of Blue Men to smite both armies. But the armies, seeing they were allies with a common enemy, joined forces and rampaged through the streets of That Lunn Don. They destroyed what they could destroy, chanting 'Can't pay won't pay,' as they battled their way toward The Snatcher's fortress with pitchforks and flaming torches.

"Many lives were lost in the ensuing bloody battle, and the armies were ultimately defeated, but the message had been sent. No longer would Yarksher put up with the tyranny of The Snatcher. The Snatcher was forced to recant her new tax, and abdicated her throne in shame soon after. She went to live in exile, where she was never heard from again for another generation.
"Scar Gill spent many years in search of The Snatcher's hiding place, so he could avenge The Under-dwellers and the people of Yarksher for the wrongs done to them.

But his search proved futile and The Snatcher remained in hiding.

"Until one day, long after Scar Gill had given up his quest, one of The Snatcher's cohorts announced she was dead and ordered the country to mourn for her passing. There was much rejoicing throughout the land of Yarksher, and street parties were held in celebration. The surviving Under-dwellers looked forward to the day when they could visit The Snatcher's grave and urinate on it, but The Snatcher's cohort decreed that she should be burned at the stake and her ashes sealed in a vault to protect them.

"Some say, before she died, The Snatcher passed her spirit to a new body, leaving an empty shell behind, so that she could continue her evil work from beyond the grave. Others say she made a pact with the devil and lives on to this day, plotting her revenge on the people of Yarksher, using the scabbed ones to do her bidding just as she did during her reign of terror. Nobody knows for sure.

"And so we remain vigilant, and watch out for the scabbed ones. We guard our homes, we guard our sheep, and we guard our children's milk. Because these things are important to us. And we will never let them be taken from us again."

"Amen," chanted a chorus of children.

"Amen," whispered Scar Gill to himself. He looked out to his sheep, satisfied himself they were safely grazing in their field.

A flutter of movement in a nearby bush caught Scar Gill's attention. He watched, raising himself up from the ground. A stranger, his hairless, naked body covered in scabs and boils, darted out from the bush.

"Scabbed ones!" Scar Gill shouted. He pulled an axe from his belt and ran at the stranger.

Gifts of the Garden

Andrew J. Wood

This short essay is a work of what some might call philosophical fiction. That is, it is an imagined conversation meant to invite and challenge readers not necessarily to take sides, but to self-examine, reflect, and question on the ideas herein. Dialogue has been utilized as a stylistic device of philosophy for several millennia, though its prominence has faded in recent centuries. As Dial House is a place of imagining alternatives and talking with others as equals, it seems only fitting to honor its legacy through such a dialectical treatment. Some of what follows is clearly indebted to actual conversations I have had with my friends at Dial House. Other parts are completely invented by me to grapple with ideas and the art of life. I prefer to leave the 'truth' of what these people have 'really' said to other contexts, leaving fact and fiction ambiguous here. I invite you to join the characters inspired by Penny Rimbaud and Gee Vaucher as we sit in the back garden…

P: I wonder if life events ever occur to those within them as anything more than just what happens.

G: What do you mean? Do you mean that we can't always make sense of what's going on?

P: Think, for instance, of those poor slaves in America. Now we look at that as horrible, one of the worst crimes ever. But, I wonder if those that were in it had thoughts like that, or if you're born into something awful it just presents itself to you as just what happens.

G: Just what happens? Are you fucking mad? It's not just what happens when someone is doing it to you.

P: I don't mean it wasn't bad, I'm just wondering if it seemed especially bad to those that were in it, or if we look back on it differently than they experienced. If you're born into something, it doesn't present itself as unusual does it?

G: But can't things be recognizable as horrific, even if they are considered usual? Look at all the institutions we don't like that we want to change. I think sometimes the painfully normal stuff is completely what we do want to change. You don't need to change the abnormal now, do you?

P: But is the change sought really a change, or do we just tell ourselves it is? We imagine changes, you're right, but maybe changes are only appearances. I'm just wondering how things persist, for so long, if they're seen as worse than regular occurrences.

A: Well, it's not like historic crimes are universally recognized as such. Some bystanders might not even have been aware of the horrors until they were over. Those who were perpetuated the system had serious economic interests in creating and maintaining such exploitation. That doesn't mean that people exploited and abused within weren't aware that it wasn't right, but when the owners and the capitalists are getting rich off the system and they have all the guns, it's awfully hard to escape. Not that there weren't successful cases of escape, which are the most interesting to me.

P: That's a really materialist response, especially to a psychological question.

G: But we're talking about people within context, and their suffering was physical and mental.

A: Right. But, I'm pointing to the complexity of existences that we want to eliminate in facile ways. For instance, when the government wants to eliminate an enemy, they declare them as 'insane,' rather than have to deal with the actual logic that they follow, especially when it is similar to their own. So, we look at past atrocities and dismiss them in an effort to distance ourselves from it.

G: That's true, but Pen's talking about people within these systems and institutions. They certainly don't have distance from their own suffering.

P: That's my point, to them it was just what happens.

G: I think in some circumstances, that's simplifying, and perhaps assuming an ignorance that might not be there.

A: I think I see what you mean, that only in later contexts can we narrativize something, seeing the context. We have a tendency to put things into a narrative so that we can describe and attempt to understand them, but events don't happen in a narrative form, or in a nice, neat sequence of events. Like, perhaps, at the time in the '80s, you weren't thinking so much about being seen as leaders of something called punk, but in retrospect that makes sense to say.

P: That's right. We weren't anarchist leaders, we were just on about how we wanted to live our lives. Suddenly, we were declared leaders of the anarchist movement and we didn't know fuck all about anarchism. That's not why we put a big A on there, it was about how we were living our lives at the time.

G: That's right, we didn't choose the label 'anarchist.' But, once we accepted it, it did allow us to do things and maneuver without the left and the right trying to get us on a particular party line. Using the term 'anarchist' gave us a bit more space, a bit more breathing room.

A: For one, the concept of anarchist leaders seems a bit like an oxymoron.

P: Of course it does. We wanted freedom for freedom, not just freedom to follow a set of rules or institutions. We weren't interested in being anarchists per se, but just in living our lives freely.

A: Doesn't that make you the best sort of anarchists then? You certainly want freedom for all, you've done things to help people struggling to survive, you share what you have, you live relatively autonomously, and you don't dictate anything to others. From what I understand, these are the best that anarchy-as-freedom can offer. Perhaps we are simply talking at crossroads, for I am thinking of anarchy as philosophy, much in the way you look at existentialism or zen. But you seem to view anarchy as anarchism, in a sort of codified sense. I'm more interested in ideas surrounding freedom and anarchy, not an ideology or programmatic stance.

G: Then why call it anarchy at all?

A: That's a good question, Gee, and one I'm not sure I have an answer to. Perhaps because we don't have another word, perhaps because there are a lot of anarchist ideas about non-governance and critiques of the state and capital that I am invested in.

P: I see what you mean, but how can you avoid all of the rotten business that anarchists have been up to for years, telling people what they can and can't do? For instance, all that rubbish about underground labels. Look, we put out our own records because no one else wanted to and no one else would have. But, I think all this about underground labels as superior is really just

nonsense. When I met with Sony, they were polite, on time, and seemed fair.

A: What of these corporations' connections to the military and prison industrial complexes?

G: Good point. Doing things yourself is always more free. That's part of why I have such a love for self-publishing.

P: Well, we're all connected to those institutions in a way, there's no escaping it.

A: But, are there not some avenues of escape or resistance? Must we be resigned to complicity, or can we also say there are instances in which we can actually, or at least attempt, to separate ourselves from what we oppose? There is still a political importance in D.I.Y.

P: Maybe idealistically, but you can only change yourself not the ways in which these companies operate. Look, if the others had been for it, I would have considered Sony.

G: Well, I would have been against it.

P: Eh?

G: Look, I haven't sought great fame or commercial success because I don't really care about it. I never really seek other people's money. Pen, come on, you know that was a big goal of ours. We've never wanted other people's money, despite how polite Sony may have been. I don't want it. We've done extraordinary things with nothing, and if we can't do it ourselves, I don't want to do it.

A: That's why I think Crass's influence on D.I.Y. culture has been so powerful. But, if I can play devil's advocate, what might we be overlooking about the embedded privilege in a lot of what's called D.I.Y.?

P: What do you mean?

A: Well, there are many people in the world whose daily struggle is just an attempt to survive.

P: They aren't trying to survive, they are surviving.

G: Well, some do, and some don't. Some are destroyed.

A: If you are struggling to survive, the idea of D.I.Y. can seem a bit insensitive. Look, I think that historically we can show that more generations of people have produced things themselves than any other form of production. However, once capitalism became the hegemonic mode of organizing production and consumption, in many ways D.I.Y. became to domain of those at the extremes, the very poor and the very privileged. Many, at least in punk, tell ourselves that D.I.Y. is a tactic of political autonomy as well as something forced upon us when other channels may be closed. I don't want to negate this argument, for at times I think it holds. However, there are other times when D.I.Y. or self-sufficiency is present for someone or some group through the exercise of privilege.

G: What do you mean?

A: Dial House, for instance.

G: Wait a minute. We've worked our fingers to the bone making this place what it is. Do you think that house was always so put together? Do you think the veggie patch planted itself? Do you think the garden maintains itself? We love our life here because we made it what it is, we chose it for ourselves.

A: That's not at all what I mean. Of course you have put forth tremendous labour to create these lovely surroundings, and any of the grateful passers-through over the last four decades can attest to that. You've also certainly led a life of sharing, and having an open house is clearly no small task. But, I'm making a deeper argument. I'm claiming that the ability, or perhaps what I mean is the freedom to work for one's self, to eat of the fruits of one's own labor, is already a privilege.

G: I agree. Well, I should say that I recognize the privilege that you're on about.

A: And to many people in the world, this is a privilege that will never be available to them.

P: Well, I'm not sure about that.

A: You think just anyone, anywhere could own such a piece of land, and a cottage, and afford to live life as they choose? Take people who are enslaved, people who are imprisoned or tortured to death, people whose race, gender, class, or whatever is oppressed?

P: Of course there's suffering in the world, and of course some people are oppressed such that they can't do just anything that they like. But look, my parent's aspiration in life was to move from being middle class to being upper middle class, and they achieved this with a fair amount of success. I, however, had no interest in such a life. I don't really know why, I just know that it hasn't ever had an appeal to me. But I have often wondered why couldn't I just have been a happy bank manager or something. But the point is, I chose something else. No one gave us permission to make an open house, to write books, paint, or put out records. We wanted it, so we did it. Does that make us privileged? Maybe, but it's not the typical 'privilege' of a criticism, but more of a zen openness. Zen is available to anyone, and it is a type of freedom that doesn't care about all that race, gender, class rubbish. Here [points with his index finger to his forehead] is the only space of freedom any of us can ever really have.

A: But I think we can still see the importance of fights for freedom and struggles against oppression. I don't think, for instance, that we can say that mental freedom is enough, you know, "question but obey" doesn't seem right to me at all, nor free. I'm also not entirely convinced that such mental freedom exists, or even can exist in physically oppressive, or even in more insidiously, hidden oppressive contexts.

G: Of course!

P: I'm just not willing to think strictly in materialist terms when we talk of freedom or privilege. The greatest privilege that I've experienced has been through meditation, as well as the greatest freedom.

G: That's individual freedom though, what about those who are denied freedom in the world? I think something like Occupy Wall Street did a wonderful job of showing our connections to each other. I mean, when you think about it, how can we sit and enjoy our own freedom when we know others can't share it.

A: Well, of course I would agree, and I think that the most exciting recent development in both punk rock and activism in the U.S. has been Occupy (both as a participant at the time and as a commentator in retrospect).

P: Well, what would you say it really accomplished? I

mean, Wall Street is still doing their thing, right?

G: But they did something, and that's important.

A: In terms of massive policy changes and changing the system as a whole, no you're right, not much changed. But, I think there are important ramifications of Occupy. For one, the lack of the typical list of demands that the media made so much out of was not a weakness, it was a strength of the movement.

P: How so?

A: If there was a set list of demands one problem is that once you start dictating goals or tactics, you begin to exclude people from within and from without the movement.

G: That was the most impressive thing about Occupy Wall Street, is that it crossed all the divides of age, class, race, gender, you know?

A: That's right, well, to an extent. We can definitely say that there was an attempt to be inclusive.

P: But what did it accomplish? It seems there was a lot of noise made, but what did it change?

G: Well, that's one thing they've said about Obama and healthcare reform too, but sometimes it's admirable to stick to your guns to get something accomplished, even if it isn't everything that you might want.

P: But that's within the system of governance, which Occupy wasn't within.

G: That's probably why it was able to be so inclusive.

A: Can we think, for instance, not about changes from within the system, but changes within activists themselves? We're always thinking and talking about resisting the system, but what if it's the system that resists us? This is what I think Occupy demonstrated, that we can live without the state, without capital, that alternatives really exist. What Occupy showed was an alternative to normative lifestyles within the context of state-capitalism. It was about finding spaces and modes of existence beyond what we are told we can and can't do. If we try to measure and accomplishment, then yes, we failed. But why should we think in terms of things that can be quantified and measured, like votes and policies and laws. These are all parts of the institutions we were demonstrating against. The powers that be would have much preferred us to put on suits and ties and lobby Congress than to experiment with modes of life beyond their understanding. The reason I think Occupy was a success and is still important is not how it changed the system, but rather how it changed participants and witnesses. I truly believe, and my project is about, how we can't have better modes of life, better organizations of society, and real freedom until we can imagine these alternatives. The target of Occupy was perhaps popular imagination more so even than finance.

G: Like us [chuckles].

P: Hmm, I see. So, it was similar to what I've been writing and saying for years, that it's truly about changing ourselves. You see, the problem isn't really the government or the bankers or the soldiers, but ourselves. We have to get beyond the blaming thing. You know, when you point at someone else, you have more fingers pointing back at yourself. The biggest blame is always right here. [Penny then points to himself, essentially in the middle of his chest, as if to punctuate the sentence with a definitive period].

A: But I think there are people who are deserving blame. I'm not claiming that the system doesn't need to be changed, that if we just change ourselves everything will be better. I'm saying that I think systematic change and individual change are interconnected.

G: That's an interesting thought, change ourselves to change each other.

P: It's the death throws of the Cartesian point, the Enlightenment way of thinking, which we must overcome. Stop being so materialist, even in anger, and start to recognize ourselves and the importance of compassion. The anger is also fed by the same phenomenon as ridiculous governance. They know they are in the last throws of the Enlightenment, that they've essentially lost control, so they pass things to seem like they are still in control. The appearance of control is all they have left. Well, if you stop thinking that they can control you, you start to think of ways that we put up obstacles for ourselves. Anger is just one of these controlling mechanisms we put upon ourselves. I spent many years saying, "oh you motherfuckers, you're such bastards" and shouting about what was wrong in the world. But I find now that if you say, "oh, well, you're a person, let's start from that" and start evaluating yourself more so than them, letting go of pure materialism, and thinking through compassion and love, it actually makes for a stronger argument. I thought in my re-write of "Yes Sir" that the insertion of love and compassion would be just as radical as the anger was in the original.

A: But that's also how so many of the horrors of the state and of capital come to be and come to perpetuate themselves. They want us to think there is no one to blame, so that they can keep being abusive and exploitative. Are you saying that we can never call a spade a spade? I don't understand, for it seems you had no difficulties openly criticizing the Thatcher administration in the '80s, yet now you seem to be saying that blame is not a proper mode of argumentation.

P: That had to be done at the time. But now? Well, for one, I don't go in for the punk sentimentality of "I still hate Thatcher." To me, that doesn't seem relevant at all politically. That type of thinking is totally useless. What I'm saying is, why are people so angry at bankers for being bankers? At the base of the crisis was greed all around, but everyone's shouting at the bankers. Look, this is the problem with the left, they are perfectly happy to benefit from greed when things are good, but then pass blame to someone else when they go bad. Bankers are greedy, but so is everyone else. If you don't like it, don't participate. But if you do, stop complaining. It's the same with oil. If you don't like oil, don't use it. And if you do use it, use it with grace. Soldiers act like soldiers, right? And soldiers kill people, so why complain?

G: That's not how I think about it. Is critique not different from complaining, Pen?

P: Well, I mean complaining as in blaming.

G: Some deserve blame, do they not?

P: Of course, but so do we all. We can't be perfectly happy to benefit from a system of violence until it goes wrong, and then act like it's always someone else to blame when it does.

A: I think I understand what you mean. It seems you are saying that it is a little too easy and a little too comfortable for us to, for example, protest wars for oil, yet still desire to purchase petrol products at low prices.

P: Precisely.

G: However, it doesn't follow that we have to accept the system as is, or not assign blame where it is necessary.

G: That's part of why I'm against revolutions, for they say their for the people, but they're really not are they? But I don't have to be pro-revolution or pro-system, do I?

P: The left is worse than the right, for at least the right is honest. You see, the left is very disingenuous, in taking this position that they say is for the people. But it's not for the people, is it? If it were, the people would be on board. That's the problem with Marxism, and what it shares with fascism, is positioning itself in a place of power to tell the people what is best for them. Why not let the people decide for themselves? What the leftist institution actually does is give the system precisely what it needs to sustain and perpetuate itself, which is opposition. All systems are based on opposition.

A: Isn't that what anarchists have been saying for more than a century?

P: I don't think so. Anarchism became an ideology and a set of rules just like everything else. For many reasons, I feel more connection with right libertarianism than I do with left anarchism. I know it has negative connotations in America, but still I wonder, why not look to libertarianism. Anarchism has become just another institution.

A: So has libertarianism.

P: Has it? I don't think as much so in this country.

A: But libertarianism is typically associated with the conservative right because it is never concerned with tearing down or overthrowing the system. Instead, libertarianism wants to work entirely within the system to the advantage of the libertarians. But, I suppose there are some leftist libertarians as well.

P: Well, look, I for one love the concept of a meritocracy. I think it's absolutely right.

A: But not in such a context in which money itself is seen as a merit. When power is itself seen as a merit. Those in power have always justified their positions of domination by appealing to their merit, whether they claim that merit comes from divine right, industry and work ethic, racist ideology, etc.

P: That's the problem isn't it? It's not with meritocracy, but the fact that, of course, what we've seen is that meritocracy is caught up and tied into the systems of racism, sexism, and classism.

A: And you think that a merit-based system could be established that is not based on such discrimination?

P: I'm not sure about that possibility. Just do the best that you can, that's what we're doing, and that's really all we can do.

A: That seems awfully individualistic.

G: You're contradicting yourself a bit, for a moment ago you said change ourselves, for instance in Occupy.

A: Yes, but I don't think you can stop there and accomplish much. Pen seems to be saying that the self is all that can be changed and all that need be changed.

P: Yes and no. Is it a lifestyle more focused on doing the best you can in your own life than on changing other people? Yes. But doesn't that also allow other people more freedom? It's also a choice I've made to live a life of sharing with others. That doesn't seem individualistic to me. You see, at first, I thought this place would simply be a hippie utopia, and for a time it was. I thought there was nothing to do but mind the apple tree and write beautiful poetry. But, of course, there was more to do. Yeah, we had Crass and that was important, but really more important is having the house open. Having the house open is one attempt at getting beyond materialism. I once had a weekend, this was even before you were here Gee, when I invited people to come a take anything they wanted. I basically wanted a bed, a book, and a small table, and that's essentially what I was left with. But it was a very freeing moment, to not have so much material around me, defining me or confining me. But, (laughing) I've never dared to do it again.

A: But, were you escaping materialism through your changed relationship to materials? Somewhat tautological, don't you think?

P: Well, of course, we do live in the material, but we can find ways to let it go. That's why I spend the first 45 minutes of the day meditating, literally staring at the wall. Now, some would really look at this as simply a waste of time, but I find it important and indispensible for setting up everything else that I do in a way. It's a step towards letting go. Existentialism has been my savior at many times in my life, but for the fact that it only makes sense in the material world. That's the big problem with Existentialism is just how overwhelmingly materialist it really is, which I think is right on the face of it, though a lot of people don't see it. But my existentialism only exists following my engagement with zen, which was my first radical thought experiment when I was a teenager. So, whenever I think I am falling back into the material realm too much, I can cycle back to zen and try to let go.

A: It's interesting to me that you see a combination of Existentialism and zen as an escape from what you call the Cartesian mode of thinking, or more broadly what I might call Enlightenment thought. Is that correct?

P: Yes.

A: Yet, all of your explanations I've heard of your thought rely on an individual experience, your individual experience in the material, the immaterial, and the mind. Correct?

P: Yes.

A: Such individualism seems to me to be firmly rooted in the Enlightenment understanding of the self, in other words, the Enlightenment liberalism's definition of the individual, which is a modern concept. How, then, can you hope to escape Cartesian thought, which you identify as individualistic, through explicitly individualist means?

G: Maybe that's all you can do, but then again, I'm not at all interested in establishing a system of any kind. Anyway, I've got to go tend to the garden before I start cooking dinner.

P: I was going to cook.

G: Were you? Alright.

P: Now, what would you all prefer, pasta or vegetarian rolly polly.

G: Rolly polly.

A: That sounds good. Can I help at all?

P: Nope, I can manage it. We'll continue our conversation later at dinner…

And so the conversation goes on, between us, between each other, and now with you as well.

Always Another Door

Gerard Evans

I used to buy books from charity shops and one such tatty paperback was called Always Another Door, detailing the life of Pamela Russell - a woman who became confined to a wheelchair after an accident. It inspired me to the tape title.

The booklet was printed at Interaction - a hippy co-op type place with ties to International Times in London's Kentish Town. We went on to play there a couple of times later on (with Rubella Ballet & Subhumans respectively) when it had a short-lived but delightful phase of hosting gigs. The very existence of Interaction gives clues to how much space has been lost in the meantime, both literally and metaphorically.

Some of us may well have screamed, but we were more into singing and reaching out. Albeit in a basic way - the songs recorded on this tape were basically me (vox & drums) & Chas (bass & guitar). I wanted to make gentle music, not music that wore big DMs.

Looking back, I'm kind of surpised at how gothic all the pics are - again a snapshot of the times, because six months later it would have probably looked very different... such was the speed of change in our heads at the the time. At least one pic also featured in Kill Your Pet Puppy - a complete co-incidence! We must have had the same book. And we were all going to see Sex Gang Children at the time.

Some of the artwork - the front page, the naked punk and part of the businessman-egg thing were done by Lawrence Llewellyn-Bowen, who was an old friend (and ex-bandmate) of Chas. Finally the back cover was done by me (Gerard) - the phrase came from a letter written to me by Sounds journalist Johnny Waller (RIP), which was part of a written argument we were having about fanzines, appropriately enough.

The lyrics speak for themselves (I hope) but the inside front page was heavily influenced by Dexy's Midnight Runners' Too-Rye-Ay sleeve notes, which sought to expand on the songs. I loved that, and them, and that album. I found the Joe Orton quote via Adam & The Ants.

The intro text would turn up later in our 'Stranger in a Strange Land' song. But it's the poem at the bottom of the page that was a manifesto of sorts, in my mind at least.

The contact address was the first house I moved out to - where I smoked my first dope and made love for the first time and generally found out I wasn't really mature enough to live away from home (but didn't go home).

The people round there wore beaten down eyes sunk in smoke-dried faces, so resigned to what their fate was. But not us - we were far too young and clever. Or so we thought.

I expected the tape to sell nothing, but via the network of fanzines around that I often contributed pre-designed pages to (guest blogging I guess you'd say now) - it sold a few. I was pleasantly astonished. But not half as astonished as I would have been if I'd known I'd be writing this over 30 years later.

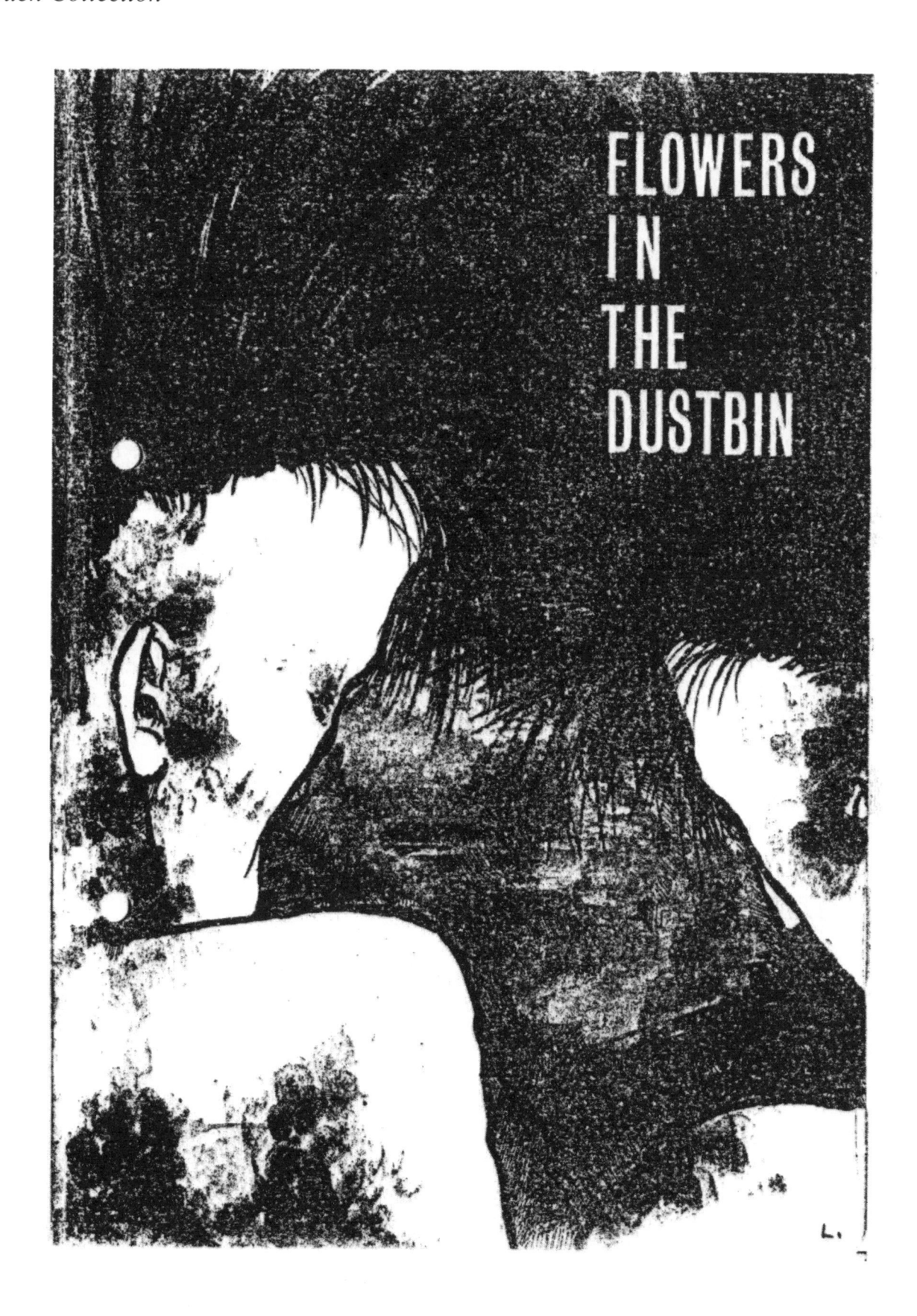

Flowers In The Dustbin Booklet

Courtesy Gerard Evans from the Nigel Crouch Collection

Flowers In The Dustbin Booklet

Courtesy Gerard Evans from the Nigel Crouch Collection

ALWAYS	tim	guitar	FLOWERS
ANOTHER	chas	bass	IN
DOOR	gerard	vocals	THE
	jo	drums	DUSTBIN

Repulsive test-tube samples of nature's mistakes run amock through flashing coloured lights. Fragments of a shattered mirror, reflected white light, memory of a wild night.
Abnormal children in the light, it's right for tonight. Wild images fall together.

"VETHIXO DISCO"

The time has come to illustrate the attitude by which we shall obtain the maximum freedom, and strive towards the Vethixo Disco.

"THE JOURNEY'S END"

And amidst all the noise, excitement and uproar, I shall pretend that I have learnt everything...but, of course, I will know that there are many mistakes still to be made, and to be learnt from.

"CASCADE"

Tears that I cry shall turn into sulphuric acid. And then, by Christ, you'll *have* to listen.

"ALL FOOLS DAY"

Remember, you don't have to smile, if only tears will do. By our pain, don't feel so all alone.

"TEMPLES"

'You must do whatever you like as long as you enjoy it, and don't hurt anyone else. That's all that matters. You shouldn't feel guilty. Get yourself fucked if you want to. Reject all the values of this society. And enjoy sex. When you're dead, you'll regret not having fun with your genital organs.' - Joe Orton

"TRUE COURAGE"

The manifesto of the lonely figure standing with himself amidst a sea of crazy colour and discarded take-away food boxes at the train station. The emotion of the freak.

```
i say i'm proud to be a freak
to cover up the fact i've got no choice
but injustices still creep
round uncertainties in my voice


flowers in the dustbin - quite a 'hip' name
putting wild images together (?)
music, use it, quite a nice game
it won't last forever

feeling ripe to be put on a sideshow
"freaks run wild in the disco"
```

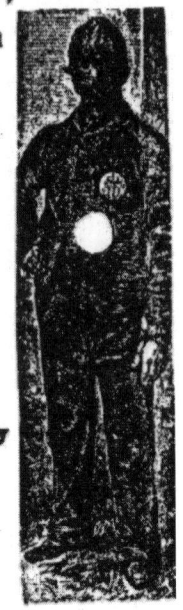

FLOWERS (IN THE) DUSTBIN

A NEW MEMORIAL
— too many followers

lithograph forms in children's brains
reinforced onstage - 'you should be the same'
groups of plural persons enforce status quo
three steps behind, they happily go

too many followers think fashion is rebelling
too many followers revel in mistakes
with mistaken identity and blind anonymity
they follow the footsteps of fakes
too many followers

kept at a distance so you'll never know
with barriers made of metal and bone
barriers that don't want to be broken down
dumb ignorance keeps the wheel spinning round

social pressure dictating particular lines
you cannot leave them, the blackmailer signs
blackmail is the murderous way
the game that i don't want to play

too many creatures that time forgot
must carve out futures, not tie them in knots
the past repeated is our only future
too many followers accept what they've got

too many followers

THE JOURNEY'S END

I've been sitting alone
While you tried to break through
I've been screaming again
There's nothing you can do

You said all the right things
And didn't understand a phrase
You've been so understanding
Are you searching for praise? (I'll try to give it all,
                                            It's only right)

I slept in your soul
You took up arms for my cause
To repay the debt
I'll try to find some applause (But I'm alone, still alone)

Arms all around and it didn't change a thing
Are you looking for something? Should I give you a ring?

You performed all your duties
With the upmost of care
How do I say you might as well
Not have been there? (I've been alone, all along).

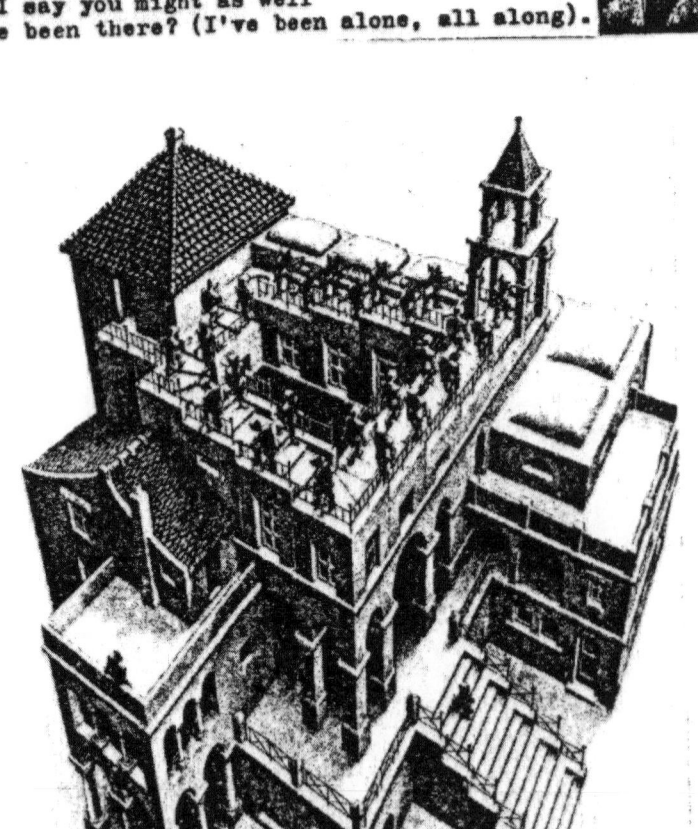

LESS THAN YOU'VE EVER DREAMED OF

You're just a prostitute to fashion
In slavery to style
Spend too much time just looking cool
To think about yourself
Is the pose real? Is it what you feel?
Or are you just out for what you can steal
From the image we present to you

Have you got your four-track mind?
Has your uniform been set?
By whatever standards you accept
- you're being dictated to

So fuck sweet innocence,
I don't like your smiles
Your vacant stare, you're going nowhere
Trapped by a sense of style

Now I'm jaded but I'm much wiser to YOU
Can criticise and I won't care
I've got nothing to prove to you

You're just a prostitute to fashion
In slavery to style
Just a worthless sad fool
With a wasted life

Just stand and stare cos we look uncool
Do you think I care when I look at you?
And does it matter if I do?
Well I feel sorry for you
Because you'll always be on the outside
Until you swallow your pride

CASCADE

Let my tears sting you
Defiance in every drop
Better forgot
You may say

But you can rap up
Warm in your silence
I'll keep my defiance
On display

Kings and pawns both dry their tears
By pulling wool over their eyes
And peer out from under covers
In moments when they feel unafraid

Never a dry eye in the house
That's the way truth often is
Until you realize
It doesn't have to be that way

But when they acknowledge their fears
And try to come to terms with their lives
No longer God's sons or lovers
Their tears run together in a cascade

ALL FOOLS DAY

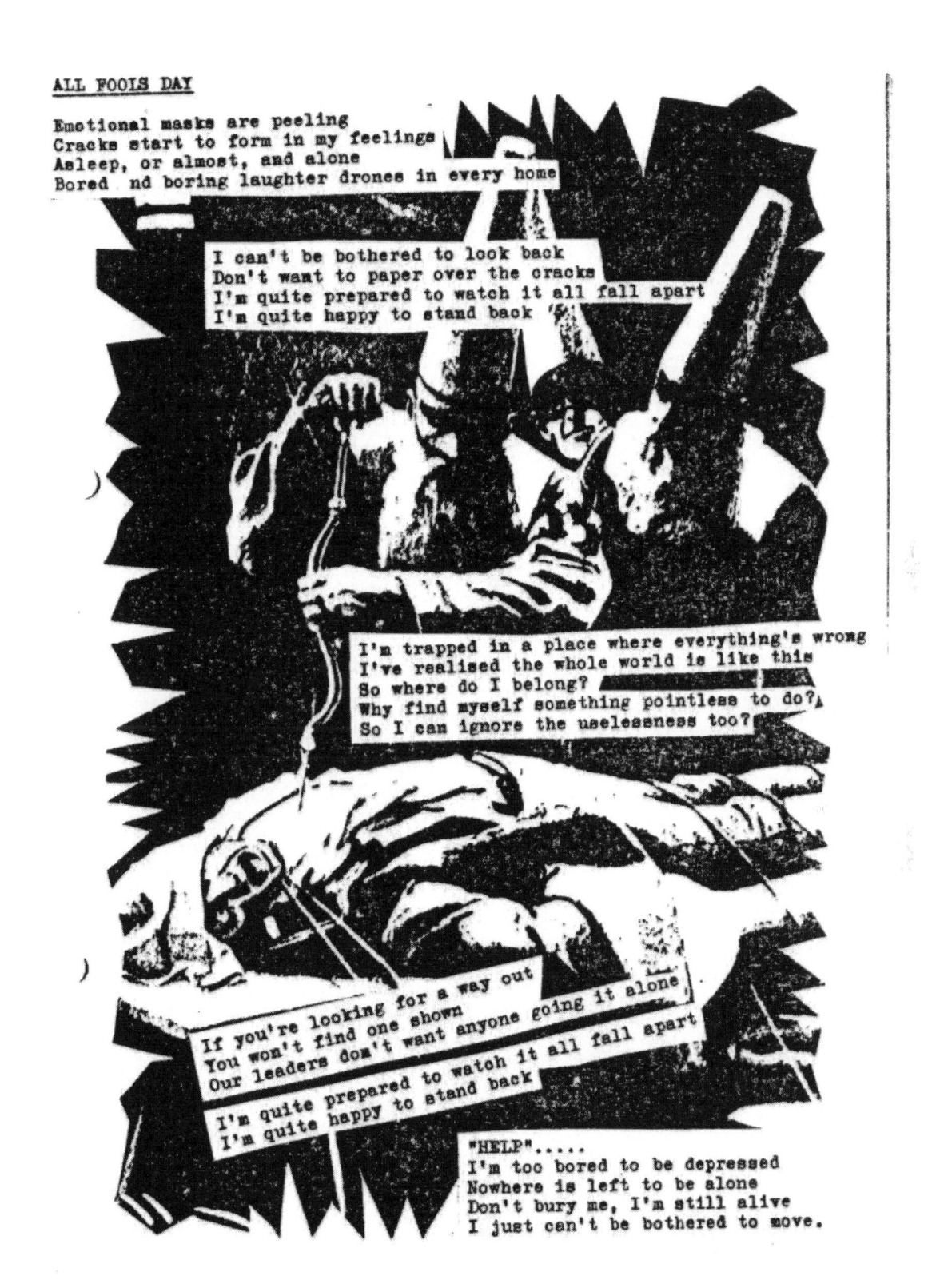

Emotional masks are peeling
Cracks start to form in my feelings
Asleep, or almost, and alone
Bored nd boring laughter drones in every home

I can't be bothered to look back
Don't want to paper over the cracks
I'm quite prepared to watch it all fall apart
I'm quite happy to stand back

I'm trapped in a place where everything's wrong
I've realised the whole world is like this
So where do I belong?
Why find myself something pointless to do?
So I can ignore the uselessness too?

If you're looking for a way out
You won't find one shown
Our leaders don't want anyone going it alone

I'm quite prepared to watch it all fall apart
I'm quite happy to stand back

"HELP".....
I'm too bored to be depressed
Nowhere is left to be alone
Don't bury me, I'm still alive
I just can't be bothered to move.

TEMPLES

The brush of a skirt against a boy's
                                  thigh
the grip of its belt,tight,round his
                                  waist
things to excite as he sets the pace
sensing his beauty,satisfying his taste

From the temples of our souls
comes the chant"We are ourselves
our bodies are our sole possesions
we won't restrict their emotions and
                                  passions

Freedom of feeling
the feeling's appealing
tied down if we want to
but never restricted
MY BODY IS THE TEMPLE OF MY SOUL

The difference between a boy's touch and
                                  a girl's
exists only in what we've been told
strength is not having to play the big
                                  man
you needn't hide the personna's you hold

These limbs are our own
designed to enjoy
our spirit's home
our soul's sensual toy

Wear what we like
as tight as we feel
unlike your suits
our rags reveal

The creatures we feel we are WE ARE.

the time may come when the tolerant will tolerate the intolerant no longer

TRUE COURAGE

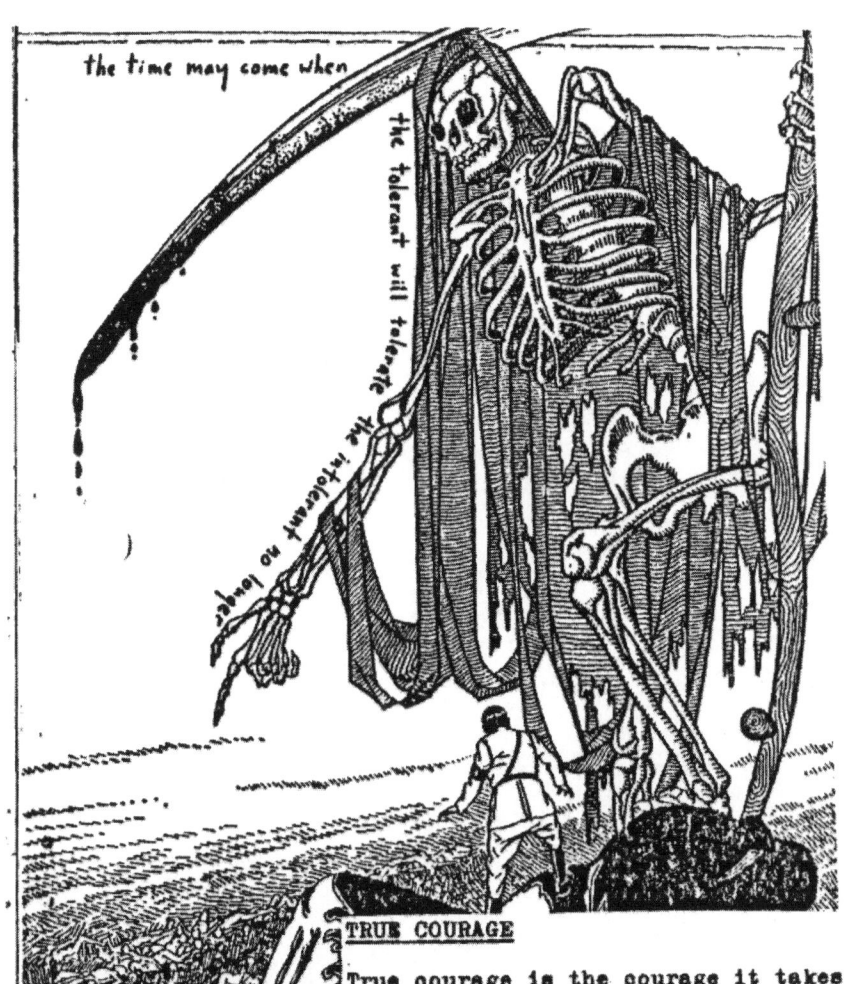

True courage is the courage it takes to say 'no'
No to the orders that tell you to kill
No to the orders that go against your will
True courage is when they say
"There's only one way" (if that way is wrong)
To look for alternatives anyway

True courage is loving when you're told to hate
To run your own life independent of the state
True courage when the orders come from above
To put them down below you when you know you
You've had enough

True courage is telling people how you feel
Even if you're "unnatural","unhip", to know you're <u>real</u>
Courage it takes to decondition yourself
From society's barriers and restrictions
And regain true health
To even consider being yourself

Oh yes, it takes <u>true</u> courage, it takes <u>real</u> guts
Because they're gonna try and scare you into violence
And mistrust
If you want to find real heroes, people who are brave
You'll find them living in peace
Not dead in war graves

VETHIXO DISCO

The time has come to illustrate our freedom
With colours to illuminate emotion of the freaks
Pushing forward lines of natural progression
We arrive scorning authority

Now is the time to advertise our lifestyle
Of deep deep souls and influences soldered
No longer will it be wasted by the work ethic
As long as we believe in this, we don't grow older

We can be told but that doesn't mean we'll listen
The teachers and preachers are only mortal men
No more preaching, we know what life's for
Proud freedom, not businessmen

Do the deca-dance at the vethixo disco

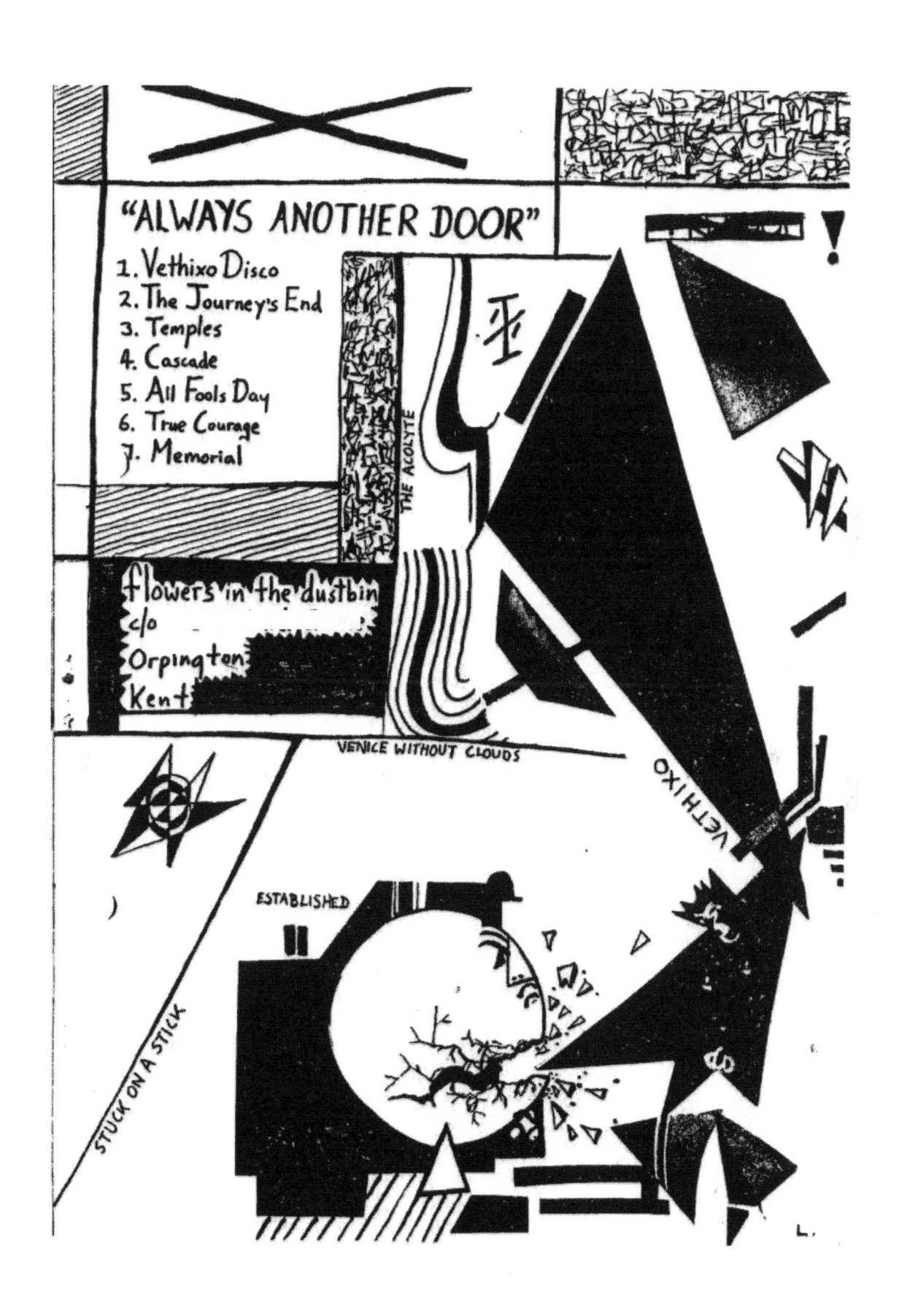

"ALWAYS ANOTHER DOOR"
1. Vethixo Disco
2. The Journey's End
3. Temples
4. Cascade
5. All Fools Day
6. True Courage
7. Memorial

flowers in the dustbin
c/o
Orpington
Kent

THE ACOLYTE

VENICE WITHOUT CLOUDS

VETHIXO

STUCK ON A STICK

ESTABLISHED

.... OR YOU'LL FALL IN THE GUTTER

To End Up on Your Table, and Shat Out of an Arse': Stinky Front Rooms, Cabbages and Animal Rights in Anarcho-Punk.

Alastair 'Gords' Gordon.

It goes without saying animal rights were –and still are - central to anarchist punk. What follows are some personal, historical anecdotal accounts of some of the experiences and activities that helped shape who I am today and also my family. For obvious reasons the personal details of some of what follows are ethically omitted to protect the guilty.

To kick off, I've always been a right fussy eater. Much of the grey, British menu of the 1970s was grim, consisting of over-boiled vegetables, fatty chunks of various meats and gravy with fat swimming in it. Let's just say I mostly looked forward to the marginally better puddings supplied by my long-suffering mother. From an early age I made the connection between death and food. Though being a vegetarian in a traditional working-class family was a rocky path indeed. My father used to loathe the fact that I hated meat. The sound of him banging the cutlery down in silence before threatening me to chew and swallow the greasy death-food is a memory that still haunts me. He used to shout "you won't have another thing to eat this week, 'laddie' if you don't eat everything on the plate". Later I would vomit the said content up causing eventual concern that I'd lost so much weight I was becoming seriously ill. When my dad was at work during the day or away on business, which was often back then, I took to eating food in the front room. Haha, I was sneaky. I used to eat some of the meals off the tray then stash the rest on a ledge on the settee in carrier bags I sneaked out the cupboard: fish fingers and cakes, lumps of liver, beef cabbage and the occasional steak and kidney pie sat un-pestered in there, slowly decomposing. Obviously my mother thought me a good boy for eating everything on the plate and things improved for a week or two. I was off the hook for a bit. Then the smell arrived: I couldn't dump the offending food in the bin as my mother was perpetually in the kitchen and being eight or nine years old I was scared of being caught. Hence, family were subject to the awful smell in the front room and turned the place over. The settee gave up its guilty secret and I was for the high jump. Once the offending bags were in the dustbin, I was taken by my father to the garage for the usual smacked arse; punctuating smacks with "don't....ever....do that....again" and expressed through his very brutal interpretation of 1970s parenthood. I was traumatised. Wanker. Now I was back to the sound of slamming cutlery and fatherly threats...great. This time they thought I was more than a little odd. I'd certainly fuck with those thoughts over the next few years.

I got into punk. This was a total lifesaver for me. The music encapsulated the early teenage rage I was feeling at the state of the fucked-up state of the world. How I came by punk is another story. Let's just say for now it seriously pissed my family off back then. The black sheep of the Gordon family? Got it in one! Aside from the my love of the UK Subs, SLF, The Clash and Sex Pistols, my mates from down the road had got into Crass. I'd already bought the (1979) *Reality Asylum* record but the politics of food came into sharp focus with the Flux of Pink Indians (1981) *Neu Smell* 7"and the Crass, *Stations of the Crass* LP (1979). Tracks from Flux like 'Sick Butchers' with lyrics stating, 'you try to stroke me in a field, then go home and eat me as your meal' and Crass' 'Time Out'...

> there's signs in the food stores advertising meat/beef-blade, chuck-roast, last you all the week/they're saying that you like it, you're saying that you do/they don't have to force it and tell you how to chew/swallow it whole, without a fucking squeak/sitting there quietly and up they creep/you think you're fucking different, you think it's you and them/if they asked you a question you'd ask them when/ you think you're hard done by, but you just want the same/chicken thighs, human-thighs, it's all the same old game.

These early lyrics were spot-on for me, making the clear connection between slaughtering animals and human-flesh as the same business. As Conflict said later: 'your blood, their blood.., serves the same'. Obviously this stuff seriously chimed with me and my distaste of meat, though most of these records were descriptive and not lyrically espousing direct-action. As I wrote in *Not Just Bits of Paper* (2014) it took a couple of false-starts for me to become vegetarian. My family were horrified and seriously worried how such a fussy eater who ate few vegetables and fuck-all else would survive as a vegetarian. Back then it wasn't easy but I managed: 'Realeat' burgers (mixed with egg) and sos/burger-mix was pretty much it as meat-substitute product. Each week, the diet became easier and I felt for the first time in my life like I was making a difference to the suffering of animals.

At school I got to be friends with a number of other punks who were on a similar path. When we met around 1981, we knew we had things in common. We hung out and discussed how we could make a difference. Let's just say this gave some of the dim-witted jocks a good reason to hate us more but we scared and confused them over the next few years to the point where they mostly left us alone. The school also noticed our change in politics, especially after one of our number graffitied 'Eat Wheat Not Meat' in letters five foot high on the barn wall. They knew we were responsible but couldn't prove it. Out of school we used to hang around and help out on the Animal Rights stall in Nottingham city centre on a Saturday morning getting the general public to sign petitions, give leaflets out and hassle fur shops, butchers and outlets selling stuff tested on animals. At one point we managed to show a BUAV (British Association for the Abolition of Vivisection) video to the entire school one afternoon. That certainly shook a few of our fellow pupils up, jocks included. As our engagement with animal rights increased our network of likeminded punks grew and so did the narrative of direct-action in the later anarcho-punk records dealing with animal rights. Back in the early to mid-eighties, things began to get militant in anarcho-punk terms. We used to attend Animal Rights Confederation meetings at the Nottingham Narrow Boat Pub deepening our involvement.

From anarcho-punk's musical output back then the whole anarcho-scene had begun to develop a real sense of urgency. The cold war threatened nuclear annihilation; Thatcher's police were shoving anyone around who didn't agree with her brave new free market world vision. Visually our clothes reflected this shift. Sex Pistols, UK Subs and general street-punk badges were swiftly removed swiftly replaced with larger 'Animals Have Rights' and 'Fishermen Smell' pins. Doctor Marten boots were replaced with cotton basketball and Rucanor shoes and espadrilles: some of us replaced leather, studded jackets for regulation donkey and jackets and replacement PVC versions. Group-discussion shifted from music to animal rights over cold-war politics. German moleskin combat trousers replaced bondage trousers etc. Similarly the music of anarcho-punk clearly echoed these shifts; most of us at this time were around fifteen years old and the sentiments and music on the records perfectly captured our feelings regarding the exploitation of animals.. Most notably, Conflict with the track 'Meat is Murder' and the more intense songs on the (1984) *Increase the Pressure* LP and *To a Nation of Animal Lovers* 7" EP (1983) perfectly summed up these feelings. Other classic songs were Rudimentary Peni's 'Pig in a Blanket'(1983); Anti-System's 'Wot No Meat' (1984) and the Subhumans *Evolution* EP. (1983). The whole UK anarcho output was notable for the unprecedented theme of explicitly discussing animal rights. For me one of the most striking songs of the time summing up our feelings on vivisection arrived on the groundbreaking (1983) Antisect LP *In Darkness, There is No Choice* LP on the track 'Tortured and Abused':

> I am an animal strapped to a chair.
> Nobody helps me because nobody cares
> Humanity injects me and injects me again
> Why am I subjected to such unbearable pain?
> Why?....
> Why Must I Die?

Likewise the Conflict track, Meat is Murder directly addressed the horror of the meat trade on the 1982 LP *It's Time to See Who's Who*:

> The factory is churning out all processed packed and neat./An obscure butchered substance and the label reads 'MEAT'./Hidden behind false names such as pork, ham, veal and beef./An eye's an eye, a life's a life, the now forgotten belief. And everyday production farms are feeding out this farce./ To end up on a table and shat out of an arse.

Conflict certainly aligned themselves with animal-rights and direct-action anarchism appealing to the urgency of doing something about the shit state of the world we all felt back then (still do!). We went to see Conflict and most of the other, numerous anarcho bands back then providing an excellent soundtrack to some of the actions we'd later be involved in. Tales of the activities at these shows takes a back-seat for the present tale. More important were the actions and activities the records and the anarcho-punk scene inspired us to become involved in direct-action politics.

The city-centre animal rights stall, the Narrow-Boat Animal Rights confederation meetings and political information-tables at gigs back then provided an information-hub allowing us to engage and network with older, more active, peers. Animal rights back then was not so much of a single-issue politics and more bound up with the political zeitgeist of the time. As a punk movement we dealt with police oppression, the miners' strike, Cruise missiles, The Falklands War and fucking capitalism in general. That said, for us animal rights went to the heart of all that seemed wrong with the world.

We were angry and decided to do something about us from super-gluing locks of butchers' shops; stickering products in chemists tested on animals; pouring paint into the pockets of fur coats, picketing fur shops and department stores selling then and my favourite Saturday activity: dropping stink-bombs in the eating areas of burger restaurants. Every little helped back then. Our confidence in direct-action was building.

Through 1983-4 we began to attend organised demonstrations against animal-abuse alongside anti-nuclear protests. Our local army-base, Chilwell-depot, was rumoured to be in preparation to store Cruise missiles. I attended a number of these 'Reclaim Chilwell, demonstrations and the ideological differences between street and anarcho-punks were made personally explicit for me at one particular event. After a rather unfortunate incident left me with two broken-wrists in plaster, I was approached by a number of 'ex'-punks and UK82 types who spotted my badges and black, spiky hair...one of them was straight in my face blasting his shitty beer-breath at me. "Are you pro or anti-peace mate?" The dumb, baiting question knocked me for six. My response came in a nervous tone: "I'm pro peace mate, what the fuck do you think I'm". Then, before I could get the words "doing here" I got caught- a vicious left hook knocking me over a garden wall and load of roses. The taste of oxygen, surprise of the cowardly sucker-punch obviously left me startled. Fucker nearly broke my jaw. My good mates carried me off with my first memory of how punks can be right bullies and rednecks (sadly the same is still evident today). This would not be the last experience of such twattery. Indeed it was the first crack in my naive teenage conception that punks were unified in their belief that peace and striving for a better world was a good thing. The small direct-actions continued and my bust wrists gradually healed in time for the next proper demonstration.

By Spring 1984 the Nottingham Animal Rights Confederation took us on a coach trip to a demonstration in Birmingham against the then notorious Singh-Gill owned Cocksparrow silver-fox fur farm. The latter was unscrupulously breeding these animals to supply the burgeoning market for fur-coats in the 1980s. Scumbag. The coach set off from outside Ye Olde Salutation Inn, Nottingham at 8am. We huddled around in the misty early morning in donkey jackets, smoking roll-ups and chatting. The bus was filled pretty quickly with a motley crew of old hippies, peace activists, anarcho-punks and a sprinkling of the general public for the smoke-filled journey to the demo.

The farm was located a couple of miles outside of Coventry and when we arrived we were met with loads of other coaches and fucking hundreds of coppers surrounding the entire farm. The whole gamut of 1980s protest was out in force; miners, CND activists, Class War and a host of others. "Coal not Dole" stickers were everywhere as the miners were getting really shafted by Thatcher's bully boys: we were about to get a taste of this 'public order management' ourselves. Memories are hazy on all the details though I remember most of the protestors left to their own devices group shouting "Human Freedom, Animal Rights, One Struggle, One Fight' at the seemingly endless lines of coppers. They stood there in silent rows and we walked right up to their faces asking if they knew what they were protecting. Often the response from her majesties 'Bobbies' was "fuck off, or I'll nick you!" The Farmer, Singh-Gill was hauled-up in his house in the middle of the farm and the central objective was one of direct action, to get through the police lines and get the animals out of their cages.

The demo seemed to be going nowhere, just one big shouting-match until the crowd mood became anger at audible animal cries from the farm. Various protestors were doing mock charges at police-lines followed by a collective.... "ah not really".
This sort of thing went on for a while until the protest reached critical mass with everyone congregated near the animal sounds. The real charge began with the police pushing back followed by a row of horses pushing us away - flash arresting people - herding us through a fence, towards fields. Collective chants of "scum, scum, scum" filled the air. Spare change from pocket's thrown at the copper went over in waves as they pushed onwards. It was chaos: and, in short, I was in the middle of it. The police charge continued into

what luckily transpired to be a ripe cabbage field. Bingo. All of a sudden the sky was black with flying cabbages flying overhead, bouncing off the coppers like some bizarre acid trip. The Police retreated under another volley of flying cabbages and the standoff continued back at square one. The chanting lasted for another hour or so with a couple of arrests before the demo wound down to a handful. We ended the day in a pub reflecting on the protest while staring at our muddy clothes and boots. Sipping my well-earned pint of Guinness, I was politely reminded by another protester at the bar that the drink wasn't vegan! This was an indicator of the later transgression of how the whole diet issue would move uncomfortably up a gear.

Back on the bus we were all slightly drunk and were treated to various sing-songs of various punk tunes with the later Pistol's Ronnie Biggs classic, 'No One Is Innocent' blasting out in a drunken chorus on the way back to Notts.

The rest of 1984 carried on as before with a good amount of us leaving school and having our first taste of a Government Youth Training scheme. We became regular faces on various demonstrations throughout that year and our covert animal rights 'actions' continued unabated. I remember being chased up a street after calling a load of butchers in the local shop "fat murdering bastards". Around Christmas that year we were arrested for causing a breach of the peace in MacDonald's for staging an impromptu sit-in demanding they stop exploiting animals. It was all good natured until the police showed up and we were charged with aggravated breach of the peace. Myself and a mate ended up facing borstal for allegedly threatening the manager of that establishment: that never happened. I remember my father coming to our court date telling me he wanted to see me sent down. Wanker. Luckily in spite of one of the witnesses lying through his teeth, we got off with a fine and a conditional discharge.

As we moved into 1985 things got more extreme with various Notts folk smashing butchers and fur shop windows. This culminated with a serious of mass-arrests leaving a lot of the animal rights activists facing jail. Jail did happen for a couple of mates, found guilty of crimes though I escaped with the above breach of the peace conviction. With Crass ending their project in 1984 and Conflict and others inspiring fresh waves of direct action, things got heavy before tailing off to the thrash-metal years beyond the scope of this piece. Arguments began to surface about who was the most vegan or most active; the collective struggle we'd embarked upon was beginning to fracture. In short, certain individuals were hell-bent on making value judgements not based on the action undertaken but whether or not a packet in your cupboard back then contained a suspicious non-vegan 'e' number. Fuck off! I found a lot of this showing-off of scene plumage tiring, and to be honest, after the chaos of 1984 and the turmoil of 1985 exhausting. Also in the spring of 85' I took the plunge into veganism though with my severe distaste of vegetables my diet plummeted to new un-nutritional depths. Glandular fever hit me hard and virtually wiped me out for six weeks. I remember being out of it and hallucinating into the anarcho record sleeve posters on my bedroom wall. The doc put my illness down to a lack of nutrition from a shit diet. That said by '86 I was on an entirely different punk path.

The legacy of all this is the whole animal rights and vegan/vegetarian politics are ubiquitous in the DiY scene with some many genre variations in new styles of music it becomes scarcely recognisable to the movement that grew in the early eighties. With a new bastard Tory government at the UK helm and the possible reintroduction of hunting with dogs coupled with blatant neo-liberal attacks on the poor and disabled the new barricades against the current scary neo-liberal onslaught against us all. The personal legacy is in spite of a couple of tiny lapses, I'm still vegetarian and my daughter's been and still is vegetarian from birth.

Meat still fucking stinks!

> AN ANIMAL HAS BEEN TORTURED IN THE MANUFACTURE OF THIS PRODUCT!

Non-Violent Direct Action Notes:

A few final thoughts!

1.) DON'T DO ANYTHING YOU ARE NOT READY FOR.

Don't let ANYONE push you into an action that you don't want to do. We all have our own levels of uncertainty, don't rush yourself. Try things in stages and gain some confidence in your own personal strength. If you've never tried flyposting or leafleting before, then more 'direct' and risky actions might leave you frightened and confused. Only YOU know what you're ready for.

2.) DON'T GET YOURSELF NICKED FOR THE SAKE OF IT

To my mind there's no point in getting yourself arrested if you can avoid it. Obviously, in some actions there is a great risk of arrest, sometimes it's almost certain — it's a case of whether you think the action is worth that or not. But in cases where people deliberately get nicked, I think there's an element of ego-tripping going on. We are much more of a threat at liberty, than we are when we're in a police cell...

3.) DON'T GET YOURSELF HURT FOR THE SAKE OF IT

This applies especially at blockades. Much of the time you've no control over police violence and brutality (and make no mistake — for every cheery faced bobby there are half a dozen hard headed thugs who enjoy causing you pain) but we can minimize the damage they can do. We don't want, or need martyrs. Challenge the police verbally, demand to know why they are trying to hurt you. Look them straight in the eye. We're not lumps of flesh, we don't have to mutely accept their violence.

4.) DON'T BRAG ABOUT ACTIONS

We're not supposed to be in this for personal glory. If you brag about what you've done you'll just get yourself nicked. DON'T TALK, DO. If you become active, chances are they'll tap your phone, and they'll almost certainly search your mail. Take care, it's not a game.

5.) LETS DO IT.

It is time for despair to end and tactics to begin. We have the strength, we have the power, our actions can AND THEY WILL HAVE AN EFFECT.

Laboratory Animals have waited over 100 years for proper legal protection.

This Government now proposes to take away the little they've got.

Oppose the Government proposals on Animal Experiments. Protest to your MP. And write to us at the BUAV to find out what you can do.

BUAV AGAINST ALL ANIMAL EXPERIMENTS

Please find enclose our cruelty free cosmetic list, sorry we do not print a list of companies that do test on animals as sadly the list would be too long.

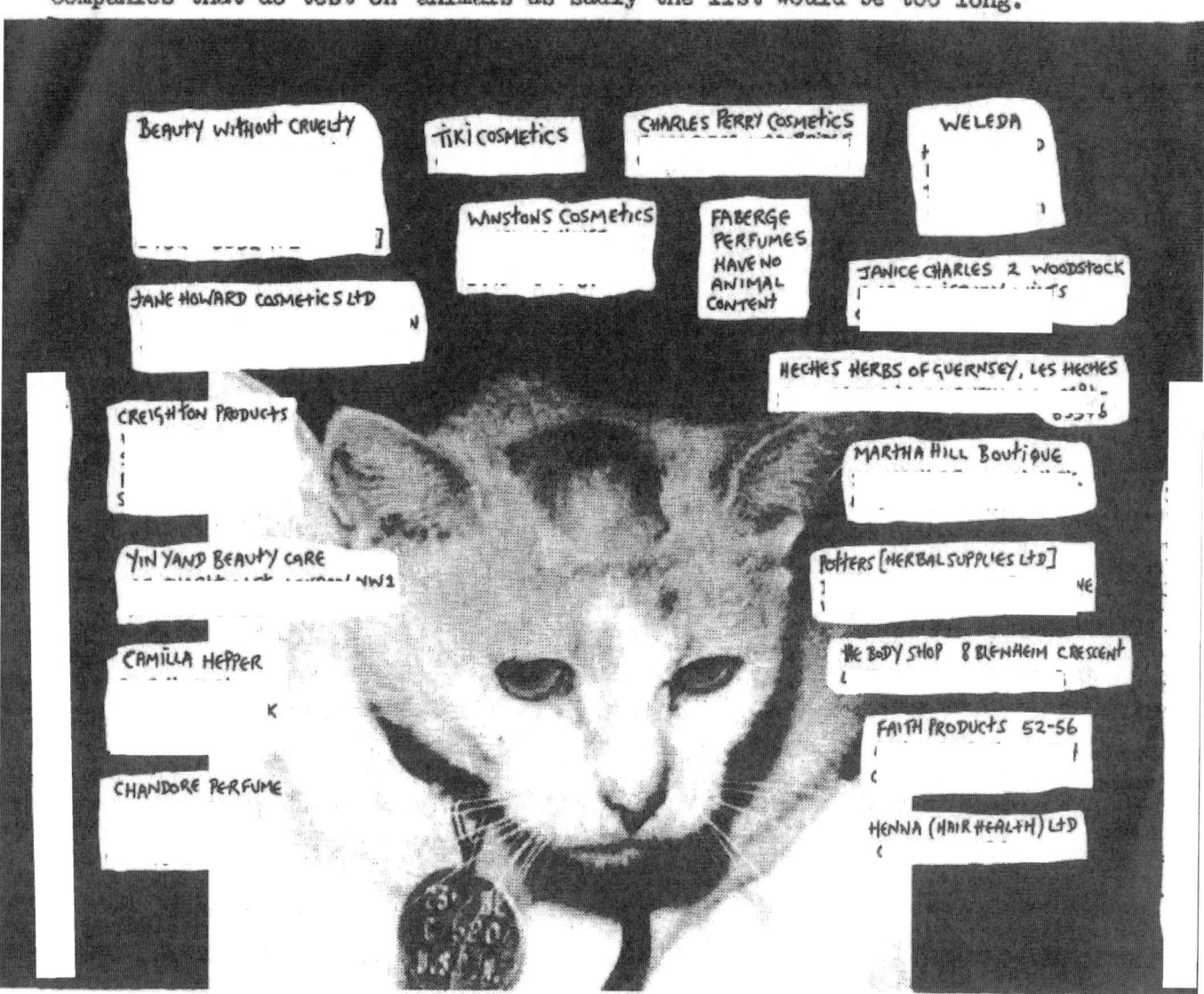

- Beauty Without Cruelty
- Tiki Cosmetics
- Charles Perry Cosmetics
- Weleda
- Winstons Cosmetics
- Faberge Perfumes have no animal content
- Janice Charles 2 Woodstock
- Jane Howard Cosmetics Ltd
- Heches Herbs of Guernsey, Les Heches
- Creighton Products
- Martha Hill Boutique
- Yin Yand Beauty Care
- Potters (Herbal Supplies Ltd)
- Camilla Hepper
- The Body Shop 8 Blenheim Crescent
- Faith Products 52-56
- Chandore Perfume
- Henna (Hair Health) Ltd

BLUURG RECORDS

fish 2

I Changed My World

Stephen Fleet

From 1979 I felt that I needed to overthrow the Government and change the world.

I started with a zine, a band and a leaflet home production line.

Progressively, I organised a couple of squat gigs, a regular run of Anarcho bands playing in my town and a number of infamous direct action campaigns.

This urgent period of my life brought me into contact with many great people, some formative life experiences and a type of radical politicisation that has stayed with me over the subsequent decades.

The simplicity and clarity of the message was crucial for me back in those days.

The campaign couldn't wait.

The scalpel knife, the lettreset, the old Gestetner printer, the car spray paint, a bag always full of leaflets, the letters, the soapy stamps, the mail art...

I changed my world and that was good enough.

Various Handouts and Missives

Courtesy of the Stephen Fleet collection

"LET THEM EAT SHit !!!"

6 Years ago when the Tory's took power, they openly declare war on the poor. Now the miners strike has shown the barbarity and ruthlessness they are prepared to use in their pursuit of absolute power.

The miners strike was constantly in the public eye, but mostly going unheard is the unemployed who are continualy having their rights scrapped away. Slowly but surely they're taking away our only means of survival. Gradually grinding us into the dirt.

The latest denial of human rights will be in action from April 29th. From then the government will have introduced new rules for DHSS payments to people living in Bed & Breakfast accomodation. The amount of time you can live in such accomodation has been cut to a minimum. For people living in London, Birmingham, Manchester and Glasgow you will be paid for up to 8 weeks. Elsewhere in the country it will only be 2 or 4 weeks before the DHSS stop your claim.

After you've had your money stopped you will have to move at least 10 miles in order to claim dole again and you wont be able to move back into the same area for up to 26 weeks.

The Tory's have with this legislation lowered the amount of money that can be claimed in Bed & Breakfast. In London the upper limit will be under £50 and in many places as little as £20.

These rulings affect 140,000 people, many of these being one parent familys, old people, people with no dependants, people with no one to fall back on. And they just dont fucking care. A lot of people are going to be left without a roof over their heads. But I suppose the tory's arent that dispicable after all, for theyve given us these new restrictions just in time for summer.

If your on the dole be warned, it may be soon before it becomes a privilage and not a right. Take what you can from them while you still can!! • slag, (the heaped one!!) •

Sunday the 7th — Stereotype Detector

YES IT'S QUIZ TIME FOLKS,COMPILED BY,YES,WAIT FOR IT,*ME*
A QUIZ COMPILED TO SEE HOW FALSE YIU ARE,ARE YOU A STEREOTYPE?
LOOK AT THE ANSWERS THEN LOOK AT YOURSELF.

1. DO YOU GO TO WORK EVERYDAY ?

2. DO YOU ENJOY IT ?

3. ARE YOU AMBITIOUS ?

4. DO YOU ARRIVE BANG ON TIME ?

5. DO YOU LIKE YOUR BOSS ?

6. ARE THE CLOTHES YOU WEAR COMFORTABLE ?

7. HOW OFTEN DO YOU WATCH T.V. ?

8. DO YOU FOLLOW FASHION ?

9. DO YOU DO THINGS JUST TO IMPRESS PEOPLE THAT YOU WOULDN'T OTHERWISE DO ?

10. WHY DID YOU WEAR THE CLOTHES THAT YOU DID LAST TIME YOU WENT OUT?

11. HOW MUCH MONEY DO YOU SPEND ON CLOTHES THAT YOU DONT NEED ?

12. DO YOU SMOKE ?

13. WHY ?

14. WILL YOU VOTE IN 1983 ?

15. WHY ?

ANYONE WHO ANSWERED YES TO NUMBERS 3,4,8,9,&14. FUCK OFF.

IF THIS QUIZ MAKES YOU THINK,ASK YOURSELF,WHAT AM I GOING TO DO ABOUT IT ?

Grasping Life

Have you ever wondered where you are in a society where people control your life, where rules are constantly being enforced? Do you really believe that those rules are there for the benefit of the public? For the benefit of you? Is the world so very bleak, so desperate? Are individuals so far from a passive existence, that a pre-planned mode of control has to be enforced?

Question after question after question. The same old open-ended attitude towards change. A predictable frame of mind that only questions, offering no solutions. It is so very hard, though, to offer any real answers when we are constantly battered from side to side by the technological, authoritarian world. Many of us have been pumped so full of shit, that the only feeling left is that of frustration. Others find short-term 'release' by adopting roles and actions that were the original cause of the mess that we are now crawling through. The creation of the imaginary 'class-war', when the only real change will come through destroying such systematic insults as 'class' and 'war'. There can be no serious alteration to a male-controlled world when we ourselves adopt the shit-filled macho-stance. Organised violence is only a reflection of what all Governments have been doing for years. We desperately need to look for other ways of thinking and acting. We need to completely disassociate ourselves from the ethics of dominance. How can we expect anyone to become liberated when they are being kicked in the head?

The attitudes towards serious rebellion has gone beyond a joke-it has become fucking hilarious! The anarchy symbols on mass produced 'punk' T-shirts selling at a mere £3.50. The money that has been handed over the counter to buy these pieces of garbage will contribute to a tidy profit for some greasy-shit of a company boss. Is this revolution? Is this anarchy? Don't make me laugh! It has been the commercial game for years now. It is the ultimate in good old rock n' roll principles-create an image, sell the product, keep the kids divided, and make a fast buck. Yet still those who think of themselves as being so 'rebellious' are funding this attrocity!

SEX PISTOLS. ANARCHY IN THE U.K. (EMI 2566)
Available from your cleverest
NEW MUSICAL EXPRESS
PUNK MAGAZINE
£150,000

Then how can we expect to achieve 'real' change? - Another question? Another stab in the dark? Well, it has been said so many times before, but still it holds true. The only real change can come through you changing yourself, changing your attitudes, changing your life. It is no longer enough just to buy the records and sing the songs, there is much more than that. Our minds and thoughts need to be turned towards each other. We have to learn to live together, in peace and on our own terms. We should never accept others trying to control this earth and our lives. No one has exclusive rights to make laws and wage wars-no one has the right at all! Government actions and the politics of inequality have been around for too long. It is high time that we work towards reclaiming what is rightfully ours. We are denied a peaceful world, we are denied our own future, we are denied equality-they have gone on for too fucking long. We must create an enviroment of our own.

SING, DANCE, SHOUT, SPRAY, SCREAM YOUR DEFIANCE - <u>ANARCHY NOW!</u>

THE Sun — Top of the Pops — VIRGIN PRESS RELEASE — Sounds

<u>DISTURBANCE FROM FEAR</u>: C/O Fleaty,

TERMINAL NUCLEAR SUICIDE DISASTER

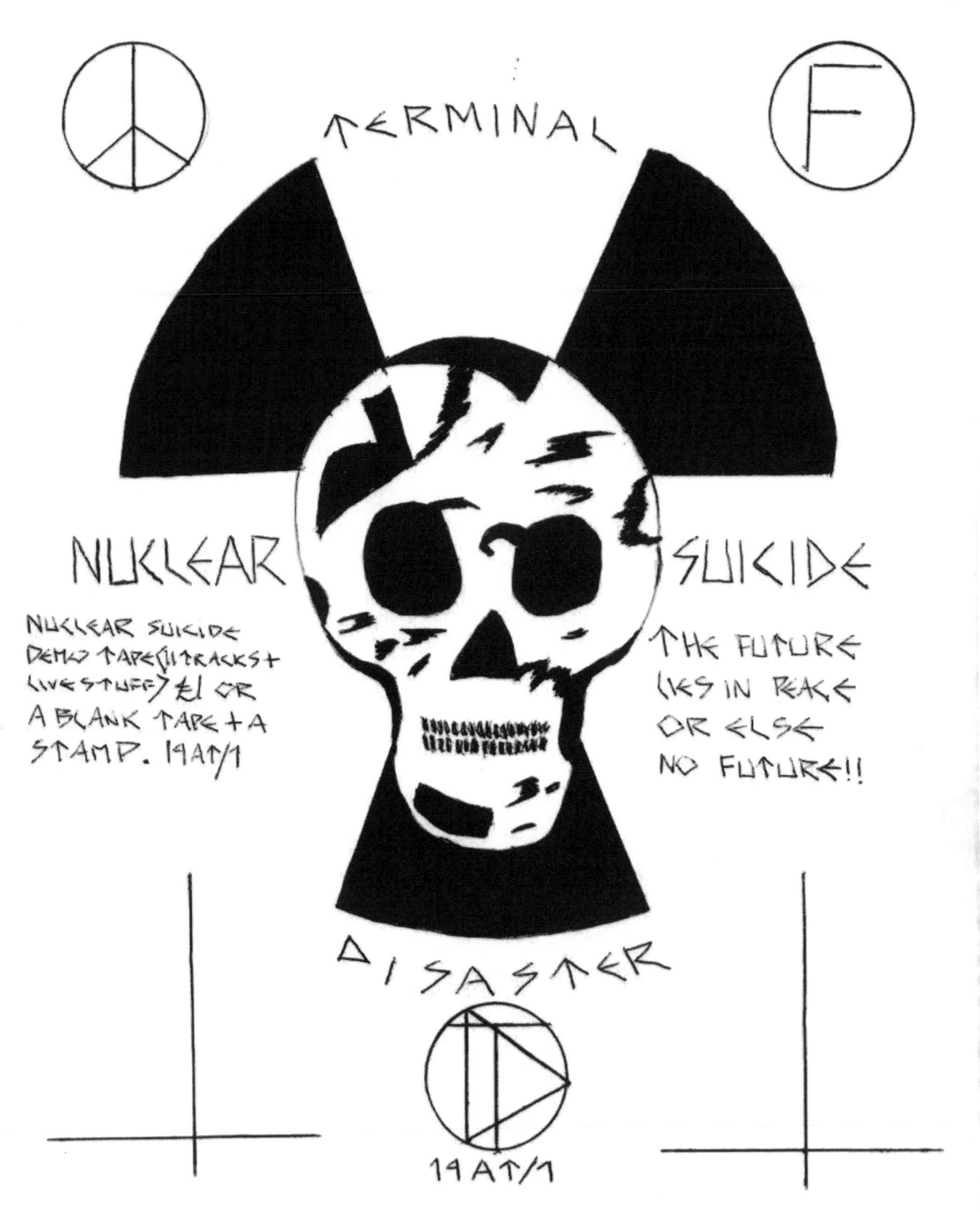

Nuclear Suicide demo tape (11 tracks + live stuff) £1 or a blank tape + a stamp. 19 AT/1

The future lies in peace or else no future!!

14 AT/1

For info, tapes, gigs, please write to Paul →

RUN FOR IT

HOW MANY TIMES WERE YOU RENOWN TODAY?
DID IT MAKE YOU FEEL GOOD?
HOW MANY TIMES WERE YOU NOTORIOUS TODAY?
DID IT MAKE YOU FEEL DANGEROUS?
HOW MANY TIMES DID YOU LIE TODAY?
DID IT MAKE YOU SOME GAIN?
HOW MANY MASKS DID YOU WEAR TODAY?
DID IT MAKE YOU LOOK GOOD?
HOW MANY TIMES DID YOU HIDE TODAY?
DID IT MAKE YOU SECURE?
RENOWN FOR FEELING GOOD
NOTORIOUS FOR FEELING DANGEROUS
LYING FOR SOME GAIN
MASKS FOR LOOKING GOOD
HIDING FOR SECURITY
RUNNING FOR YOUR LIFE
OR RUNNING FROM YOUR LIFE?

Dave A. Apostle

The APOSTLES

1 Blow It Up, Burn It Down, Kick It Till It Breaks! 1st EP
2 Rising From The Ashes. 2nd EP
3 The Curse Of The Creature. 3rd EP
4 The Giving Of Love Costs Nothing. 4th EP
5 Smash The Spectacle! 5th EP
Mob Violence (Part 2) on The Fight Back compilation album We Don't Want Your Law. Rainbow Warrior on Animal Rights compilation album out soon. Hello, Black Flag! on CFC compilation album. After The Fact & The Island on Rot Records compilation album.

The Apostles were formed in November 1980. Six demo tapes, five records (7"EP) and four compilation albums later and Dave and myself are the only original, seminal members of the group left. We are an art group, not a rock band and this distinction is an important element in comprehending our motivation, methods and material. Dave and Scruff are atheists, I am a strong believer in God and the teachings of Jesus – but I believe a person who is an atheist and works towards the abolition of oppression, prejudice and exploitation, is far more worthy than the plastic 'Christian' who visits a church every Sunday and is no different from every other selfish, bigotted moron — all three of us are vegetarians and we each hold some libertarian views, although these differ in intensity and direction according to our upbringing and background. We are opposed to the class system as we are also opposed to political parties, including anarchism, which is merely another form of moral servitude, hypocrasy, prejudice and rules to oppress us anyway. Pacifism is commendable if it means resisting war – but it is despicable if it means allowing the state to get away with its murders, infringement of personal freedoms and exploitation of animals and the planet we live on. Earth – it's the only one we have so let's look after it. Anarchists want the freedom to abuse their (and our) bodies with drugs and inflict their rules on us — we want freedom for everyone who is willing to share the world. The Reverend Andy Martin.

The Apostles. C60 1st Demo, The Second Dark Age. C60 2nd Demo, Libertarian Propaganda. C90 3rd Demo, Topics For Discussion. C90 4th Demo, Swimmers In The Sea of Life. C60 5th Demo, from BBP. Will I Ever Be Free? C90 6th Demo, from Andy Martin. CFC, 53 Hollybush Hill, Snaresbrook, London, E.11. BBP, 90 Grange Drive, Stratton Street, Swindon, Wilts. Anal Probe, 77 Solstice Drive, Amesbury, Salisbury, Wilts.

SUPPORT YOUR LOCAL D.I.Y. DEALER!

from CFC.

SCRUFF.

CRASS ALIVE IN 1985!

The Reverend Andy Martin.
Dave Fanning.
Stephen Lewty (Scruff).

HELLO JESS, LARRY, JABBS, WIDNI, TREV, PETE, CRASS, OLLY AND THE 281 CREW.

Dave...
Dave...

The Nouveau Hippies

Paul Platypus

> NEWS:
> Punk rock group CRASS have signed an eight year contract with Virgin Records, a large label based in Portobello Road, which rose to fame courtesy of Mike Oldfield's 'Tubular Bells' LP. CRASS' first release will be an 18-album-boxed-set album, retailing at 30p.

"News" Item from Son Of Wombat Weekly 1983

I first tasted soya milk in a squat in Offord Road, where Duncan was living. It would have been 1981 or 1982. The kitchen was bright and clean, not the kitchen of an archetypal squat. I don't remember how many squats Duncan lived in, or how many I visited, but I do have odd memories of the squats and their occupants - a slightly intense conversation with a guy who had a very camp-sounding Manchester accent; a party where people all seemed to be either taking smack or having sex (I was doing neither!); a large gang of us walking down Caledonian Road to go to a gig, with some of the group slipping into a small grocery shop along the way to shoplift alcohol.

Duncan's whole raison d'etre at this time centred on his desire to take in new experiences. He'd been working as a telecomms apprentice and living in a bedsit in Hornsey that was so cold he had to put his clothes over the two-bar heater each morning before he could brave getting out of bed. He left the bedsit and the job so he could go on the dole, live in a squat and experiment - with music, drugs, food, love, sex, you name it. Every fortnight he'd buy enough tobacco and lager to last him till his next giro, then live as best he could on what was left. The drugs would be given to him free by various questionable characters. The disquiet this caused me was one (but only one) of the reasons we eventually fell out. I have many letters from him expressing his bafflement - and sadness really - at why I disapproved of his life at this time. He was trying to live out the philosophy of the libertine - 'do what thou wilst be the whole of the law' - but couldn't see that this choice itself could trouble the people he cared about, whilst our negative reaction to what he saw as a lifestyle that hurt nobody else, in turn hurt him.

I'd met Duncan through the network of people swapping their home-recorded tapes through the pages of Sounds and NME. In contrast, Elaine and I met indirectly through our mothers - but she ended up being part of the same crowd as Duncan. Our mums were both secretaries at an electronics research lab in Wembley. We both got temp work there after our A Levels in the summer of 1982, lugging huge ancient scientific tomes around the research library, mostly to the stores in the rafters of the building. I was completely besotted with Elaine, but completely inexperienced with girls, and I lacked any understanding of - or interest in - what it might mean to have 'a girlfriend'. My social life was dominated by music - band rehearsals, going to or playing at gigs, hanging around at Rough Trade, hanging around anywhere else whilst talking about music. It never occurred to me to ask Elaine out, and I wouldn't have known what to do next if I had, other than to do the things we did anyway. Elaine used to talk about somebody she wanted to ask her out - which I took to mean I had no chance even if I'd known what to do. I was too naive to realise the person she talked about was me (as a colleague told me much later), and was happy just to see her at gigs.

Elaine's favourite drink was snakebite. She dressed in black, spiked her hair, used black make-up on her face - I later came to see her and her friends as proto-goths, since this was before the term goth began to appear. The music they liked - bands such as Blood and Roses, the Sex Gang Children, Southern Death Cult - was being referred to in the music press as 'positive punk' (what made it positive I'm not entirely sure - I have no memory of any of the lyrics) but there wasn't a great divide between that and the anarcho-punk bands that Elaine, Duncan and I also listened to, went to see and in the case of my own band, Twelve Cubic Feet (which Duncan joined for a period), did the occasional gig with.

These band were only a small part of my musical world, and of Duncan's. I don't know what else Elaine liked, but whilst she was more rooted in pre-goth/anarcho-punk circles than me, we had plenty in common, and came to realise whilst lugging books that we had many mutual friends who were completely disconnected from the very straight suburban world where we'd both grown up and were working. Like Duncan, Elaine eventually moved out of her parents' house into a squat somewhere in north-east London, and even became a singer in an anarcho-punk band. Both Elaine and Duncan were meant to move into a shared house I tried to organise in late 1982, which fell through. Instead I got a flat by myself, which Duncan then moved into after a couple of weeks - at the same time as I began to mix with another group of musical misfits at Alan McGee's Communication Club. I lost touch with Elaine, and with most of the anarcho-punk/proto-goth scene, not long after.

All this is the backdrop to the 'nouveau hippies' cartoon I published in my fanzine *Son of Wombat Weekly* in 1983 (like the original Wombat Weekly which I'd produced with a group of friends, SOWW combined sarcastic/cynical humour with an occasional piece about music). Looking back, this was probably the harshest piece I have ever written. I remember thinking it was mildly satirical, but it actually reads to me now as quite vicious, and in retrospect fairly undeserved. Duncan was very unhappy about it, as he felt it laid into his friends as a front for attacking him. To an extent, he was right, especially the political snipe. Duncan often switched himself off from the wider world for several weeks whilst life in the squat passed by, as far as I could tell, very slowly. Most notably, it turned out he had been entirely unaware of the Falklands War till several weeks later. This appalled me, as the words make clear. But as well as Duncan, the characters I described were an amalgam of the various people I met in his and other friends' squats and at gigs. Ros Picklehype was a spoof of the name of Jo Brocklehurst, the artist who drew many anarcho-punk squatters at the time (I wrongly assumed she was part of that scene). For the most part, I found these people naive in the way they convinced themselves they had something important to say, whilst often being a bit too stoned to actually say it. But I also had some affection for them, though perhaps it's taken rather a long time for me to realise it.

In common with Duncan, but in contrast with Elaine, I was never one to join a specific musical tribe, and both my broad musical tastes and my dress sense (or lack of one) set me apart from most of them, whether down-

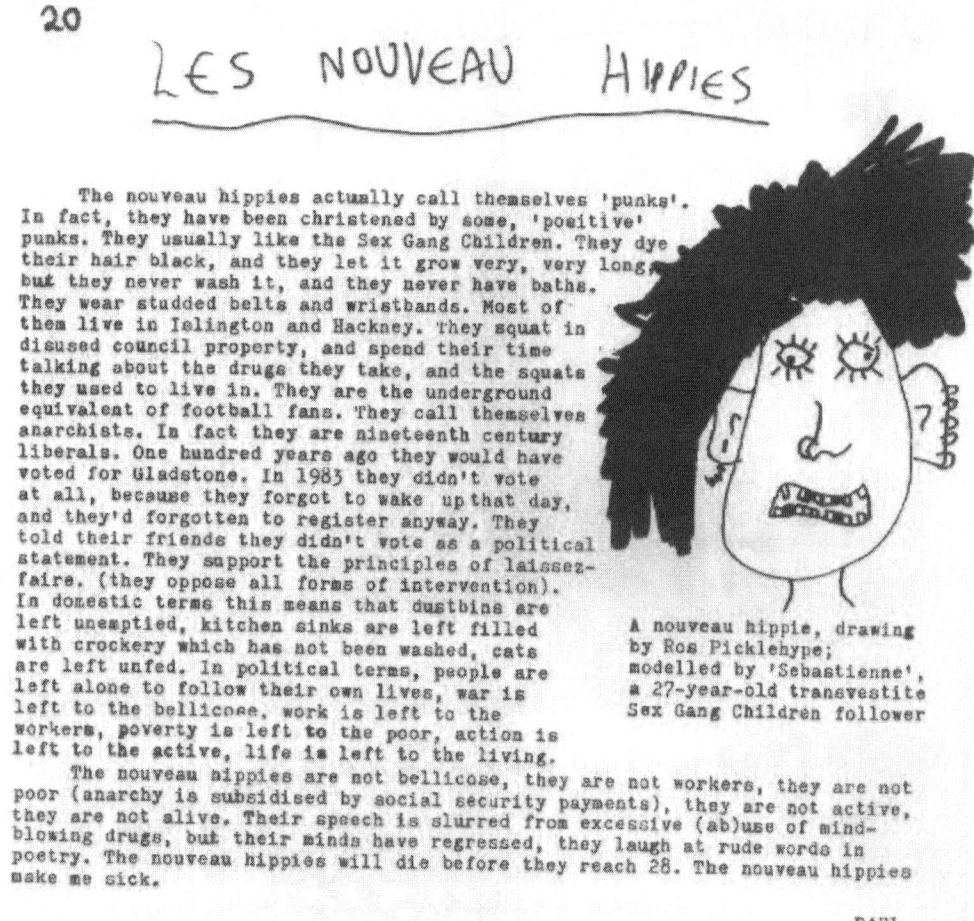

LES NOUVEAU HIPPIES

The nouveau hippies actually call themselves 'punks'. In fact, they have been christened by some, 'positive' punks. They usually like the Sex Gang Children. They dye their hair black, and they let it grow very, very long, but they never wash it, and they never have baths. They wear studded belts and wristbands. Most of them live in Islington and Hackney. They squat in disused council property, and spend their time talking about the drugs they take, and the squats they used to live in. They are the underground equivalent of football fans. They call themselves anarchists. In fact they are nineteenth century liberals. One hundred years ago they would have voted for Gladstone. In 1983 they didn't vote at all, because they forgot to wake up that day, and they'd forgotten to register anyway. They told their friends they didn't vote as a political statement. They support the principles of laissez-faire. (they oppose all forms of intervention). In domestic terms this means that dustbins are left unemptied, kitchen sinks are left filled with crockery which has not been washed, cats are left unfed. In political terms, people are left alone to follow their own lives, war is left to the bellicose, work is left to the workers, poverty is left to the poor, action is left to the active, life is left to the living.

The nouveau hippies are not bellicose, they are not poor (anarchy is subsidised by social security payments), they are not active, they are not alive. Their speech is slurred from excessive (ab)use of mind-blowing drugs, but their minds have regressed, they laugh at rude words in poetry. The nouveau hippies will die before they reach 28. The nouveau hippies make me sick.

A nouveau hippie, drawing by Ros Picklehype; modelled by 'Sebastienne', a 27-year-old transvestite Sex Gang Children follower

PAUL

the-line punks, positive punks or indeed anarcho-punk squatters. But then being an outsider was itself part of the self-image of punk in its broadest sense, and the fact that these close and intense - but actually very short-lived - friendships have stayed with me so long after we lost touch says something about their importance to me, and also reminds me that I was in fact a part of this group even whilst standing very close to its outer edge.

"Advert" from Son of Wombat Weekly 1983

Publish And Be Damned.

Nick Hydra

Back in the dim distant past of 1987, I'd finally got tired of being poor and got a job as a labourer (naturally, I carried on signing on, usually rocking up to the dole office in my mud-spattered work clothes. No one seemed to notice, let alone care), the upshot of which was that for the first time in seven years, I had some disposable income.

Years before I'd started work on an Artzine called Nails in Flesh, which was going to be images of the crucifiction interposed with 'erotic' photography (religion, sex and death juxtaposed; because no-one's ever thought of that before), which I abandoned, partly because of lack of funds, but mainly for lack of decent 'erotic' photographs.

So when I actually had some cash I thought about resurrecting* the idea; but going back to the few pages I'd managed to complete, I realised it was a bad idea poorly executed and gave it up. However, I still thought doing a 'zine was a good idea, and set about drawing up a list of bands I wanted to include.

By this point I'd drifted away from the Anarcho scene, as the most of the good bands had split up or gone down musical routes that didn't appeal to me, and I'd been getting heavily into the post-industrial/ EBM stuff that was starting to appear.**

I wanted the 'zine to have a strong authorial voice, so I decided to ditch the question/ answer format, and go with something more impressionistic. I also decided that I was going to hand write it (which, when I look at my idiot scrawl of the time was a terrible idea).

I had already been writing to In The Nursery for some while so I had enough stuff from them to cobble an article together. I did a face to face interview with Veg Ranking Bass (at the time in the reasonably successful We Are Going To Eat You) about Birth Complex, a noise band I had been in with him for roughly 10 minutes, partly because there was a direct line of influence running via Eat Shit (from Nebraska USA) to God Told Me To Do It, but mainly to make sure the influence of La Monte Young, Terry Riley and other minimalist composers on our work wasn't overlooked.

I was pulling together a standard list of questions that (with tweaking for each individual band) would hopefully give me a framework to write interesting articles, when out of the blue, Amebix (who I had assumed had split up) released Monolith. To be honest it wasn't their finest hour, and was significantly too metal for me to fully embrace, but their early releases on Spiderleg were some of my favourite records of the whole anarcho era, and I thought their interest in the occult would make for an interesting set of replies, so I promptly shot off a set of questions.

After considering and discarding 'Twilight' (too Goth), 'Warzone 5' (a reference to Alan Moore's 'Ballard of Halo Jones') and 'Seventh Circle' (a reference to Dante's 'Inferno'), I settled on 'Necropolis' (because London's a city of the dead innit?). I even wrote an editorial inking the 'living dead on the commuter trains' to the cattle trucks transporting Jews to the death camps. This was all completely serious and po-faced you understand.

I then got the reply back, and I was fully intending to send off a follow up letter to clarify and expand on some points when the fickle finger of fate*** intervened and I never did any more work on it.

Naturally being the hoarder that I am, I kept all the bits and pieces in a file for the day when they would become useful. I don't know if 'useful' is exactly the word I would use to describe my childish scratching, but what the fuck.

I can only offer my heartfelt apologies to the many innocents crushed by the repressive machinations of the state apparatus as a result of my lapse of judgement, and promise to try harder next time.

*See what I did there?

** Taking the heretical position that the cover wouldn't feature any combination of Thatcher and/ or Reagan (whether in corporeal of skeletal form), skulls, Mohicans, skulls with Mohicans, mushroom clouds, or cut-up BUAV leaflets was obviously commercial suicide, but it was undoubtedly my failure to include a giant WH Smiths stencil headline of 'A STATEMENT' with a typed shopping list of things I considered wrong with society overlaid onto a photo of a rabbit smoking a Rothmans on page 2 which meant the system wasn't brought to its knees.

***I forget exactly what now, but it almost certainly involved someone breaking my heart and the resulting search for a lake of beer to cry into.

Hello!

At the moment I'm trying to put together a fanzine (Warzone 5) which was going to include an article on Amebix in the form of an overview/potted history/obituary - simply because it was generally believed that the band had ceased to function; there were rumours of mental institutions and smack O.D's flying round for a while. Judging by the sleeve notes on 'Monolith', you did go through a bad time for a while - could you give me a little background on this so I can bring the article up to the present day; also can you a) send me the lyrics for 'Monolith' plus the lyrics of 'Belief' and 'Curfew' off the "Who's the Enemy" EP

and b) answer some questions which rather than print in the usual Question/Answer format will hopefully get a clearer idea of what you're about these days

① The Logo you use is taken from a painting by Austin Spare - does this imply any acceptance of the theories of Atavism he tried to express in his work, or did you just like the picture?

② Are the lyrics of 'The Power Remains' meant to be taken literally ie - do you actually believe in the LeyLine/Earth Power/Old People mythos or is the song meant allegorically?

③ What are your favorite films/filmmakers
　　　　　　　　　　　Bands
　　　　　　　　　　　records
　　　　　　　　　　　Books
　　　　　　　　　　　Comics
　　　　　　　　　　　Artists/Artistic style

④ Are you the same Amebix that did 'University Challenged' on Bullshit detector 1

Well thanks for listening and I hope to hear from you soon

Bye Nick Morfit

P.S. You'll be getting a copy of the fanzine once it's finished.
P.P.S. Any chance of a London Gig?

AMEBIX

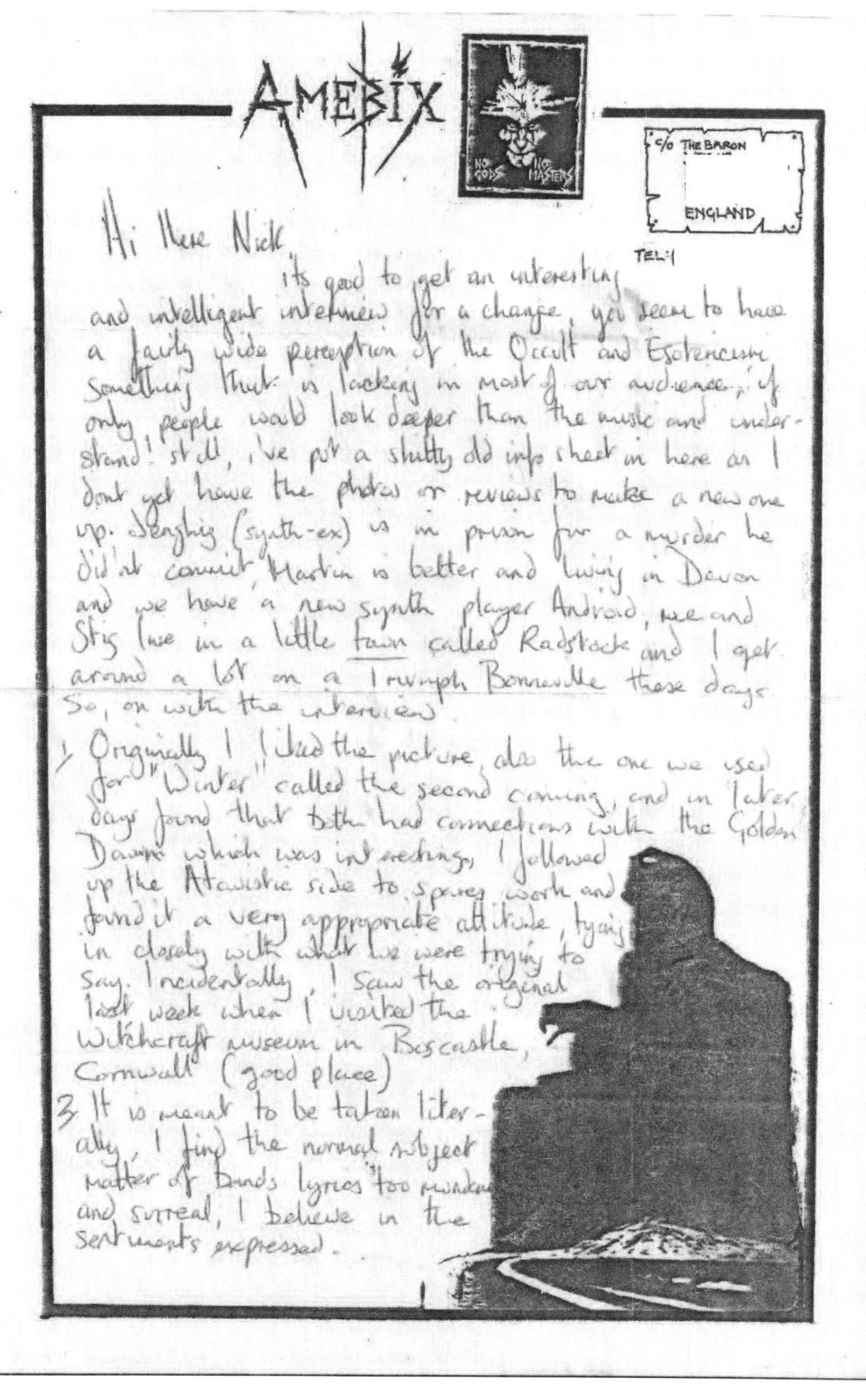

c/o THE BARON
ENGLAND

TEL: /

Hi there Nick,
 it's good to get an interesting and intelligent interview for a change, you seem to have a fairly wide perception of the Occult and Esotericism, something that is lacking in most of our audience,; if only people would look deeper than the music and understand! Still, i've put a shitty old info sheet in here as I don't yet have the photos or reviews to make a new one up. Jenghiz (synth-ex) is in prison for a murder he didn't commit, Martin is better and living in Devon and we have a new synth player Android, me and Stig live in a little town called Radstock and I get around a lot on a Triumph Bonneville these days. So, on with the interview.

1, Originally I liked the picture, also the one we used for "Winter" called the second coming, and in later days found that both had connections with the Golden Dawn which was interesting, I followed up the Atavistic side to sigils work and found it a very appropriate attitude, tying in closely with what we were trying to say. Incidentally, I saw the original last week when I visited the Witchcraft museum in Boscastle, Cornwall (good place)

3, It is meant to be taken literally, I find the normal subject matter of bands lyrics too mundane and surreal, I believe in the sentiments expressed.

3 Films - Highlander, Mask, Nosferatu, Spaghetti Westerns
Filmmakers - Sergio Leone
Bands - Queen, Civilised Society, Mercyful Fate, Accept, PiL, Metal Church, Jethro Tull, Clannad — etc etc
Records - My fave record of all time is Mercyful Fate's 'Don't Break the Oath' from a purely musical angle
Books - Macbeth the King - Nigel Tranter
The Occult - Colin Wilson
Phaid the Gambler - I forget who wrote it
The Longships - Bengt T. Bengtsson
Comics - 2000 AD (of course)
Freak Brothers
Heavy Metal
Warrior
All sicko stuff like R. Crumb etc
Artists/style - Giger, Salvador Dali, Turner

4, 'Fraid so, that was me and Stig in my Bedroom at home, I was 15 he was 17.

Hope that is OK, I would write more but my typewriter is fucked so me old wrist is aching. A copy of the 'Zine would be great and yes, we should be playing in and around London at the end of November. Take care for now.

The Byron

AMEBIX

'Twas in the year Nineteen Hundred and Seventy Eight, the great Shadow of Punkdom had fallen upon the land, in many places motely groups of spotty individuals gathered together in secret places to form bands to spread the word. One of these groups had its inception in the Small Devon Town of Tavistock, this group later came to be known as AMEBIX.

In the early days the group was comprised of Billy on drums, Chive Bass, the Baron on Vocals and Stig on guitar, however, many trials and tribulations led to an assortment of members joining or leaving over the preceding years. And yea....they did play their vile music in front of local, albeit unsympathetic audiences for nearly three years, in which time the infamous Martin had joined and left the band, spending the rest of his days in mental Institutions, Stig and the Baron had lived with him in a manor house on the edge of Dartmoor so after he left they had to find new lodgings. A cornishman by the name of Norman helped by telling his uncle that he had visitors for a few months and Norman came to play synth.

Becoming dissilusioned with the responses of the local Knaves they uprooted themselves unto a carreer of squatting and poverty on the streets of Bristol City, there meeting with Virus who at that time played for Disorder, and politely stealing him from them. They all clubbed together what few meagre pennies they had left and spent a day in a local Recording studio, the resultant piece of music being sent to Siderleg Records who in turn released it as the Whos the Enemy EP, enjoying a modicum of success they then released the Winter 7" and No Sanctuary 12"EP through the same label. At this time they played a lot in England as well as Touring Italy, and began to get a trusty, crusty following throughout the land. Virus went on to pusue other matters after the Italian outing, and the band were left drummerless, despite having a studio date in three weeks time. The new label was Alternative tentacles, AMEBIX being the first British band to grace their Vynil. Spider came forward from Local thrash heroes SCUM and spent the three weeks unlearning the mediocre hardcore rythms and getting to grips with the new Material. In the end he mastered it all and they recorded the LP Arise! the first true Testimony to AMEBIX's sound, refreshingly Individual as once qouted! The LP has sold out of the first pressing and Tentacles will not print anymore, obviously the band were'nt too pleased with the lack of promotion and faith and have since left them to look for another label.

At time of print there is no news but hopefully when you read this the situation will have changed. AMEBIX have just completed Tours of Switzerland, and Yugoslavia, we now await news and expect to be touring Britain in March 87...Coming your way soon!

Spider...Drums
Stig...Geeetar
The Baron...Bass and Vocals

The Baron
Sept '86.

UPDATE........UPDATE........UPDATE........UPDATE........UPDATE...

REVIEWS

SLEDGEHAMMER PRESS (USA)

Amebix : Arise (Advance tape) [BLACKTHORN]

*****(5 stars)
AMEBIX-NO GODS, NO MASTERS (Alternative Tentacles Records)

Goddamn it, I lost the fuckin' bio sheet to this band-Excuse the slip on professionalism here, 'cause I want to make sure you are informed about Amebix (I'll give you some more details next issue—I PROMISE!).

The band is from England and they sent me an advance tape of their upcoming debut album, and if played at maximum volume - it is truly MONSTEROUS! Reminds me a lot of CELTIC FROST/HELLHAMMER, not so much on actual musical deliverance as in the mood they create. This is definitely graveyard-mode music. Death Metal at it's darkest, gut-level heaviest and best!

The opening track, "The Moor", as well as other tunes like "Drink and be Merry"-For tomorrow you may DIE!!!, "Arise"-Get off your knees! "The Darkest Hour") are straight out of a horror movie soundtrack. 100% and 100 proof heavy! Watch for the Amebix album, and buy it-then take it home and kill yourself!

BEST CUTS!; "Drink And Be Merry", "Arise", "The Darkest Hour", and many more! A very consistant album! GET IT!

A British band. Maybe the British Metal scene isn't as quiet as I thought. This band hails from Avon. Their new album, a 10-tracker, is featuring some brilliant tracks. First time I heard I thought it was bad. A New Wawe album. But I wasn't listening, so I had to hear it once more, if it should have a decent review. I now realized their style. I presume it's an old New Wave band, and they've found out that Metal is the style. Their countrymen from Venom must have inspired them quite a lot, to a rare Metal style. Slow Black Power Metal combined with a little New Wawe. Tracks like "Slave" and "The Darkest Hour" are more New Wawe than Metal. Their lead singer is especially Venom (Cronos) inspired. He's got the same crazy way in singing as Cronos. This can be noticed in "Axeman" where he sings like another lunatic. Definately a great album. It should be out soon, but I don't think it'll be released world wide, so please contact the following address, Amebix, ning, [...] land.

THE HIT

THE AMEBIX
Arise
(*Alternative Tentacles*)

What? An English crew of loudmouth punks on The Dead Kennedys' very own Alternative Tentacles label? But it's true.

The Amebix are the first UK riot squad to enter the Tentacles hall of infamy, and well deserved it is too. 'Arise' is a savage drone, a churning noise. Their screeching guitars rival the likes of Dio and Venom for metal supremacy but there's more bite to these boys and the pace never lets up.

Far removed from The Sex Pistols, Clash and Buzzcocks school of speaking, The Amebix owe more to Crass and Conflict. But the dirty edge and aggressive sound are more than sharp enough.

'Arise' is not a compulsive necessity but it is an urgent plea for recognition. The Amebix are hot.

DAVE HENDERSON

NME 16th November, 1985

THE AMEBIX
Arise (Alternative Tentacles)

SWIRLING, SWARTHY, powerful, rather mean, actually. Not the most cheerful-sounding of albums but all the more mesmerising for that. Coming across in a similar vein to early Killing Joke or Blackpool's own Vee V.V.—a 'boy's own' record as it were—dragging (draggling?), insistent—insistently insistent repetition; one riff bludgeoned after another with suitably archaic titles. 'Axeman', 'Fear Of God', 'The Darkest Hour'.

Alternative Tentacles as a label is ALRIGHT by me (D.O.A./Dead Kennedys/Butthole Surfers) and this record is a worthy stablemate to the others. Entombed in a tunnel-vision of their own choosing, pounding wretched, driving—it must be that old lobe 'punk/rock' again. The message? 'arise! Get off your feet!' Ok, OK, I'm a-rising.

The Legend!

Arisesplittingly Powerful Stuff from this Punky Trio THE BARON(AMEBIX WEEKLY) GREATest!.... Beyond groovy; hurry the Guitar work, SMIG(BIG ME Magazine) Hurtling balls of intense grating sheep shit melting faces in its awesome path of total destruction,mega power indiscripable absolutely squelching blobs the Drummer is absolutely brilliant and no relation despite having the same name (honest).... SPIDER(No Relation Zine)

SO NOW BUY IT!

SOUNDS October 19

AMEBIX 'Arise' (Alternative Tentacles VIRUS 46) ****
STRANGE HOW a peaceful Monday afternoon can be so definitely disturbed in a half-hour. The sun shone before, the first mutterings of 'Arise' had dispersed themselves around the room. Ten minutes in; a horrific, claustrophobic feeling has enveloped the room, and the sky is filling with clouds. Twenty minutes in: a positively putrid feeling of violence exists whilst the clouds start to burst. Thirty minutes in: it's pissing down while inside the pressure has further intensified.

'Arise' commands you to do just that. An orgy of bass belches, grating guitars and guttural groans, it surfaces as an indohesive bundle of unrestrained malevolence. Smatterings of Venian haunt the vocals but, overall, it's a deliciously independent affair. Amebix don't even thrash their message home, they studiously shove it down the throat with their steady, thumping numbers.

The threatening tone of 'Axeman' is just a personification of the everyone, and this almost asphyxiating undercurrent lies behind other titles like 'The Darkest Hour' and 'Largactyl'. Its trance-like qualities are almost dangerous, and undoubtedly designed to be so - sheer blood-splattered horror on vinyl.

STEFFAN CHIRAZI

'Why do you think that they are laughing?'

Rich Cross

In the winter of 1982, to promote the release of the *Where's the Pleasure?* album, Poison Girls were out on tour around the country with Rubella Ballet. After ending their period of close collaboration with Crass, Poison Girls were clearly enjoying the experience of renewed independence and were revelling in the advantages of autonomy. *Where's the Pleasure?* was the LP which cemented the distinction and difference of the band's rich reinterpretation of the original raw anarchist punk impulse. Heff and myself had already caught up with them at the Bradford gig, and decided we'd head off to catch them again at the Old Town Hall, Greenmarket, Carlisle on 10 December; despite the fact that it was a long and difficult hitchhike in short daylight hours.

Both bands had been fantastic and we were really motivated to see them again, but there were other incentives too. The Carlisle gig gave us the chance to catch up with Sean McGhee from Psycho Faction and Tricia and Ali, the two young women from *Kind Girls* fanzine who we'd been in correspondence with since Poison Girls put us in touch with each other, after seeing the similarities in our approach to fanzine publishing (including our shared poor production values and limited print runs!).

It turned out to be the most memorable Poison Girls' gig I ever attended; although not for reasons I'd been expecting. It was also the night that I first met Raf from *Acts of Defiance* fanzine, one of the very few black faces (if not the only black face) in the audience; the start of an important new friendship and alliance. When we arrived the organisers told us that Psycho Faction had been dropped from the bill after splitting up, and that another local punk band had taken their place. When Psycho Faction turned up (having replaced the guitarist who'd quit), it was agreed that time would be set aside so that both bands could play.

It was reasonably busy inside the hall, and it was striking how *young* the average age of the audience was (mostly aged about 12-15) and that it was about one-third female in composition (a positive shift in the usual gender balance which Poison Girls were explicit about wanting to encourage). Notable too was the presence of a distinctive all-male group of older punks and skins, whose intention to intimidate and 'squad mentality' was unmistakable; as they sauntered, brooding, through the hall, giving everyone the evil eye. They perhaps could all have worn 'Right-wing naughty boys on tour 1982' T-shirts, but I'm not sure it would have added anything much to the identity they were broadcasting. It was later confirmed that this 'crew' had been put together by the Carlisle branch of the National Front, and that their intention to wreck the gig was part of a new, co-ordinated local Rock Against Communism campaign.

My memory of the first band (who I've had to be reminded were called Aftermath) is that they were by-the-numbers, join-the-dots Exploited wannabes whose political orientation was opaque. What caught the attention of a good proportion of the crowd was that their underwhelming, derivative 'punk rock antics' drew an oddly over-enthusiastic response from the 'squad'. Like *weirdly, inauthentically* over-the-top. Just how bad a choice was this stand-in support booking? Looking at the squad's attire. it soon became apparent just how many union jacks and swastikas they were sporting.

The squad's confidence grew as Psycho Faction took to the stage. They began the tedious, predictable chants of 'Sieg Heil' (and the accompanying salutes) and made their bid to take total control of the gig. They produced a swastika banner, which they began to wave around, and they gobbed and leered at Psycho Faction, doing everything possible to disrupt their performance. The atmosphere was toxic. Psycho Faction did their level best but, as the squad's disruptive tactics worsened, it became impossible to continue under these conditions and they cut their set short. To begin with, given the average age and make-up of the rest of the crowd, it seemed that it would be down to those individuals who felt brave or foolhardy enough to challenge the rightists' wrecking crew.

One young woman, who had a child with her, marched up to a group of skinheads and challenged them directly, arguing with them and refusing to back down until they surrendered their swastika banner. Surprisingly, they gave it up without a fist fight. As Rubella Ballet readied themselves, the squad returned en masse to the front of the stage. Quietly and without fuss, Richard Famous and Lance d'Boyle from Poison Girls slipped in amongst the group, breaking up their 'ownership' of the space and, by dint of a difference in age that was more than 15 years in some cases, posing a direct challenge to the gang's bravado. Would these thugs lash out at those so much older than them, who - while standing amongst them - were clearly not spoiling for a fight? Would they still feel confident enough to harass and attack those on stage? As it was, the squad was completely confused by the arrival of Rubella Ballet on stage. With their their dayglo attire, gloriously petulant pop tunes and joyously cartoon-style presentation: these were not the pasty, whiny hippies in black cotton that the squad had been briefed to expect.

While Rubella Ballet delivered their set with commendable panache, suffering few direct interruptions from the squad, the poisonous mood in the hall is worsening and it feels like things will shortly reach the point of 'kicking off'. As they finish their final number, and make their way from the stage, there is almost total silence in the room.

There is of course no question of Poison Girls backing down in the face of these attempts at intimidation. Right-wing thugs have been unwelcome interlopers at many a Poison Girls' gig; and the band's determination not be cowed into silence by bully-boy threats has been demonstrated time and again. Vi Subversa walks out onto the stage to adjust and reposition microphones. From the rightist mob came whistles, cat calls and a cry of 'hello sexy!'. 'Fuck off', she replies calmly. In the complete absence of any bouncers or security staff, Poison Girls' unassuming, implacable refusal to buckle in the face of the mounting sense of threat in the hall was as impressive as it was unforced.

With an opening that could scarcely have been more fitting, the band's choral arrangement of the song *Take the Toys from the Boys* erupted from the speakers, and Poison Girls appeared on stage. The sense of anticipation was so palpable you could have cut through it with one of the knives that we hoped that the skins weren't carrying. They opened with the majestic *Fear of Freedom*, a layered and complex song which holds back on its full, soaring power until it has fully suckered you in with its cabaret sensibilities. This was not what the squad were expecting and not the cue they had planned for; and, in their confusion, they seemed unsure of what to do. When the song reached its mid-point crescendo and Poison Girls let rip, the squad leapt into action; jumping around, knocking into anyone in the way, and flinging boots and fists around with abandon. Recalling the gig later in *Catalyst* fanzine, I wrote: 'Every time I hear the song now, it makes me shiver. "Why do you think that they are laughing? Why do you think that they are laughing? Because they've got you where they want you?". Your only fear? "The fear of freedom." Is was so fucking ironic.'

One of the squad wrenches a foldback monitor from the front of the stage, and it crashes to the floor with a loud 'whump'. Poison Girls all stop mid-song, and there is a brief, eerie moment of silence as those in the room decide (consciously and unconsciously; collectively and individually), what will happen next. Things teeter on the brink. This could explode into an enormous ruck, or (more likely, given the make-up of the audience) a sustained assault on unprepared, peaceable young punks by vindictive, violent bullies. Subversa speaks first. 'We're going to put that monitor back on stage and carry on', she says. A simple statement of fact. But the squad has other ideas. Then things happen really fast.

In an act of insane bravery, Sid from Rubella Ballet races from the side of the stage and launches himself directly at the squad. 'What the fuck do you think you're doing here? Fuck off! We don't want you here!', he screams at them. The gang are taken aback, and flinch from the confrontation. They had clearly been told that these drippy hippies were easy pickings and wouldn't stand up for themselves. Where could they have got that idea from? Recovering themselves, the gang grab hold of Sid. And that's what did it. Suddenly, from the sides of the hall where so many of the audience had retreated, a surge of people came forward. We mass in front of Poison Girls, inserting ourselves between the band and the thugs; shouting, and yelling at them as Sid is freed from their clutches.

The thugs flinch, surprised by the sudden assertiveness of the crowd. The hall splits in two. The retreating squad, trying to rally itself with renewed chants of 'Sieg Heil'; facing a newly united opposition. Some of the older punks in the group want to lay into the retreating squad, but to avoid a full-scale ruck with so many very young teenagers around, they hold themselves (or are held) in check.

The caretaker has called the cops, and when a solitary local bobby wanders in, the rightist gang scramble and scarper from the hall. The moment was amazing. Jubilant people began racing and dancing across the floor, retaking the territory and asserting their ownership of it. Poison Girls took their cue, and launched into their next number with abandon. It would have been the start of a triumphant, wild culmination to the evening; as all of that repressed energy exploded. But the caretaker and police were having none of it; and Poison Girls' sound was cut dead when the power was switched off. Despite the howls of protest and vocal objections, the gig was shut down and, as more cops arrive, the hall is emptied.

We're all staying overnight as guests of Sean and *Kind Girls*, and we all busy ourselves with packing down the rig and loading up the van. By the time that we've nearly finished, spotters for the squad are seen circling the area, trying to size up how many of us remain. As the last equipment is loaded into the van, the squad reappears (their numbers swelled by an impromptu recruitment tour of local pubs). They are clearly bent on trying to recover their tattered reputation ('What? Scared off by a bunch of *little punks*!'), intending to smash up what they can and pick off any stragglers.

In a mad rush, everyone piles into the van and, as the gang race towards us, we fire up the engine and tear off; escaping the impending wave of fists and boots with only seconds to spare. Tension and excitement mix in equal parts as we navigate the streets of Carlisle, expecting to be ambushed at any moment, before we find our way out of the city. Packed into the back of Poison Girls' van, having made a last-minute escape from a rightist hit squad, adrenaline racing as we head off into the dark of an icy December night: it is easy to see why this is one of my abiding memories of that time.

As Sean from Psycho Faction directs us to our overnight accommodation, Sid spots a road sign, pointing to a local village. '*Cockermouth*?', he blurts out in disbelief. And then laughing: 'Cockermouth? *Cock-er-mouth*!'. No-one else in the bus thinks it's quite as funny as Sid thinks it is; but an infantile knob gag can usually be relied on to break the tension in the most unlikely of places. Even in a van full of relieved Poison Girls.

What becomes clearer in retrospect is how evenings like this put into the sharpest focus possible the issue of how anarchist punks would respond to threats of violence from those determined to attack them and disrupt their gigs. Poison Girls were always less instinctively pacifist in outlook than Crass, and by late 1982 the implicit nonviolence of anarcho-punk was just beginning to be challenged by more physically assertive forms of anarchism. The willingness of that night's audience to resist the invasion of their gig and stand up for themselves was impressive; but it took a long time to reach that tipping point and we conceded far too much of the evening before then. There was, though, something really significant revealed through that 'snap' decision that we all made to take matters into our own hands and reassert our shared ownership of that space, repelling those who sought to deny us that. No, we didn't 'win the night', but we took joint responsibility for our collective self-defence: even though few of us were more than twenty years old, and many of us considerably younger. Under attack, we didn't back down, and we didn't ask anyone else to do it for us. 'Invisible people, show yourselves,' Poison Girls urged. 'People in hiding, come out.' That night, I think maybe we did.

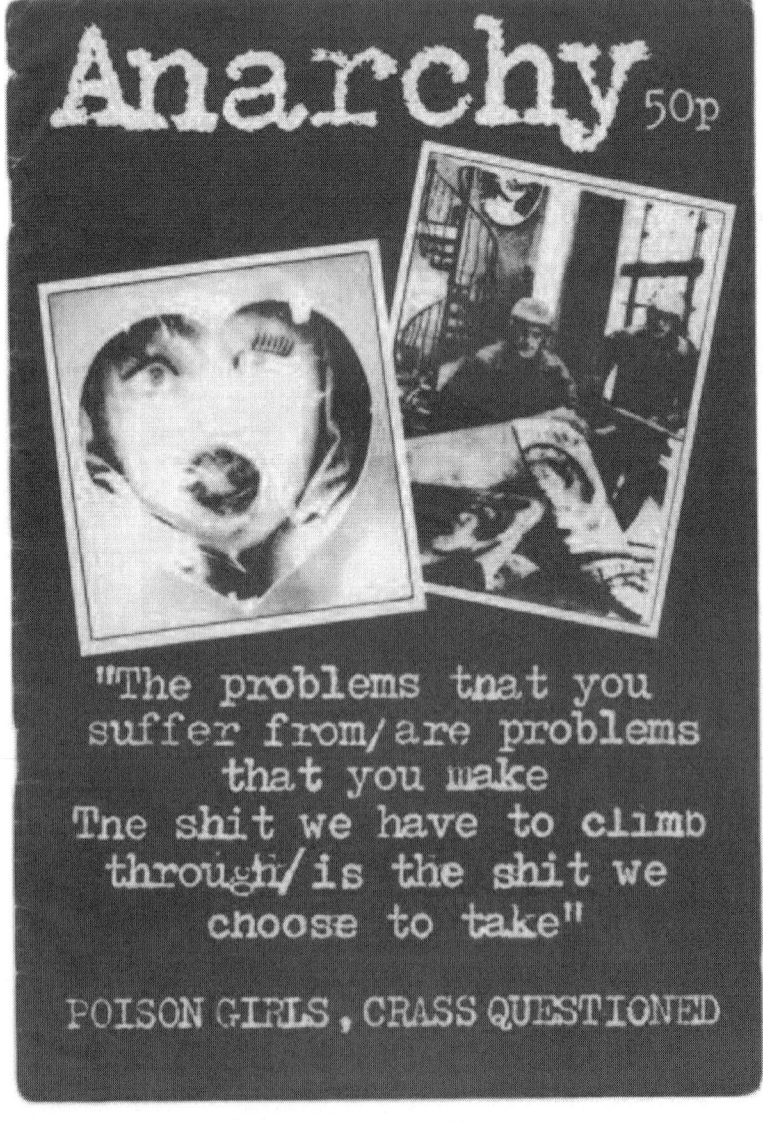

Your Life in Their Hands

Antisect

"TRAPPED WITHIN THE DARKNESS
THE DARKNESS THAT ELUDES ALL HOPE
A BLIND BELIEF IN ANOTHERS VALUES,ANOTHERS TRUTH
NO QUESTIONS.NO ANSWERS.
EVERYTHING IS PERFECT (?)
WITH EYES CLOSED NOTHING IS SEEN.NOTHING CHANGES
THERE IS BUT AN ENDLESS ACCEPTANCE OF A FUTILE EXISTANCE.......

YOUR LIFE IN THEIR HANDS

THE WORLD,AS IT IS TODAY AND HAS BEEN FOR HUNDREDS OF YEARS,COULD BE DIVIDED INTO TWO MAIN CATEGORIES.THE FIRST BEING THAT OF THE RULING CLASS (GOVERNMENT,AUTORITARIANS,ETC.).THE SECOND BEING THOSE THAT SERVE THE RULING CLASS (THE WORKFORCE,ETC.).THE OBJECTIVES OF THE FORMER ARE TO KEEP THE LATTER FIRMLY WHERE THEY ARE AND TO FOOL THEM INTO BELIEVING THAT THAT IS THEIR RIGHTFUL PLACE.THE LATTER,UNFORTUNATELY,ARE SUCCESSFULLY CONNED INTO ACCEPTING THE RULING CLASS AS PART AND PARCEL OF THEIR EXISTANCE,THEREFORE MOST OF THEIR LIVES ARE SPENT WORKING FOR AND SERVING THE RULING CLASS.

FROM THE AGE OF FIVE UNTIL WE ARE SIXTEEN WE ARE FORCEBLY MADE TO ATTEND SCHOOL.THE REASON BEING THAT WE SHOULD INEVITABLEY COME OUT OF THE PROCESS WITH THE IDEA FIRMLY IMPLANTED IN OUR HEADS THAT IT IS RIGHT AND PROPER FOR US TO WORK FOR THE STATE.THE ABOVE MENTIONED CON IS SO SUCCESSFUL THAT CERTAIN FACTIONS BELIEVE IT CORRECT AND IN SOME CASES NECESSARY THAT THEY SHOULD OFFER UP THEIR LIVES TO DEFEND THE STATE AND,IN EFFECT,THEY BECOME PART OF THE KILLING MACHINE KNOWN AS THE ARMED FORCES.MEANWHILE,THE REST OF THE WORKING POPULATION PROVIDE THE MEANS FOR THIS KILLING MACHINE TO EXIST.(TAXATION)THIS,IS PROBABLY THE MOST CALCULATED AND CALLOUS PART OF THE CON.THE POPULATION IS LED TO BELIEVE THAT BY PAYING TAXES TO THE STATE,THE STATE WILL, IN TURN,PROVIDE AMENITIES THAT THEY SHALL BENEFIT FROM.I.E.BETTER HOUSING, IMPROVED HOSPITAL FACILITIES,ETC.HOWEVER,THE MAJORITY OF MONEY PAID IN TAXES IS SPENT ON THE MEANS TO PROTECT THE STATE.IF,AT ANY TIME,THE STATE IS THREATENED BY THAT OF ANOTHER NATION,THE AFORE MENTIONED KILLING MACHINE IS PUT INTO OPERATION AGAINST THAT OF ITS "ENEMY".THE REST OF THE SERVING POPULATION ARE THEN DECIEVED INTO THINKING THAT THE WAR IS TO PROTECT THEM.THEREFORE THEY BELIEVE THAT THE WAR IS A "WAR OF JUSTICE",AND ARE TOLD TO SUPPORT THE "WAR EFFORT" IN EVERY WAY POSSIBLE TO ENSURE THAT THEIR NATION "WINS" AND JUSTICE IS THEREFORE DONE.THE FALLACY OF THIS COULD BE EXPOSED IN THIS QUESTION."HOW DOES ONE JUSTIFY KILLING,IN ORDER TO RETAIN JUSTICE".IT SHOULD BE OBVIOUS FROM THIS,THAT IN ACTUAL FACT,THE ARMED FORCES DON'T EXIST TO PROTECT THE ACTUAL POPULATION,THEY EXIST SOLELY TO PROTECT THE STATE.WHILST THE ARMED FORCES ARE OUT KILLING AND BEING KILLED TO SUPPOSEDLY PROTECT THE POPULATION,IT SHOULD BE NOTED THAT THEIR GOVERNMENTS ARE SAFELY TUCKED AWAY IN THEIR RESPECTIVE PARLIAMENTS.(OR,IN THE EVENT OF FUTURE WORLD WARS,IN THEIR (TOP SECRET) NUCLEAR BUNKERS).IN WAR,NO MATTER WHICH COUNTRY SUPPOSEDLY "WINS",THERE IS STILL A RULING CLASS AND THE REST OF THE POPULATION ARE STILL FORCED TO SERVE THAT RULING CLASS.IT DOESN'T REALLY MATTER WHICH GOVERNMENT IS IN POWER,AS THEY ARE STILL IN POWER,AND THIS IN ITSELF STANDS AS A GROSS VIOLATION OF INDIVIDUAL FREEDOM.

ONE OF THE MAIN REASONS WHY SITUATIONS LIKE THIS ARE ALLOWED TO CONTINUE IS BECAUSE OF THE PASSIVE AND "BLIND" ACCEPTANCE OF THE RULING CLASS BY THOSE WHO SERVE THE RULING CLASS.AND PERHAPS THE MAIN REASON FOR THIS BLIND AND PASSIVE ACCEPTANCE IS,TO PUT IT INTO A SINGLE WORD,IGNORANCE.THE IGNORANCE THAT HAS BEEN FORCED UPON US AND,AT EVERY CONCIEVABLE OPPORTUNITY,EXPLOITED BY THE RULING CLASS.

(I)

DADDY SAYS TO LITTLE JIMMY,"GO TO THE SHOPS AND FETCH ME "THE NEWS OF THE WORLD"AND I'LL GIVE YOU TWENTY PENCE FOR SOME SWEETS".THIS,SEEMINGLY INNOCENT SITUATION IS REPEATED AT THE OTHER END OF THE SCALE,WHEREBY THE RULING CLASS ASK US TO WORK FOR THEM AS THEY WILL,IN TURN,OFFER US A WAGE.(OF COURSE THEY DON'T MAKE IT QUITE AS OBVIOUS AND EASY TO UNDERSTAND AS THIS,BUT IN SIMPLE TERMS THIS IS WHAT THEY ARE SAYING.)UNFORTUNATELY,BECAUSE OF THE NEED TO SURVIVE,PEOPLE ARE FORCED INTO WORKING FOR THE STATE BECAUSE THE STATE OFFERS NO ALTERNATIVE.(APART FROM CLAIMING UNEMPLOYMENT BENEFIT,WHICH IS SEEN IN THE EYES OF MOST AS BEING A DEGRADING EXPERIENCE.IT IS,HOWEVER, THE STATE THAT CREATES THIS ATTITUDE,BECAUSE IT KNOWS THAT IT IS MORE PROFITABLE FOR THE STATE THAT PEOPLE SHOULD WORK FOR IT,RATHER THAN FEED OFF IT .AFTER ALL,THE GOVERNMENT HAS MORE IMPORTANT THINGS TO SPEND OUR MONEY ON (NUCLEAR WEAPONS,MURDERING PEOPLE IN THE SOUTH ATLANTIC,CHARLES AND DI'S WEDDING ARRANGEMENTS,ETC.)BESIDES TRYING TO IMPROVE THE SOCIAL STANDARDS OF THE LIVES OF THOSE THAT THEY ARE SUPPOSEDLY SERVING.)

(QUOTE:)"PERHAPS THE MOST CONSTRUCTIVE THING A GOVERNMENT COULD DO TO AID ITS PEOPLE WOULD BE TO DISBAND INDEFINATELY AND LEAVE THE POOR FUCKERS ALONE".(ASUB VERSIVE,1982)

THERE ARE MANY FORMS OF MODERN DAY INDOCTRINATION/MANIPULATION.PERHAPS THE MOST DAMAGING AND EFFECTIVE OF THESE BEING THE MEDIA.(NEWSPAPERS,TELEVISION,ETC.)THIS IS ALMOST TOTALLY CONTROLLED BY THE STATE,WHO ONLY LET US KNOW WHAT THEY WANT US TO KNOW.THE MEDIA HAS TO FALL IN LINE WITH GOVERNMENT STANDARDS OR ELSE FACE THE CONSEQUENCES.(IMPRISONMENT.OR,AT THE LEAST, DAY TO DAY HARRASSMENT AND INTIMIDATION.)A RECENT EXAMPLE OF THIS WAS WHEN A FACTUAL BOOK WAS RELEASED ABOUT GOVERNMENT PLANS IN THE EVENT OF NUCLEAR WAR,OR IF THERE EVER WAS A REVOLUTION.THE BOOK WAS CALLED "BENEATH THE CITY STREETS"(GRANADA)AND THE AUTHOR WAS A MAN CALLED PETER LAURIE.A LARGE PROPORTION OF THE CONTENTS OF THIS BOOK ARE FACTS THAT THE STATE CONSIDERS "TOP SECRET" AND THEREFORE THINGS THAT THEY DON'T WANT US TO KNOW ABOUT.IT WAS BECAUSE OF THIS THAT CERTAIN PEOPLE INVOLVED IN THE COMPILING OF THE BOOK WERE ARRESTED AND THEN PROSECUTED UNDER ALLEDGED INFRINGEMENTS OF THE "OFFICIAL SECRETS ACT".(INCIDENTLY,THE VERY FACT THAT A GOVERNMENT WHO SUPPOSEDLY EXISTS TO SERVE "ITS PEOPLE" SHOULD HAVE AN "OFFICIAL SECRETS ACT" THAT PREVENTS THE PEOPLE FROM REALISING WHAT IS REALLY GOING ON,SEEMS RATHER DUBIOUS TO SAY THE LEAST).IT SHOULD ALSO BE NOTED THAT A FILM COMMISSIONED BY THE B.B.C. ON THE EFFECTS OF NUCLEAR WARFARE,("THE WARGAME")WAS BANNED BY THE GOVERNMENT OWING TO ITS "ATROCIOUS SCALE OF SHOCK/HORROR CONTENT".IN FACT THE FILM IS A VERY THOROUGH TREATMENT OF THE FACTS OF NUCLEAR WAR.(OBVIOUSLY SO THOROUGH THAT THEY ARE SCARED OF THE CONSEQUENCES OF WHAT MIGHT HAPPEN SHOULD THEY ALLOW THE PUBLIC AT LARGE TO SEE IT)."THE WARGAME" WAS MADE IN 1967.AN UPDATE ON IT,CALLED "THE TRUTH GAME" BY JONATHON PILGER WAS ALSO BANNED.

ONE OF THE MOST POWERFUL FORMS OF MEDIA MANIPULATION IS THAT OF TELEVISION.ON THE SURFACE IT IS A NICE,SECURE COMPANION (LIKE RADIO) THAT NO HOME SHOULD BE WITHOUT,BUT REMOVE THE GLOSSY ILLUSIONS AND WE ARE LEFT WITH WHAT ONE PERSON CALLED,"THE MOST ADDICTIVE DRUG IN EXISTANCE".TELEVISION CAN SOMETIMES BE SAID TO BE EDUCATIONAL.(BUT,NINE TIMES OUT OF TEN,FOR THE WRONG REASONS)THE ANIMALS FILM FOR INSTANCE,WAS MADE BY PEOPLE WHO FELT GENUINE CONCERN FOR THE ISSUES RAISED IN ITS CONTENT.HOWEVER THE COMPANY THAT SCREENED IT,IN ALL PROBABILITY,HAD VERY DIFFERENT MOTIVES FOR DOING SO.IT IS A KNOWN FACT THAT THE MORE VEIWERS A TELEVISION CHANNEL CAN ATTRACT,THE WEALTHIER ITS SHAREHOLDERS SEEM TO GET.THEREFORE,IF WE PUT TWO AND TWO TOGETHER ,IT'S QUITE PLAIN TO SEE THAT THOSE WHO CONTROL WHAT WE SEE ON OUR SCREENS ARE MERELY USING THEIR POSITION TO CAPITALISE ON ANYTHING THAT WILL MAKE THEM A QUICK BUCK.WE HAVE STATED THAT ONCE EVERY SO OFTEN,TELEVISION CAN PRODUCE SOMETHING OF SOME VALUE.HOWEVER,FOR THE REST OF THE TIME IT OFFERS NOTHING MORE TO THOSE WHO WATCH IT,THAN A DISCREIT INSULT TO THEIR INTELLIGENCE.

MEANS FOR THE RUNNING OF CERTAIN CHANNELS IS PROVIDED BY OUTSIDE COMPANIES "BUYING TIME" ON THE SCREEN TO PROMOTE,ADVERTISE,AND HOPEFULLY SELL THEIR PARTICULAR PRODUCT TO THE "GULLIBLE" PUBLIC.ADVERTISMENTS ARE SKILLFULLY DESIGNED TO MANIPULATE THE VEIWER INTO BUYING A COMMODITY THAT,IN ALL PROBABILITY,THEY DON'T REALLY NEED.SUCH IS THE EXTENT OF THE POWER CONTAINED IN THE LITTLE RECTANGULAR BOX,THAT INVARIABLEY THE PUBLIC DO BUY THE PRODUCT ON OFFER.IT THEREFORE SEEMS UNFORTUNATE THAT SO MANY OF US HAVE BECOME MORE OR LESS DEPENDANT ON TELEVISION AS ONE OF THE MAIN SOURCES OF ENTERTAINMENT,AS,FOR ALL INTENTS & PURPOSES,THE TELEVISION IS NOT THERE TO RAISE THE LEVEL OF OUR AWARENESS,IN ACTUAL FACT ITS MAIN PURPOSE SEEMS TO BE TO MAINTAIN "NORMALITY",OR,"THE STATUS QUO".

HAVING TOUCHED (ALL BE IT BRIEFLY) ON THE SUBJECT OF THE MEDIAS PART IN THE CON,WE WILL NOW MOVE ON TO THE STATE ITSELF,AND HOW IT MANIPULATES US INTO ACCEPTING THE MILITARY AND NUCLEAR WEAPONS.

"BUT WE MUST HAVE NUCLEAR WEAPONS,OR ELSE THE RUSSIANS WILL INVADE". THIS IS A COMMON THEORY THAT CROPS UP FREQUENTLY WHENEVER THE SUBJECT OF NUCLEAR WEAPONS ARISES.HOWEVER IT IS NEITHER A PRACTICAL ASSUMPTION,NOR A LOGICAL CONCLUSION THAT THIS SHOULD BE THE CASE,FOR,AS FAR AS TECHNOLOGY GOES,RUSSIA IS BETWEEN FIVE AND TEN YEARS BEHIND THE UNITED STATES.THERE SHOULD THEREFORE BE NO DOUBT THAT THE EAST FEELS JUST AS THREATENED BY NUCLEAR WEAPONS AS THE WEST.(IF NOT MORE SO.)THE ONLY WAY IN WHICH WE CAN EXPERIENCE TRUE PEACE IS BY MUTUAL TRUST,AND BY CARVING OUT AN ENVIRONMENT WHERE WE CAN SOLVE ANY HOSTILITIES BETWEEN NATIONS IN A DIGNIFIED AND HUMANE MANNER.ANY SITUATION WHEREBY TO PRESERVE SO CALLED PEACE,WE MUST THREATEN AND BE THREATENED BY CONFLICT,IS NOTHING MORE THAN A CONTRADICTION OF THE ORIGINAL AIM.(WHAT SORT OF PEACE IS THIS? CERTAINLY NOT PEACE OF MIND.)

IT SEEMS HORRIFIC THAT WHILST COUNTRIES ARE SPENDING BILLIONS OF POUNDS/DOLLARS/ROUBLES/YOU NAME IT,ON THE ARMS RACE,(NUCLEAR AND CONVENTIONAL)THERE ARE MORE THAN TWO THIRDS OF THE WORLD LIVING BELOW THE ACCEPTED POVERTY LINE OF THEIR RESPECTIVE NATIONS.IT SEEMS HORRIFIC TO THINK THAT,IN THE MIDST OF ALL THIS POVERTY,THE ARMS RACE IS ESCALATING AT AN EVEN FASTER AND MORE TERRIFYING RATE THAN EVER BEFORE.

THE AMERICAN GOVERNMENT,IN COLLABORATION WITH THE BRITISH GOVERNMENT ARE DUE TO SITE ONE HUNDRED AND SIXTY CRUISE MISSILES IN THIS COUNTRY WITHIN THE NEXT YEAR.FOR MARGARET THATCHER TO CLAIM,AS SHE DOES,TO DESPISE NUCLEAR WEAPONS,IT SEEMS A BLATANT CONTRADICTION THAT SHE SHOULD BE A WILLING PARTY TO THE EVER INCREASING NUCLEAR WAR PREPARATIONS.SHE AND THE BRITISH GOVERNMENT HAVE PROVED THEIR HYPOCRISY BEYOND ALL DOUBT.SIX MONTHS AGO THEY WERE OPENLY ATTACKING ALL THINGS FASCIST AND CONDEMNING THE ARGENTINE MILITARY JUNTA FOR THEIR VIOLATION OF HUMAN RIGHTS,DURING THE FALKLANDS WAR.NOW WE LEARN THAT THE VERY SAME SCABBY MAGGIE AND HER SENILE SIDEKICKS HAVE BEEN DISCUSSING THE TRADING OF NUCLEAR TECHNOLOGY TO CHILE.(WHICH ITSELF IS RULED BY A SIMILAR REGIME TO THAT OF THE ARGENTINE.)THE WHOLE DISGUSTING AFFAIR SEEMS TO US TO BE VERY MUCH A CASE OF SINISTER DOUBLE VALUES.

TO GET BACK TO THE SUBJECT OF NUCLEAR WEAPONS AS A "DETTERENT FOR WOULD BE AGGRESSORS",THIS IS SIMPLY NO LONGER THE CASE.THE NEW CRUISE AND TRIDENT MISSILES ARE FIRST STRIKE WEAPONS.THE CRUISE MISSILE IS A VERY COMPLICATED AND INTRICATE PEICE OF MACHINERY THAT IS DESIGNED TO TRAVEL TO ITS TARGET AT A VERY LOW ALTITUDE,SKIMMING OVER LAND AND SEA AT SUCH A LOW LEVEL THAT IT IS NEAR ENOUGH IMPOSSIBLE TO DETECT BY RADAR.ITS AIM IS TO DESTROY "THE ENEMY" BEFORE THEY KNOW THAT IT'S EVEN ON ITS WAY.THUS,THE CRUISE MISSILE IS A POTENTIAL "WAR WINNING" DEVICE AND ITS BASES WOULD BE PRIME TARGETS FOR "THE ENEMY".(THEREFORE,THE ELEMENT OF DETTERENT IS NOTHING MORE THAN A DOWNRIGHT LIE.) YET STILL WE ARE TOLD THAT IT IS FOR OUR OWN GOOD AND NECESSARY TO PRESERVE THE "PEACE".(WHAT PEACE?)

SO FAR WE HAVE ONLY "TOUCHED THE TIP OF THE ICEBERG",AS THEY SAY.THE EXTENT OF MAN/WOMANKINDS SELF ABUSE GOES A WHOLE LOT FURTHER THAN THE POINTS WE HAVE TRIED TO MAKE UP UNTIL NOW.THE ATROCITIES WOULD TAKE A LIFETIME TO EX-

PLAIN.WE'RE NOT TRYING TO IMPLY THAT WE KNOW OF EVERYTHING THAT'S GOING ON, IN FACT WE KNOW VERY LITTLE,BUT WHAT WE DO KNOW WE'RE PREPARED TO PASS ON TO OTHERS,IN THE HOPE THAT SOME DAY EVERYONE WILL BE ABLE TO EXPERIENCE A TRULY AUTONOMOUS AND UNTROUBLED LIFE.WE ARE NOT TRYING TO CHANGE THE WORLD,WE ARE MERELY TRYING TO AID A FEW PEOPLE IN CHANGING THEIR ATTITUDE TOWARDS IT.TRUE PEACE AND TRUE FREEDOM WILL NOT BE REALISED BY VOTING FOR ANY POLITICAL PARTY,BE THEY LABOUR,TORY,CAPITALIST,COMMUNIST,THISIST,THATIST,OR THE OTHERIST. NOR WILL THIS STATE OF BEING COME ABOUT BY VIOLENT REVOLUTION OR UPRISING. (VIOLENCE IS UNFORTUNATELY PART AND PARCEL OF THE PRESENT,AND IF WE WISH FOR A BETTER FUTURE,WE MUST STRIVE TO ALIEVIATE VIOLENCE,OR,MORE IMPORTANTLY,THE VERY REASON BEHIND ITS EXISTANCE).

"SO WHAT ARE THE ALTERNATIVES?" THERE ARE MANY.SMALL COMMUNITIES,(NO LEADERS)WHOLE NATIONS COULD BE TURNED INTO PLACES WHERE PEOPLE WORKED FOR THEMSELVES AND EACH OTHER,SHARING,CO-OPERATING,RESPECTING AND TRUSTING EACH OTHER .NO BOSSES,NO LIFE SUCKING PARASITES,NO ONE TO SAY WHAT YOU CAN AND CANNOT DO,EXCEPT YOURSELF.USE YOUR IMAGINATION AND THEN WORK TOWARDS TURNING THE DREAM INTO REALITY.

FREEDOM CANNOT BE OBTAINED BY THE SIMPLE PROCESS OF BUYING A BADGE WITH AN "A" ON IT.NOR BY PURCHASING THE LATEST EDITION OF "BLACK FLAG".IT WILL ONLY COME ABOUT BY REALISING YOUR RESPONSIBILITIES TO YOURSELF AND THE REST OF THE WORLD.(MAN AND ANIMAL).LOOK AROUND YOU.DON'T BE AFRAID TO ASK QUESTIONS. WITHOUT QUESTIONS THERE ARE NO ANSWERS.IT'S SO EASY TO AGREE WITH IT ALL,BUT IT'S A LOT MORE CONSTRUCTIVE TO MAKE THE EFFORT TO CHANGE THINGS.YOU MAY FEEL THAT TO STRIVE FOR A BETTER WORLD IS MERELY A LOAD OF OVER-AMBITIOUS NONSENSE.BUT THE TRUTH IS,WE'LL BE LUCKY IF WE HAVE A WORLD LEFT AT ALL IF WE LET OUR(?) GOVERNMENTS CONTINUE TO LEAD US ALL UP THEIR MILITARISTIC PATHWAY TO NUCLEAR OBLIVION.IF YOU FEEL THAT YOU'VE HAD ENOUGH OF THEIR OPPRESSION AND THEIR WAR,IT IS YOUR RIGHT AS A HUMAN BEING TO REFUSE TO BE A PART OF IT. IF YOU REALLY THINK THAT YOU DON'T GIVE A FUCK WHAT HAPPENS TO YOU,YOU MUST BE IN A VERY SORRY STATE OF MIND.IF YOU'RE REALLY SO WEAK AND SO PASSIVE TO THE EXTENT OF ALLOWING YOURSELF TO DEGENERATE SO FAR,THEN,AS FAR AS YOU'RE CONCERNED,THINGS CAN ONLY GET WORSE.UNTIL YOU REALISE WHERE YOUR LIFE IS LEADING YOU,YOU WILL NOT BE ABLE TO CHANGE ITS COURSE.(SHOULD YOU WISH TO DO SO.)

WE ARE ALL A PART OF THE WORLD,WHETHER WE'RE BLACK,WHITE,SIXTEEN OR SIXTY, "PUNK","SKIN","HIPPY","STRAIGHT",OR WHATEVER,AND IT IS UP TO US TO ENSURE THAT NOBODY TAKES IT AWAY FROM US.IT IS UP TO US TO SORT ITS PROBLEMS OUT,AND IT IS UP TO US TO PREVENT IT BECOMING THE STAGNANT,LIFELESS,CORPSE THAT IT IS SLOWLY TURNING INTO.EVERY DAY WE LEARN OF ANOTHER NEW ATROCITY THAT HAS BEEN COMMITTED,AND EVERY DAY THE ATROCITIES WORSEN,AND GROW MORE CONSUMING. THE EARTH IS OURS,SO WHY SHOULD WE LET ANYBODY HOLD IT TO RANSOM,OR THREATEN TO DESTROY IT.(OR US,FOR THAT MATTER.)LIFE SHOULD AND COULD BE AN AWE INSPIRING EXPERIENCE SHARED BY ALL.NOT THE PATHETIC SHAMBLES THAT IS ON OFFER TO US BY OUR OPPRESSORS AND WOULD-BE OPPRESSORS.YOUR FREEDOM IS THERE FOR YOU TO HAVE,IF YOU REALLY WANT IT (AND,SPEAKING FROM A PERSONAL POINT OF VIEW,I MOST CERTAINLY DO.)

IT IS OUR BELIEF THAT WE HAVE TWO CHOICES.WE CAN EITHER CARRY ON AS WE ARE (OR AS SOME OF US ARE),AND EVENTUALLY END UP EITHER TOTALLY CONTROLLED BY OUR PRESENT DAY OPPRESSORS (OR THEIR SUCCESSORS),(THAT IS,OF COURSE,MOMENTARILY FORGETTING THE OVERHANGING THREAT OF NUCLEAR WARFARE),OR,WE CAN REACH FOR THE SECOND OF THESE TWO CHOICES,AND THAT IS TO START WORKING TOWARDS A WORLD WHERE WAR,OPPRESSION AND VIOLENCE OF ANY KIND ARE THINGS OF THE PAST.

..........UNTIL YOU OPEN YOUR EYES,SOME THINGS CANNOT CHANGE.
AND UNTIL SOME THINGS CHANGE,YOU CANNOT OPEN YOUR EYES.

ANTISECT

Well, Sir. I Might

Willie Rissy

I need to be clear from the beginning. This story ends with me *loathing* Crass. For a good couple of months, at least. I get over it, and relations are repaired; we work together again, and I have a somewhat different perspective on things looking back. But I need to set out where this story is headed; so that it's not a complete surprise when we get there. It's me *resenting* Crass; me *losing confidence* in Crass; me feeling Crass had enticed me up the garden path, only to shove me into the compost bin. You have been warned. So now (much like when you select *Yes Sir, I Will* from the CD stack) you can't claim you didn't know what was coming.

In the cold mid-winter of 1983, me and the small network of anarcho-punk comrades I had close connections with were pretty much fully immersed in the work of the direct action wing of the anti-nuclear movement. That was our focus and preoccupation and sat at the core of our subcultural politics. At the time, we remained nonviolent in orientation but militant and highly motivated in temperament. The arrival of the first flights of American Cruise missiles at military bases on British soil was imminent and, as the countdown to what increasingly felt like an inevitable nuclear conflagration accelerated, we were *impatient* to escalate the temper and confidence of the anti-war opposition in confronting its enemies. Really, really impatient. The music of Crass, Poison Girls, Flux and Dirt was both the playing-in-your-head-as-you're-doing-it soundtrack to our actions and the inspiration and rallying cry for them.

That month, coordinated protests were being held at military sites across the country, and, realising that we could join an event at the Tornado jet base at

RAF Cottesmore in Rutland on the same day that Crass were playing in Birmingham, we hatched a cunning plan. Horribly early on the morning of 16 December 1983, me, Phil, Jimmy and Judith crammed into my faithful Mini-Clubman and set off from Peterborough to Cottesmore to join an early morning blockade of the base; that would attempt to shut down, or at least to disrupt, the operation of the site if only for a few hours.

It was the kind of action we'd been involved with numerous times before (and would join in with many times again in the future), at military installations the breadth of Britain. RAF Cottesmore was an isolated location and, as we arrived and joined the small throng of other demonstrators making their way to the main gates, the demonstration had something of an otherworldly quality. Clutches of protesters moved through the the mist and frost in the weak early-morning light, in the near-silence of the countryside around the base, under the watchful eyes of police patrols. It made for an eerie and unsettling sight. Phil recalls: 'we could see the tail fins of the Tornadoes through the mist. That's how close we were to the machines of the war machine!' The demonstration had drawn a familiar profile of peace activists, but, aside from our black-clad foursome, there are unusually few other punks in attendance. Turnout was not great (the number of different regional demonstrations being mounted that decisive month stretching our mobilising powers), but we split into groups to cover the entrances as best we could; intending to mount a bodies-in-the-road blockade of the main approaches that might together generate the impression of the base being 'under siege'. All symbolic stuff, of course. But then symbols have their uses, and can be powerful things. As David King once explained to Crass.

Sometimes the symbolism of such anti-nuclear encounters played out without descending into bruising brutality. But this particular blockade quickly becomes pretty hardcore, and the conflict ratchets up. As traffic approaches, we lunge into the roadway, evading the frustrated cops; and they step in to manhandle us out of the way while the vehicles slow; waiting for the path to be cleared. The wintry isolation of the setting reinforces the surreal quality of this ritualistic tussle for the temporary control of a few yards of tarmac. As the morning unfolds, the blockade battle loses any vestige of 'good humour' on either side.

Then one more nondescript vehicle approaches the blockade line, its driver the only occupant. He's probably a civilian contractor. As we move into position, the car driver shows no signs of slowing down, and the cluster of activists in the roadway quickly realise that a pretty unevenly matched game of chicken is now underway. As he races towards the group, the cops watch impassively. He's clearly going to push it to the last minute before hitting the brakes, ensuring he is as intimidating as possible. Only he doesn't slow down. At all. And just before he strikes the line of blockaders, we realise what's now become inevitable and we all try to scramble out of harm's way.

But we don't all make it in time and, as this unconscionable fuckwit races into our line, several protesters are struck by the vehicle. One is smashed onto the bonnet of the car, and is carried probably 10-15 feet along the roadway before being flung from the vehicle into the verge. The car races towards the gates of the base without slowing. We jump to our feet and, pushing through the police lines, race after the vehicle. The gates of the base open and the car is ushered inside. A few of us reach the fence line as the gates slam shut; shouting obscenities at the disappearing vehicle. The MoD police inside and the civilian cops outside regain control of the situation, and drive us back from the perimeter; ignoring our vocal protests. The callousness of the action is ugly and unexpected, and pulls us all up with a renewed feeling of vulnerability; here in this middle-of-nowhere winter hinterland.

Incredibly, the unwilling hitchhiker has only suffered minor cuts and bruises, and is remarkably composed. Despite being badly shaken up, the mutual refusal to be intimidated by this assault is immediate; an unspoken act of collective defiance. Together we continue to mount what becomes an increasingly ineffective blockade, against mounting odds. It's cold, muddy, exhausting, sporadically painful (as the cops tire of dragging us from the road with any kind of restraint) and - as was so often the case - comes to feel completely futile. We stick it out to the end, and then disperse with the other demonstrators - attempting to find some joint affirmation in our efforts, however inadequate our methods.

Tired, battered and pretty mucky, we head from the base into Birmingham city centre and towards Digbeth Civic Hall, hopeful of being re-energised by the shared experience of righteous indignation and passion of a large anarcho-punk gig. Even though it's the city of my birth, and somewhere I returned to and spent a lot of time in in the early 1980s, I've never properly warmed to Birmingham. In fact, I've been to more dire punk gigs (and been hit more times at dire gigs) in Birmingham than in any other city I've been to in the UK. And I've been to Bristol. *To Bristol.*

The Digbeth area has always felt pretty grim to me (and has still missed out on the multi-million pound 'regeneration' that has rebuilt other sections of the city centre). Its civic hall sits right next door to Digbeth Police Station and always seemed a deeply unsympathetic setting for anarcho-punk. With its old-style musical hall sensibilities it was an equally surreal place to arrive in, its own way, as the environs of RAF Cottesmore. It would have been the perfect venue for bingo nights, choir concerts and Bernard Manning. Punk shows, not so much. The place was staffed by a team of male ushers, all in their 50s and 60s, wearing garish purple jackets and sporting Brylcreemed slicked-back grey hair (in the style like what The Old People had in Those Days). To begin with, as their hall filled with hundreds of punks, skinheads and assorted, wayward Young People, they looked bemused and uncomfortable. Later, at things soured, and recognising they were way out of their depth, they disappeared; sensibly taking shelter in some locked up office backstage.

Somehow large scale anarcho-punk events rarely seemed to 'fit' well to the cultural contours of 1980s' Birmingham. And I may be guilty of a huge disservice to anarcho comrades from England's 'second city', but it always seemed to me as though Crass, failing to find local organisers, booked their Birmingham shows directly with the venue. I have no memory of paste-and-run flyposting in the city for the Crass gigs of 1983 and 1984. There were never any bookstalls, local campaign displays; no-one doing veggie food, and none of the few fanzines on sale seemed to be produced in the city. It's also hard to imagine local punks producing tickets and flyers using the spartan commercial templates that were the design signature of the Digbeth gigs. There was nothing much to suggest that anyone immersed in the local punk scene was *looking after* things. These gigs attracted several hundred people from across and beyond the city, but they always felt *unsupported*; some kind of unasked-for import. The acoustics in the place were never great either. Sizeable PA rigs could rarely marshall the sounds bouncing off the walls and balconies every which way, and the mix was usually muggy. It was liveable with, when what was projected from the stage was a clean, powerful punk rock sound. Good thing then that no-one that night was planning a massively loud deconstructed sound collage overlaying a complex multi-voice spoken-word performance...

Sometimes anarcho gigs felt powerful and celebratory; other times unsettling and unpredictable - and no less thrilling for that. Not that night. The atmosphere was bad-tempered and sullen from the beginning. It felt *dangerous*, alright. But not in a good way. Predatory skinheads, rockabillies and psychobillies, who always seemed to be present at Birmingham anarcho gigs, were soon in evidence, excited by the easy pleasures of soft targets. The vibe was alienating and edgy. There was little in the room which spoke to the idea of liberating collective empowerment. If everyone seemed *angry*, they seemed just as likely to be pissed off with each other as with the state of the world. It was a pretty foul environment to find yourself a part of.

After tense performances from Flux, D&V and the redoubtable Annie Anxiety, Crass appeared on stage. Steve Ignorant, Eve Libertine and Joy De Vivre took up positions centre stage, each studying lyric folders. Within seconds it became clear that Crass planned to perform *Yes Sir, I Will* in its entirety. Now, in my humble opinion, *Yes Sir, I Will* is a peerless testament to the power and passion of anarcho-punk; and arguably the most important musical and political statement that Crass ever recorded. In my book, it's a mesmerising, compelling album. It also has real artistic purchase in its disturbing, impassioned film incarnation. It could have worked well as an unplugged or semi-acoustic cabaret piece or as a poetry 'happening'. But as a live rock 'concept' show, projected to an audience of hundreds, it made for a relentless and remorseless forty-five minutes of aural battery.

A few months earlier, I'd been at a Flux gig in Evesham (marred by endemic and horribly casual outbreaks of violence) at which a poet had read his work while his colleague hacked at the strings of a distorted electric guitar with a Stanley knife. I remember feeling pretty conflicted about the performance: was this a powerfully dramatic expression of creative *ennui*, or a form of 'cultural nihilism' as pointlessly fucked-up as whatever the inaudible words of the poet were denouncing? Why not just *lose* the guitar? I felt similarly ambivalent about the live experience of *Yes Sir, I Will*.

Several months later when I visited Dial House to discuss arranging a second Crass gig in my own home town, I made clear that I didn't want to do it if what Crass were offering was an unexpurgated, undiluted performance of *Yes Sir, I Will*. 'If you're convinced that the music is getting in the way of the message', I suggested, 'then dump the music. Completely. Go on stage and *read out* the text of *Yes Sir, I Will* without any of the distractions of rock'n'roll.' The suggestion was greeted with a short, confused silence. 'But what would everyone in Crass who's not a vocalist do?', asked Eve, not unreasonably. 'I don't know', I answered, irritated. 'Maybe they could wander through the audience with handouts or banners or something?' And then, sounding more dismissive than I intended: 'But I don't think that worrying about finding jobs for other members of Crass is really the issue.' Eve and Steve looked unconvinced, but nodded.

That night in Birmingham, Crass delivered *Yes Sir, I Will* with conviction, with energy and without a hint of self-doubt. Large sections of the audience (like audiences at other nights on that tour) had come in the expectation of being able to sing along to songs from Crass's crowd-pleasing back-catalogue; but there was to be no accommodation to that. There was so little in their performance which suggested they were reaching out to, and seeking connection with, their audience; and so much evidence of them pushing that audience away. In return, the mood of the crowd spoke of boredom and bad-temper.

Many years later, Penny Rimbaud proclaimed that: 'most anarchist punks were just as happy tearing down the barbed wire fences of military bases as they might be going to a gig.' It would have been fantastic if that had been true. But in reality, anarchist punk culture contained a good percentage of 'punters'; who bought records and went to concerts, and whose relationship to the scene remained that of *consumer*. That meant the goal, surely, had to be to find ways to encourage those punks to develop the confidence and the willingness to *contribute* and *create*?

As the performance approached its jagged, breathless conclusion, it reached the accusatory section about the role of the 'passive observer'. Listening to this on record, it was easy to connect with a sense of righteous indignation that both artist and listener could share. But in the context of that evening, Crass seemed insistent that the audience was the *subject* of the attack, not part of the *agency* jointly responsible for the message. In recent years, Steve Ignorant has been keen to distance himself from any accountability for the political rubric of Crass. But on that night in 1983, there seemed nothing tentative or reluctant about his sense of political identification. Ignorant took the section to heart. 'It is *you* the passive observer who has given them this power', he screamed indignantly; his arm outstretched, his finger pointing out over the crowd and sweeping slowly around every inch of the auditorium. 'You are being used and abused and will be discarded as soon as they've bled what they want from you', he continued. No-one was excluded from his withering condemnation; and in those few moments Ignorant encapsulated the experience of the whole evening.

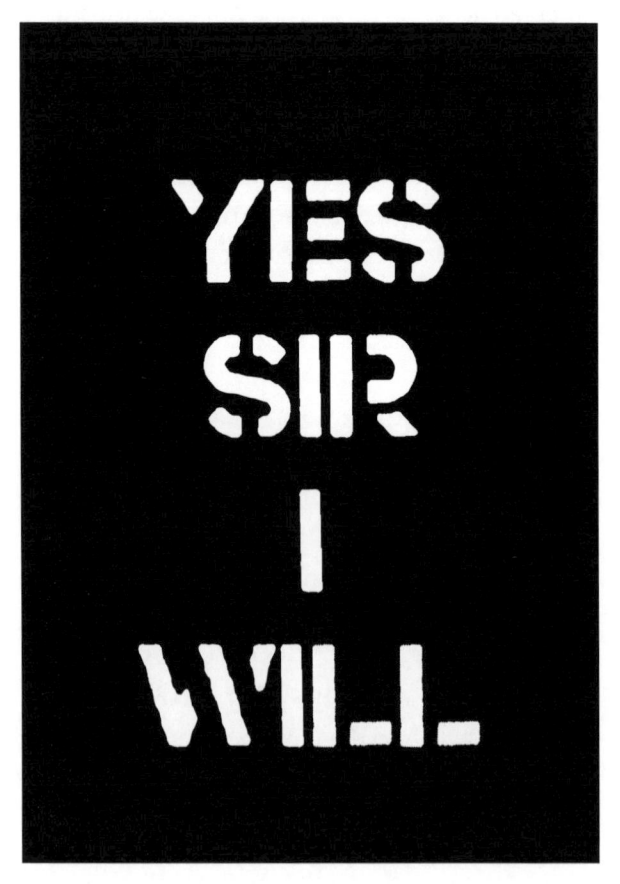

We'd gone to the Crass gig in the hope of encouragement, inspiration - of reaffirming the hope that the looming nuclear apocalypse might yet be averted by the cumulative actions of a people rising in unconstrained revolt. We'd wanted to feel *together*; while Crass seemed to want to declare their separation from us. They weren't *angry* with us. They were *disappointed*. No, hang on. That's not right. They were angry *and* disappointed. 'We' had come up painfully short against Crass' high standards. Crass were announcing that *we'd* failed *them* and the common cause we were all supposedly committed to. Individually and collectively, the four of us were incandescent at this hubris, leaving the menacing after-gig loitering of Digbeth behind, as we set off deflated and seriously pissed off. Despite our best efforts, were we simply not *good enough* for them? We we 'part of the problem' in a way that only they had sufficient insight to comprehend? Arrogant, dismissive, judgemental *fuckers*.

On the final track of the studio disc of *Christ: The Album*, Crass had sampled a speech at a CND rally by social historian, anti-nuclear polemicist and dissident former Communist Party member E P Thompson. From the stage of the rally, looking out over the multitudes in the park, he had declared: 'Looking at you now, I know one thing. We can win. We can win... I want you to... I want you to sense your own *strength*.' That crappy night in Birmingham, after that shitty day at Cottesmore, it was difficult to feel any of that optimism or self-belief. Despite the mental and physical exhaustion of the day, I struggled to get to sleep when we were finally able to climb into our beds at the end of a 20-hour day. If, as so many of us feared, the world really did stand teetering on the edge of the nuclear abyss, this was surely the worst possible time for committed anti-militarists to shun and separate from each other. If Crass seemed to be at risk of losing the plot at this critical moment, in a welter of recrimination and reprimands, then maybe the time had come to look elsewhere for anarchist inspiration.

Walk away from Crass?

Well sir, I might.

THERE IS NO AUTHORITY BUT YOURSELF

Memories

Tim Voss

The 1970's had promised so much and spectacularly failed to deliver, government was pushed around and about by union power who in turn were governed by left wing agitators who should have been fighting the rise of the right wing movement instead of battering a notionally left wing government. Out of the boredom and frustration of the black, white and grey colours of England, punk rock blew everything apart, or so the myth goes. By 1980 the Sex Pistols had dissolved into a dead circus horse being flogged around the arena of the music business, The Clash whilst playing top rock n roll had moved stateside and seemed less and less relevant, The Damned were little more than a damned good night down the venues the band were performing in. These bands belonged to our older brothers and sisters, our older uncles and aunties. Whilst we loved the poses and the music, it offered little more to us than the fallen labour government offered to the union members and workers who had blindly supported it… In short punk was dead and buried.

But out of the darkness and the grey, out of the sneers and gobbing a new set of groups jumped off the stages, into the record shop racks and through to the front pages of the music press. The Ruts, the UK Subs, Crisis, the Newtown Neurotics, the Angelic Upstarts, Theatre Of Hate and most importantly, dressed in black military uniforms and boots, rattling like a machine gun and shouting to us, about us, came the huge alternative musical, political and art movement that was spearheaded by Crass. Although Johnny Rotten had screamed 'get off your arse' here was something, a movement that seemed to mean it. Our year zero had arrived for us.

Necro, were a group of school friends with similar interests in music who spent most of their time sitting around each other's bedrooms listening to records we had bought with pocket and paper-round money and cooking up ways to form a band. Andy's older brother played bass and mine played guitar so we could talk a bit about the practical side of music. Andy, after much saving, bought a Les Paul copy guitar, covered it in CND stickers and paid an acquaintance to build an amp with built in fuzzbox (don't forget, purchasing instruments back in the early 1980's was much more expensive than they are now). I eventually saved the money to buy a small drum kit (thanks to £100 left to me by my gran).

[Tim and Andy at the very beginning of Necro being formed – Photograph from Andy Lane's collection]

The band, a band, in theory, had been formed. During Saturday afternoons in the autumn of 1981 the curtains were drawn in my parents backroom as they 'went shopping' for the afternoon, bless them. The amps were fired up, drums were attacked mercilessly. It was glorious, out of time, out of tune and chaotic… Friends came around with various instruments and then left.

My inept drumming was matched by Andy's belief that all you needed to know was open E and then bar chords to play any tune. We attempted to play Clash songs, Crass songs and UK Subs songs. Steve, although not around during the initial rehearsals had the best record collection of us all, and who was quite wordy, joined on vocals and by late autumn or early winter the group had settled down to have Steve on vocals, Andy guitar, Bill on bass and me on drums. Andy and I had spent the half term school holiday writing half a dozen songs, Steve had come up with the name Necro. We would settle for that as a decent name to shock some of the public who actually would know what the name meant. All that we needed now was for the world to listen.

Revolution rarely happens in isolation and whilst we were planning and rehearsing to take the world on there was a whole bunch of other groups in the Ware / Hertford area doing the same. From the angry to the arty, from poets to the punks. Bands like Onslaught, Virus V1, Moscovite 5, Rig Veda And The Twins, Dicotoledan, Timmy And The Wheelbarrows, The Plugs, The Frets and a whole other set of bands I can't remember the names of with so many years passing. Some bands were real runners, some bedroom pipe dreams, but all were coming out of the mire at the same time in the same place. Necro were first and foremost mates, and we would go along to hear Onslaught (the then top punk band from the area) practice and the floor shook they were so loud! Rig Veda were arty like Orange Juice and were cool. Each one of these bands and people were a crucial ingredient in the very scene that was emerging. You couldn't walk down the street on a Saturday afternoon without bumping into someone from one of the bands. Also worth noting was the relative close proximity to towns like Welwyn Garden City, Stevenage and Harlow. All these three areas having vibrant punk scenes already established with venues, record shops and fanzine culture. The centre of London was a forty five minute train journey away. Small Wonder records in Walthamstow was only around an hour away via all the public transport connections.

The winter of 1981 going through to 1982 was cold and long. A number of gigs were being arranged by friends at the Pioneer Hall and at the Richard Hale School in Hertford. All gigs were CND benefits, though probably not big fund raisers as they were about 30p to get in and only around seventy people in attendance!

[Penguin remembers Onslaught performing at Richard Hale school when the bassist Sam who had missing front teeth and a one string Rickenbacker bass tried to explain to a mixed race skinhead the irony of wearing a YNF shirt and hanging out with the handful of other white YNF skinheads that had turned up for the gig.]

Posters were made and photocopied. Evenings were spent fly-posting them, usually alongside CND posters. Some nights it was so cold and damp the posters fell off the lamp-posts and walls as soon as we pasted them up. Occasionally we were stopped by the police, usually when Steve mentioned his surname we got a 'take care son' and were left alone (Steve's dad was in the police). It was always good fun, there was a feeling of I fought the law and got away with it (I was never sure of the punishment for a 14 year old bill stickerer if anything had not gone right on the night). The early gigs were chaotic and brilliant fun, the audience being made up of mates and people from other bands. Necro played at the local Hertford conservative party club; surely we could convert the ruling classes with our blend of music, lyrics and slogans written on the back of our leather jackets? A teacher at school was a club member and we asked if we could play on the night (he had no idea what sort of music we played). He got us a spot on a Saturday disco night. A friendly art teacher with a penchant for The Clash drove us to the club. After arriving things clearly weren't going to go as planned, and after just one song the microphone we borrowed off the DJ was pulled and Andy's lovely fuzzbox bearing amp unplugged. We were 'banned from the Tory club… ok…never much liked playing there anyway…think they only wanted well behaved boys…etc etc'.

Top street cred ratings and the teacher went onto state "you should never dismiss seeing a band twice, but I think Necro is the exception to the rule".
We should remember that the early 1980's were highly politically charged times. Unemployment had hit three million, industry was being shut down, riots in Toxteth, Bristol and Brixton, the nuclear arms race and possible use of those nuclear arms was a very real possibility, public services were starting to get demolished by chunks (except the police and army who were given generous pay rises), and led by one Maggie Thatcher who made it clear that she was not only made of iron, she certainly wasn't for turning. Oh yes, then she declared war on Argentina, more of that later. This war was as illegal as the recent Iraq war. On top of all this, the nazi right in the form of the National Front was on the rise and certainly on the march. The mainstream politics was either right (Tory) or left (Labour), the mush of consensual right wing politics of today was a long way away…

The songs we wrote in Necro were about the world around us and how we wanted it to change. Songs were written about the right wing press, about the (then soon to be) development of Stansted airport, about the arms race, about the police state and Maggie's stooges. In fact we wrote about all the usual political targets. As we played more we got slightly better, we recorded the rehearsals on hand held Binatone and Soundhog cassette recorders, to us they sounded great. Andy showed up one day with a new fuzzbox, it made his guitar buzz even more like an angry wasp caught in the Ramones guitar amp! We walked around like a gang and all was going well until…

Our prime minister, Maggie Thatcher, whilst festering in the opinion polls engaged in an illegal war with Argentina, the start of hostilities from the UK was the sinking of the Belgrano whilst it was sailing away from the exclusion zone around the Falklands. After a jingoistic build up 'our lads' sailed to the Falklands and fought a war resulting in the deaths of between 900 and 1300 soldiers and the maiming and injuring of several hundred others. From feeling we could change the world the world had been changed in front of our eyes, the carpet pulled from under the punk and wider protest movement and the political landscape in this country was changed forever…

Andy left Necro to sing for his brothers band Virus V1. (Skinner on guitar, Andy on vocals, Richard on bass and Russ on drums). Necro was left directionless and a bit let down. Steve, Bill and I toyed about but without Andy's bar chords and one string guitar leads driving us forward we didn't know what to do. Another Andy joined us on guitar briefly but it didn't quite work out. As Virus V1 and Onslaught gained a reputation and played more gigs, Necro languished in those bands shadow. Into the Autumn of 1982. Paul, another friend and a proper bonafide guitarist came to our rescue. We rehearsed new songs, landed a CND benefit gig at the prestigious Times club in glamorous Stevenage and were ready again to take on the world. We swapped the fuzz box for a more 'pop' Clash influenced sound. I'd learnt to keep time, Bill could walk a bass-line, Steve's lyrics were intelligent and personal. The first song we wrote during this line up was about the self-expression of spray-painting. At this time 'graffiti' artists were not about getting exhibitions at art galleries. Walls and hoardings were fair game and there for political slogans and ideas to be painted onto. For the Times club gig, we took a coach load of mates over and got the blame for the windows being smashed later that night!

[Penguin remembers Virus V1 had a distinct Discharge sound and Andy had spikes which were similar to Cal from Discharge at that time; Virus V1 and Necro went to Stevenage Bowes Lyon house for a Subhumans / Omega Tribe gig and Virus V1 were first on support for that night.]

In true Necro form things fell apart again, Paul left to pursue a more musical direction, and Bill petulantly declared he needed to play with proper musicians. The gloves were off and Steve and I were looking for a guitarist and bassist. Rob Baxter came along with a bass guitar and a top record collection no doubt some pilfered from elder brother Mickey (at some point much later in the 1980's to be known as 'Penguin'). Simon was a friend from another band who joined on guitar. Although Simon was a good friend he didn't really get what we wanted to do and after a disastrous gig at the Triad club in Bishops Stortford, noted for all four of us travelling in Rob and Mickey's dads car with a guitar amp across our collective legs, a confrontation with skinhead nazis and sadly missing out on a trick as Steve and Simon from the Newtown Neurotics along with Colin from Flux were in the audience to witness our band Necro's performance. I very much doubt that performance impressed them.

[Rob at fourteen years old at the time of Necro with donkey jacket and Spurs scarf.]

Simon left and we were on the search for another guitarist. We rehearsed with a heavy metal freak called Martyn, but those rehearsals were thankfully short lived. So the solution came from within the band itself. Rob was learning the guitar and Steve the bass, so it made sense to follow our noses and become a three piece. I think rehearsals were probably torturous for my mum and dads neighbours, but we battled on and the sound took on a more raw quality. The cassettes of these rehearsals sounded ok and we had a couple of gigs to aim for. Rob developed a nice trebly sound to his guitar, which was exciting and angular and Steve could hold a simple bass-line down as he shouted along.

[Penguin remembers Rob painting a back drop for Necro on an old bed sheet – He used the wrong kind of paint so it was not that easy to fold the sheet after the paint had dried onto it, in fact impossible, it was like folding a garden fence!]

Gig number one as a three piece was at the Rye Road youth club in Hoddesdon in February 1983, it had been a snowy, cold, wet winter and a thick layer of slush lay on the roads as the mini-bus we were using with mates in pulled up outside the youth club. Myself and Steve not really knowing the Hoddesdon scene that well, chatted to the other bands and got to know each other. Rob and his brother Mickey lived just around the corner to this youth club in this rather unglamorous town with a large skinhead population on the Essex / Hertfordshire border. Necro played, we were quite good, there was a bit of agro from some Hoddesdon skinheads and then the Malteser incident happened! What was a single malteser wittily sent flying at the band by someone in the audience, which I thought was hilarious, soon turned into Necro being maltesered off the stage in local Hoddesdon folk-law! I only wish our exit had been that dramatic! Some of the local skinheads threw lighted match boxes (full of a complete set of now ignited matches) at Rob's head several times throughout the heckling, but that was good natured (I think) as Rob and Mickey vaguely knew those skinheads.

[Penguin remembers Necro also performed at the Rye House Tavern in Hoddesdon in front of the same skinheads around this time and it was well behaved, it had to be as in those days the landlord ruled those skinheads with an iron fist. The band were not allowed to drink alcohol in the pub though, being at least two or three years under age.]

By the summer of 1983 Thatcher had singlehandedly claimed victory in the Falklands, had broken much of the trade union movement and weathered the storms of northern Ireland and the riots. She was returned to power in the general election with a landslide majority, for those who thought the battle was being won, how wrong we were. Worse (or at best more of the same) was to come in the form of the breaking of the miners' strike during the Orwellian year 1984, the dismantling of local government as it then stood and the erosion of personal freedoms. Whatever in-roads the movement had made, or believed it had made, were spat back out. The in-roads became personal journeys of awakenings and realisation for individuals and groups of likeminded people, but any sting we hoped we'd make on the government or the 'system' was swatted away by the media, the police and the army. A vivid memory of this time is going on the CND demonstration at Greenham Common on April 1st of that year. We arrived early and stood around talking to each other and groups of police, who were quite chatty and kept telling us that not many protesters were going to come along. Then some coaches appeared on the horizon, followed by some-more; then a never ending convoy headed towards the air-base, 'fair-cop gov'! The US airbase was surrounded and we marched in tight formation, as you got to the top of one hill the ground would dip down to reveal thousands upon thousands of people, wearing black (the chosen colour of the movement), in a sea of protest, there was certainly no lack of a feeling of strength.

[Penguin remembers Necro, Virus V1 and I think Onslaught were billed to perform with Conflict at the Tudor Hall in Hoddesdon, a gig that Tim from Necro part organised but sadly never happened due to threats to the venue from the NF skinheads in the area, later to be highlighted by Tim as the main article in the Sounds music paper letter pages.]

The next gig was to be at the Hartham peace festival in Hertford. Myself, Steve and other friends had been instrumental in organising the festival. A friendly lorry driver had been persuaded to park his lorry there to form the stage, it was true DIY and we had bagged Flux Of Pink Indians to headline. Necro were to be performing second on the bill with a host of other local bands in what was planned as a celebratory afternoon in aid of CND, but in true fashion things didn't quite go according to plan.

[Rob with some school friends turning up to the Hartham common gig ready to support Flux Of Pink Indians; which sadly did not happen.]

We and other CND factions marched from Ware to Hertford and arrived on Hartham common to be greeted by a large group of NF skinheads. Peace festival this was not going to be. Some of the NF skinheads were from further afield, Harlow and Stevenage, but many of them were idiots that could be seen in and around Hertford starting fights and generally being arseholes. With these also came a largish police presence, who were unwilling to ask the NF to leave. Wonder why? Me too…!

[Penguin remembers the march to Hertford County Hall at the end of the CND march where Steve, the vocalist from Necro unfolded a Crass 'Nagasaki Nightmare' sleeve and read from it word for word to the crowd in attendance whilst the poster was being blown around by the wind. I think it ended up ripped in half!]

It became clear that the tight time plan for the festival had gone and the time slots allocated to the support bands had just slipped away, Flux were planning to meet the NF face on was the little information that I had to explain this to other people and band members. Apologies were made to the local bands as we all walked around with guitars and drumsticks looking lost. Flux had brought a band called D & V with them who played a short set, then Flux took the stage and Derek Birkett, in an attempt to show the stupidity of the NF's arguments offered them some of their set time to debate the issues on stage, refer to a previous KYPP post for a recording made on my Binotone cassette recorder for the full debate. Flux's strategy worked and the NF 'intelligensia' took the stage. He could string three words together almost coherently, he contradicted himself, said he'd prefer to be called a nazi and generally proved what a bunch of misguided and nasty bastards they were. Flux then played a glorious set with the steps up to the 'stage' being guarded by a single police officer!

The PA during Flux Of Pink Indians set was so loud that a wedding in a nearby church had to be stopped as they couldn't hear what was being said. One of the elders of the festival organisers did mention to me that he hadn't been told that this would happen… Truth was, no-one knew…

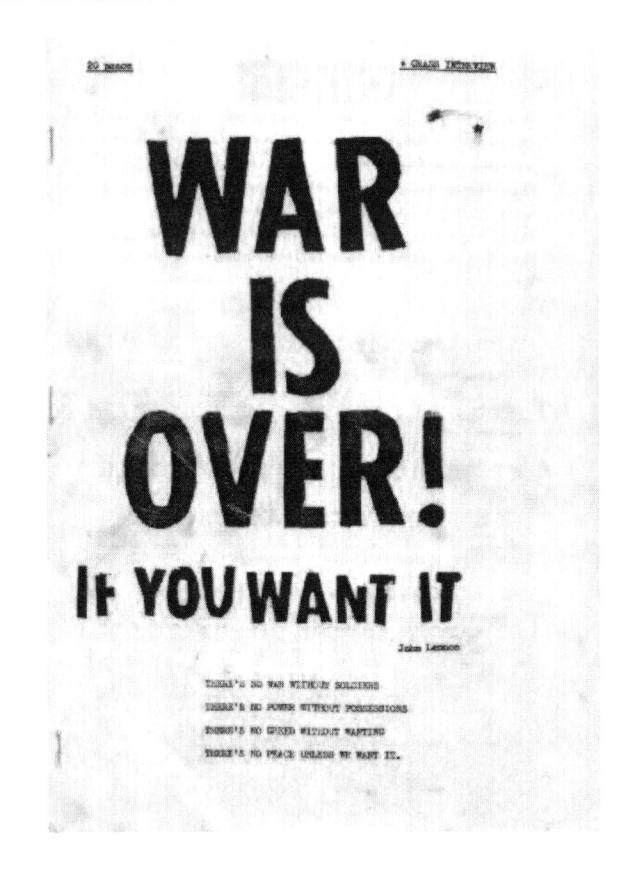

[Penguin remembers around this time Tim from Necro produced the only issue of his fanzine 'War Is Over' which had pieces on animal rights, the riots from the previous year and of course the obligatory Crass interview (with Pete Wright on a visit to Dial House) amongst its pages.]

After the Hartham peace festival, Steve who I had a feeling had been thinking of moving on decided to leave the band. I was quite upset. Steve had become my closest mate and the band had been a platform for that friendship. But I knew that he'd had enough of it and wanted to concentrate on other things in his life. Although I'd formed a good friendship with Rob, and we both tried to carry on for a short while, Necro wasn't going to work without the main lyricist and vocalist so the band just drifted to an end. I did feel a little bit guilty about the band finishing just as Rob had started to stamp his mark on it but that's rock'n'roll folks!

Although only a tiny bubble in our local music scene, the era of Necro and the other bands Onslaught and Virus V1 was a gloriously creative time where almost all things seemed possible and maybe they were. The bubble burst around the time of the Hartham peace festival. The backdrop of politics at the time was crucial to both the development and ending of the movement and maybe moving onto to try and change things in different ways was the right way to go…But above all the times were fun!

[Penguin remembers buying The Onslaught 7" single from Kensington Our Price record shop towards the end of the summer in 1983, a rare and fine record indeed. It was released by Mark Flunder who was a well known face in the Hertford scene. Mark had a stint performing and recording with the Television Personalities in 1982 and was also involved (in an organisational way) with The Marine Girls and Ten Cubic Feet. He performed later on in the McTells, and much later on in Sportique and Cee Cee Beaumont – Matt the guitarist of Onslaught joined up with west country band Idiot Strength as that bands drummer. Matt sadly is no longer with us.]

Rob as a guitarist helped to form other bands throughout the rest of the 1980's

[Penguin remembers one of Rob's latter bands were banned from the Harlow Square due to the vocalist taking all his clothes off and hanging upside down from the lighting rig. Rob performing the gig at the time did not notice this oddity on the stage but only knew when I told him later on after the band had wandered off the stage. How he missed that I still do not know! Rob must have been well out of it. Rob was also in a band with one of our dear friends Simon N who later on became known as Ossian Brown. Ossian now performs in Cyclobe. Rob has now lived in Sheffield for decades and is an art teacher.]

I joined a band from Hoddesdon called Strontium 90 (of which Paul, ex Necro, was already in), Andy was sacked from Virus V1 for singing too weirdly and shortly afterwards trained to become a P.E teacher. Bill got a tattoo!

ALL MATERIAL FROM MICKEY 'PENGUIN'S COLLECTION except the photographs credited which are from Andy Lane's collection.

Photograph of Tim taken by Mickey 'Penguin' at Steve Ignorant's last night of performing Crass songs. Thanks for the essay you wrote for Kill Your Pet Puppy Tim.

Tumbleweeds.

Ted Curtis

WILDLY I DRIBBLED ON A HIGH ROCK

Poems and other Gems by

DESMOND FAIRYBREATH

It's the night of the last ever Subhumans gig, a proper farewell concert, so long and thanks for all the vegan fish, and they've booked out the all-seater Warminster Arts Centre theatre to make it a proper spectacular. You may think that makes this a recent history story but no, it's the summer of 1985, and the farewell gig will be, as with Status Quo, the first of many. You have never seen them, you missed all the legendary Walcot Village Hall 50p concerts with sex and cider in the graveyard, the Julian Barnett inspired near-riots, breezeblocks through the windows, fighting in the middle of the road. You had seen their records in Cruisin' and Records Unlimited but thought they must be some class of anti-intellectual morons to actually call themselves the subhumans, and so you hadn't bothered with them. Since then you've acquired their music osmotically, through their LPs and singles being played so incessantly in freezing squats like Railway Place, Railway Buildings, Comfortable Place, Cleveland Row, and you've grown to like the majority of it, although their attempt at aping Yes Sir I Will, From the Cradle to the Grave, doesn't quite hit it with you. Reality is waiting for a bus.

You get the train from Bath, along with Taff, Owen Llewellyn Grainger Jones, from school – known as the man with the sun in his hair on account of an orange sideways Mohican, which he believes to be completely original, as if he has never been to London and walked down the Kings Road. His major claim to fame, other than the haircut, seems to be that he went to boarding school in Surrey with Joe McClaren, son of Malcolm and Vivienne Westwood, and later proprietor of Agent Provocateur, and he likes to talk about this a lot. Also along for the ride is Adrian Armit, a Royal Navy absconder who hangs out with the smartpils and claims to have invented the genre gothick punx. He is a thoughtful and enthusiastic solvent abuser, who calls and styles himself Merlin De'Ath. He has brought fruit, he's fun to travel with.

Your journey is uneventful and you manage to dodge the fare. At the Warminster end, the station is like a ghost town in a horror film from the previous decade: the 1970s have not yet become fashionable again, they are too recent, they are still profoundly naff. For some reason the day chosen for the big farewell concert is a Sunday. You are walking down the deserted high street, wondering which way you ought to be going. You have no clue where the arts centre is, the flyer didn't say and you didn't bring it with you anyway. You thought it would be easy to find, what with it being such a momentous occasion and all. Usually with underground punk gigs, if the venue is in a distant small town, all you have to do is wander around for a little while until you bump into some other punks who are wandering around, then ask them where the gig is. Someone always knows, but those gigs are invariably held on Fridays and Saturdays, never on a Sunday. The three of you wander down Station Road in abject silence and wonder, it's the right side of the tracks but there's still nothing happening, walking in the opposite direction would have taken you to Copheap Lane and the West Wiltshire Golf Club. The footfalls of your vegan espadrilles echo in the eerie quiet as you look from side to side, watching the tumbleweeds blow across your path in the eerie quiet, such a tiny place, nothing all like the sophisticated big city vibe of metropolitan Bath, no, nothing like that here, the Sunday licensing laws religiously observed. Then you reach the bottom of Station Road. It's a T-junction: do you turn left, or do you turn right? You look back up at the station. It is topped off by a clock, you see that it's 4pm. You look at the others, they have stopped walking too. It's like the first crucial point in a video game. The first decision. Their faces are completely blank. Taff rubs some dust from his eyes, then Merlin De'Ath does the same. Their hands drop back to their sides in unison. Maybe you really are in a video game, although the only one you've ever played is Binatone tennis. Ba-doink. Ba-doink. Ba-doink. Merlin De'Ath licks his lips, swallows, sniffs. Then you speak.

At first your throat is too dry. You have to swallow some saliva in order to begin.

"Is it left or is it right?" you say, before blinking some dust away and swallowing again. You can feel it in your nose now too, irritating the little hairs.

"Ah, the eternal question, young Frank!" says Taff, with a smug grin, his head cocked to the side. He is taller than he looks. On his bass guitar he has written IRA=crap. You have no idea what this means. He's not really a musician. He can play the bassline for tube disasters but his timing is all out. On the train journey here he'd told you how negative you always are, then looked out the window at the fields and the trees, grinning. Always grinning.

"Have either of you been here before?" you ask, looking first at him, then at Merlin De'Ath, who has begun nervously chewing on a fingernail.

"Never in me life mate, and I've been to a lot of places!" says Merlin De'Ath. He is always telling you this. For some reason it makes you think of the Philippines.

"There's a sign behind you, look Frankie!" says Taff, pointing over your shoulder. He's still grinning. He seems to have grown another inch.

You turn around. Across the street there it is, give us a sign Lord you think, you were expecting it to be obscured with thick dust but it seems that the dust is mostly in your head, a tendrilsome outgrowth of the vibe from the dead Sunday afternoon and the dead little town in the middle of Nowhere, Wiltshire. The sign points right. The sign says, town centre.

"It's right," says Taff. "It's not left, it's right. C'mon, let's go."

Taff leads the way now. His stride is purposeful, his head up as he walks down the centre of the road, he's way ahead of you. Neither you nor Merlin De'Ath speak. Your heads are both down. It still seems dusty, a couple more tumbleweeds blow across your path. Merlin De'Ath seems not to notice them, you are not sure whether they are real. Two minutes later you are in the town centre. There are a few shops that look as if they ought to be boarded up, but aren't. There are a couple of benches and some large concrete basins filled with vegetation, not quite flowers. It's the right time of year for flowers but there aren't any. You stop, look around. Nothing. Taff stops suddenly in his tracks, looks up at the sky, sniffs the air like Hannibal Lecter. He closes his eyes, inhales deeply, holds it there. He spreads his arms wide, then lets his breath out slowly. And just as this happens, Pete the Roadie appears, emerging from a red telephone box you hadn't noticed was there, its door permanently askew at twenty degrees, one of the hinges rusted clean through. He has to clamber around it to exit the phone box. He sees Taff standing there in the road, silently beseeching the heavens, eyes closed, grinning.

"Taff!" yells Pete the Roadie, striding over towards him. When he gets nearer they hug, Taff dwarfing him. He is so tall that his head is on Taff's chest. His pork pie hat is knocked askew by the closeness of the embrace. Pete the Roadie is grinning too, his eyes squeezed shut. He is not a particularly short man. You are sure that Taff was not this tall on the train. You are not sure what is happening.

Finally they break, stand half a foot apart, their fingertips still touching, considering one another. They talk very quietly about you-don't-know-what, you can't hear what they're saying, they seem to be whispering. Eventually Taff gives a brief backward nod of his head in your direction, and Pete the Roadie looks over, straightens his hat on his head, sees you there. He beams, raises one eyebrow. Walks across to you. Neither you nor Merlin De'Ath have moved so much as an inch this whole time.

"Merlin De'Ath me old mucker, as I live and breathe!" says Pete the Roadie as he skips into Merlin De'Ath's personal space like a jester, simultaneously mock-punching him playfully in the shoulder. The crusty-mockney thing is just catching on in Wiltshire. Merlin

De'Ath is definitely at least a whole head taller than Pete the Roadie, he's still taller than Taff even after Taff's mysterious growth spurt, it must be a navy thing you think, Merlin De'Ath was in the navy, and you notice that Pete the Roadie has to properly stretch his arm out just to reach Merlin De'Ath's shoulder. It's a bit of a strain just for a playful gesture. It's all a bit homo-erotic, you think, as you stand there looking sheepishly down at your vegan black espadrilles, letting them get on with it. Then they do the hugging thing too, Pete the Roadie's face crushed sideways onto Merlin De'Ath's sweaty chest, his cheek adhering to his pectoral muscles through his black string vest, his pork pie hat once more askew. Merlin De'Ath looks over at you with a kind of deadpan smirk, letting you know he isn't taking any of this BFF nonsense too seriously. When they break, Pete the Roadie has to almost peel himself off Merlin De'Ath's chest. He stands there, momentarily dazed, then looks across at you. His eyes seem to glaze over. Behind him, another tumbleweed blows across the street.

"Who's this cunt?" he finally asks, his eyes demisting as he stares straight at you. You've met before, you've drunk Special Brew and Buckfast wine and scrumpy together on countless stone steps outside innumerable community halls, as bands who are either not worth watching or who play so often that one more time won't make any difference one way or another, have gone through their paces or the motions inside. You've sat up late afterwards in damp freezing squats and deserted bus stations, putting the world to rights and waiting for the next big thing to happen. But he doesn't recognise you. Even with his eyes demisted, he doesn't recognise you.

"You two know each other dontcha?" Merlin De'Ath says, after a moment.

"Yeah, course" Pete the Roadie says, looking you in the eye again, smiling slightly, one half-closed, as though trying to focus. He looks a little like the crowman from the Catweazle television series. The crowman often appeared bemused, but the unspoken constant was that he always knew exactly what was going on. Like Pete the Roadie.

"Um, Chris, right?" Pete the Roadie says.

"Frank, Pete," you tell him.

"Frank. Yeah, course, how you doing Frank?"

He puts out his hand for you to shake, and you grasp it briefly, moving it up and down. He has a very light handshake, it's almost limp. There will be no hugging between you, you at least have that much to be grateful for. Then he turns in the opposite direction from Taff and starts walking.

"Come on lads," he says, calling over his shoulder, "everyone's at East Street. This way!"

Taff and Merlin De'Ath start after him. You skip past them to catch up with Pete the Roadie, wanting to chat, thinking that perhaps he does remember you after all. All those drunken amphetamine nights, all those conversations, you often more pissed than him, surely something must have stuck in his head? It doesn't occur to you that not everybody is like you, that hardly anyone is like you, that most people have a lot more friends than you do, that somebody like Pete the Roadie probably has about a million friends.

"How come you're not at the gig yet Pete?" you say, "you know, all busy-busy doing your thing and that?"

He turns to you, a cheeky smirk on his face, a glint in his eye. Just for a moment you see the Pete the Roadie you remember from those million nights, the Pete the Roadie you had almost begun to believe was nothing but a figment, and you regret spot-judging him on his handshake, you feel bad about feeling a little put out that he didn't remember you, and a sensation of guilt rushes in. Maybe that's how the world is for me you think, it's either rage or guilt. I wonder how it is for everyone else.

"Big place like that, they got their own people, Frank mate," Pete the Roadie says. "It's all over for the little guy, even in Warminster." And then he chuckles, looks back down at his boots as he walks. You still don't think he remembers you though. Why would he? He's just being nice. You look back over your shoulder at Taff and Merlin De'Ath, you see that Taff is now bringing up the rear, head down, his £5 vegan black baseball boots scuffing through the dust, little puffs of it rising up to obscure his turnups. He hasn't shrunk any though. The mystery deepens. Behind his powdery heels, two more tumbleweeds blow across the street.

Number 44 East Street is crammed to the gills. There is

overspill onto the pavement, people stand around talking ten to the dozen and drinking weak lager from half-crushed tins, making the most of the summer weather as the boiling red sun lowers in the sky above the treetops across the street. Pete the Roadie seems to know them all. He nods and says hello to each and every one of them as he passes, squeezing through a little at a time, hunching up his shoulders, heading for the open door. The three of you do likewise and follow him. You nod and smile at random individual as if it is the thing to do. Then you are inside.

The hallway is even more crowded than the street: innumerable lank and greasy crazy-coloured mohawks sit cross-legged in the demi-monde light all the way along both walls, topping off variform perfect punk uniforms who are busy making roll-ups, rolling joints, swagging scrumpy from plastic gallon containers, like active participants in a game of post-apocalyptic sardines. There's a level of background chatter not unlike the beginning of that Omega Tribe song that begins people talking all around me, all their words just seem to drown me and there's the smell of cider and sweat, it's everywhere, it's making your eyes sing just stumbling through it. Still following Pete the Roadie's lead, you squeeze through and step over them all, force your way after him into a large sitting room where there is air, where there are upturned sofas, gutted armchairs, posters from the 1960s and 1970s hanging off the walls, Why? a cartoon Jimi Hendrix with burning joint, space-case lettering informing the casual observer that it's 1969, do whatever thou wilt, a promotional poster in identical script for the Windor Great Park Free 1974. Here as in the hallway, people sit wherever they can, but here there are not that many of them and there's room to breathe. The fug in the hallway surely could not have been tolerated for more than the minute it took to negotiate its length, without specialised breathing apparatus. You put your hands on your hips, look up at the ceiling and immediately think of the current pop song living on the ceiling. The ceiling itself is nondescript, it's just a ceiling. Pete the Roadie stops in the centre of the room, turns, says something. Although the room is quiet he seems to be speaking at you from a distance, as if at the end of a long tunnel, perhaps a disused sewage pipe that surfaces somewhere in the middle of some stretch of wasteground in West Swindon, the ash pits, fire pits, the pipes. Perhaps there is dust in your ears, real or otherwise. You ask him to repeat himself.

"I said I just got to see a man about a dog, you know what I mean Frank? You three'll be alright here won't you? Make yourselves at home and that, like."

Then he turns and disappears into the kitchen.

Taff looks around, then immediately recognises somebody leaning against the wall next to the doorway you just walked through. He is dressed all in black in the underground punk style: black drill jeans, black Doctor Marten boots, black leather jacket. Apart from that, he seems to have modelled himself on Dick Lucas from the Subhumans. The hair is the same, but he seems to have the same face too, as if they are somehow related. Perhaps they are you think, maybe everyone in rural Wiltshire is, like everybody in Western Europe is supposed to be descended from Charlemagne. Years later you will be present at the Longacre Hall in Bath as Neil from Wroughton, also in Wiltshire, winds Bill from Calne up with stories about how Dick Lucas from the Subhumans is a pop star now, how he drives a Porsche Turbo home after gigs, refusing to help with the gear, refusing to give anybody a lift because of the restrictions of his expensive motor insurance. Bastard, Bill from Calne will say. Yeah, Neil from Wroughton will reply, trying not to laugh.

"Bill from Calne, how you doing mate?" Taff says enthusiastically, as he strides over to him.

How's your cat?"

Bill from Calne begins detailing veterinary procedures and you tune the conversation out, sit down on the floor. Merlin De'Ath doesn't know Bill from Calne either so he sits down next to you. You cross your legs. Neither of you say anything. Then a large buxom woman who looks a bit psychobilly, a bit Rubella Ballet, comes into the room from the kitchen. It's Merlin De'Ath's girlfriend, Tracey. You recognise her. She made you and Chris Palmer a roast dinner once. Nutroast with all the trimmings, syrupy sponge pudding with custard for afters. You look at Merlin De'Ath and see that he has his head between his knees, his eyes closed. You rap him on one of his knees with your knuckles and he does a little textbook kneejerk reflex then looks up, sees Tracey. She's stopped and she's standing over him, her hands on her hips.

"Trace," he says. "What the fuck are you doing here? I thought you were at your mum's."

"She's gone over to Laycock with that Mr Develish again," she says. "Thought I'd better come keep an eye on you. Alright there Frank?"

You look up, nod.

"So, you want some cider then, or what?" she asks Merlin De'Ath.

"Do I ever!" he exclaims, springing up in one deft movement, like a cat.

"Come on then, droopy wrinkleskin," she says, and together they stroll back into the crowded hallway.

"Alright there Taff, hello again Bill mate," Tracey says as they pass.

"Hello there miss Tracey!" Taff beams at her cleavage, prominently displayed in a lilac and black basque.

Bill from Calne looks up and grunts something vaguely sociable, then goes back to telling Taff all about his grandmother's haemorrhoids. You look around the room. Hardly anybody else is here now. Everyone seems to be either in the kitchen, the hallway or the street outside. You look directly opposite you and see a youth with short black curly hair, wearing a herringbone overcoat and black jeans with the knees out, monkey boots, swagging from a glass bottle of Tizer, perched on one end of an upturned sofa. You think that he is slightly overdressed for a summer's evening. But you remember Tizer. Originally from the north, the name a contraction of the appetizer. The Corona lorry used to bring it round door to door when you were very young and lived just outside of Trowbridge. Since then it seems to have all but disappeared. You nod hello at him and he raises his eyebrows, hands you the bottle. You take a swag, then hold it up to the light that's streaming into the room from the kitchen. There are UFOs inside the bottle. He must have been eating a sandwich before. You wonder what might have been in the sandwich, then hand the bottle back to him.

"Good bit of stuff that, mate," you say as he takes it from you. He smiles, replaces the cap, puts it into one of the large pockets of the herringbone overcoat. He is looking at you now, not saying anything.

"Do I know you mate?" he eventually asks.

You frown, feigning deep thought. For some reason it occurs to you that he is John from Evercreech, three miles from Shepton Mallet in North Somerset. You have been corresponding with John from Evercreech for about six months, you have never met him, you don't know what he looks like but you have a picture of him in your head. John from Evercreech runs a miniscule underground punk tape distro, Evercreech Tapes. You have bought a couple from him, a compilation called killing to be clever that's a fundraiser for the South Devon Hunt Saboteurs Association, and the mob live at meanwhile gardens, '83. Killing to be clever is a sarcastic nod to the Culture Club LP Kissing to be Clever. You lean forward.

"I don't know," you say, still frowning. "You aren't John from Evercreech are you?"

"No, mate," he says with a sigh. "No, I'm not." He looks down at his monkey boots. He doesn't say who he is. He seems to have no accent. Certainly not Somerset. In your head, you hear the sound of tumbleweeds blowing across the street again. You rub at one eye as if there is dust there. All of this makes you all the more certain that he really is John from Evercreech.

"Are you sure, mate?" you ask him. "Are you sure you're not John from Evercreech?"

This seems to really rankle him. He stands, wraps his herringbone coat around himself as though it has suddenly got very cold in the room, although you're pretty sure it hasn't.

"I've fucking had enough of this," he says, standing and sashaying out into the hallway.

"I'm sure you're John from Evercreech," you call out after him. "It's near Shepton Mallet!" It's the best you can do.

The sound of wind and tumbleweeds in your head ceases as Pete the Roadie comes back in from the kitchen, or wherever it is he has been all this time, which has really been no time at all. The room is still empty except for Taff and Bill from Calne leaning against the doorframe, discussing grandmothers, cats and piles. You stand. Pete the Roadie stops just short of you, grins. He slaps himself around the face a couple of times with the palms of both hands.

"Ooh, that's better Frank mate," he says, "I feel much better now."

You stand.

"Who was that just now?" you ask him.

"Who was what?"

"That bloke who was sitting there," you say, pointing at the upturned sofa. "Herringbone overcoat, black curly hair. Thought I recognised him."

"Didn't see him mate."

"You know a John from Evercreech? Near Shepton Mallet? Evercreech Tapes?"

Pete the Roadie pulls a thinking face, squints, looks up into one corner of the ceiling for a few moments. Then he comes back down to earth. His face returns to normal. His cheeks are still slightly flushed from the slapping he's just given himself. His pupils are like pinpricks. His breath smells of mouthwash.

"Nah, don't think so Frank," he finally says. He puts his hands on his hips, exhales. "I've got to get down to the gig now, mate. You wanna come? You doing anything here?"

You look around the empty room with your eyes for comedic effect, give a slight shrug.

"Come on then," he says, laughing. "Hey, where'd Merlin get to?"

"Tracey came and spirited him away to the off license for cider."

"Good luck with that, mate," Pete the Roadie says. "It's a fucking Sunday afternoon in Warminster."

You walk out into the hallway. It's still crowded as all hell, only there's a slight tang of puke in the air now too. Taff moves to one side as you pass, puts one palm up in silent acknowledgement. Bill from Calne looks up at you, then down again. His lips don't stop moving as he tells Taff all about how GDP interacts with the RPI.

He's been reading all about it on Ceefax.

Making your way down the street, back towards Warminster central, you notice the midges in the air for the first time. Your veganism forbids you from swatting at them. If one flies into your mouth and down your throat, it's a sin. But it's a perfect summer's evening. Pete the Roadie seems lost in thought.

"I feel weird," he says as you walk. "The Subhumans are playing and I've got the night off, sort of. That hasn't happened since, what, 1980?"

"You're like the fifth Beatle, Pete," you say.

"I am like the fifth Beatle. No I'm not, I'm the fifth Subhuman!"

Pete the Roadie laughs. You laugh. Pete the Roadie laughs again, and then you are there. It's taken you five minutes to get from the suburbs of Warminster to the downtown. There's a slight crowd milling around Warminster Arts Centre now. You scan it for familiar faces. There's a billboard planted in a small flower garden out front, advertising a forthcoming poetry recital, Wildly I Dribbled on a High Rock, a new collection from Desmond Fairybreath. You look at the billboard but that's all the information given, other than the date, which is tomorrow. You wonder whether it will be any good. You wonder whether it will be better than the Subhumans, more transformative. You doubt it, and anyway, you wouldn't like to travel to Warminster on consecutive days. It might get to become a habit. You might end up moving here.

You look around again, see a face in the crowd you think you know. It's Steve Membury, a part-time punk from school. He wasn't at your school, you knew him through Nicky Baylun from Larkhall, you hung out with him a couple of times, together with another Larkhall punk named Mess, a bastardization of his Italian surname, DiMassimo. Mess was known for deliberately pissing himself rather than sort out which was his fly zipper from among all his bondage straps. That may have been a joke, you never saw it happen. You're pretty sure you saw Rowan Atkinson almost doing it on Not the Nine O'Clock News once. You ran into him again, Steve Membury, at a Stiff Little Fingers gig at the Colston Hall in Bristol, where Steve from Crass saw The Clash all those years before and got himself all inspired. Steve Membury didn't have a ticket for the Stiff Little Fingers gig, he had snuck in with some other people through the fire escape, and in the bar he had persuaded you, against your better judgement, to hand over your ticket stub. You'll be all right mate, he had said, they won't be looking for you. You were there with the future DCI Stephen Rowe and Clare Murphy, his current squeeze from the upper sixth. When they came round looking for people without tickets, you had made yourself small behind a big fat exploited fan who looked like Big John, their bass player. You had a narrow escape. Afterwards, the future DCI Stephen Rowe had called you an idiot. Stiff Little Fingers were good, they had played OK. The support group were The Wall. They were shit. It was the Go For It tour.

Tonight Steve Membury is still looking very Stiff Little Fingers. He has black jeans, white Rucanor baseball boots, one of those biker jackets with the lapels stained white, like Jake Burns wears. Lightly spiked hair, no soap. You walk over to him.

"All right mate," you say. He squints at you.

"You seem familiar," he says.

"I'm Frank from Ralph Allen." Ralph Allen was the name of your school, it was named after the man who made all the money from Bath Stone. "Mate of Nicky Baylun's," you add, for emphasis.

"Oh, right." He says. "Yeah think I remember you. You got a ticket?"

You crinkle your nose at the memory of the Stiff Little Fingers gig, but he doesn't notice.

"Nah mate, think I've got an in with someone," you say. "You see any of the old gang around still? Mess? Sheridan?"

"That cunt owes me a fiver," he says, spitting onto one of his Rucanors. This surprises you. You haven't seen anybody do that before. It must be some new mainstream punk thing you haven't heard about yet. Then, without even a cheerio, he wanders off, over to some young and local gothettes, begging for change and cigarettes. He seems very spick and span for a beggar.

When you look around again, you see that Pete the Roadie has gone. You look up at the sky. The sun is lowering behind the trees, it seems to have only dropped an inch since the last time you looked. The night is about to begin.

The Squatting Years

Gail Thibert

NIGHTINGALE ESTATE, HACKNEY

Cheryl; whom I'd met via my Sounds advert a few years before and her boyfriend Mal, lived in a squatted flat on the top floor (the 21st floor) of a tower block on the notorious Nightingale Estate in Hackney. It was such a dump that it's nickname was the 'Nightmare estate'. Many of the other flats near the top floor were also squatted and there was a small community amongst the squatters, including a group of Italians who were running away from conscription, all looking out for each other.

Cheryl knew I was depressed living back in Morden. I was isolated and lonely and there was nowhere decent to go out to - all the good things were happening in London, a tube ride away. They had a spare room and offered it to me.

My dad had also suggested I leave home after my ferrets caused him an embarrassment - they had somehow found their way into my parent's room one morning and then came running back into mine. Verity [the ferret] had with something in her mouth. I took it from her and realised with horror that it was actually a sex toy!

Unsure of exactly where she'd found it, made it difficult for me to return it with no one noticing.

There was no avoiding it; wherever I put it, it was bound to be the wrong place. So I left it on my parent's bed. No point hiding it I'd probably have put it back in the wrong place and that would arouse even more suspicion- besides, they might think I had borrowed it and I didn't want to even think about that! I waited to see what was said about it. I said nothing. Later that evening, my mum approached me.

'I think you found something of ours…' she started a little awkwardly.

'Oh! I'm sorry about that,' I replied, realising what she was referring to.

'It was my ferrets- they found it and I didn't know where they got it from.. .' I replied equally embarrassed.

Well, it's erm, your dad's… you know what men are like - never think they are big enough…' she tried to explain, giving me more detail than I wanted or needed.

Well, dad was embarrassed and it was a case of the ferrets go or I go. I was very attached to my pets, so decided it was time for me to move on once again.

Consequently, I eagerly accepted the spare room in Hackney and moved in right away. There was also a big room for the ferrets to run around in, a large cupboard in the hallway, but as it had no windows, we kept the lights on in that room most of the time.

Looking back, I shouldn't have taken the pets on. I had little idea how to look after them, but Mal liked them and we would both let them have the run of the flat on a daily basis. They were cute and entertaining, like hyperactive squirrels, all bends and bouncy, they were a delight to watch.

Moving my few bags of possessions into the room, I was confronted with about 50 dead flies on the floor by the window. I duly swept them up and thankfully no live ones re appeared. We had no idea where they came from! Again I had a single mattress on the floor provided by Cheryl and Mal. I had no idea where it came from. I still had very few possessions, but my keyboards travelled everywhere with me. The flat had just a two bar electric heater in the living room- no other heating anywhere else, so the bedrooms were freezing in the winter. We were paying for the electricity and always careful of what we used as we were all skint and out of work.

Mal and Cheryl were very sociable. Cheryl came from Devon and Mal from Cornwall. They often had friends staying over who would sleep on a spare mattress on the floor of the living room after we had been to gigs together.

Cheryl's hair was so outrageous people would stare at her in the street. She had huge foot long spikes formed from her hair. Green on one side and orange the other, with black sides and shaved bits. Very original. It could take her 3 hours to form it into spikes and she wouldn't leave the flat until it was perfect. She would start by crimping and backcombing and then form it into the spikes with half a can of hairspray. I swear us punks were responsible for the holes in the ozone layer!

I was still friends with Addy, whom I had also met via the Sounds advert, had competing punk hair and clothes. Addy's hair was bleached blonde and soaked up into huge foot long spikes that we referred to as 'ice-cream cones' because it looked like someone had stuck a whole load of inverted ice cream cones on her head. One day, out of the blue, she told me she had got married. I didn't even know she'd been seeing anyone. Turned out she married a man she'd only met two weeks previously. He'd just come out of jail and wanting to make a good impression to his parole officer, had asked Addy to marry him. When I met him, he had a skinhead hair cut and a moustache that didn't suit him. Addy soon had him clean shaven and next time I saw them, he had a double Mohican with pink tips. Addys husband was friendly. But he soon took over conversations. If I was talking to Addy at a gig, he would join in and the take over, pushing her out.

Soon Addy was pregnant with her first child and he became even more possessive and domineering. They visited me at the squat and we sat about drinking beers before going out. Although punk looking, Cheryl was neat and tidy and clean. She went to use the toilet shortly after Addy's husband had come out. And had found urine on the floor. She confronted him about it, but he denied it was him. There was no way it was anyone else but he just wouldn't own up. It got cleaned up and later he whispered to me that it WAS him.

It was becoming impossible to talk to Addy when he was around. He pushed all her friends away. I later heard, after she'd had her second child with him that she moved back to her mum's after he had punched her. They later divorced.

Another visitor was a punk called Pus. He was part of the 'Hackney Hell Crew' with whom Cheryl had stayed with when she first came to London. A lot of the punks became 'wasters' and 'Crusties' a waster was someone who didn't want to do anything with their life - just take drugs and get drunk. And a Crusty was someone who let their looks go, but took pride in that. They would wear the same clothes with rips and holes without ever washing them, and let their hair grow into matted dreadlocks. They'd compete over who could get the crustiest. I think Pus fell into both categories of Waster and Crusty, although he didn't have dreads.

Some of the Hackney Hell Crew wouldn't take their Doc Marten boots off for days or weeks at a time and even sleep in them. We heard of people getting gangrene.

Pus turned up on our doorstep one night to visit Mal and Cheryl. He ended up sleeping over, as they couldn't get rid of him. He bought a small puppy with him, which widdled on the floor, much to Cheryl's horror. As soon as Pus was in the flat, his stench penetrated every inch of space. We threw the windows open but it was the middle of winter and it was a choice between breathing or freezing. When I woke the next morning, Pus was still there, asleep on the floor of the living room in front of the electric fire, with both bars on full. Mal never let us use both bars, he always said to put more layers on if we were cold . We would often sit there in jumpers and coats with our duvets round us, huddled in front of the one bar. Pus eventually left and there was a deep black mark on the pillow he's used, that never washed out. The flat stank for weeks despite open windows and air fresheners.

Years later we heard Pus had died. Some stabbing incident over drugs.

Like myself, Cheryl had gone to art school and had aspirations of being a clothes designer. She had done a course in textiles and knew how to pattern cut. She started making punk clothes mainly in black cotton drill and had her own 'Damage' label printed. She knew another girl - Jan, who was making jewellery out of old computer components and circuit boards. We decided to take on a stall in Camden market together, splitting the rent three ways. Jan gave up after a few months as she wasn't selling much, but me and Cheryl persevered and I stated selling big chunky silver rings with skulls on-suitable for Goths, bikers and punks. I did ok with that and the ear piercing. Cheryl did ok too but we were never rolling in money, mainly covering the rent and our materials and stock and a few quid extra for beers and clubs at the weekend. We were never going to make it a full time business.

Our stall was in the 'Electric Ballroom' just by Camden tube station. We were casual traders at first, having to put our names down for the pitch at 4am. Cheryl was often the one to do this as she liked to go clubbing and was often going home at that time. I would then turn up at 9am to claim the pitch. We were eventually offered our own permanent pitch which previously belonged to

'Psychic TV' a well known 'Alternative' band.

Trading in the Electric Ballroom was fun. We were going there on the Friday night for a club known as 'Full Tilt' and it would be transformed into the market on the Sunday daytime. A different club ran on the Saturday night but not our sort of music. Every stall was taken with unique original stalls. By the entrance was record traders, stripy tights in every colour combination, spiky rubber bags and then in the main foyer were designer clothes, when designer meant the person selling it was the person who had made it- no Dolce and Gabbana! Although the Ballroom was often crowded, we often struggled to make a decent living from it and decided to call it a day.

Whilst living in Hackney, I had gone to a squat party with Sebastian. I was single, having split up with Martin some time ago and noticed a handsome man with a floppy black Mohican staring at me. I looked up, smiled and ignored him. He seemed to be with a girl anyway. I sat in the living room of the house chatting to Sebastian. We went to a lot of places together and people often thought we were a couple, but we were just mates. When I'd been living in Morden, he was the nearest to me, living in Elephant and Castle, so I often called round to his, on my way to gigs. Sometimes I just turned up and we drank cider . He'd got the ferrets running about the house and they would make tunnels in his dilapidated sofa, disappearing down one end and reappearing at the other. He also had a pet rabbit called 'Stew', which was ironic for a vegan. Sometimes I'd stay over on his sofa and wake up with the ferrets running all over me. I met some of Sebastian's other friends- Dave , Steve and Fiona and Sharon had all been round his at some point when I visited.

We were having a conversation one day about school and Fiona described her old school and spoke about a nun who looked like Batman as she chased pupils across the quad, her habit flowing behind her. I described a similar nun at my old school who I also thought we named Batman.

'Yeah, I think her real name was Sister Beatrix.' I remembered.

'Hang on' said Fiona, 'what school did you go to?' she asked.

Turned out we both went to the same school in Wimbledon- the Ursuline Convent High School for girls! She was in the year younger than me though. we hadn't known each other at school and it was odd finding another punk from the same background. Turned out Fiona lived in Tooting, two stops from Morden.

Anyway, back to the party…

Sebastian was sitting next to me chatting and the handsome man came in on his own and started chatting to us. He introduced himself as Nigel. I thought it was an old fashioned name for someone his age, but it didn't matter, it was just a name. His girlfriend was in another room, passed out. He still kept giving me the eye. He made some reference about me being Sebastian's girlfriend, and Sebastian freaked!

' YUK! No way! I wouldn't go out with HER!' he joked, referring to me, making sure I heard him and got the message.

About a month later, I was at a gig at the Clarendon in Hammersmith. I was sat on the bar, swinging my legs and chatting to some mates, when I saw Nigel. He came over and told me he'd now split with his girlfriend and did I want to go out with him?

We started seeing each other and going to a few gigs together. He always dressed in black and wore pointed black suede Chelsea boots. I would often stay over at his flat in Sunbury while he worked as a fork lift truck driver at a factory. He told me the flat was haunted- there was the ghost of a man who'd come to look for his girlfriend or wife. Nigel had seen him a couple of times, but it didn't bother him, he said.

One night, Nigel had stayed over with me in Hackney. He had to be up super early to get home in time for work. I heard him leave and the door shut behind him. I imagined him taking the lift down all 21 floors, walking out of the estate and down the road to the station, as I snuggled into the warmth of the duvet. Suddenly, I was aware of my bedroom door opening, only it didn't open. I was aware of a 'presence' in my room, just to the side of me. By then I was working in Oddities market and friends with the witches. I had always believed in the supernatural, but I was scared of ghosts. I froze in terror, aware of this presence being aware of me. It hovered nearby, close to the bed and whizzed off to the window.

Maybe I was dreaming?

I pinched myself to check [that's what you are meant to do isn't it?] I checked my eyes were open, that I was really awake, yes, my eyes were open, I felt the pinch and I could still sense something in my room.

Just as I thought, 'If I go back to sleep and ignore it, it'll go away.' I then felt this spirit entity whoosh through me, entering me by the soles of my feet. I felt it inside my body, wrestling with me, trying to suffocate me. I honestly thought I was going to die. I had never experienced anything like it before.

Fear shot through me. I didn't know what to do.

There was no way I could fight it and I succumbed to the idea that everyone has to die sometime and maybe this was my time, I relaxed. Just as I relaxed, I felt the spirit lose hold of me. I psychically tuned in to what it was and what it wanted before it whooshed away, straight out of my head, through the door and felt the door bang behind it, even though physically, the door didn't move. And that was it. It was gone!

My heart raced as I tried to take in what had just happened. Nigel had told me about the ghost in his house. It must have followed him, attached itself to him. I had heard of spirit attachments, and it must have left him when he went to work and jumped into me. I figured out the spirit was male and looking for his missus. He was angry with me: how dare I be alive and his Mrs not? Maybe he didn't realise he was dead. I'd heard that could happen too.

I couldn't get back to sleep. I didn't sleep for three whole nights, terrified it would happen again- terrified it was still in the flat. I told Cheryl and Mal what had happened, fearing they wouldn't believe me, that I was making it up, but I must have overdone the description because they couldn't sleep that night either.

The morning after it happened, I went to Oddities market as usual. I tried to tell Bill what had happened, but he only half believed me.

'Spirits don't go jumping from one person to another, Gail.' He said when I told him what had happened and that I was scared I had bought it in with me and that it might jump onto him or someone else. I am sure he just thought I was attention seeking.

Later that afternoon, Bill approached me and asked me to repeat what I had told him in the morning. A startled looking woman stood with him.

I described in detail what had happened and the woman was nodding, saying

'Yes! Yes!, that was it!'

She'd been standing by my unit, when she felt the same thing enter her body, stifle her breathing and then leave as fast as it came. It had jumped briefly onto Bill, who'd experienced it for himself.

Now he believed me.

Bill talked me through some psychic protection exercises to stop it happening again.

Nigel was shocked when I told him what had happened. He thought it was attached to the house. It'd never followed him before. He then told me about a friend who'd had a dream about him.

'She dreamt I was at a funeral, but it was MY funeral. She was there, but so was I, alive and following the coffin. She said I was with a girl with bright orange hair and a green army jacket. '

We were both stunned. I was the girl she had described. My hair was bright orange at that time and I always wore bright colours and a green camouflage jacket I had designed and made myself. The girl had never met me yet described me so accurately. We wondered what the dream could mean, but thankfully, Nigel was still alive and well several years later when I last bumped into him, it could have been she foresaw the end of the relationship as we parted not long after, and yes, I was sad.

A Selection of Crass Handouts

Courtesy of Chris Butler

A MESSAGE TO THATCHER, HER GOVERNMENT, THOSE WHO SUPPORT HER AND ALL THOSE WHO ARE WILLING TO SEND LAMBS TO THE SLAUGHTERHOUSE OF WAR.

We never asked for war, nor in the innocence of our birth were we aware of it. We never asked for war, nor in the struggle to realisation did we feel that there was a need for it. We never asked for war, nor in the joyful colours of our childhood were we conscious of its darkness.

*

'The sky is empty and it's turning different shades of colour,
It never did before and we never asked for war.
My mind is empty and my body different shades of torture,
It never was before and we never asked for war.
The buildings are empty and the countryside is wasteland,
It never was before and we never asked for war.
The playgrounds are empty and the children limbless corpses,
They never were before and they never asked for war.
No-one is moving and no doves fly here.
No-one is thinking and no doves fly here.
No-one remembers beyond all this fear.
No doves fly here'.

The Mob 1982.

*

We never asked for war; this glib, horrific indifference, that leads young men barely old enough to have experienced anything of the joy of life to kill and be killed, is something that *you* have imposed upon us. You snatch these young bodies from the brain-washing cradle of the schoolroom to be maimed, mutilated and slaughtered in the cold grave of your cynicism. You tear these young bodies from their homes to die in the foreign soil of your barren, blood-stained minds. How perverted you are, how distorted and twisted, how divorced from the simple joy of existence. You dare to threaten the one life that we have with your pained violence. In the crystal light of our lives you are the darkest shadow.

Each body that you shovel into the mass graves of history is another darling boy that you have bled, another precious life that you have defiled, another act of creation that you have dared to violate. What is birth to you but another rag that you may wring and slap and beat and discard? What is life to you but another plastic body-bag into which you defecate? What is death to you but the disfigured bodies of our children upon whose angel faces you smear your rancid droppings?

How grand you must feel as you chart out your battlefields; each feature on that map describes the desolation of your mind. How powerful you must feel as you order the plunder and rape of those battlefields; each bayonet that turns in some contracting stomach is the pointing finger of your right hand. How omnipotent you must feel as those young men stumble in the death of those battlefields; each death is part of *you* that dies.

How glorious war. How rich the experience of war.

Those castaway boys, deranged, dismembered, crying, homeless, are the reality of your horror, the actuality of your insanity. That horror is the heritage that you create. That insanity is the tradition that you leave to those as yet unborn. The frightened corpses of the living are shadowed by your arrogance. The limbless corpses of the dead are devoured in your lust for power. The maggots that inch away at the rotting flesh are your true compatriots, you keep them fed, they are your true companions. Those bodies were my brothers that you have destroyed. That battlefield is my home that you have burnt in your fire.

Your minds are filth. Your lives are corruption. You are the walking dead, the parasites who bleed this earth of ours, that dry the waters from the river-beds that give us blood in its place.
YOU STAND ACCUSED OF PREMEDITATED, CALCULATED AND COLD-BLOODED MURDER. YOUR CRIMES ARE WELL DOCUMENTED. YOUR GUILT IS THE RESPONSIBILITY THAT ONE DAY YOU WILL HAVE TO REALISE.

Crass. 3rd June 1982.

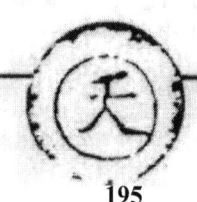

Twelve die in war games

Boostedt, West Germany (Reuter, AP) -- An American Harrier plunged into the Baltic yesterday and its pilot became the twelfth man to die in three weeks of Nato manoeuvres.

Six other Americans and five British soldiers died in a series of accidents (there were 500 in all) and 100 people, including civilians, were injured. More than £2m of damage was caused.

LAST WEEK I PICKED UP A COPY OF A NEWSPAPER THAT I LAYING ON THE SEAT OF A TRAIN, A CRUMPLED SCREWED UP OF PAPER AND INK, ENDLESS WORDS, THE TOP PEOPLES PAPER, TH GOOD OLD 'TIMES'. THE FALKLANDS PANTOMIME WAS OVER, THREE MONTHS OLD AND ALREADY THE FEAR AND THE SHAME HAS BEEN FORGOTTEN. EVERYTHING'S OK AGAIN NOW, THE DEAD HAVE DIED, THE PUBLIC HAD CRIED FOR BLOOD AND THEY'D GOT IT AND WHEN THEIR OWN HAD BEEN SPILLED ON THE ICY MOORLANDS OF THOSE DISTANT ISLANDS, THEY'D CRIED AGAIN, BITTER AND BIGOTTED TEARS THAT MEANT NOTHING. BOY SOLDIERS HAD BEEN GIVEN A TASTE OF WAR, A TASTE OF STEEL, A TASTE OF MUD. THOSE THAT RETURNED AS HEROES ARE FORGOTTEN NOW, LEFT FOR THE REST OF THEIR LIVES WITH THE IMAGES OF CRUELTY AND BRUTALISATION TO WHICH THEY WERE EXPOSED. AS THE TRAIN RUMBLED ITS WAY TOWARDS LONDON I WATCHED THE LITTLE HOUSES WITH THEIR NEAT GARDENS, WASHING BLOWING IN THE LATE SUMMER BREEZE, OLD MEN BENT OVER THEIR VEGETABLE PATCHES, CHILDREN HIDING AMONGST THE BUSHES, EVERYTHING LOOKED SO ORDERED, SO COMFORTABLE, I WONDERED IF ANY OF THEM REMEMBERED. I TURNED BACK TO THE NEWSPAPER, BLACK AND WHITE STATEMENTS, CONTROLLED CONTAINED; MASSACRE IN THE LEBANON, NEAT LIKE THAT ON THE PAGES. ANOTHER BLOODY BODY PILE, TORN BODIES, WORN BODIES, BLED BODIES, DEAD BODIES. OF COURSE THE RESPECTABLE ELITE WERE NOT UPON THAT BODY PILE, WHAT BODY PILE WAS EVER CONSTRUCTED WITH THE BODIES OF THE RICH AND PRIVILEGED? JUST MORE BLOODY PEASANTS, MORE BLOODY SERFS, MORE BLOODY COMMON PEOPLE; JUST BLOODY PEOPLE BLEEDING ON THE BODY PILE. STACK 'EM UP HIGH JOE, PILE 'EM UP JOE - JUST MORE BLOODY BODIES, BLEEDING. AND OF COURSE IT WAS NO ONES FAULT THAT THOSE PEOPLE DIED, IT'S AN ACT OF WAR AFTER ALL, WE'VE GOT TO ACCEPT THE REALITY OF LIFE AND PART OF THAT IS THE REALITY OF WAR. OH NO, IT IS NOBODIES FAULT, WE'RE ALL SO FUCKING GUILTLESS AREN'T WE? ANOTHER BLOODY BODY PILE AND ANOTHER GREY SUITED SHIT RATIONALISES AND LIES, JARGONISES AND CHEATS THEMSELF AWAY FROM THE RESPONSIBILITY THAT THEY ARE INCAPABLE OF ACCEPTING. LEAVE THE BODIES JOE, LET THEM ROT JOE, LET THEM GO JOE. AND ON THE MARBLE FLOORS OF THE TEMPLES OF POWER NOT ONE DROP OF BLOOD FALLS, NOT ONE WAXY MAGGOT CRAWLS ITS WAY TOWARDS THE STENCH; BEGIN AND REAGAN AND THATCHER BEND AND BOW AND CREEP AND CRAWL AND ARE SO DIVORCED FROM REALITY THAT THEY PERHAPS DO NOT EVEN REALISE WHAT IT IS THAT THEY ARE DOING TO THIS EARTH OF OURS. BLINDED BY THEIR ARROGANCE THEY PILE THE BODIES HIGH; SO FAR FROM THE FEAR AND THE SHAME. I LOOK OUT FROM THE TRAIN AGAIN, CLOSER TO THE CITY NOW, THE HOUSES ARE SMALLER, THE BACK GARDENS MORE CONCRETE THAN GRASS, EVERYTHING IS WRAPPED IN INDUSTRIAL GREY AND IT SEEMS THAT HERE THE WIND NEVER BLOWS. STRUNG ACROSS THE PORCH OF ONE OF THE ENDLESS ROWS OF TERRACES WAS A FADED FLAG AND A HAND WRITTEN SIGN, I COULD NOT QUITE READ IT ALL, BUT I THINK IT SAID 'WELCOME HOME SON'; ANOTHER BOY HERO RETURNS, ANOTHER WAR OVER. THATCHERS ARMY, DRAWN FROM THE RANKS OF UNEMPLOYED, IN A SOCIETY OF THREE MILLION UNEMPLOYED THE FORCES BECOME AN OPEN DOOR TO THOSE WHO SEEK SOME KIND OF SECURITY AND SO THOSE WHO HAVE MOST CAUSE TO OPPOSE THE SYSTEM COME TO SERVE IT. HOW ELSE WOULD THAT FLAG AND THAT HAND WRITTEN MESSAGE HAVE FOUND ITS WAY ONTO THAT PORCH? 'WELCOME HOME SON', you're one of the lucky ones. THERE'S OTHERS STILL ON THOSE ISLANDS, HEAPED INTO THEIR COMMUNAL GRAVES AND WHEN THE PARENTS AND LOVERS OF THOSE CORPSES ASK THAT THEY BE BROUGHT BACK, THEY ARE TOLD THAT IT ISN'T POSSIBLE - AND WHEN THE PARENTS AND LOVERS OF THOSE CORPSES ASK THEY THEY MIGHT BE TAKEN TO THE SITE OF THOSE PITS, THEY ARE TOLD THAT IT ISN'T POSSIBLE, THEY ARE TOLD THAT THERE ARE NO TOILETS ON THE PLANES, THAT THE FORCES DO NOT POSSESS THE CORRECT FACILITIES TO GET THEM THERE AND THAT THEY MUST WAIT FOR TWO YEARS BEFORE THEY CAN EXPECT ANYTHING AT ALL. SO MUCH FOR RESPECT, SO MUCH FOR CARING, JUST ANOTHER BLOODY BODY PILE. ANOTHER WAR IS OVER, THE FALKLANDS HAVE BECOME A VIDEO ADVENTURE STORY, ANOTHER HOLLY- WOOD PRODUCTION AND THATCHER, THE WOMAN DIRECTLY RESPONSIBLE FOR THE DEATHS OF OVER ONE THOUSAND PEOPLE IS ALLOWED TO CONTINUE HER RULE OF TYRANNY OVER OUR LIVES. HER ARROGANCE KILLS PEOPLE IN IRELAND WITH THE PLASTIC BULLETS THAT HAVE BEEN INTERNATIONALLY CONDEMNED, HER ARROGANCE KILLS PEOPLE IN HOSPITALS WHERE SHE REFUSES TO ACCEPT THE NEEDS OF OTHERS. HER AND HER KIND ARE PERMITTED TO STRUT UPON THE BODY PILES THAT THEY HAVE CREATED WHILE WE PASSIVELY SIT BY. I TURN AGAIN TO THE TIMES, 'TWELVE DIE IN WAR GAMES'..............................

"....guess what, I saw this bloke on the train today, looked like a punk, all torn clothes and things, a grown man dressed like a fucking tramp and reading a copy of the Times and crying, a man of his age crying..........what a fucking crank."

...y is the only form of political thought that does not seek to control the individual through the use of force. Right-wing and left-wing politics are concerned with the control of people through the use of power, state-control. Under both left and right-wing governments, people are secondary to the state, they are seen as nothing more than the machinery of the state and they are expected to live, and if need be die, for the state. Anarchy is the rejection of that state and its control and represents a demand by the individual for a life of PERSONAL CHOICE, not one of POLITICAL MANIPULATION. Anarchy is the first demand made by those seeking a life of personal responsibility, by refusing to be controlled by the state, you take your life into your own hands and that is, rather than the popular and ignorant idea of anarchy as chaos, the first step towards TRUE PERSONAL ORDER. The people who talk about anarchy and chaos are talking out of their arses, stupid little heroes who can't see that the world IS IN CHAOS ALREADY, and that their idea of anarchy is blowing rasberries at policemen. The world is in a fucking mess and the idiots who advocate chaos simply want to add to that mess. Anarchy is a state of mind, not another government, you can't vote anarchist, YOU CAN ONLY BE ONE, and being one isn't just a matter of wearing bondage trousers and talking out your arse, it's a matter of hard work and hard thought, it's a matter of learning to trust your own judgement and learning to live your own life. If you trust yourself to live your own life you become more able to let others live theirs. If you are able to make your own choices in life you are more able to let others make theirs. The state of anarchy is anywhere that individuals live with other individuals in trust and mutual respect and NOT a chaotic bedlam where everyone is out for themselves. Chaos is already the structure of this system, mindless, self-interested and destructive, what's the future in that?

People ask," what if there were no government, or police, or army?What if there were no laws?Wouldn't a state of anarchy just mean chaos? What fucking stupid questions. Anarchy isn't about imposed control, it's about SELF CONTROL, it's about people, not politics, it's about people living, loving and learning TOGETHER. If there were a state of complete anarchy (which there probably won't ever be) everyone would be HELPING each other BECAUSE THAT'S WHAT ANARCHY IS ABOUT, not hindering with competitive and self grabbing natures that we are taught is the right way to be. You wouldn't NEED laws and controls because people would WANT to help each other, that is what anarchy seeks to do, it believes that we are capable of living together without agression, it believes the we are basically good, not the evil shits that our system would have us believe we are. People would want to help because of the sense of their own responsibilit that we are never permitted to develope in our oppressive society. It is because of this sense of responsibility that very few anarchists advocate physical violence and revolution, the people that do are generally Marxists who spend a lot more time waffling with a beer glass in their hand than actually doing anything. If force is used to achieve political ends, it means that someone has had to accept something against their will and that can only lead to resentment and the desire to fight back, which is the never ending circle of violence that you can read about in any history book, so how can real peace be achieved through violent means?Peace can only exist where there is a real desire for it, a recognition of the rights of individuals to live their OWN life, free of restriction and free of oppression. It is a matter of personal choice, a matter of personal responsibility and through realising that it is a responsibility to work towards a world of harmony and mutual respect.

No regime, be it communist, fascist, tory, labour etc. etc. will ever achieve anything of real value because regimes seek to control and manipulate people into FORCED responsibility and that is a CONTRADICTION of terms. Nationalism, socialism or whatever, all imposed ideas all ways of saying that the STATE is more important than the INDIVIDUAL. Anarchy quite simply says that the INDIVIDUAL is more important than the STATE. Responsibility and coexistance can only be achieved through FREE CHOICE, it can't be forced on people, it is an act of faith, NOT A POLITICAL DOCTRINAIRE. As with pacifism, anarchy is a personal choice, an act of commitment, a decision in your own head to pursue a life that is ENTIRELY your own, free of restriction, free of fear, free of intimidation. OK, so you won't change the world tomorrow by becoming an anarchist today, but it's a start, everything has to start somewhere, where better than in yourself? ANARCHY AND PEACE ARE ONE OF THE SAME THING, the complete state of anarchy WOULD BE PEACE in the way that NO OTHER way of life could b because as long as people are forced into accepting things that they don't want to accept, there can be no peace. On a social level perhaps it's all a dream, but on a personal level it can be a reality. It's stupid to say,"Oh I won't do that, there's not enough people to make it work", that's sheep-like, it can ONLY work if you are prepared to stand alone and MAKE it work, it can only work if you are prepared to make it work on your OWN. Other kinds of political thought can easily do without your help because people don't matter in party politics, they're just numbers. It doesn't matter what you think if there's a fascist government in power, because, like it or not, you're going to have to accept it, the same applies to ALL GOVERNMENT, you have to tow the party line, or, at best, suffer it. PEOPLE DON'T MATTER TO SYSTEMS, THEY NEVER HAVE AND THEY NEVER WILL. ANARCHY HAS NO PARTY, NO LINE TO TOW, IT'S YOU, YOU ALONE. Anarchy and peace are internal, personal facts, decisions made in your own head to live your own life. Stop blaming others for the mess you're in and get on with making your own life, YOU'VE ONLY GOT ONE, USE IT.

IF YOU'RE NOT LOOKING FOR THE ANSWER, YOU'RE PART OF THE PROBLEM.
Marxism, Maoism, Fascism, this ism and that ism can only give you books and words and words and books and books and words and books,
ANARCHY GIVES YOU YOURSELF, ANARCHY IS YOU.....GET ON WITH IT.

(A note on pacifism)

Pacifism is not a wishy washy cop-out that says "OK, I don't mind if people shit on me", it simply says that on no account will I be drawn into acts of violence against my fellow beings on this earth. Some pacifists might claim that self defence, if it uses physical force, is unacceptable, this, I feel, is, in todays violent climate, a dangerous stance to take. It is imperative to defend oneself against acts of physical violence, that defence may take the form of running like hell to get away, or it might take the form of counter-attack, whatever the individual under attack feels is the best and safest course of action. Perhaps it is worth following the example of many feminists and learning self defence (judo, karate etc), through learning to handle attack we are much more able to control a situation rather than allowing ourselves to become victims to it. On no account should any more force be used than is necessary to protect oneself, otherwise one is part of the escalation of violence that one is standing against. Pacifism is, primarily, a stance against STATE VIOLENCE, be it in the form of WAR, or in the form of STATE CONTROL (police etc). Pacifism says that it is foolish and wrong to attempt to solve problems through the use of force, it also believes that force against force can not be justified, that is, it believes that to prevent organised attack through organised attack (war) is a contradiction of terms. It is important though that it be understood that this is an ATTITUDE OF MIND and where the body is in REAL DANGER of attack it would be foolish NOT to defend it. Because we are pacifists, certain idiots seem to imagine that we are easy game for their idiot games of intimidation, well they've been reading the wrong comic books, we are not prepared to stand by and watch the cattle-trucks roll by, we will defend what we believe to be our rights and we will attempt to understand those that seek other visions, but we will NOT permit ANYONE to impose their vision on

BE EXACTLY WHO YOU WANT TO BE, DO WHAT YOU WANT TO DO, BUT DON'T SHIT ON OTHERS IN THE PROCESS.

ANARCHY/PEACE/FREEDOM/IF YOU'RE NOT LOOKING FOR AN ANSWER YOU'RE A PART OF THE PROBLEM.
THERE IS NO PEACE/WE ARE AT WAR/WAR HAS BECOME A PERMANENT STATE OF REALITY.
THERE IS NO ANARCHY/WE ARE IN CHAOS/CHAOS HAS BECOME A PERMANENT STATE OF NORMALITY.
THERE IS NO FREEDOM/WE ARE IN BONDAGE/BONDAGE HAS BECOME A PERMANENT STATE OF LIFE.
WAR IN IRELAND/WAR IN THE HOME/CHAOS IN THE STREETS/CHAOS IN THE HOME/BONDAGE AT WORK/BONDAG
IN THE HOME/WHAT'S THE DIFFERENCE?IT IS ALL A STATE OF MIND/WAR CAN ONLY BE FOUGHT IF THERE
ARE PEOPLE TO FIGHT AND SUPPORT IT/BY OPPOSING WAR YOU ARE STANDING AGAINST ONE OF THE OLDES
INSTITUTIONS OF MAN.BIG M.A.N./BY BEING A PACIFIST YOU ARE CEASING TO BE A PART OF THE MACHI
ERY OF WAR/
IF EVERYONE WAS A PACIFIST THERE WOULD BE NO WAR.
BY BECOMING A VEGETARIAN YOU WON'T STOP THE SLAUGHTER OF INNOCENT ANIMALS,BUT YOU AT LEAST
ARE NOT CONTRIBUTING TO THAT PAIN.IT'S THE SAME WITH PACIFISM,OF COURSE IT ISN'T GOING TO
STOP WAR TOMMORROW,AT LEAST YOU'RE NOT A PART OF IT.BY STANDING AGAINST SLAUGHTER,VIOLENCE
WAR YOU HAVE MADE YOUR OWN DECISION TO MAKE A START TOWARDS A SANE WORLD.PEACE IS SOMETHING
THAT YOU FEEL FROM INSIDE,YOU WON'T GET MUCH HELP FROM THE OUTER WORLD.BY FEELING THAT DESI
FOR PEACE AND SANITY AND BY SHARING THOSE FEELINGS YOU ARE CREATING HOPE.HOPE IN A FAIRLY
HOPELESS WORLD IS LIKE WATER IN THE DESERT.WE ARE TOLD AT HOME,AT SCHOOL,ON TV,IN FACT JUST
ABOUT EVERYWHERE,TO ACCEPT RAPE,VIOLENCE,MURDER AND WAR AS A PART OF EVERYDAY LIFE,A PART O
THE NATURAL WAY THINGS ARE,THEY ARE NOT.FEAR IS A REALITY THAT WE MUST LEARN TO REJECT.IF
SOMEONE TELLS YOU THAT THAT'S JUST THE WAY IT IS THEY ARE TRYING TO PERPETUATE THOSE ATTITU
THAT OPPRESS US ALL.UNTIL WE CAN SHOW THAT IT IS NOT NATURAL TO HURT AND DESTROY NOTHING MU
IS GOING TO GET BETTER.WE DON'T HAVE TO ACCEPT LIFE AS AN ORDEAL,IT SHOULDN'T BE A TRIAL OF
FEAR AND INTIMIDATION,LIFE SHOULD BE A WONDERFUL EXPERIENCE NOT THE SHITTY HORROR THAT PEOP
HAVE MADE IT INTO.YOU'VE ONLY ONE LIFE,WHY WASTE IT ON DESTRUCTION?BY STANDING AGAINST THES
VIOLENT WAYS OF SEEING THE WORLD,BY OPPOSING THIS SO CALLED TRADITION,WE CEASE TO BE A PART
OF ALL THAT CRAP,WE WITHDRAW OUR SUPPORT.NOTHING MUCH MIGHT SEEM TO BE CHANGING BUT WE ARE
TRYING,WE ARE DOING SOMETHING ABOUT IT AND AT LEAST THAT IS A STEP TOWARDS SOME KIND OF
DIGNITY.
DON'T BE CONNED WHEN PEOPLE TELL YOU THAT NOTHING WILL EVER BE DIFFERENT,IT WILL BE,BUT IT
ONLY WILL BE IF YOU AND I ARE PREPARED TO DO SOMETHING ABOUT IT.

LITTLE BOYS ARE GIVEN LITTLE SOLDIERS TO PLAY WITH,LITTLE TOY SOLDIERS,LITTLE GUNS,LITTLE
WARS,LITTLE CORPSES.
LITTLE GIRLS ARE GIVEN LITTLE PEOPLE TO PLAY WITH,LITTLE DOLLIES TO NURSE,LITTLE WOUNDS,
LITTLE BANDAGES,LITTLE CORPSES.
PREPARATION FOR ADULTHOOD.HOW FUCKING STUPID.
BIG BOYS ARE MUTILATED AND DESTROYED BY WAR(EVEN IF THEY NEVER GO TO REAL WAR THEY HAVE
GONE THERE A THOUSAND TIMES IN THEIR FANTASIES,MURDERED,RAPED AND DESTROYED,A THOUSAND TIME
IN THE MOCK BATTLEFIELD OF THE PLAYGROUND).THE BIG,DOMINANT,GUN SHOVING,PRICK PUSHING MALE
NOW A REAL MAN AND IS LOOKED AFTER IN THIS FUCKED UP REALITY BY THE SERVILE LITTLE LADY WHO
BY NOW HAS BEEN TAUGHT TO COOK,NURSE,SUPPORT HER MAN.THE GIRL HAS BECOME A REAL WOMAN,A SLA
IN THE VIOLENT WORLD OF MAN MADE WAR,MAN MADE POWER,MAN MADE PAIN.PASSIVE ACCEPTANCE IS ALL
THAT IS EXPECTED FROM HER,ANOTHER LITTLE NIGHTINGALE TO PATCH UP THE WOUNDED HEROES.BOYS
MUST BE BOYS,RUGGED,MEAN,TOUGH AND MEATY........GIRLS MUST BE GIRLS,SOFT,GENTLE,MEEK AND SWE
................................FUCKING RUBBISH................
WE ARE TAUGHT TO ACCEPT THESE ROLES SO THAT THE SYSTEM CAN CONTROL US.GOD QUEEN AND COUNTRY
NEED THEIR SERVANTS AND SLAVES AND AS LONG AS WE GO ON ACCEPTING THEIR CRAP THEY'LL GO ON
OPPRESSING US.THEY GIVE US IGNORANCE SO THAT THEY CAN MAINTAIN THEIR STRUCTURES OF POWER AN
GREED AND VIOLENCE AND WAR.MEN ARE TAUGHT TO DESTROY THEIR FELLOW MEN AND WOMEN ARE TAUGHT
TO PATCH UP THIS TATTERED REALITY,TAUGHT TO PATCH UP THIS DESTRUCTIVE REALITY AND PRODUCE
MORE RAW MATERIAL(CHILDREN)FOR IT.WOMEN ARE TAUGHT TO ACCEPT THAT THE CHILD THEY BARE MUST
CLAMBER FROM THE WOMB READY TO MAKE WAR........IS THAT REALLY THE FUTURE THAT WE WANT TO OFF
THE UNBORN CHILDREN OF TOMORROW?

it's your
life...
live it.

VICTORY PARADE

THE MILITARY PARADE AT THE END OF WAR HAS ALWAYS BEEN A GRAND DELUSION, ESPECIALLY IN COUNTRIES THEMSELVES NOT RAVAGED BY WAR. LIKE TELEVISION MOVIES IN WHICH BLOOD AND GORE ARE NEVER SEEN, THE PARADES OF THE PAST WERE GREAT DEMONSTRATIONS OF VITAL VICTORIOUS MANHOOD. IMAGINE A PARADE FOR HUMAN CRABS WITHOUT LIMBS, MEN WITHOUT FACES, MEN WITH MINDS AND TESTACLES BLOWN AWAY, FRAIL YOUNG MEN DYING FROM CANCERS CAUSED BY CHEMICAL WARFARE. AND WHO WOULD TAKE THE SALUTE FOR SUCH A PARADE? THE GENERALS? THE POLITICIANS? THE ARMS MANUFACTURERS? NOT LIKELY.

heroes return home

WOUNDED Falklands heroes are to be left out of big victory parade.

"It's a parade for marching troops. Those recovered from their wounds will be able to take part but wounded men in wheelchairs are never included in this kind of parade.

"That's not the way we do things—not in a military parade."

Prime Minister Margaret Thatcher will make a speech at the slap-up luncheon at the Guildhall.

The war resulted in 255 British deaths and 777 wounded.

The money required to provide adequate food, water, education, health and housing for everyone in the world has been estimated at $17 billion a year. It is a huge sum of money . . . about as much as the world spends on arms every two weeks.

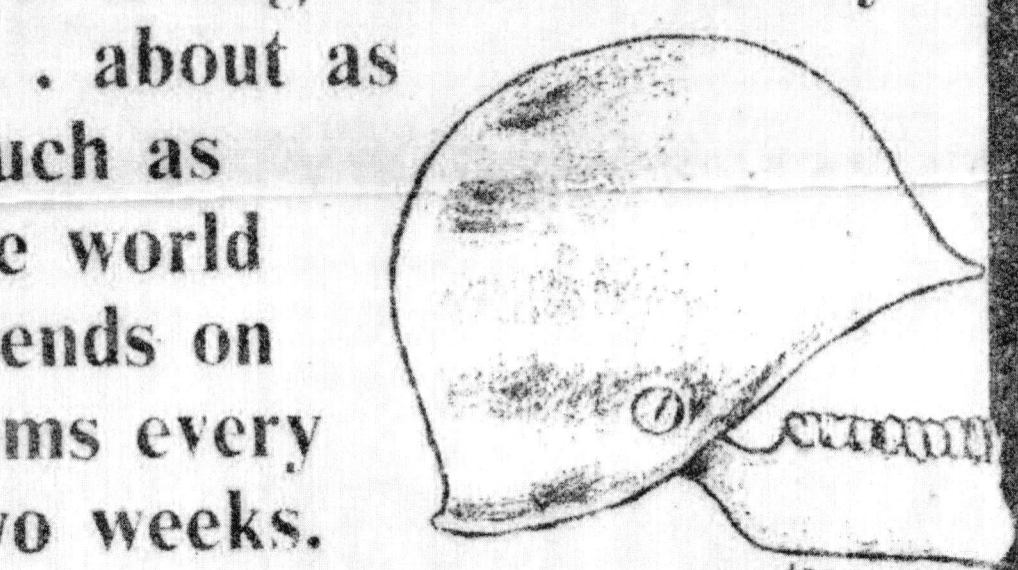

...ons with 20/20 vision.
Missiles that hide and seek.
Now what can we do for you?

World Inaction
Thirty million people die of hunger each year, a figure which could double by 1980. Ten days' world armament expenditure would buy enough grain to feed them for this year.

Nuclear-war food for dogs
A CALIFORNIAN firm called Country Roads is producing nuclear-war dog food, writes Geoffrey Lean.

The dehydrated food called 'survival' is packed in pressurised nitrogen and designed to stay fresh for 20 years. People are also buying it to keep their pets happy and fed through a depression or another Californian earthquake.

'A lot of people are getting panicky, and are concerned about their dogs,' said Colt Tarman of Country Roads.

They believe that an alignment of the planets next year will alter gravitational forces and cause California to fall into the ocean — or are just worried about plain old fashioned nuclear war.

IN ALL OUR DECADENCE PEOPLE DIE

THIS IS A SAMPLE OF SOME OF THE SPRAYS THAT WE USE FOR VARIOUS GRAFFITI PROJECTS.IF YOU CUT THIS STENCILS OUT,PERHAPS IT WOULD BE BETTER TO COPY THEM ONTO THIN CARD FIRST,YOU COULD USE THEM FOR DECORATING CLOTHING,IN WHICH CASE SILVER SPRAY IS THE BEST TO USE IF IT'S ONTO BLACK CLOTHES,OR IF ITS ONTO ANY OTHER LIGHT COLOUR ANY CAR SPRAY PAINT WILL DO.YOU CAN BUY ALPHABET STENCIL KITS IN MOST SHOPS THAT SELL ART MATERIAL,YOU CAN ALSO BUY CRAFT KNIVES WHICH ARE THE BEST TYPE FOR CUTTING STENCILS.SOME OF THESE STENCILS ARE THE ONES THAT WE USE ON POSTERS ETC. TO LET PEOPLE KNOW THAT WE DON'T AGREE WITH THE SHIT THAT THEY PROMOTE.IT'S A GOOD WAY OF SPENDING AN EVENING,BUT DON'T GET CAUGHT.GRAFFITI IS A REALLY EFFECTIVE WAY OF LETTING YOUR OPPINIONS BE SEEN.IF ALL THE ARMY RECRUITMENT OFFICES IN THE COUNTRY WERE SPRAYED WITH A FIGHT WAR STENCIL MAYBE THE MESSAGE WOULD GET THROUGH A LITTLE. GOOD LUCK WITH THEM.

WHO DO THEY THINK THEY'RE FOOLING: YOU?

WEALTH IS A GHETTO

FIGHT WAR - NOT WARS

CRASS

ANARCHY PEACE & FREEDOM

Poetry

Ruth Harvey Gasson

Warrington 1977

He nodded at the bouncers
Doug and fat-man Will,
in 'is tartan brothel creepers
and black punk-rock kilt.
Giro's in 'is wallet,
rubber's in there too,
he felt a million dollars,
a shag long overdue.

Dave loved it down the Carlton
the music made 'im spin,
or maybe it weren't the music
but the beer in 'im.
At the bar he sees 'er,
looks like Poly Styrene,
but she's with a geezer,
who's lookin' really mean.

He picks up his pint of Greenalls
leans over the DJ's decks
and in a Northern drawl says,
'Oi mate got any X-Ray Spex?'
The music starts to pound
Dave winks at Poly, gets a frown,
then 'e think 'e sees 'er smile
nods at 'er, 'Outside for a while?'

The fella she's with gives 'im the look,
Dave raises a middle finger
the bloke snarls a little
then launches a left-winger
a bottle follows, then a fist,
full right and head-butt back
'e's sure 'e sees 'er smiling
as 'e gets kicked in the sac.

Dave loved it down the Carlton
the music made 'im spin
or maybe it weren't the music
but 'is face smashed in.

Brockwell Park, August 1984

Flanked by two coppers,
the girl in the red pixie boots
was only fifteen.

One made a joke about
showing the picture to is boss,
she laughed.

The morning was spent
in a pub while rain stopped play.
Later the park.

Tie-died stalls and GLC
lined the pavements, pot lined
the air.

Polka-dot Switchblades
got canned, Kirk Brandon's
face got cut.

Zephania spilled calm
before the squall that was
the Damned.

It was the Captain's last,
the girls first, on the way home
she was sick.

Searching for Satori

"Just sit down and listen." He said
so I did. The music was all elbows and knees,
it matched how I felt, punching a hole
in Mainstream. He watched me.
I closed my eyes, lids heavy with the beat,
my skirt rose up uncovering white.
The music finished, replaced by the reverb
of the needle on the centre. Velour indented
my legs, as I listened, eyes still closed,
to his breath. I wanted to cling to the missed
beats, bury my head in his web covered chest.
He returned the needle to the start.

Poetry

Ruth Harvey Gasson

Hammersmith Palais 1984

We caught the train from Aldermaston
left our day clothes on the back seat.
Black bondage was the order of the day
our faces painted death white in wing mirrors.
I did my hair in a tube station, extricated
fellow passengers will Elnett XX hold.
No one smiled at me, no one ID'd
The red plushness of the ballroom
alcohol and sick stank drapes.
Skins and Rockabilly's edged round
us wagon-train like. Then the lights dimmed.

We ran for the train, missed the encore,
slept haunted by music in the car,
faces washed clean with baby-wipes.

The Poet in My Heart

'Sarah' your name conjures up
images of magic and wonder,
of Boudicca the warrior princess,
of CND rallies and sharp contrasts.
The undulation of womanhood,
strong and passionate.

The stories people tell of you,
of poll tax protests and solstice rituals.
The books you left on the shelves,
of Plath and Barthes. The lives people
shared with you, your legacies,
your delicate children and grandchild,
the Umbrella party in the park.

The empty pages that you left.

Fanzine Articles and Clippings

Persons Unknown

ANTI-SYSTEM/THE ABDUCTERS/PUBLIC DISTURBANCE
The Station, Gateshead, 3-9-83

The Station in Gateshead is a similar venue to the Bunker in Sund--erland, a semi-derelict, graffiti covered black hole with no rules and no rulers. With no authority present, the atmosphere in a venue of this type is less tense and much freer and a gig, any gig is more exciting.
I missed the first band, THE FIEND, although after hearing their tracks on the Still Dying tape and seeing their stupid 'axed to death' logo, I wasnt too bothered. Apparently they'd been dogged by sound problems anyway. Unfortunately, so were PUBLIC DISTURBANCE and they were little more than a wall of noise. Strongly in the Discharge mould (they even played 'Realities of war') I think they could be quite impressive through a decent PA.
It was now time for the pub, so we missed another band (Morbid hum--our, it said on the tickets) but we arrived back in time to see the ABDUCTERS. It was the first time I'd heard this band and now that the PA was sorted out, they were simply brilliant. Sounding a bit like early Anti Pasti they churned out some great powerhouse tunes and I just can't wait to hear the demo.
Naturally the Abducters got loads of people dancing and it was a pity that the headliners came on straight after. Speaking for myself I was fucking knackered and needed a rest.
ANTI-SYSTEM deserve to be big, more than that they deserve to be mega because tonight they were absolutely devastating. They play simple songs but they are direct and very effective and they put a hellof a lot into them, and could give most of today's so-called punk bands a good boot up the arse. Great 100 mph songs that don't run away from themselves and a thundering beat that doesn't get lost in the noise; Anti-System know what they are doing. They blast--ed through all the songs off their EP and the two Pax compilations and showed us what a good band sounds like. Naturally the audience went berserk and the dance floor became a surging mass of flailing bodies. Never have I been so exhausted but I can't praise this bands performance enough. Tonight Anti-System were THE BEST, noth--ing less!

D.A.N./Famous Imposters   The Station 18th Feb 84

Soon you'll be able to write a book on the bands that have failed to turn up here! Tonight the offenders were Amebix and Anti-Sect...so much for preaching animal liberation!
Anarka and Poppy were also supposed to play, but were fined for doing animal rights activities-that's the only acceptable excuse that i've heard yet for a band not turning up at the Station, oh yes, the Alternative had a good reason too.
I had seen the Famous Imposters in quite a few zines, and this must be partly due to having someone from Acts of Defiance in the band. With the guitar, in places, being much in the style of the System's "White Youth", they went down very well, and quite rightly too.
Ian T.O.R., bassist in DAN, later rated his band's performance as "appaling", and sorry Ian, but you were right. He later sent me a list of excuses but the main one must have been that they were pissed out of their heads. It was luckily for them that the crowd were in the same state, because there were quite a few dancing. The only thing I could make out in their set was the tune to "Magic Roundabout".
Rumours were going round that Public Disturbance were to finish off the night but this was not to be, although their singer got up to recite "Postman Pat", which was incredibly funny on the first hearing, but with the crowd feeling pissed off, didn't raise many laughs tonight.

Stalag 17/Asylum/Anathema/Sons of Vengeance The Station, 13th July 85. Yet again the full line up played so I hope we've seen the last of bands that don't turn up, tho' I think the Sons of Vengeance would've been better off stopping at home! They'll take that in the best possible taste though, with me being a music lover, and who can make Disorder and Venom songs sound good anyway? The only interesting thing about their set was watching Simmons who on this occasion sang for them. Looking, as usual, like the star role in a "before" Persil ad, he did wierd movements about stage which, for a moment, took my mind away from the dreadful noise the band were making.

Anathema were next, with a female singer and bassist that swapped duties half way through the set, not that it made any difference, as both sounded like the one from DIRT (for those of you who still haven't heard DIRT yet, I mean like a car's brakes squeaking). On the whole they didn't really impress me until the rather fabby last song they did, but by then it was too late.

Anyone who thought Mensi was a dead cert to win the Blown to Bits "Mr. Ugly Bastard" competition would have to think again if they saw the frontman of Asylum (listen who's talking!) but that didn't stop them doing a good set, hard and tuneful stuff. ← HONEST!!!

Ironically my camera broke after taking piccies of Asylum so I was a wee bit pissed off when Stalag 17 came on, but not to worry, they soon cheered me up with their rough tough and tuneful set, most of the songs knocking shit out of their track on the Mortarhate/Fight Back comp. Never since the Chumba's gig at the Bridge Hotel have I regretted having to leave and miss some of a band's set.

Righteo, time for more nagging..Asylum and Stalag 17 came all the way from Ireland only to be greeted by a half empty hall (Anathema came a long way too) so half the people that suddenly emerge when Subhumans, Conflict, play etc couldn't even be bothered to travel a few miles, probably the same people that used to moan "why isn't there gigs at the Station every week?" If this keeps up, you'll be saying that again, so get off your arse and be there..or is the Station not good enough for you?

SUBHUMANS/FACTION/INSTIGATORS/ PHANTOMS OF THE UNDERGROUND/ FREAK ELECTRIC. STATION, G/HEAD.

This has taken the place of an article i did on violence at gigs and the gig review page cos it had to be said.This is exactly what i saw and was told by other

Anyway read on and form your own views....................
Igot there at about 7-ish and there was only about 25 people in. By the time FREAK ELECTRIC came on the station was filling up.FREAK ELECTRIC suprised me cos I'd never seen them before. They use two drumers one feamale who also sings along with the guitarist. They reminded be a bit of rubbela ballet and a lot of the banshees. But then again they were quite origional really.After a short while the next band PHANTOMB OF THE UNDERGROUND took the stage and theywere excellent. I'd never seen or heard them before and I'd been told they were good. They sounded like the uk subs in places and were really heavilly influenced by 77 stle punk. by now the station had filled up a bit.Infact it was packed !!!!!!!!!!! Next on were FACTION because the INSTIGATORS had dissapeared. I've heard FACTION before cos they've got a single on BLUURG records.They started off with a few I didn't know so i took this oppotunity to rest on the front of the stage. Then they did the best one on the single,TURN AWAY.It was amazing !!!wwwwoooowwwweeeeeeee !!!!
Then they did more songs from the single and demos.The one before last was brill but i can't remember what it was called and i even asked the guitarist at the end. IF ANYONE KNOWS WHAT IT WAS PLEASE WRITE IN AND TELL ME.It was more like the toy dolls, it really cheered me up.This was when the firsts reports of trouble came becaise someone had been sniffing glue in the corner.Then INSTIGATORS came on and did all the favs like OLD SOLDIERS,BEHINED CLOSED DOORS,MONKEY MAN ,THE CHURCH SAYS,ALL CREATURES,UGLY PEOPLE etc etc.This was when the trouble started On one side of the stage some ignorant idiot (singer of   according to friends) grabbed a mike and stand and pulled it into the crowd. He was stopped by a boy in a white shirt. Then the singer of   . and friends preccede to kick and punch the boy in white.Then at the end of the song smed got on the stage and said "can you all look at the bunch of idiots in the corner,have you got turds for brains or something" The INSTIGATORS stopped and the majority of the crowd started to chant "OUT" to the idiots in the corner. Despite this the idiots in the corner were waiting for a fight.Another fight broke out and the singer of INSTIGATORS was yelling "STOP THEM FROM FIGHTING,GO ON STOP THEM" so a bunch of people went to stop it and then a bunch of people went in to cause more fights.Then a tall lad in black tried to rescue his mate. Then the singer from   jumped on the lad in black and started to punch him.The lad in black got up and shouted at him why he hit him. THE SInger of   backed off (they cantstand up to questions it hurts there brain (if they've got one))and then the next thing i knew was the lad in black was on the ground in the corner with a mohicand maniek on top of him who was being restrained by a friend. Some stupid idiot was shouting "its allright he's on our side he's on our side " it made me sick,there are no sides.I was trying to get this lad out of the corner along with others so i said to this idiot "can you calm down and let him out please" he looked at me as if to say "f. off or i&ll kill you" so i left. The lad in black got up and he started to tell them to get out.then suddenly a fist hit him and resulted in his brow being cut open.He had managed to stay non-violent so far but he had to be pulled away by his mates cos he lost his temper.This was understandable with stupid idiots laying into you for no reason at all.The n more fights broke out and people inc. me were yelling at people to stop the fighting but no-one was listening.Blood was splatted all over peoples clothes and faces. Then this lad got up on stage and said "lets stop fighting and watch the gig,no more fights" Everyone cheered and INSTIGATORS were getting prepared to play again but more fights broke out.This time the lad who had just been on the stage jumped in and laid into everyone including two girls (wow what a real hard man eh?????)

Mark Wilson [The Mob]

Irene Frizzera

The Last of the Mohawks

Tom Laimer-Read

Spike Mayhem sat uncomfortably on his broken toilet glaring at the small bottle of pills that he held in one hand and the large bottle of vodka that he held in the other and thought about ending it all. He looked forwards in a sad, musty fug. As he peered listlessly, almost lifelessly into the cracked mirror in front of him he recalled his earlier salad days, or so they called them, even though he didn't really like eating salad now or at any point in his life, and reflected, badly as it turned out, on how it had all been so much easier back then, even though times were hard.

Spike had moved to the bustling, industrious city of Manchester in the northwest of England from the not-quite-so-hectic town of Hull in the northeast England in 1977 when he had heard that something new and exciting was happening there that people were calling "punk rock". He didn't really see what all the racket was about until he attended his first punk rock show at the Electric Circus in the August of that heady, humid year. He was transfixed by what he witnessed; a corruscating group called The Adverts supported by the energetic 999. As it happened, 999 were rousing enough to grab Spike's attention from the outset. They hurtled about the stage, a morass of energy exploding in front of him, causing his brain to short fuse and his mental faculties to all but implode at the amazing wonder of it all.

"This is the dog's bollocks!" he roared into the hazy ether.

Then came the headliners, The Adverts. Their ecstatic cacophony caused a feeling akin to euphoria in Spike's crazed cerebellum that shuddered across his body. The raw energy of the band hit him with a full-on body blow and he became an instant on-the-spot convert, undergoing a punk epiphany right there and then. That show was to change his life - forever.

Back in his home town of Hull the girl who had initially told him about this rowdy new sound that was going around was one Tammy Windles, a girl that he'd had a crush on since early high school. He was besotted by her and would follow her to the ends of the Earth. Well, to Manchester, at least, which was a bit like the end of the Earth back then anyway, with lots of dilapidated buildings and World War II bomb craters around that hadn't been filled in yet because there wasn't any money to cover them up. Tammy got herself a job as a barmaid at the Electric Circus so that she could get to see the bands that came there for free, at least while she wasn't serving drinks, anyway, and maybe even get to meet them at some point in between the sound check, if they did one, or hanging around after the show, if they bothered staying. Spike's real name was Greg Mayhew, who got labelled 'Greg the Egg' or 'Eggy Greggy' or occasionally 'Greg On Your Face' in high school due to the rhyming of the word with his name and the fact that he also had an ovular-shaped noggin. Kids can be particularly cruel where poetry and poultry-produced products are concerned, so it would seem.

Spike realised that he had to start off his own band if he ever wanted to compete for the affections of his amorous intentions, Tammy, who by this point called herself Tammy Tampon in true punk fashion, as well as wearing all of the new punk fashion, occasionally featuring used tampons for added shock value. Spike got himself a day job as a refuse collector, using a long spike to pick up rubbish on the floor, which is where he got his punk nickname from. He turned the 'w' in his surname around to create 'Mayhem'. He formed a band shortly after that from a group of slobs and yobbish layabouts that he fell in with. They called themselves The Purple Sloths, because they were all quite lazy in their own ways, and Tammy liked the colour purple. There was Monkey Joe, who had massive sideburns that caused him to resemble an ape, who took up the bass, Terry the Hedge, who liked to jump into hedges and looked as if he was dragged backwards through one most of the time, which most likely would have been the case, who played rhythm guitar, Donny Rosco, a suave Italian drummer, Shaved Dave, who was a black guy with a shaved head named Dave, on lead guitar, and Jimmy Two Shoes on trumpet, whose thing was that he always wore two different, mismatched shoes, mostly because he had stolen them from various shoe shops while the assistants weren't looking. He should really have been called Jimmy Two Different Shoes, but that didn't scan half as well. Neither did his shoes, not that there were scanners back then or anything, so it doesn't really matter that much at all. This was the motley crew that Spike Mayhem, the singer, had self assembled, badly, and with a few pieces missing, as it usually the case with self-assembly products. They were a D.I.Y. outfit, not to mention their outfits, some of which were made from scouring pads, bits of sandpaper and tinfoil. A haphazard bunch of scrapyard dogs you were never more likely to find.

"Right, lads! We gotta get our shit together and start playing, write some songs and that, then we can stick it to The Man and shake this whole music industry and political sham to its foundations! Anyone seen my mohair jumper?!"

The band practised for a bit, got a handful of relatively acceptable songs together, and managed to book themselves in to the Electric Circus in late October of that monumental year, 1977. They were all geared up to play, but then - the venue got closed down by the council before they could perform.

"What a bunch of absolute bureaucratic bastards!" spat Spike.

Spike knocked back a pill and took a tentative sip of vodka from the bottle, swilling it down and shuddering as the vile, acrid liquid slipped icily along his throat. He groaned, wiped his mouth, and reminisced some more, his vision beginning to blur.

After the abject failure of their Electric Circus gig, if you can even call it a failure at all, since it never even happened to begin with, Donny Rosco left the band due to musical indifferences, and became a successful local radio disc jockey. Not knowing very much about music helped him greatly in this respect. Monkey Joe went off to become a zoo keeper at Chester Zoo, feeling an affinity with his ape brethren and sistren there, and Terry the Hedge departed to become a traffic warden, oddly. Tammy didn't have her job as a barmaid anymore since the Electric Circus had closed down, so she decided to start a career as a psychic, giving people predictions about their future, telling them reassuring things about people that they'd known who had recently died, and that kind of thing. She sometimes held seances, but she never had much success. Somebody had wanted to talk to Elvis, who had recently died during the summer of that year, but when she was asked to perform a rendition of one of his famous songs, she didn't know the lyrics, and the gathered fans didn't believe her when she said that The King had just had a temporary lapse of concentration and couldn't remember the songs as he was a little rusty and hadn't been doing so many shows in his new place of residence.

The remaining members of The Purple Sloths wanted to pursue some kind of further musical achievements, however, so got themselves another gig booked in at the Band on the Wall venue, another Manchester hotspot, and one that wouldn't be closing down - for the foreseeable, at any rate. Shaved Dave had the guitar side covered, and taught Spike how to play the basics of the bass, which worked out well enough for most of their songs. Jimmy Two Shoes switched to drums, and they became an efficient and effective three piece. Dave grew a beard and large Afro hairdo, so they renamed him Unshaved Dave, and they all wrote a cheeky song about their ex bandmates who'd deserted them which they called 'Sod Off!' and which eventually became a minor hit on the punk club circuit scene. This caused repercussions further down the line at a gig where Terry the Hedge had tried to get their van clamped outside a venue because they were parked on a single yellow line, but the rest of the band went and poured a tin of prunes into his hat and trousers as a joke, which squared things, in a way, and they became friends again. Terry became their driver, because he owned a van, knew his way around, and exactly where it was safe to park.

Tammy got fed up with the psychic predictions (she should really have foreseen it sooner) and moved down to London for a while to become a stylish hairdresser. It was the beginning of the nineteen eighties, and such matters were becoming big business. Being still enamoured by the flame of his heart's desire, Spike convinced the band to relocate down south to the Big Smoke too, in a bid to get more attention for the group, and they reluctantly agreed. They moved into a squat in Forest Hill and had to fend off rats and bailiffs on a regular basis. They got to play some shows down the Hope and Anchor and at The Marquee on Wardour Street a few times, as well as at any venue that would have them, and built a small, but dedicated following.

Sadly Jimmy Two Shoes got arrested for attempting to rob a load of pencils from a stationery shop - he was caught and asked to remain stationary and also for the stationery to remain. This left the band in a bit of a fix, without a steady drummer they wouldn't have been able to play proper shows, but they managed to get someone to fill the empty spot on the drum stool, a guy named Fresh Phil, who did a number of neat drum fills, and possessed a sparkling, winning smile, aptly. Tammy liked to spend time with the band, she was their contractual hair stylist and came up with all of the new styles that were to emerge in the nineteen eighties, such as the waifish back-combed look, the elegant gothic sweep, the jaunty rockabilly quiff and one that nobody really knew what it was, but it was a kind of sideways ski-slope thing that went upwards and then sideways again somehow.

None of them were very good looks, in hindsight, but it was the eighties, so it didn't really matter. What mattered was MONEY! And the band had none. Zilch. Zero. They decided to get an agent, which didn't help financial matters at all either. They met a man who went by the name of Micky McGee, although they had suspicions that this wasn't his real name. They wondered if he was related to popular television magician Paul Daniels' wife Debbie McGee, but were always too frightened to ask, Micky being an imposing, threatening, highly irrationally violent and unpredictable fellow in general. He once threw a television out of a window because he didn't like the result of the horse race that he'd just seen, as if doing that could change the result in any way. They assumed, quite rightly, that he could do the same to them if they ever got on his wrong side, and made every attempt not to.

"Er, Micky?" asked Spike, cautiously.

"WHAT DO YE WANT?!" roared Micky.

"Um, when are we gonna get paid? We need a bit of money up front to buy, know, food and stuff. We haven't eaten in days, apart from some out of date mayonnaise that I found in a bin that I think is making me hallucinate slightly."

"Ye WHAT?! Ye wanna get PAID?!"

"Er, yeah, that was the general idea of what we were enquiring about," added Unshaved Dave through his voluminous beard.

"Well, we'll see about that, my boys. I got some money coming in, but it'll be another few days. Until then, all I can suggest is that you do some buskin'. Yer musicians, ain't ya?"

"Yeah, well..."

"Yeah, well, great! SEE YA!"

Tammy had taken quite a shine to the new drummer, Phil, which irked Spike immensely. He had been getting on well with her up to this point, even though he felt as if she was leading him along a little. He could never quite build up the confidence to ask her out though, for some weirdly inexplicable reason. He had tried on quite a few occasions, but the words always got stuck in the back of his throat like a mis-swallowed fishbone. This made Spike rather resentful of many people and things. He wished that he had the confidence that some guys had, but he could never quite work himself up to saying anything. Coming from Hull gave him a sense of inadequacy, maybe. People from Hull felt as if they didn't have a say in anything, as nobody from Hull ever really got listened to. That's why they lived in Hull. It was like Hull on Earth. To move out was almost unheard of back then, and Spike had been rather brave to do so, but he was following his heart like a lovelorn fool, which nobody could blame him for, but was not always the best of options. Still, there were far worse things that he could have done with his time.

Things came to a head at a gig at The Duke's Head when Spike caught Phil putting his hand down Tammy's top. They almost came to blows, Phil threatening Spike with a drumstick at one point, but Micky McGee intervened and broke it all up by smashing the bar to pieces himself. Spike, being the original convener of the band, managed to get Phil to leave. However, Unshaved Dave wasn't happy with the direction that the band were going in, and decided that it was a good time to split too. He invested in computers and became a highly paid business executive through his shrewd investments and business acumen. The group was in tatters. Spike was distraught, but knew that it was time to move on. Music had changed anyway, and he was ready for a new challenge. He started a completely new outfit, The Sadists of Satan, a punk band with more of a heavy metal edge, who caught a lot of public attention for their raunchy stage antics, such as live fornication and allegedly a goat sacrifice, although this was thought to be just conjecture by the religious right, rather than any proof of it actually happening. Tammy was not so interested in these raucous rock excesses, and went off with Phil who became a quantity surveyor somewhere in the Midlands. Not quite so Fresh Phil anymore. To express his anger and annoyance at Tammy's departure, Spike had cut his hair into a mohican style crest, a bit like Travis Bickle in the film Taxi Driver after he went postal, showing his abject resentment towards the world at large.

Spike was most upset. Sitting on the porcelain throne as

he was, he looked gloopily into the broken mirror, a broken man himself. This rejection had hit him hard, and he had hit the bottle even harder, as well as whatever else came his way. Rock and roll had virtually stolen his soul. He had made a pact with the devil of hard rock, and now it was perversely punishing him persistently. He peered again at the bottle of tablets, steeled himself, then knocked back a handful and slugged another gulp from the vodka to wash them down. He was getting more hazy as the pills and booze did their work. This was it, Judgement Day. Time all was in the balance. His life really was flashing before his eyes, and so, he thought, this must almost be his time.

The career of The Sadists of Satan had gone quite well for a while, considering that they were mostly awful, but began to hit a nosedive in the early nineties when people lost their fondness for trashy hair metal bands, and instead preferred a grungier sound. Spike deftly renamed his group Nosedive, as this concept seemed to suit his situation generally. He had worked hard at being a musician, without much general attention or recompense for it, but would continue while he still relatively enjoyed what he was doing, even if most other people didn't seem to. They appeared to prefer slick, sickly boy bands like East 17 and Take That. Where would they be in twenty years' time? They had nothing to contribute musically or lyrically, they were just musical fluff without any substance, whereas Spike had a fair amount of technical skill on bass by now and his words were wise and world-weary. Nosedive got a spot on a Lollapollooza tour and did a decent stint in the U.S., but never really got the recognition that at least that Spike felt they deserved.

Spike glared again into the gloomy face that gazed despondently back at him in the mirror. What kind of life was this? Was it really worth it? What good did anything do anyone? Nobody appreciated him or his music. He'd be better off dead, wouldn't he?

The 2000s were not any kinder to Spike. He had managed to get work as a house musician in a band at an Italian restaurant now run by Donny Rosco back in Manchester, who he still occasionally kept in touch with. There was talk of a Purple Sloths revival, but nothing ever quite came of it. Somebody was always busy, or out on traffic warden duties. Spike had tried to get back in touch with Tammy after he had heard of her divorce from Phil, but she didn't return his phone messages.

As the years spun by, Spike's head swirled more wildly, like water down a flushed toilet. Life hadn't been good to Spike, real name Greg, and he felt like the proverbial turd hurtling down the cistern. But wait. What was punk all about? Smashing the cistern, wasn't it? Yeah! He could fight back! Why shouldn't he? You didn't have to be a young man to play from the heart or sing about what you knew and had seen of the world. Age gave you experience and insight. Use it! He would call his new band 'The Proverbial Turds'! The time for rising up was NOW!

Spike got up, but his head whirled and he fell back into the pan. As he fell he grabbed the chain and held it in a misplaced attempt at levelling himself. He pulled hard on the dangling handle and it came off in his hand, but not before sending the cistern above him veering forwards, pouring the full contents of the cistern onto his head. Fortunately for him, this burst of water woke him up, reinvigorating him with the cold shock, and he seemed somewhat awake for the first time in a long time. This was his own toilet-based baptism. He didn't want to die. He looked down at the bottle. It said, 'LAXATRON' on it in large letters. Why hadn't he noticed this before? Slip of focus, most likely. There was a deep rumble in Spike's belly. Things never really went very well for Spike. He hastily pulled down his trousers and pants and then sat sturdily on the seat as his bowels exploded, gushing out in a gooey stream of dirty gunk. This was all part of Spike's cleansing process. After the flow had subsided he felt at ease, at one with himself, empty, void of all excess shit he'd built up over the years. He could now get up and move on. Well, after wiping, obviously. He decided to give Tammy a call. Maybe she'd answer this time?

Rich Hill and Pete Boyce [Antisect]

Irene Frizzera

Various Handouts

Courtesy Nigel Crouch Collection

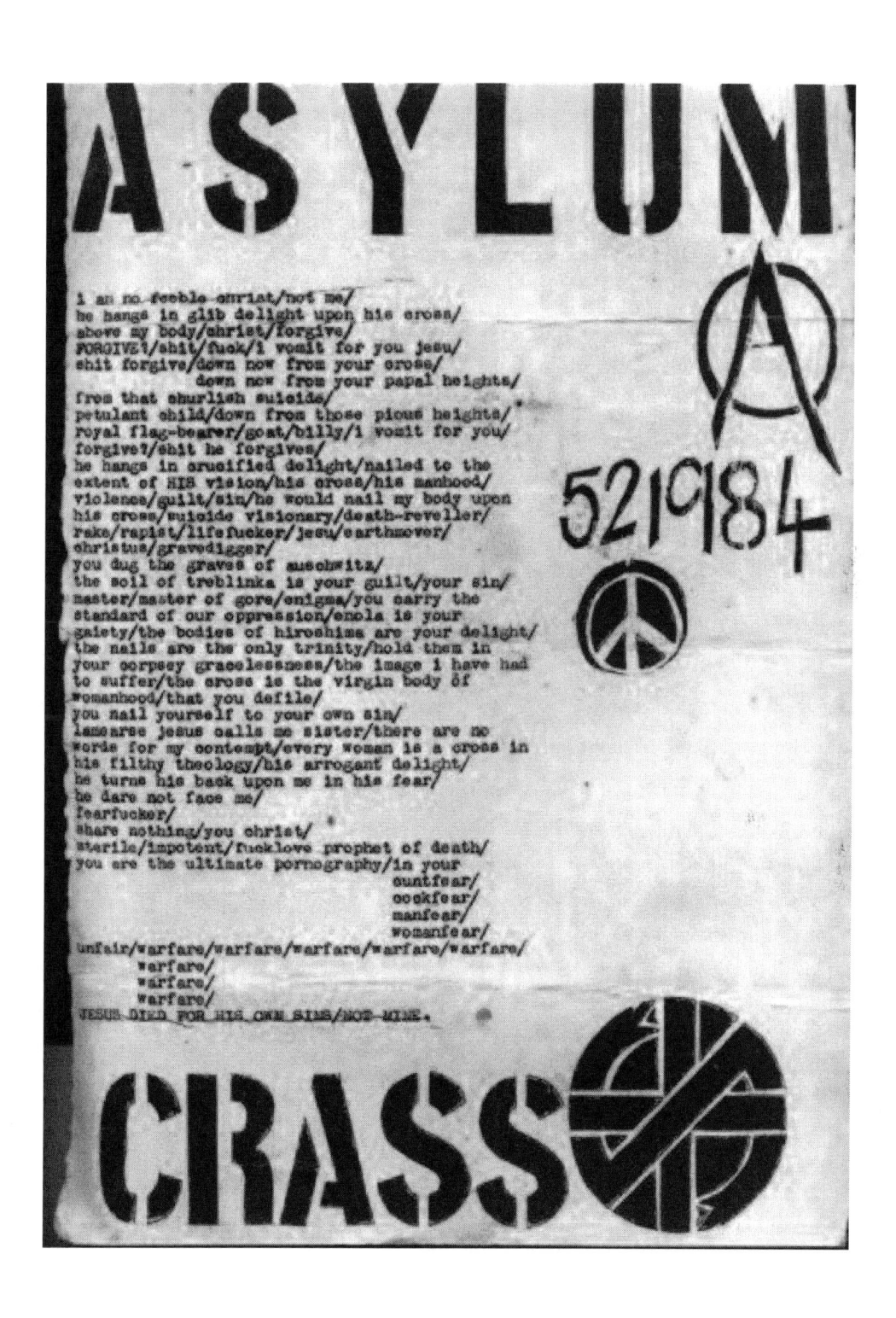

TOTAL CHAOS = TOTAL SHIT

WHAT NEXT?FOR FIVE YEARS PUNK HAS BEEN MAKING PROMISES,HOW MANY OF THEM HAVE COME TO EFFECT?YES,THE BANDS ARE STILL AROUND,THE FANZINES KEEP ON COMING OUT,A LOT OF PEOPLE WEAR THE OUTFITS,BUT NOT A LOT REALLY SEEMS TO HAPPEN.SO WHAT NEXT?WHAT ARE YOU DOING?YES,THE BANDS AND THE FANZINES ARE PUTTING OUT THE MESSAGE,YOU CAN SEE THE SLOGANS WRITTEN ON A THOUSAND LEATHER COATS,BUT WHERE'S THE ACTION?SO THE EXPLOITED CAME ALONG AND GAVE US ANARCHY AND CHAOS AGAIN AND AGAIN AND AGAIN,BIG DEAL.TOP OF THE POPS, THAT'S REAL ANARCHY AIN'T IT?BUT THE SAME OLD SLOGANS AND BADGES ARE STILL THERE.BARMY ARMY?TOO BLOODY RIGHT;IF YOU STILL BELIEVE IN THAT SHIT YOU'VE GOT TO BE BARMY.YES,THERE IS A CHANCE OF CHANGING THINGS IF YOU'RE PRE- PARED TO DO A LITTLE BIT MORE THAN TO ACCEPT THE SHIT THAT'S CONSTANTLY THROWN AT US ALL.THE GOVERNMENT IS PUSHING THROUGH A DEAL WITH AMERICA THAT WILL GUARANTEE A MASSIVE ESCALATION OF NUCLEAR ACTIVITY IN THIS COUNTRY,WE'RE ALREADY A NUCLEAR SCRAP-HEAP FOR THE USA,DO WE REALLY NEED MORE OF THEIR SHIT ON OUR DOORSTEP.OK,SO THE LOCAL CND ISN'T TOO INTERESTED IN PUNKS,WELL START YOUR OWN MOVEMENT,GET TOGETHER WITH OTHER PEOPLE WHO ARE PISSED OFF WITH WHAT'S GOING ON IN YOUR AREA AND DO SOMETHING ABOUT IT. SEE IF YOU CAN GET HOLD OF A SHED,MAYBE THE LOCAL SCOUTS SHED,OR SOME VILLAGE HALL FOR ONE OR TWO DAYS A WEEK AND START HAVING MEETINGS TO DISCUSS WHAT'S GOING ON,ARRANGE FILM SHOWS,CND WILL OFTEN COME DOWN TO PLACES WITH FILMS;ARRANGE GIGS,THERE'S LOTS OF BANDS LIKE OURSELVES WHO ARE PREPARED TO PLAY IN SMALL OUT OF THE WAY PLACES;WHEN YOU RUN OUT OF MONEY,ARRANGE A JUMBLE SALE,YOU CAN GET ALL YOUR OWN GEAR THAT WAY AS WELL; SET UP A RECORD AND BOOK LIBRARY SO THAT YOU CAN SHARE THE EXPENSE OF BUYING NEW ONES.THIS MIGHT SOUND A BIT YOUTH CLUBISH,BUT SO FUCKING WHAT? IT'S A FUCKING SIGHT BETTER THAN STANDING AROUND ON STREET CORNERS MOANING ABOUT HOW NOTHING EVER HAPPENS,IT'S YOUR FUCKING FAULT IF THERE'S NOTHING HAPPENING IN YOUR AREA,IT'S YOUR RESPONSIBILITY TO DO SOMETHING ABOUT IT.

DON'T FUCKING COMPLAIN- IT'S YOU THAT FUCKING PAYS.

THERE'S LOTS OF PEOPLE WHO DO WANT TO CHANGE THINGS AND ARE PREPARED TO DO SOMETHING ABOUT IT.OK,SO IT'S HARD TO FIND THEM,BUT WHAT HAVE YOU DONE TO TRY?PEOPLE LIKE PEACE NEWS,CND,THE ANIMAL LIBERATION FRONT,THE PEACE PLEDGE UNION,ETC.CAN ALL HELP YOU GET IN TOUCH WITH PEOPLE LIKE YOURSELVES.HAVE YOU TRIED WRITING TO ANY OF THOSE PEOPLE?WE GET SO MANY LETTERS FROM PEOPLE WHO DON'T SEEM TO DO MUCH MORE THAN MOAN.WHERE DOES THAT GET ANYONE?THE ONLY WAY IN WHICH THINGS ARE GOING TO CHANGE IS IF YOU DO SOMETHING ABOUT IT YOURSELF.WHAT DO YOU KNOW ABOUT WHAT'S HAPPENING IN YOUR AREA?WHAT KIND OF ARMY ACTIVITY IS THERE?WHERE ARE THE LOCAL GOVERNMENT BUNKERS?IS THERE A SLAUGHTERHOUSE IN THE AREA?IF THERE IS,ARRANGE TO VISIT IT AND YOU'LL NEVER EAT MEAT AGAIN.PRINT A PAMPHLET ABOUT WHAT YOU FIND OUT,LET OTHER PEOPLE KNOW WHAT'S GOING ON AND LET THEM KNOW WHAT YOU THINK ABOUT IT.IT'S TIME THAT WE ALL STOPPED BEING SO APOLOGETIC AND TRIED TO REALLY DO SOME- THING.IF YOU THINK THAT PUNK IS JUST A WAY OF AMUSING YOURSELF ON A SAT- URDAY NIGHT,YOU'VE GOT IT ALL WRONG,YOU'D BE DOING A LOT MORE GOOD GOING OUT & SPRAYING GRAFFITI THAN JUST MINDLESSLY POGOING TO SOME SHIT-HEAD BAND WHO DON'T WANT TO DO ANYTHING BUT TAKE YOUR LAST QUID.IT'S TIME TO REALISE THAT PUNK IS ABOUT DOING IT YOURSELF,ABOUT BEING CREATIVE RATHER THAN DESTRUCTIVE,HOW ARE WE GOING TO CHANGE THE WORLD BY SMASHING UP A BOG?IT'S TIME TO GROW UP AND STOP BEHAVING LIKE SPOILT CHILDREN.IT'S OUR WORLD SO WHY THE FUCK DON'T WE START USING IT RATHER THAN LETTING IT USE US?NO ONE ELSE IS GOING TO HELP,IT'S UP TO US TO GET TOGETHER AND DO IT.

THE GREAT ROCK 'N' ROLL SWINDLE

EIGHT YEARS AGO THE 'PUNK MOVEMENT' ROSE OUT OF THE DESPERATION AND ANGER THAT WE HAD ALL BEEN FEELING, ABOUT THE WAY IN WHICH OUR LIVES, AND OUR WORLD WAS BEING CONTROLLED AND RUINED BY THE STATE.

AT THIS TIME WE HAD NO WAY OF MAKING OUR VOICES HEARD, SO WE CREATED ONE.

WE BEGAN BY TELLING THE BIG BUSINESSES TO FUCK OFF - WE DIDN'T NEED THEM. WE ORGANISED OUR OWN GIGS AND PUT OUT OUR OWN RECORDS, ALL UNDER OUR OWN CONTROL AND AT PRICES WE COULD ALL AFFORD.

ROUGH TRADE AND THE OTHER 'INDEPENDANTS' FORMED AN ALTERNATIVE DISTRIBUTION NETWORK, AND IT WASN'T LONG BEFORE WE HAD OUR OWN WORKABLE ALTERNATIVE TO THE MUSIC BUSINESS - MUSIC FOR THE PEOPLE, PLAYED BY THE PEOPLE, AND ORGANISED BY THE PEOPLE.

OF COURSE WE WERE LET DOWN BY THOSE WHO WERE UNABLE TO RESIST THE TEMPTATIONS OFFERED BY THE MUSIC BUSINESS - THE CLASH BECAME THE NEW ROLLING STONES, AND SOME OF THE SO CALLED INDIE LABELS MADE BUSINESS DEALS WITH THE MAJORS.

BUT WHILE THERE WERE A FEW THAT GRABBED AT THE CHANCE OF A FEW SECONDS GLORY STRUTTING IN THE ARENAS PROVIDED BY THE MUSIC BUSINESS, MANY MORE OF US WENT ON TO TURN OUR VISIONS OF LOVE, HOPE, SHARING, AND CARING INTO A REALITY.

WE BELIEVED THAT BY SHARING OUR VISIONS, IDEAS AND EXPERIENCES; BY MAKING AVAILABLE INFORMATION NOT NORMALLY AVAILABLE; AND BY ACTUALLY LIVING A WORKABLE ALTERNATIVE WE COULD CREATE AND BUILD UP SUFFICIENT DESIRE FOR CHANGE; THAT WOULD EVENTUALLY LEAD TO SUCH A CHANGE COMING ABOUT.

EIGHT YEARS LATER IT HAS BECOME OBVIOUS THAT THIS IS NOT ENOUGH. ROUGH TRADE AND THE CARTEL HAVE NOW GOT SO MANY BUSINESS DEALS ARRANGED WITH THE MAJOR LABELS, THAT THEY HAVE BECOME JUST ANOTHER MAJOR.

THE ALTERNATIVE CHARTS HAVE BECOME A COMPLETE AND UTTER FARCE - HOW CAN ANYBODY BELIEVE THAT THE SMITHS, OR ELVIS COSTELLO, OR THE COCK TOE TWINS OFFER ANYTHING ALTERNATIVE. YOU ONLY HAVE TO HEAR THEIR RECORDS OR SEE THEM ON TOP OF THE POPS TO SEE THAT THEY ARE JUST THE SAME AS THE REST OF THE MINDLESS PAP.

I'M TRYING NOT TO PUT TOO MUCH IMPORTANCE ON THE PUNK MOVEMENT - AFTER ALL IT WAS JUST A LABEL CREATED BY THE MEDIA TO PIGEON HOLE THESE 'DIFFERENT PEOPLE'. TAKE AWAY THE LABEL AND ALL YOU HAVE LEFT IS THE PEOPLE - AND THAT'S WHAT REALLY HURTS.

I BELIEVED IN PEOPLE LIKE THE CLASH AND ROUGH TRADE, I BELIEVED THAT THEY CARED AND MEANT WHAT THEY SAID. I BELIEVED THAT ALL OF US TOGETHER WERE CREATING AN ALTERNATIVE TOGETHER.

BUT FOR EACH OF THE DISHONEST SHITS THAT HAVE LET ME DOWN THERE HAVE BEEN MANY MORE THAT HAVN'T - AND I STILL BELIEVE THAT DESPITE THE SELLOUTS AND CONTRADICTIONS WE CAN STILL MAKE OUR ALTERNATIVE WORK - NOT JUST WITHIN THE MUSIC BUSINESS - BUT WITHIN THE WHOLE WORLD.

SOMEONE ONCE CAME UPTO ME AT A GIG AND SAID WE WERE IN DANGER OF BECOMING AS VICIOUS AND PERNICIOUS TOOL AS DALLAS. HE WENT ON TO SAY THAT THERE WAS VERY LITTLE DIFFERENCE BETWEEN THE WAY DALLAS ENTERTAINED AND APPEASED PEOPLE; AND THE WAY IN WHICH ANGRY FRUSTRATED PEOPLE CAME TO OUR GIGS - ENJOYED THEMSELVES, AND WENT AWAY FEELING RELIEVED ONCE THAT ANGER AND FRUSTRATION HAD BEEN GIVEN SOME FORM OF ESCAPE.

TO A CERTAIN EXTENT I AGREE WITH HIM - BUT WHEN YOU'RE TRYING TO USE 'MUSIC' TO GIVE A MESSAGE YOU FIND YOURSELF TRYING TO GET A WORKABLE BALANCE BETWEEN 'ENJOYMENT' AND 'COMMUNICATION'. IF YOU'RE TOO ENJOYABLE AND UNDEMANDING THE CONTENTS OF THE MESSAGE GET LOST, AND IF YOU'RE NOT ENJOYABLE ENOUGH NO ONE IS PREPARED TO LISTEN TO WHAT YOU HAVE TO SAY.

DURING THE PAST FEW MONTHS I HAVE BEEN FEELING MORE AND MORE FRUSTRATED WORKING IN A BAND - HOW CAN YOU KEEP PUTTING OUT RECORDS AND DOING GIGS THAT ARE INEFFECTIVE - AND HOW DO YOU AVOID BECOMING JUST ANOTHER ROCK 'N' ROLL BAND?

I KNOW THAT THERE IS SO MUCH GROUND THAT CAN BE EXPLORED IF PEOPLE ARE PREPARED TO DEVELOP AND PUSH THEMSELVES FURTHER, WITH IDEAS AS WELL AS WITH MUSIC.

WE CAN'T GO ON RETREADING THE SAME GROUND WHEN WE KNOW THAT WE ARN'T GETTING ANYWHERE.

REASONING WITH THE AUTHORITIES HAS NOT WORKED - THE RECENT C.N.D. PROTEST MARCHES (AND COUNTLESS OTHER PROTESTS) HAS HAD NO EFFECT ON CURBING THE GOVERNMENTS MILITARY BUILD UP.

Protest, Resist, Live: An Interview with SLUG

Mike Dines

To be honest, this turned out to be a bit of an odd interview. Three days earlier to meeting Phil, JJ and Trev on a sunny afternoon in the 'Our Black Heart' pub in Camden, London, they had announced that SLUG were no more. Posting a pensive-looking shot of them sitting on Brighton beach (very tongue-in-cheek) the band had decided to move on to other projects. At first, I wondered whether they would cancel the interview, but was relieved to find they still wanted to meet. It was also odd in meeting Phil again for the first time in just over 15 years. In a previous life I had taught him music in a college in Portsmouth. Although at home I listened to Crass, Culture Shock and other noisy shenanigans, I taught Schubert, Mozart and Debussy, all of which are a far cry from the stuff that Phil plays today.

Formed in London, SLUG consisted of Brickett on vocals, JJ on guitar and vocals, Campos on Bass, Phil on guitar and vocals, and Trev on drums. With members from Active Slaughter (JJ and Trev) and Bug Central (Trev), the band played fast, aggressive punk, dealing with subjects such as animal rights, Britain First and class war. Discography includes the album Detect, Denounce, Destroy (2014) and the split Echoes of the Past…Reverberate into Our Future (2014) with Piss on Authority. I started with the obvious….

Me: Pleased to meet you all. Would you like to introduce yourselves?

JJ: Normally I answer 'no comment' [Laughs]. JJ, guitarist of SLUG, and Trev sitting next to me, we started the band three years ago, a few weeks before Phil joined. For about 10 years we both used to be in a band called Active Slaughter. So we started SLUG and then we dragged in Phil and Sam and a fella called Bruce who was in a band called Bug Central, which used to be Trev's band as well. Bruce stayed for about 6 months and then left and we brought in Campo on bass.

Phil: I'm Phil, I play guitar in SLUG. I met the other members in a squat called Kernels, in South London. That was roughly about five years ago. Me and the singer [Bricket] joined the band about three years ago with the guys sitting with me. Yeah, and I'm from Pompey.

Me: Thanks. I've been listening to your album Detect, Denounce, Destroy, and I particularly like tracks such as 'Class War,' 'Shoot to Kill' and 'To The End.' I'd really like your thoughts on definition and thought I'd start with a loaded question: do you see yourself as an 'anarcho-punk' band?

Trev: Personally, I have real trouble with the whole 'naming' everything different 'sub-genres.' I know, I understand, why people do it, but personally, I don't like labels.

Me: Yeah, I can fully understand that. I mean, do you see Bug Central as an anarcho-punk band?

Trev: Yes, if you're going to 'abide' by the divisions then yes. But personally I'm not in favour of sub-dividing it. To me, it's all punk; it's that simple.

Me: I see what you mean. I remember hearing Penny Rimbaud's thoughts on this and he said that defining punk in this way could be pretty divisive.

Phil: Yeah, I think it's pretty difficult. Don't forget that music is only a medium of expression, so like the question it's a pretty loaded position to be in, as well. I think from some of our perspectives – as with the outset of anarcho-punk – anarchism in general is seen as something that is completely free from the clutches of the State. That's what anarchism could mean as to some people it could be different to other people. And that kind of feeling, a feeling you get when you're free from the State, so I don't think being a band, being in a punk band, as an active band, can give you that feeling. And I think there are certain aspects of life where you can get that feeling, like squatting, for example. During those two years where I was squatting there were some parts of that feeling where I was completely free from the State. I had no troubles and I was doing things creatively and I had little trouble doing it at all. And also, from the animal rights perspective that came from the '80s [to JJ and Trev] you'll be able to answer this better, but that has always been a big part of it.

Trev: I think the thing with the anarcho-punk label as well is that it's kind of a convenient way of basically saying what your politics are. I mean, if you just take for example anarcho-punk and Oi, if two bands had those labels you would pretty much be able to determine what the politics are and the people who would be into them were into to. And I think that's just a convenient way of describing something.

JJ: I agree, it can cause divisions, but I don't think the labels do that people do that themselves without the labels. Then again, I'm giving it all that, but to be honest, some of punks out there I wouldn't wanna stand side-by-side with. I might wanna stand side-by side with somebody else who don't even like punk – they might be into Celine Dion or something! It's not about what music they like or into, it's about who they are. There's all this punk unity stuff but at the end of the day but I don't wanna unify with a lot of people and that includes punks.

Phil: It's quite important to separate anarchism and anarcho-punk as well. I mean, you go to protests [and the people who attend] are not necessarily into punk music they're into other stuff and so it is quite important to separate anarchism and anarcho-punk in that sense because you can't sort of like say that everybody dressed in black down in the local estate is looking to smash the State or are into anarcho-punk or into anarchism, whatever that might be.

Me: We talk about what anarcho-punk might mean in the 1980s – lyrical content including animal rights and anti-religion – do you think that this political sloganeering is just as important? [To JJ] I read your statement about HLS [Huntingdon Life Sciences] and SHAC [Stop Huntingdon Animal Cruelty], so that's really important to you, isn't it? [JJ was one of those involved with SHAC, an international animal rights campaign involved in the attempted closing down of HLS, a company that tests medical and non-medical substances on over 75,000 animals every year. In 2009 and 2010, 13 members of the group were jailed for between 15 months and 11 elevens on charges of conspiracy to blackmail or harm HLS and its suppliers]

JJ: Yeah, more than the music is. At the end of the day, anarcho-punk is just music to me. I have more important things, my beliefs. Music is like a subdivision of that – like an extension – and I'm into all different kinds of punk and not just anarcho-punk, and not just punk. But if it's changed, then Trev was there in the '80s so….[everyone laughs]

Phil: What was that band you were in?

Trev: The first band I was in was The Miscreants…

Phil: and Anthrax as well…

Trev: Well, I knew Anthrax, yeah.

Me: Capitalism is Cannibalism was '82 and of course there are arguments that this so-called first-wave of anarcho-punk was over by '84. Where do you think it came from? Why did anarcho-punk develop such a political message from '77?

Trev: It's entirely Crass, it's all their fault. Everything is their fault. Well, for me it was. I'm sure Penny Rimbaud has said this countless times but after hearing the Pistols and stuff like that, it was kind of the next logical step to make. If you believe in the notion of anarchy as in 'Anarchy in the UK,' then, they…what did someone once say…that the Sex Pistols told us about anarchy and Crass told us what anarchy actually was. And I think that was essentially what happened.

JJ: And also, they were a cross between hippies and punks weren't they? They mixed the both together and I think that's where the passion came from and the politics because of the '60s and '70s and they'd done a lot.

Trev: And older people. I think if it had just been up to seventeen-year-old punks…if they'd just left it to the kids they would have fucked it up [laughs].

Me: Do you think it was more like a counterculture, of it being a little more 'thought out'? There was certainly a sense of ideology around the movement.

Phil: I don't think it was too engineered though. It was more like a natural progression to make out of first wave punk.

Trev: Yeah. I mean, Dial House. There's the perfect example of putting peace into practice, basically.

Me: And you think that these ideals are still relevant today?

JJ: For the anarcho-scene today, if we're gonna go back to the labels, there are a lot less anarcho-punk bands around than in the early '80s. I think, perhaps, the majority of band in the early '80s were anarcho bands….

Phil: I would say though that kids today are more pissed off than when I was younger. The squat where I lived in south London for a good few years…like so many kids came through and basically they just got younger and younger. They were so disillusioned, with some of them being homeless, and many of them wanting a real say in how they live their lives – so much more than 10 years ago. Back then everyone seemed to have jobs and stuff and people were like doing well. But now, it's completely different. Like our singer, for example, he's in the clutches of this government's Workfare Scheme, [a Conservative-led policy in the UK where individuals must undertake work in return for benefits] which has made him more pissed off than I ever was as a kid. I think kids have more of a say, but not under the influence of anarcho-punk as a label, but are still as influenced by what we term as punk today. Some of the messages that come out of the scene can still be deemed under anarcho-punk, but wouldn't necessarily be described as that, if that makes sense? It kind of highlights the difficulties with labels and stuff.

Me: And what about the DiY scene? Do you think the scene is as prominent as it was in the 1980s?

Phil: I think there is more of a friendly collective of people but some people like to position themselves outside of DiY. You know, 'I don't wanna be part of that scene,' but it's just like one of those dumb things. There's nothing wrong with doing stuff for charity, there's nothing wrong with doing benefit gigs.

Trev: I think the thing is about DiY is that it's incredibly easy to be DiY. You can do it in your own bedroom – although you could always do it in your bedroom but it was on a cassette tape….

Phil: I mean you can run your own label from your own bedroom…

Trev: Yeah, it's dead easy to be DiY, but I don't think it's as prominent…

JJ: The thing is, is that I think that everything is split up now into different types of punk, and not even punk. You know, the majority of anarchists out there are not into punk and people seem to be split up into other groups. So the anarcho-punk scene seems smaller, but the amount of anger that the kids have now and how politically aware they are, it's just as big now as it was in the '80s.

Me: [to JJ] And of course, tied in with the anger and that political awareness, I read your statement online about what happened to you. It reminded me a little bit of Mark Barnsley and the pressures that he encountered whilst in prison and what happened to him when he got out.

JJ: Yeah, I used to write to him when he was in prison.

Me: Because I was listening to the track on your album about HLS. Are you able to write about HLS now? In your statement you talked about going to see Conflict and you were pulled up for it.

JJ: Yeah, it turned out that someone who worked at probation was into punk and he was there at the gig. Out of all the places, you know, small world. So a few days after that, someone from Scotland Yard, from like the anti-terrorist unit, he used to come once a month to have a chat with me and see what I've been up to and that – basically to put a bit of fear into me – he turned up a few days after and all he wanted to talk about was that gig and who was there, who I spoke to. So yeah, they weren't happy about that. So, it just shows that obviously back in the day Conflict was really well known band in the political movement – alongside Crass as well – and Scotland Yard are still thinking that Conflict are a powerful part of the movement today. We're saying that anarcho-punk isn't as powerful, but Scotland Yard are still interested in what Conflict do.

Phil: Yeah, apparently Scotland Yard have parked up outside Colin's house in the past…

Me: And of course what you've written about Scotland Yard putting undercover individuals in with you whilst you were planning the HLS stuff. A bit like the McLibel Trial fiasco with Helen Steel and stuff.

JJ: Hopefully there might be a little more of that stuff coming up in the future as we're talking to barristers at the moment about this. They're the barristers who are involved with all the undercover police stuff that we've been hearing about at the moment.

Me: What you went through sounds horrendous.

JJ: One of my co-defendants went through even worse. That was just my story.

Me: I think there were 31 other defendants and because you pleaded guilty to a lesser chance this meant you got a shorter sentence. However, some of the other defendants got pretty long prison-terms, like 10 years.

JJ: Heather got the worse. She got 11 years. Then a few got 9 years and below that a few got 7 years. And quite a few got 5 years, and few got like 2 years and 3 years.

Me: Was it true that HLS were on the verge of closing down?

JJ: Yeah, due to us. We basically closed it but the government stepped in and gave them a bailout.

Phil: They were about to float on the stock exchange weren't they?

JJ: That was after then. They were stopped, but they did afterwards. But there was one point when there was basically a victory and then the next day we found out that the government had stepped in and bailed them out with taxpayers' money. The government basically said we're gonna keep you open no matter what and then the pharmaceutical companies started to step in, people like Glaxo, Merck and Roche, and they put pressure on the Blair and Brown government and they said to them look, if you don't sort them out these activists, we're gonna leave the UK and that was when they brought in the new laws. So it was the big pharmaceutical companies influencing government.

Phil: Also, many politicians have financial interests in pharmaceutical companies anyway so it was obviously in their interests to keep it open. In fact, I think it was more about that issue than the animal welfare issue.

JJ: It's like either the second or the third biggest industry in the UK, the pharmaceutical industry, so it's pretty powerful…

Trev: It's after anarcho punk….[all laughs]

Me: We've talked about the past. Where do you think punk is going? Where would you like it to go?

JJ: To inspire people, that would be my dream. Some kid off the street, he's angry, and he doesn't know where to point his anger towards and suddenly he gets into punk and listens to whatever band and he thinks 'I like these lyrics, I agree with them' and so gets into the scene, meets similar people and then suddenly he becomes influenced by other people's ideas which are similar to his and he's got direction then. Yeah, giving people a direction, inspiring people, bringing them together.

Phil: I think there are two ways to look at this. There is the personal and the collective. From the personal point of view we each have our own politics, our own ideas and thoughts about how we express that. In terms of the collective, I think there needs to be a bit more, er…not 'leadership'…but collective determination to protest. We go to demos – like housing demos for instance – but we need more people there. In also goes for animal rights – and also, I think people should leave Facebook alone. Stop clicking stuff and actually go out and do it!

Trev: I think the way in which we all grow together, like JJ says, is that we get together and go 'we agree with this, or agree with that.' I guess that's all we can hope for really. I mean, when we make music, everything we write has to be somehow political, otherwise, what's the point? And that's it, you play it and hopefully inspire somebody to do something, say something, or be active.

JJ: And we have, over the years, in Active Slaughter and SLUG, we've had people come up to us and say you know, 'you've changed my life. You've turned me vegetarian, you've turned me vegan, you've turned me into an activist.' One bloke I know he got into Active Slaughter years ago and within a couple of years he was doing time for animal rights. It was amazing.

Trev: I mean, there has to be that, doesn't there? Somebody does have to influence somebody else, that's how ideas spread. It just so happens we're doing it in musical form, other people do it in other ways.

JJ: I can relate to that. Trev influenced me quite a lot within punk, especially with his bands Bug Central and Intensive Care. Musically and also about ideas round punk and that. I mean, I liked him so much I stole him out of the band for Active Slaughter [laughs]. But Trev probably influences me more than people like Steve Ignorant or Dick Lucas [Trev gets up and buys a round] I was just gonna say, you owe me a drink after that! So, you don't have to be someone like, 'famous,' – I hate saying that word – like Dick Lucas or Steve Ignorant, you can just be someone who not many people know.

Trev returns with our drinks and we continue chatting in the sun. The conversation moves away from punk towards Kanye West at Glastonbury, Steve Reich and the Criminal Justice Bill. With a band tuning up in the pub and regulars turning up for a night's drinking we walk down towards Camden Underground Station where, although it's late afternoon it's still hot and there are still plenty of tourists milling around wanting to see the 'famous' Camden Market. Phil tells me that he still listens to Schubert and I tell him we shouldn't leave it so long next time.

It's a shame to see the end of SLUG, but I have a feeling that there's something else to come from Phil, JJ and Trev……

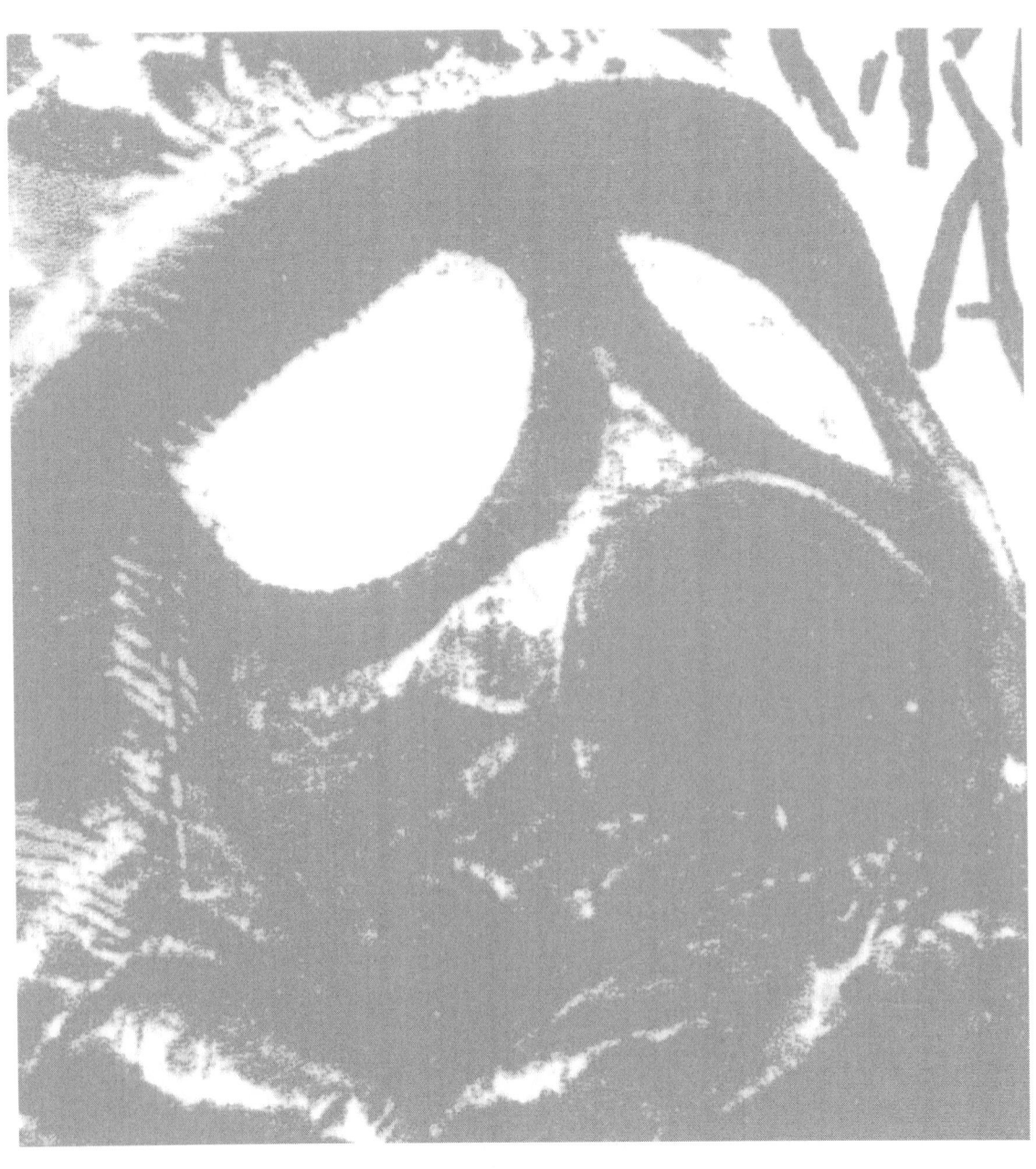

Various Handouts, Flyers and Information and Advice

Courtesy Johnny Reynolds

Anorexia

SEXIST TRADITION

HAVE YOU EVER STOPPED AND THOUGHT ABOUT THE HUMILIATION AND DEGRADATION THAT WIMMIN GO THROUGH IN EVERYDAY LIFE? PEOPLES WAY OF LIFE EVOLVES AROUND THE EXPLOITATION OF WIMMIN. FROM THE HARD-CORE PORN ON THE SHELVES OF THE 'MARITIAL HARMONY' SHOPS TO THE ATTITUDES OF THEIR FRIENDS AND RELATIVES AROUND THEM. THE INDOCTRINATED BELIEF THAT MAN IS THE STRONG, FORCEFUL, DOMINANT TYPE AND THAT WOMAN IS THE WEAK, GENTLE, SUBMISSIVE TYPE IS PUT INTO EVERYONES MIND FROM DAY ONE, SO IT IS EASY TO UNDERSTAND HOW PEOPLE CAN BELIEVE THIS CRAP.

PEOPLE ARE MOST EASILY INFLUENCED WHEN THEY ARE YOUNG, AND SO THE MOST DANGEROUS FORM OF SEXISM IS INTRODUCED FROM AN EARLY AGE. TO BACK UP THE SEXIST MYTH CHILDREN ARE GIVEN TOYS THAT MATCH THEIR SEX BY PEOPLE WHO HAVE ALREADY BEEN PUT THROUGH THIS SEXIST TRADITION. LITTLE BOYS PLAY WITH ACTION MEN, CARS, TANKS, GUNS AND VERY LITTLE ELSE WHILE LITTLE GIRLS PLAY WITH DOLLS, TOY COOKERS, IRONING BOARDS AND USUALLY VERY LITTLE ELSE. CHILDREN ARE TOLD THAT BOYS PLAY RUGBY AND FOOTBALL AND GIRLS PLAY NETBALL, AND THAT WHEN THEY GROW UP THE BOYS WILL GO OUT TO WORK IN A FACTORY OR AS A MECHANIC, AND THAT THE GIRLS SHOULD BE HAPPY TO STAY AT HOME AND DO THE HOUSE WORK AND THE WASHING. AND SO THE PROCESS OF A SEXIST WAY OF

LIFE HAS BEGUN.

School will generally reinforce the myth, that the boys do the wood and the metalwork while the girls do the needlework and the cookery. After school boys will usually find it easy to get employment, easier that is than a girl, who would face ridicule if she applied for a job in a factory or as a mechanic. In the business world, although all business people are greedy, profit making scum, a woman is looked upon as being aggressive and pushy, while a man with the same attitude is looked upon as being competitive and determined. Is it no wonder why it is men who occupy powerful positions at the top.

Pornography is avaliable in many forms, both strong and mild, and can usually be found cropping up in many areas of everyday life. It can be found not only within 'traditional' pornographic literature, but also in easily accesable newspapers, magazines, books, films, t.v and advertising boards. All using wimmin for the female body to add 'spice' or to sell a product, portraying wimmin to be toys and always willing to please. They all degrade wimmin and allow them no respect.

The result of pornography is the main cause of sexual crimes. Because men begin to beleive that it is right for them to be able to dominate wimmin and use them for selfish pleasure, that it is right to take out their anger and frustration on the 'always willing to please' wimmin that they see so often. This kind of violence is a direct result of the media dominated pornography. Wimmin are not ours to control and exploit, wimmin are not lesser than men, they are not our 'mississ' or our 'bird' they are our equal.

   1 in 6 wimmin have been raped.
   1 in 12 rapes are reported to the police

(whose attitude to the victims of rape is intimidating, uncaring and often suspicious)
3 in 4 attackers are known to the victims
(this does not include incest)
1 in 2 rapes occur in the home of the rapist or the victim.

In particular the advertising media exploits wimmin, merely as objects and tools, that if by revealing enough of their bodies then that will sell the product. Since when has a woman in a bikini had any relevance to a sausage, none whatsoever, but this can be seen on a television ad. Wimmin are used to advertise make up, by using 'pretty' models, they leave the 'ordinary' wimmin feeling inadequate and so maybe they ought to try this 'beauty' product too. Look at the adverts for the washing machines and powders, it always seems to be the wimmin that do all of the washing and the men with the authoritive voices and the smart suites that tell them they are using the wrong washing powder.

Wimmin as well as men are capable of being conned by this sexist tradition, and usually are. How many times do wimmin allow themselves to be left at home gossiping while the man is out drinking with his mates. How many times does the man come home from work with his dinner on the table and his shirts washed and ironed. Even if the wimmin realise that this position they are in is wrong, they often find it difficult to escape. They are in an ideal position for the man to be able to blackmail them as he usually earns most or all of the money they live on.

Things are indeed changing, but slowly. Its about time we all realised our potential for independance, that we all tried to understand and come to terms with the ingrained

IDEAS THAT INFLUENCE US. WE MUST BREAK AWAY FROM THE ROLES WE HAVE BEEN FORCED INTO, WE CAN, AND MUST, ALL WORK ALONGSIDE EACH OTHER, AND IT IS TIME FOR THE TYPICAL MAN TO GET OUT OF THE WAY, OR BE PHYSICALLY REMOVED FROM THE PATH OF THIS DEVELOPEMENT.

       OBSESSION
       POSSESSION
       OPPRESSION
PORNOGRAPHY IS WIMMINS DEGRADATION.

IN THE STRUGGLE FOR THE LIBERATION AND EQUALITY OF THE PEOPLE - MALE AND FEMALE
       LOVE ANOREXIA.

COMMUNICATE :- DAVE (ANOREXIA),

IT'S UP TO YOU
THERE IS AN ENEMY
AND A FENCE THAT DIVIDES
WHICH SIDE ARE YOU ON?
LIBERTY
time for action
LIBERTY
'OUR VOICE IS TOMMOROW'S HOPE'
LIBERTY'S 4 TRACK EP.
99p MORTORHATE RECORDS
OUT NOW
We are gonna stop all forms of abuse, but
not by giving peace signs we're gonna
use force, we won't stand back and
let it happen it's gone on far too long
we've got to stand together and prove
those murdering bastards wrong.
'Liberty'
MASTERS FAKE
BEG FOR THEIR BONES
They turned against their own
people and worked for the Nazis to stay
alive: Jewish policemen during a
round-up in the Ghetto.

BOYCOTT COCA KILLER

Everyone knows that Coca-cola rots your teeth and guts,but heres a few facts that perhaps you didnt know.Apart from the obvious accusations of dirty fingers in dirty pies,and the muffled screams of the multinationals crimes,and apart from the fact that one of the additives in coca-cola is carcogenic(cancer causing) the bastards have gone too far in Guatemala.

In february 1984 the workers of the coca-cola plant in Guatemala City occupied their workplace ater being told of the franchise owners supposed insolvency but he was lying because he'd fiddled by undercharging othercompanies that he owned.

The workers demanded that:

1. Coca-cola international should take over direct running of the plant until a new franchise owner could be found. 2.That the current workforce be retained and Union rights should be respected.3.That the workers should be paid for maintaining the plant during occupation.

So the military set up road blocks and said they'd shoot people on plant property.

One person was shot, two injured and four just disappeared. So a boycott was launched and solidarity strikes undertakenan and after four months workers solidarity triumphed and the workers were rehired, But the bastards refused to reopen the plant till a new franchise owner could be found and they only paid the workers partial wages for maintaining the plant during the occupation.

During a previous dispute with the previous franchise owner, the bastards tried to break the union with paid hit squads. He had five union officalls killed and six others disappeared. After another boycott and other workers giving solidarity coca-cola was forced to revoke the operators franchise and to make monthly payments to the widows and orphans of the murdered unionists.Coca-cola stopped these payments during the occupation.Since May 1984 Coca-cola has violated every single aspect of the agreement.After trying to starve them out by waiting till November 1984 before securing a new franchise owner, the new owner is just as much of a bastard as the previous ones.He refuses to honour the promises on employment levels,he has declared the may 1984 agreement defunct and he has demanded concessions on wages and benefits.FOR THE CONTINUED SAFETY OF THE WORKERS WE MUST PUBLICISE THE DISPUTE AND HIT COCA-COLA WHERE IT HURTS THEM MOST - IN THE BANK BALANCE..........BOYCOTT THE BASTARDS!!!

COCA-COLA POLITICAL KILLER/COCA-COLA RIGHTS DESTROYER/ALL THEY WANTED WAS TO HAVE A UNION/A BASIC HUMAN RIGHT.

Generic.

CONFLICT

ON SUNDAY 23 FEB AT THE CLARENDON HOTEL IN HAMMERSMITH A FESTIVAL AGAINST APARTHEID IS BEING HELD, WE WOULD LIKE EVERYONE TO COME AND SHOW SUPPORT FOR THE ANTI APARTHEID MOVEMENT,............
ON THE NIGHT THERE WILL BE CONFLICT AND SIX OTHER BANDS FROM VARIOUS PARTS OF THE COUNTRY.
AND MEMBERS OF A FLUX OF PINK INDIANS WILL BE SPEAKING.

TICKETS ARE AVAILABLE NOW FROM PO.BOX 448, ELTHAM, LONDON, S.E.9. AND WILL BE AVAILABLE FROM ROUGH TRADE FROM THIS WEEKEND, TICKETS COST £1.75p AND PEOPLE MAY ALSO PAY AT THE DOOR

Smash Apartheid

THE UNGOVERNABLE FORCE IS COMING

CONFLICT

LIBERTY SPEAKERS
ICONS OF FILTH EXITSTANCE
PLUS MORE

ANTI APARTHEID FESTIVAL sunday 23 feb.

AT THE CLARENDON, HAMMERSMITH BROADWAY, LONDON.

DOORS OPEN AT 7pm

£1·75

THE UNGOVERNABLE FORCE IS COMING

THE CENTRE
AT THE CRYPT
UNDER St PAULS CHURCH
DEPTFORD HIGH STREET
LONDON S.E.8.

ALTERNATIVE NIGHT
EVERY MONDAY 8-12
LIVE BANDS

SOUNDS BY SAV - YOUR VINYL CARETAKER
RECORD/MERCHANDISE STALL + INFO ON GIGS
AND ACTION

BANDS WISHING TO PLAY, SEND TAPE TO CRYPT
MARKED 'MONDAY NIGHTS' OR ADDRESS TO 'THE
CENTRE'

ALL PROFITS TO THE BUST FUND!
PRICE £1.50

BUSES: 47,199,53,188,1. BR: DEPTFORD 2 MINS/NEW X 10 MINS

NIGHT BUSES: N47, N72, N77, N74, N82, N85, N86 !!!!!

Do you know that at least 70% of the human population of this planet starve & many more do not get enough to eat? You must now be familiar with reports of the famine in Ethiopia, where the weather has been so dry that crops fail, where the people are so hungry they have to walk many miles to the nearest relief station where there might be food if people have been generous. In any 1 station at least 40 people a day die, totally shrivelled. They haven't the energy to brush away the flies that are waiting for THEIR meal. These people are the victims of our western governments. In Britain alone there are massive great food stores where surplus grain sits, in the EEC there are food mountains, in America farmers are paid to destroy part of their harvest, while big corporations plunder the 3rd world countries at the expense of the natives. Why is this - economics, the science of greed, that which says people must pay western prices for their food. Naturally starving countries can't afford this, especially when their government takes the best first. The western governments have plenty of money. They tax us on our income, then they tax us on what we buy. They take the money we have worked for & use it to buy arms. They would rather be able to destroy the world 12 instead of 10 times over than transport surplus food to those who die. Indeed, they become ill through obesity. Must we tolerate these obscenities? When soon even we may be starving because of their taxes.

Some people don't see the connexions between big business & destruction. The biggest murderers are MacDonalds. Not only do they breed & slaughter millions of cattle, great rain forrests are pulled down to make way for grazing ground. This destroys hundreds of unique species each time not to mention the fact that we need the trees to produce oxygen for the planet. Many birds in North America migrate to these forests, on arriving & finding no forest they die. The drop in population of birds means more insects & the Americans only answer to that is pesticide. We all know about factories who manufacture pesticide, you know about Union Carbide. They're an American company who set up dangerous plants where if anything goes wrong it doesn't matter. Nearly 3000 Indians are now dead due to their callousness, thousands have strokes & injuries that will never heal. Innocent people who had done nothing, whose life is not easy anyway, & why? So America can steel food from the starving millions.

Nearly all big business is based on exploitation of the worst kinds. Cosmetic companies use dead animals to make their products, then poison many more by feeding it to them with the end result of encouraging sexism by convincing men & women to look the same as each other. Advertising promotes this & advertising of any kind usually portrays woman as a sex object only, there to be raped. Drug companies (like Roche & ICI) claim to invent new drugs to cure imagined diseases. Thousands die at the hands of their useless research. They try to make drugs to cure heart disease which was originally caused by the sufferer eating meat & dairy products to excess. Booker McConnell own everything from butchers to health shops, as long as the cash rolls in who cares? Other companies who make machinery & domestic appliances (like Thorn EMI,) also make defence gadgetry. British Aerospace specialise in fighters in favour of passenger jets. Governments pay more for weaponry than domestic consumers pay for domestic items. That's why many many companies world wide clamour for defence orders, some would go bankrupt without them. The final industry, uranium mining, sponsored in Britain by RTZ plunders the landscape, kills the wildlife expoits the natives & gives them cancer. The product makes bombs to kill all & is used for nuclear fuel. The kind of power that produces waste which can be pumped into the sea in Cumbria. Deformed babies & children dying of leukaemia are coincidences we are told.

How many more lies must we listen to.

THE CENTRE!
THE CRYPT DEPTFORD S.E.8.

THE BENIFIT CONTINUES!!

Monday 24th Feb. 8-12

with

Potential Threat (Blackburn)
Unknown Colours
Mentacide
Under The Gun (Exeter)

£1.50

Be there or get your arse home Sunday!

CONFLICT

Liberty
Sat May 24th
Hand & Heart, far gosford street, cov
£1.50

CONFLICT.
LONDON, S.E.9. ENGLAND
TELEPHONE:

HELLO,

SORRY ITS TAKEN SO LONG TO REPLY TO YOU BUT WEVE HAD A VERY HECTIC YEAR, WHAT WITH THE RUNNING OF THE RECORD LABELS THE BUST FUND, THE CENTRE, AND MORE IMPORTANTLY KEEPING THE BAND CONFLICT ON THE ROAD THROUGHOUT THE YEAR.
AS YOU WILL SEE THIS IS JUST A PRINTED FACT SHEET, THE REASON BEHIND THIS IS WE SIMPLY HAVE NOT GOT ENOUGH TIME TO REPLY IN PERSON AS WE ARE IN THE MIDDLE OF RECORDING OUR NEXT L.P. AND ARE BUSY ARRANGING OUR FIRST TOUR OF THE YEAR.
IT IS ALSO NOT A CASE OF US NOT CARING ABOUT YOUR LETTERS SO IF YOU NEED A PERSONAL REPLY PLEASE WRITE AGAIN AND WE WILL DO OUR BEST TO MAKE A PERSONAL REPLY QUICKLY.

THE CENTRE

AS SOME OF YOU ARE AWARE WE (CONFLICT) PLANNED TO OPEN A TOTALLY INDIPENDANT VENUE FOR BANDS TO PLAY IN LONDON.
THIS IS NOW IN OPERATION AND THE ADDRESS IS:
THE CENTRE, UNDER SAINT PAULS CHURCH, DEPTFORD HIGH STREET, DEPTFORD, LONDON, S.E.8.
THE CENTRE IS OPEN ON MONDAYS (EVERY MONDAY) BETWEEN 8-12pm.
AT THE CENTRE THERE ARE ALSO RECORD STALLS, VIDEOS, ALTERNATIVE MUSIC, AND AT LEAST ONE BAND PLAYING.
ANY BANDS WISHING TO PLAY PLEASE MAKE CONTACT WITH US AT THE PO.BOX AND PREFERABLY SEND A SAMPLE TAPE OR RECORD.

THE BUST FUND

THE BUST FUND IS NOW IN FULL SWING AND IS DOING WELL ALTHOUGH FUNDS ARE RUNNING LOW AND ANY OFFERS OF FUND RAISING ARE WELCOME.
FIRST ACCOUNTS ARE PRINTED IN THE BATTLE CONTINUES PAPER (ISSUE I.) WHICH IS INCLUDED FREE WITH OUR NEXT L.P. "THE UNGOVERNABLE FORCE"

RECORDING

AS PREVIOUSLY STATED, WE ARE AT THE PRESENT PUTTING THE FINAL TOUCHES TO OUR THIRD L.P. "THE UNGOVERNABLE FORCE"
THE L.P. WHICH IS ALL NEW STUDIO MATERIAL WILL BE AVAILABLE FROM THE END OF MARCH.
ALSO WE ARE RECORDING A NEW TRACK FOR OUR SHARE IN A JOINT 7" SINGLE WITH A FLUX OF PINK INDIANS.
THE SINGLE "SMASH APARTHEID" SHOULD BE RELEASED IN MAY AND WILL BE ON MORTARHATE RECORDS.

TOURING

WE (CONFLICT) ARE PLANNING TO TOUR THROUGHOUT BRITAIN FROM APRIL 28 TO THE END OF MAY, ANY PERSON WISHING TO HELP US ARRANGE A GIG IN YOUR AREA PLEASE GET IN CONTACT SOON, AS THIS IS THE ONLY PERIOD WE WILL BE FREE TO PLAY FOR A WHILE.
(MAKE CONTACT AT THE PO.BOX, OR THE PHONE NO.ABOVE)

FOR FULL INFORMATION ON CONFLICTS ACTIVITIES IN 1985, AND FUTURE PLANS SEE ISSUE NO I. OF THE BATTLE CONTINUES PAPER.
ONCE AGAIN SORRY FOR THE PRINTED FACT SHEET BUT TIME IS SHORT, WE HOPE WITH THE ENCLOSED LEAFLETS YOU WILL HAVE ALL THE INFO YOU REQUIRED.

.....MAKE 1986 THE YEAR OF THE FIGHTBACK.....
CONFLICT

DIRECT ACTION IN ANIMAL RIGHTS

What does direct action mean?

It means that you are no longer prepared to sit back and allow terrible, cruel, abominable things to happen.

The camera man in Ethiopia took direct action, he filmed the worst disaster that has happened to human beings. He realised it was too enormous a problem to handle himself - so he took films in the hope that other people would help. They did.

Are you prepared to sit back any longer?

Direct action in animal rights means causing economic damage to those who abuse and make profits from exploitation.

How do you start?

It is possible to do things on your own, e.g. slash tyres, glue up the locks of shops (butchers, burger bars, furriers, fishing tackle, gunsmiths, etc); smash windows, throw paint over shops/houses, throw paint stripper on cars, stick chewing gum on fur coats (after you have chewed the gum).

Stop contributing to the abuse yourself - don't eat meat, don't wear leather or fur; buy non-animal tested make-up, soap, shampoo, etc.

Try to form a small group of people you know and trust, and plan more ambitious actions. Use a camera to get photographic evidence - go into hospitals, schools, colleges, universities, laboratories, slaughterhouses, factory farms, in fact any place where animals are abused.
If you do manage to get into any of these places do as much damage as possible, especially to computer and electrical equipment. In other words, damage the most expensive equipment - the less money these establishments have, the fewer animals they can afford to buy and abuse.

Many shops, etc. which are attacked find that the Insurance companies put the premiums up so much that they cannot afford to pay it, and they are therefore forced to pay for the damage out of their own pockets. Several businesses have been compelled to close down as a result.

Of course, try to rescue animals whenever possible, including your neighbour's dog if it is being ill treated. Cruelty goes on all around us every day - will you let it continue?

The world is made up of people like you and me. What goes on in the world is our responsibility.

WE CAN, WE MUST, and WE WILL stop the suffering.

STARTING NOW . . .

ARREST - WHAT TO DO AND WHAT NOT TO DO

If you take part in direct action or if the police don't like the look of you, it might lead to arrest.

If you are arrested you don't have to say anything at all. NOTHING.

It is advisable (but your choice) to give your name, address and date of birth. AND THEN NOTHING ELSE.

If you do not give your name and address they will hold you longer while they try to establish your identity.

If you have previous convictions decide whether or not to give your date of birth. You will be on their computers in date of birth order.

You are not obliged to answer any questions AT ALL. NONE.

I keep stressing that because most people are caught out by their own evidence. The police are cunning but thick. Don't hand it to them on a plate.

Whether you have done what they are accusing you of or not, keep your mouth shut. They are probably bluffing, they might (only might) have some evidence against you. Remember if they really had a good case they wouldn't need to keep asking you questions.

You do not have to give your fingerprints - if you refuse they will probably apply to the Magistrates Court for a warrant. Magistrates do sometimes refuse especially if the evidence is flimsy.

You most definitely must not let them take your photograph. That is only compulsory after you have received a prison sentence.

You can demand suitable food, i.e. vegan or vegetarian or sugar free if you are diabetic, etc. You might not get it but keep on and on insisting. You are entitled to make phone calls but often they refuse to let you. As with the food, just keep insisting. If nothing else it relieves the boredom!

Memorise the numbers of the arresting officer or any of the police who treat you badly. You can then make an official complaint afterwards. That is worth doing because every complaint is recorded and if one particular officer has a lot of complaints against him he can be demoted or at least not promoted. Look and act bored but stay polite - when they ask you questions reply "no comment" or "I don't want to say anything" or something similar. EVERYTHING you say is written down and may be read out in Court. So while you might feel better at the time if you say "fuck off you fascist pig" it won't help much in court.

They will try to trick you by saing things like "secretly I admire what you do but I have to do my job" or "people have probably told you not to answer our questions but it is better if you do" or "you have to answer our questions, the person who told you not to is an idiot" and so on. They might ask you your views on the exploitation of blacks in South Afric for example - IGNORE THEM, they are just trying to get you talking.

Don't admit to any weakness such as fear of the dark (they will remove the light) or claustrophobia (they will shut you up in a small cell).

Remember they are trained to be absolute BASTARDS.

One girl who was arrested was told if she didn't talk they were going to go to her house to get her animals and have them put down. It was a lie., there is no way they can do things like that so don't believe any of the crap they talk.

I have been arrested quite a few times, but I was only charged on two occasions and only found guilty once. BECAUSE I KEPT MY MOUTH SHUT otherwise I might by now be serving a prison sentence.

Being arrested is not fun, but if you know your rights and stick to them it is not that bad.

Whatever you go through in a police cell is nothing like the suffering of countless animals in laboratories, factory farms etc.
Remember that and GOOD LUCK!

CONFLICT

THE MAJORITY OF PEOPLE DESPISE CHANGE/CHANGE UPSETS THEIR DAILY LIFESTYLE/A LIFESTYLE DULL & MUNDANE BUT SAFE & SECURE/SCARED TO VENTURE OUTSIDE OF THEIR LIMITED VISION/AFRAID TO OPEN BOTH EYES & MINDS FULLY/TO NEW POSSIBILITIES/SCARED OF ALTERNATIVES TO THAT WHICH HAS BEEN CAREFULLY & METHODICALLY INSTALLED INTO THEIR HEARTS & MINDS BY A SYSTEM WHICH THEY ARE TAUGHT IS RIGHT/ THEY ARE CONTENT TO SUFFER THE INJUSTICE THEY SEE AROUND THEM/ THEY NEVER SHOUT/THEY MAY WHISPER/THINKING IS LIMITED/STUPIDITY UNLIMITED/WE TALK OF ANARCHY THEY LAUGH/WE TALK OF A SYSTEM CORRUPT & VIOLENT/THEY LAUGH/THEY ARE AFRAID TO LOOK/TO HEAR/TO THINK/CONDITIONED THEY ARE SUBSERVIENT/CAGED & TRAPPED/OUR ANARCHY IS WITHIN OUR OWN MINDS/WE ARE THE SYSTEM/WE ARE ALSO THE PROBLEM & SOLUTION/BY THINKING & REJECTING WHAT IS REGARDED AS SACRED & NORMAL/WE REJECT THE SYSTEM/BY HAVING OUR OWN VALUES & MORALITY/ WE REJECT THE SYSTEM/BY ACTING AS INDIVIDUALS AS WE SEE FIT/WE REJECT THE SYSTEM/BY LIVING/WE BEAT THE SYSTEM/WE TRY TO LIVE TO OUR BELIEFS AS CLOSELY AS POSSIBLE/WE DO NOT ALWAYS SUCCEED/WE SOMETIMES MAKE MISTAKES/WE HAVE FOUND OUR PEACE/ITS UP TO YOU TO FIND YOURS/BY LISTENING & LEARNING WE GROW STRONGER/BY OPENING OUR MINDS WE GROW STRONGER/WE ARE HUMAN/WE ARE NOT ALWAYS RIGHT/ OUR ANARCHY RELIES UPON THE INDIVIDUAL BEING RESPONSABLE FOR THIER ACTIONS/ORDER & DISCIPLINE LAY WITHIN EACH AND EVERY ONE OF US/IT DOES NOT HAVE TO BE INFORCED/ITS OUR FUTURE/OUR CHOICE/OUR LIFE/GRAB IT/CREATE YOUR OWN ANARCHY WITHIN YOURSELF/FIND PEACE & SHARE IT/CARE FOR OTHERS HOW YOU WOULD LIKE OTHERS TO CARE FOR YOU/QUESTION & THINK/DO NOT JUDGE OTHERS AS BEING WRONG/UNDER- STAND & COMMUNICATE/LOVE PEACE FREEDOM/
      EXIT-STANCE

EXIT/STANCE '84

OH ROSE, thou art sick!
The invisible worm
That flies in the night,
In the howling storm,
Has found thy bed
Of crimson joy:
And his dark secret love
Does thy life destroy.
EAT THE RICH

Rob Miller [Amebix]

Irene Frizzera

Deviated Instinct Lyrics, Artwork and Gig Flyer

Courtesy Dion Fen

WHATS THE DIFFERANCE BETWEEN AN ONION AND A POLICEMAN?
YOU CRY WHEN YOU CHOP UP AN ONION

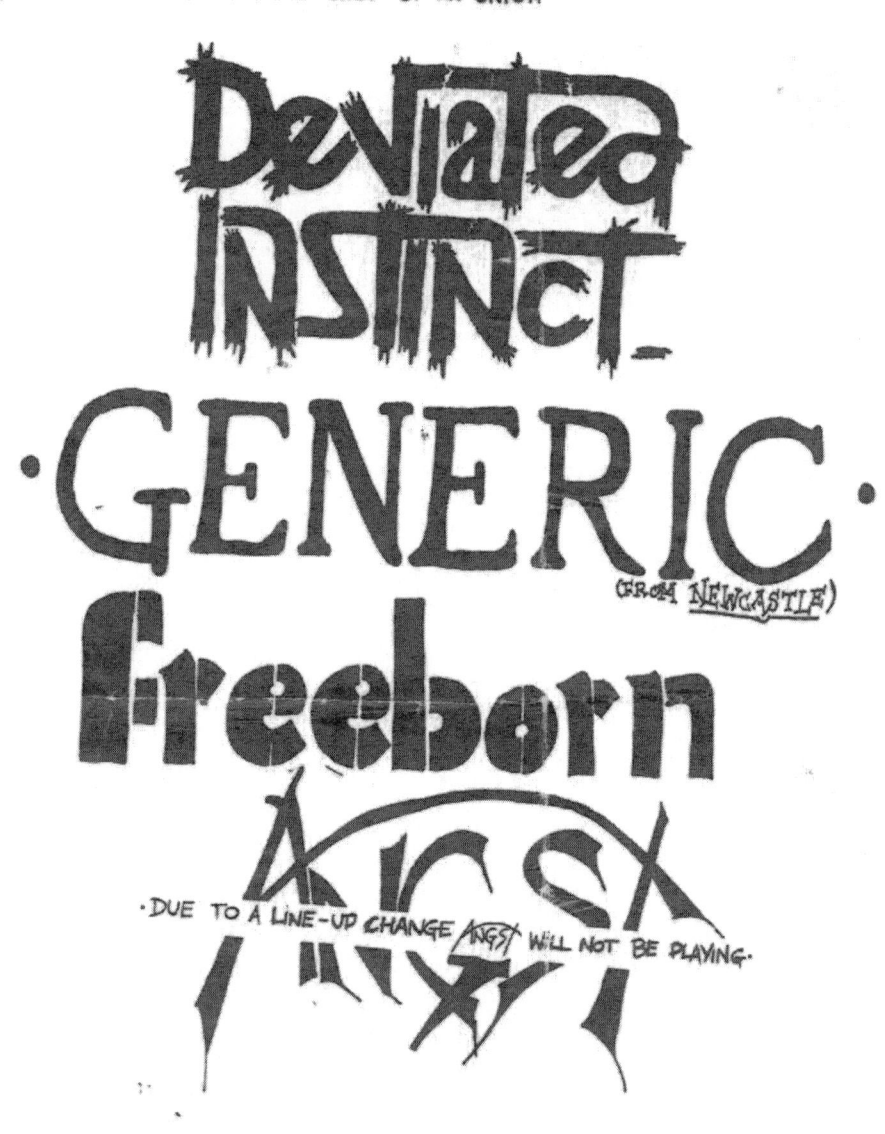

Deviated Instinct
GENERIC (FROM NEWCASTLE)
Freeborn
Angst

· DUE TO A LINE-UP CHANGE ANGST WILL NOT BE PLAYING·

AT SANTANAS
MAGDALEN STREET
NORWICH

APRIL/WED 9TH
START – 9:00 PM
FINISH – LATE
FIRST BAND ON AT 9:30

A NORWICH BUST FUND BENEFIT
TOGETHER WE CAN.... WE MUST... AND... WE WILL.

THERE MUST BE MORE.

Forever I cry,
Forever I die,
In desperation I plead my insanity.
A scornful look,
A thick bound book.
I look in despair,
The sky reflects the grey.
The raven watches with a knowing eye.
From within the dark a faint light grows dimmer,
Destiny disapearing into oblivion.
Four walls and a door.....open,
As a butterfly pulls at my senses,
So near,yet so far.
To have to pass the crowds of laughing people,
Only to be greeted by the palm of a hand,
Of one.....always watching.
Smug superioity,
Intense inferioity.
Knowing im right yet condemed to be wrong.
Forget the fight and sing another song.
Couldn't there be more ?
A pre-packed existance...
For a pre-packed mind,
There must be more!
The green laid to waste as the dustbin overflows.
Was that the note of a bird ?
Or another signal ?
A cry of hope ?
Or time to begin ?
Another day...The same day,
To be followed in the same way.
The path is wearing deep,
Another rut....
I stumble,fall and am lost.
Losing sight of the warmth,
That is so teasingly kept on the outside,
While we freeze inside.
To resist is to give in...or so im told.
Yet to exist is to live...not to die,
How can i give in to life ?
I cannot support my own slavery,
While they distort my destruction.
Am i being too greedy to ask for more ?
When more is only the right to myself ?
Im afraid of fading,
So that all that remains is a lifeless flag,
A reminder.....of a fool,
The ridicule bites hard,yet makes me strong,
Carries me forever on,
One step forward...two steps back.
As the jaws wait to close upon me,
Only to be spat out again.

                    CONTINUED .....

Artwork by Rob "Mid" Middleton

```
but the scent fills me with an optimism,
Knowing there is more,
That beyond the crowds of umbrellas,
The twenty storey tombstones,
The blood drenched pollution,
That the breeze is forced to bear.
We can all here the screams,
but daren't look for the voice,
I dream its a nightmare,
But i needn't close my eyes,
I so much need to take your hands,
Alone all i see are the same walls,
bars,
Chains,
Bondage,
Shackles,
But we have a key.
```

Artwork by Rob "Mid" Middleton

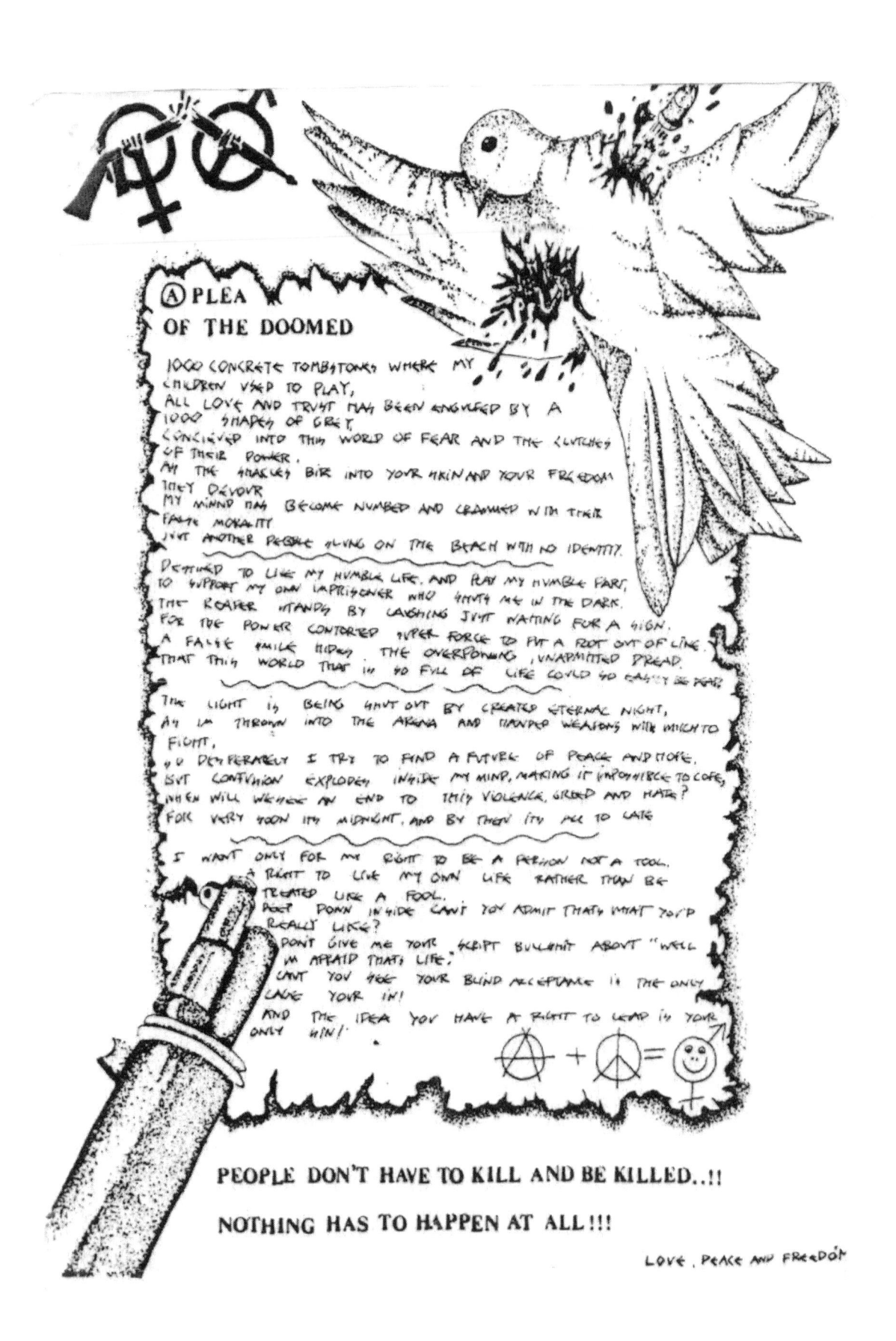

Artwork by Rob "Mid" Middleton

How I Finally Learnt to Love Grindcore! And in doing so Reclaimed a Very Close Friend.

Matt Grimes

(For Stevie G-my punk soul brother)

I still remember it to this day, the sheer feeling of shock and surprise when, my then best mate Stevie G, played me the opening refrain of "You Suffer" by Napalm Death. Just as I heard the first few seconds of aural assault coming from the speaker on Stevie's cassette player it was over, as if it didn't happen, as if it was an acoustic hallucination-all 1.3 seconds of it; a momentary blast of noise, that seemed to be made up of pure unadulterated, visceral anger and despair. In an instant it seemed as if anarcho-punk was destined to morph into another more extreme sub-genre that was beyond my comprehension of what constituted music, well anarcho-punk music at least. Stevie had this massive smile on his face as if to say this is as good as it is ever going to get Matt-this was the future the past and the present of extreme music right there in that 1.3 seconds.

I had heard of Napalm Death before hearing this particular tune, their name had been brought to my attention through an advert in a fanzine I had picked up at a gig somewhere. It was for a demo tape they had made called 'Punk Is A Rotting Corpse' and available by mail order from the fanzine distro. Perhaps the title of the demo tape was a portent to what was to follow in the ensuing years that, for me, marked the demise of anarcho-punk as it fragmented into a number of more extreme sub-genres of music that seemed to push the envelope of sonic experimentation and assault

Stevie and I were really close mates and had been since secondary school. We had made each other's acquaintance through the tried and tested ceremony of the school playground fight. Stevie was the only outwardly visible punk at my new secondary school and when he spotted me on my first day of school, also doing my best to look as punk as I dared for a new boy, he decided that in a school of 500 kids there was not enough room for 2 punks, so one of us had to go.

As is common with school fights, no one ever wins because the teachers come and break them up before it gets that far. We were both dragged off to the headmaster's office and given 5 of the best with a Dunlop Green Flash plimsoll (the headmaster loved tennis and I was convinced he didn't like even numbers either, hence only getting 5 rather than 6 of the best). From that day on Stevie and I decided that the fight wasn't between us but was between us and the 'system' that school, our parents, the police, in fact everyone who was not a punk.

And that's how Stevie and I forged a relationship that lasted for a number of years. We did just about everything together, hitched around the country to go to punk gigs, experimented with drugs and alcohol, got into fights with skinheads and mods, bunked off school and listened to punk music whenever we could and argued with our teachers and parents about the injustices of authority.

In the summer of 1981 when it was time to leave school and the parental home it only seemed natural that we would get a squat together because that was what we had been talking about for years. So along with a number of other miscreants we had collected on the way we set off into town to liberate a building and join the ranks of the 'real' punks. Time moved on and some things changed whilst others remained the same. We still carried on squatting together, spent time with the anarcho-punks in London and Bristol, went hunt sabbing, political rallies and demos with Class War and the Anarchist Federation, even hippy free festivals such as Stonehenge, where I made my first contact with a 'tribe' of people that would later form the next chapter of my life. Anarcho-punk was in 'full flight' and Stevie and I were living the dream (of sorts), no money, and no jobs but, most importantly, no responsibilities and feeling part of a community of likeminded free people.

I'm not sure when it happened exactly but at some point the mood of anarcho-punk shifted and got darker, as did the politics and the people around it. Margaret Thatcher's decimation of the mining communities, the Peace Convoy and an escalating nuclear muscle flexing exercise with Russia, only added to the darkness as society seemed to become more fragmented. The music also started to get a bit darker and more aggressive with bands such as Discharge, Antisect and Extreme Noise Terror playing breakneck speed thrash punk with lyrics focussing on nuclear death and destruction and total state control of a near future oppressed dystopian society. Squatting became more problematic and with it came a new breed of crusty squatter, dosed up on Special Brew, Tuinal, glue and even louder and more aggressive extreme music that seemed shambolically reflective of its listeners.

Stevie had been up in Birmingham for a while, staying with some mates and came back excited about a new band he had seen a couple of times at a venue called The Mermaid, which already had a reputation for the punk scene that had developed around it. That band was Napalm Death and Stevie described the experience as likened to being hit in the face with a sonic sledgehammer; he had, he said, found what was missing from his life, something that unleashed and expressed that anger he had carried with him, something cathartic.

So this sort of brings me back to the beginning and me hearing Napalm Death for the first time. I just didn't get it, and Stevie trying to convince me by playing it over and over again, that this was the future of music. We didn't see eye to eye over this, it just didn't work for me and that's when the problems started. Stevie was always a 100%er-an all or nothing bloke and he had latched onto this sound and that would be his focus from that point on. With Stevie's forays into this extreme music, and my lack of interest in it, he started hanging out with what he called a more 'committed' group of people, who ended up at the squat and with them came an additional pervading darkness; heroin.

It was only a matter of time before Stevie got tempted into it; part of his all or nothing character, and from then on heroin became a regular feature of a large number of the squats residents. We would argue more, the music in the squat became more extreme and aggressive, personal stuff would start going 'missing' and after one of Stevie's so called new 'committed' mates threatened me with an iron bar, after being on a four day amphetamine binge, our friendship imploded.

I decided after a while and after another summer at free festivals to get away from the darkness and join the Travellers on the road. As a parting gesture of goodwill and hope I offered the hand of friendship to Stevie and tried to persuade him to come on the road with me, away from the smack and the darkness, but he was too wrapped up in his own pitiful ego by then. I left Brighton, not returning for a number of years, and sadly heard on the grapevine, a year after leaving, that Stevie had died of a heroin overdose. I couldn't bring myself to attend the funeral- a regretful decision that has always troubled me. Looking back it was almost inevitable that Stevie would not quit this mortal coil easily or peacefully-he always was a person of extremes, energetic, volatile, unpredictably violent but beautifully funny and my best mate.

I'm not suggesting that Grindcore (as this type of extreme music later became to be known by) was responsible for our friendship falling apart, it was more the smack and the company Stevie chose to keep. For a number of years I could not entertain the thought of listening to Grindcore because of the memories associated with it and my musical tastes had, by then, encompassed the E- generation as I travelled from one free techno party to another, with my new 'tribe'.

But it was certainly the highly political song titles and lyrical content of Napalm Death that had always struck a chord with me, even if the music initially didn't. Finally, after hearing Napalm Death again on the John Peel radio show one night in 1992, I decided to revisit Napalm Death, and I have done again for this piece of writing. I was intrigued by the production values of the band and the paradox they seemed to create. The sound of their music takes punk's lack of concern for formal structure and standard musical convention to another level. They offer a version of punk at its most blunt and brutal. Atonal in their approach their songs are brief, often limited to one or two minutes, and often tended to avoid formal lyrical structure in favour of short, sharp statements, revealing a pre-occupation with state control, corporate power and a dystopian society built on economic and physical slavery.

From the titles of the songs their lyrical content is seemingly important, but paradoxically is mostly indecipherable due to the mode of delivery. Deena Weinstein suggests that in mainstream Heavy Metal lyrical matter may not be of concern to the listener (1991 & 2009), however I would suggest that the importance of the lyrical matter to the artists in this case is vital: the content informs the form completely.

It would be fair to say that "You Suffer" and a number of Napalm Death's repertoire are not songs in the context of the model adopted in recent centuries, by Western culture and the formation of the Western music canon, but it could certainly be regarded as a song within the context of the musical structures of other cultures such as those I previously mentioned. While

Napalm Death's songs do not contain a formal 'story' narrative as would be common in western popular music structure, it may be possible to view a large proportion of their work as existing within an extended tradition of folk music. The folk tradition is often characterised by songs that are 'social documents' and include narratives that focus around notions of 'class struggle', 'oppression', 'poverty' and 'protest'. Those political and social issues and more contemporary ones were implicit in the repertoire of a number of anarcho-punk bands in a continuum of dissent. The political impact of extreme metal music comes into question particularly when looking at arguments such as those of Keith Kahn-Harris (2004). Kahn-Harris argues that the very nature of extreme metal is "reflexively-anti-reflexively constructed as a depoliticizing category" (2004, 98). He identifies the ways in which black metal, for example, constantly toys with the ideas of violent racism and fascism, however will never embrace it outright. Napalm Death on the other hand are not accommodated by Kahn-Harris' analysis of extreme metal because of the nature of their songs and their behaviour. I would suggest Napalm Death embrace the lyrics they sing, and support the various causes they sing about such as campaigns against apartheid, animal exploitation, global corporate and state power among others, and openly express their disgust of fascism, racism and the establishment. This is also reflective of the political stance of a large number of anarcho-punk bands and the anarcho-punk scene from which Napalm Death emerged from.

The early recording techniques and seeming lack of acoustic treatment and mastering perhaps reflect the very raw subject matter implicit in their lyrics. Where it is traditionally perceived that the meaning of the song is carried in the lyrical content, Napalm Death seem to focus on the delivery of sound and also on the way in which that sound is utilised as a carrier of meaning, both of which are key elements that seem to underpin the Grindcore genre. The actual structure of the text of the song is broken down, by the vocal delivery, into syllabic content. Listening to the vocal output, this low pitch guttural sound seems to come from another place outside of the human vocal range. It seems the voice travels from the diaphragm, from the lower points of the body, inside the resonant sounding chamber of the torso, which allows the low pitch to be sustained without damage to the throat or lack of breath to sustain the sound. This approach is not dissimilar to early Buddhist temple chanting, where monks would employ tonal variations in their meditative temple chanting in a quest to connect with divinity. The style of delivery and associated production values seems to contribute to a sense of sonic rupture, of speech being drawn to a halt and fractured, with the suggestion that the end result of this process will be atomisation, an attack upon the fabric of the text itself. A form of sonic 'rupture', where a new sphere of possibility may be opened, if only for a moment, in the space created by this rupture.

So perhaps that's what Stevie saw in this music all those years ago, that rupture and the possibilities that might have opened up for not only him but all those around him.

Perhaps If I had also seen that then things may have turned out differently for both of us.

I like Grindcore and have done for a number of years, I enjoy listening to it, albeit though mostly in a slightly nostalgic way. The good thing now is that I can listen to it and remember the better, happier times with Stevie before it all went tragically wrong.

Perhaps I should have just listened to Napalm Death a bit more then.

Bibliography;

Kahn-Harris, K. (2004) The 'Failure' of Youth Culture Reflexivity, Music and Politics in the Black Metal Scene. European Journal of Cultural Studies. 7(1) 95-111

Weinstein, D (1991) Heavy Metal: A Cultural Sociology. Idaho Falls. Lexington Books.

Weinstein, D (2009) Heavy Metal: The Music and Its Culture. Boston. DeCapo Press.

Various Handouts

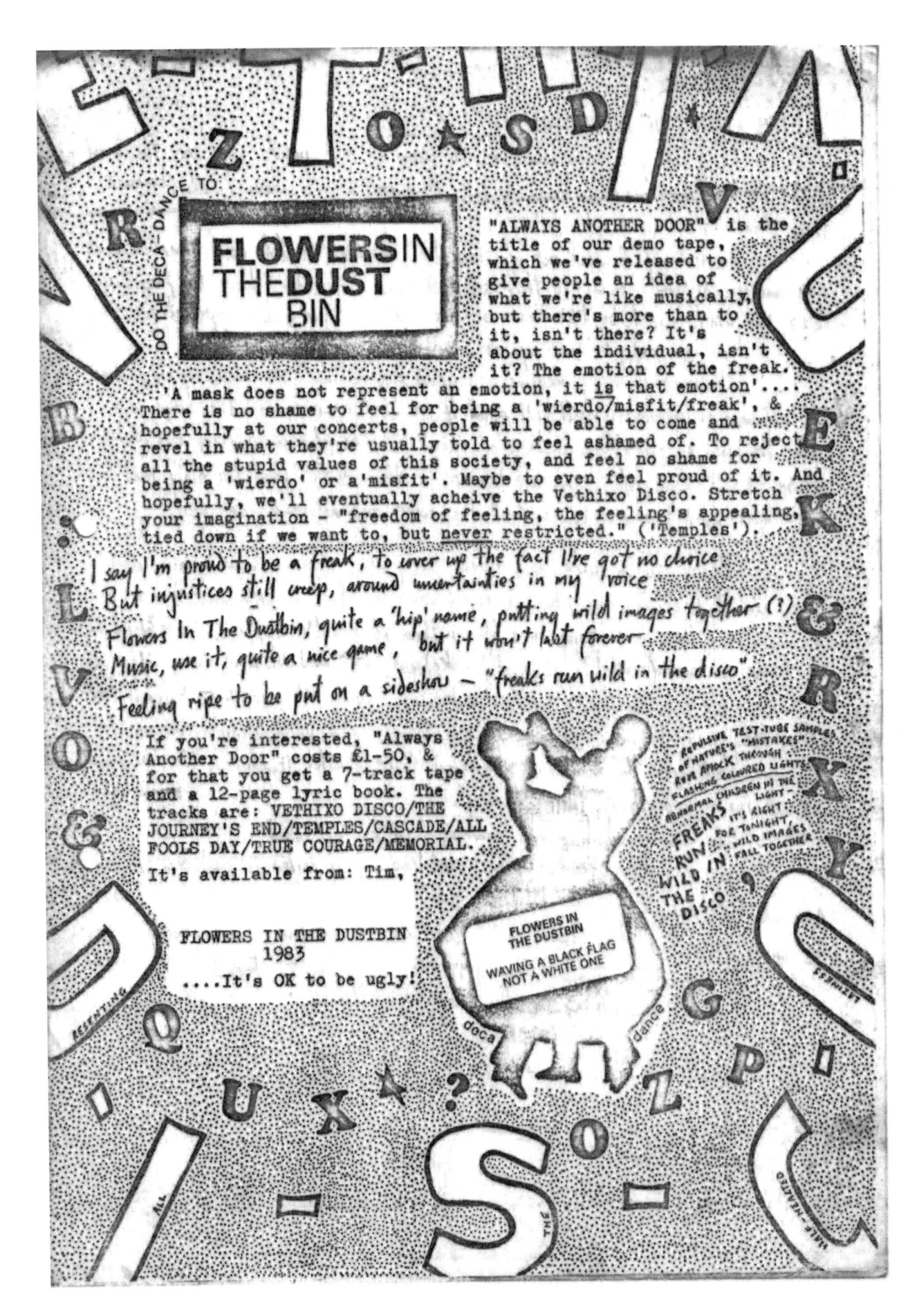

Courtesy Nigel Crouch Collection

FLOWERS IN THE DUST BIN

"ALWAYS ANOTHER DOOR" is the title of our demo tape, which we've released to give people an idea of what we're like musically, but there's more than to it, isn't there? It's about the individual, isn't it? The emotion of the freak. 'A mask does not represent an emotion, it is that emotion'.... There is no shame to feel for being a 'wierdo/misfit/freak', & hopefully at our concerts, people will be able to come and revel in what they're usually told to feel ashamed of. To reject all the stupid values of this society, and feel no shame for being a 'wierdo' or a 'misfit'. Maybe to even feel proud of it. And hopefully, we'll eventually acheive the Vethixo Disco. Stretch your imagination – "freedom of feeling, the feeling's appealing, tied down if we want to, but never restricted." ('Temples').

I say I'm proud to be a freak, To cover up the fact I've got no choice
But injustices still creep, around uncertainties in my voice

Flowers In The Dustbin, quite a 'hip' name, putting wild images together (?)
Music, use it, quite a nice game, but it won't last forever

Feeling ripe to be put on a sideshow – "freaks run wild in the disco"

If you're interested, "Always Another Door" costs £1-50, & for that you get a 7-track tape and a 12-page lyric book. The tracks are: VETHIXO DISCO/THE JOURNEY'S END/TEMPLES/CASCADE/ALL FOOLS DAY/TRUE COURAGE/MEMORIAL.

It's available from: Tim,

FLOWERS IN THE DUSTBIN
1983

....It's OK to be ugly!

REPULSIVE TEST-TUBE SAMPLES OF NATURE'S "MISTAKES" ROCK AMOCK THROUGH FLASHING COLOURED LIGHTS ABNORMAL CHILDREN IN THE LIGHT FREAKS IT'S RIGHT RUN FOR TONIGHT WILD IN WILD IMAGES THE FALL TOGETHER DISCO

FLOWERS IN THE DUSTBIN
WAVING A BLACK FLAG NOT A WHITE ONE

IT'S ABOUT THE INDIVIDUAL, ISN'T IT?......

It is the grey ones who try to keep us dead inside who are the most dead. The machine world they build controls them too, controls them totally, because they think it's their own.

Be yourself & break out of their death machine. Stretch your imagination & you can live different dreams to their sad dull excuses. You don't have to play their roles, you don't have to be like them, or live "up" to their feeble expectations of you.

You can only be yourself, or a collaborator in grey mind-death.

The mind-fucking machine will grind dry without the sweat of our bodies. The costumes of mediocrity will fall apart if we don't wear them. The stage is a world, the world, at present, is a stage of falsehood. The roles are pre-set, but if we refuse to act them out, if we live life rather than death, then the play just folds up — you can't have a play without the actors and actresses, can you?

Refuse to be ruled, and rulers lose power. Refuse to be afraid, and they cannot frighten. And when we reveal ourselves from beneath our disguises, we shall see, there are many more of us than it usually appears. We should have no shame in our (mental & physical) nakedness, it's how we were born after all.

We are the 'freaks' with the 'twisted' minds. When we look beyond their walls, they cease to exist, and we can see clearly, and build bridges. We are the children from over the rainbow, who reject their twisted teachings. We have life without the slow death of their "reality".

We are everywhere and nowhere — we are all about.

We are their freaks. Their mistakes. They failed to condition us enough. And we broke out. We opened Pandora's Box, and saw a better world out there to work for. And they cannot catch us, because we live in everybody.

flowers in the dustbin, june 1983. it is forbidden to forbid —
power to the imagination!!

rubella ballet.

rubella ballet met in Epping forest in the summer of 79. In those days there was Zillah, Sid, Gem, Pete, Annie, Womble and it. They made weird songs and weird music, but didn't agree on very much for very long. Womble and it went for a walk in the forest and never came back. Annie went to sing very weird songs in another part of the forest and Pete left to make a record all by himself. Where at least there wasn't any arguements, but it did get a bit lonely. Gem sang on lots of other people's records, Sid banged drums with some Indians deeper in the forest and Zillah + Gem made stunning dresses ready for the time when they would all get together again......

Happily Zillah, Gem + Sid got together with Andy + Eugene, two mushroom pickers from the forest and made a "ballet bag" tape which was magic and they started to play for the fairies + pixies to dance in the forest. Not long after this Andy + Eugene left to find bigger + better mushrooms in the forest + Pete was persuaded to come back so that they could keep on playing and the pixies could go on dancing. They made an EP together called "ballet Dance". Then lured by the promise of magic money Pete left to create and engineer other peoples music. But very deep in the forest lived a hermit who was pursuaded to leave his home + join the other ballerina's making magic music. Now the best is yet to come.

The End

- **ballet gear** • All available on xntrix records now.
① ballet dance 7inch single
② ballet bag, bag with lots of goodies including a 30 cassette with 9 studio recorded tracks.
all available from rough trade and local indies stockists now.

.... Stuck in a world controlled by grey businessmen obsessed by grey businessmen obsessed by grey grey businessmen obsessed by numbers written on endless 14 10/4% sheets of lined paper they call "forms." Searching constantly for a path of honesty, excitement & peace, being blocked, as we travel the yellow brick road, by the wicked bureaucracy of the south & the wicked poverty of the north. We search for the truth that is sanity, but is labelled "insanity". We put our faith in that which is real, we fight for the freedom which naturally belongs to us, the land which belongs to all of us, the produce of the land, the shelters built by us upon the land. And respect for all the creatures that walk, swim and fly upon the land. And we can never be at peace without not giving up, for freedom. And our spirits living on after our deaths, for there will always be those swimming against the tide of corruption and lies, trying to create that oasis of truth — the space to live.

And if they say two plus two makes four, who am I to believe them? stretch your imagination ---- live out Your dreams. that which we dream is that we strive for, a life free from enforced restriction, free from mistrust. And this shall not arrive through dreams alone; and different paths we shall leave up to all our imaginations. Power to the imagination my dear friends!

flowers in the dustbin / never never land / august 1983.

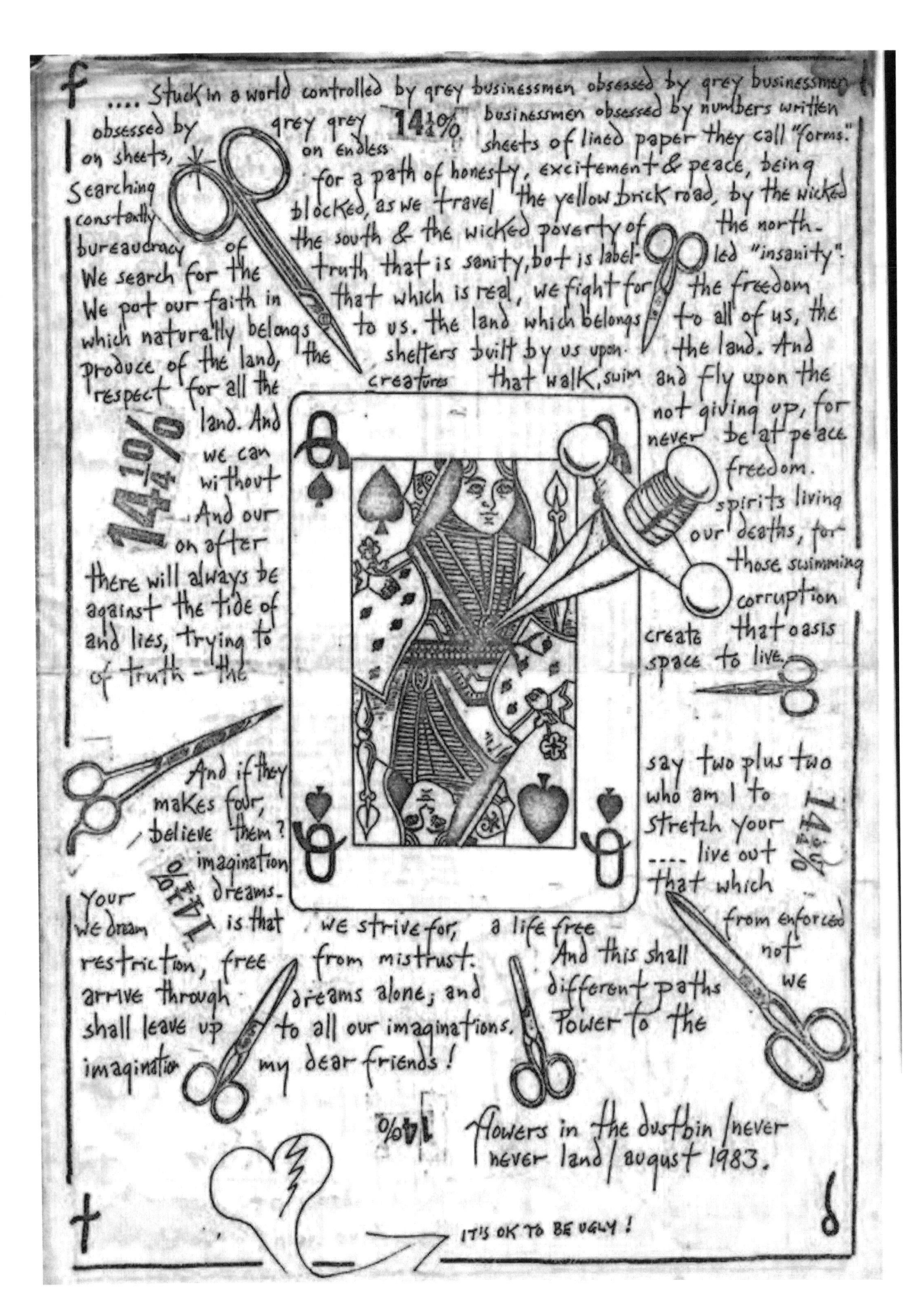

IT'S OK TO BE UGLY !

FLOWERS IN THE DUSTBIN

When enemies kiss and the world gets pissed
And love's not unhip cos I sip your lip
And we all feel high all day and all night
When there's no hate and no state....
there'll be no shit.

STOP 'THE CITY'

come and **Stop 'the City'** on Sept. 29th
6am-6pm
assemble at St. Pauls
an anti-war protest & carnival

We want a world without war, or the threat of it. All over the world, people in their millions are realising that the process towards destruction of life and our planet has to be halted. In this country the growing protests and actions to close military bases, along with the protests in the towns, are showing that it's up to ourselves to stop the plans of the State.

This summer nuclear missiles are being secretly installed all over Europe, East and West. While the bases are the last of the steps to military confrontation, the first seem to be, the whole system of finance for war - where profits and power are calculated and decisions made.

In London there's one area where such decisions are concentrated - "The City". People once lived there but now it's full of Banks, Companies Headquarters, Government buildings and places like the Stock Exchange.

For the sake of ourselves, our children and generations to come we have to stop this madness. So we are calling on everyone to come and help CLOSE DOWN 'THE CITY' (especially the Stock Exchange) on Thurs SEPTEMBER 29th.
On that day, profits for the summer are reckoned up by accountants -
A DAY OF RECKONING.
A day when people will show that human life is more important than money.

We also call on people working in the area to **stop**, for the day, and to consider how the financial empires which exploit their labour contribute to the war machine.

And together in the streets we can have a **carnival** as we reclaim the old area for the people once again. (It's 502 years since we were last there - during the 1381 peasants revolt.)

Assemble from 6am onwards at :
Steps of St Pauls...Tower Hill...Finsbury Circus

FLOWERS IN THE DUSTBIN
WAVING A BLACK FLAG NOT A WHITE ONE

STUCK ON A STICK

Hey Alice, where's your wonderland?
The land you live in through your unseeing glass
I want to run, a fugitive from the shops
Full of props and plastic tops

Two and two can make three if you want
They'll tell you it always makes four
Take inspiration, stretch your imagination
Watch the law of averages fall to the floor

Now I'm stuck on a stick in a polythene bag
But my eyes aren't aimed at the drawing board
So I'm black and white, not grey and thick
But I'm still stuck, stuck on a stick

LAST TANGO IN VIETNAM

have an orgasm in oslo bay-bee
take a trip to the u s s a
we're sitting on a time bomb baby
we might be gone tomorrow but we're here today

dancing in the deca-dance....your perfume smells
not paying any pittance......and your complex tells
in open wounds of countries..they're staring at your make-up
dancing in the disease......wild huh?

drop all your chains.........let yourself go
claw out your brains........leave them at home
pull a stupid face..........don't work, get a tan
let's leave the human race...in vietnam

destroy your wildlife
cut yourself with a knife
see you feel so happy
dancing in a third-world war-torn country

make up for years of being trussed
for all those boring years, get one year sussed
dancing with malaria, dancing with polio
dancing in your wheelchair go go go

Write to:
Flowers In the dustbin

Do the decadance at the vethixo disco!

A Haunting

Lucy Robinson

Let's start this piece backwards. Because we don't live our lives in straight lines, and we live in ways where our past is constantly nagging at our present.

When I wrote the original piece below, Greg sent me his responses to it.

Let's start with his responses and then move backwards.

Greg Bull:

As the distance, measured in time, between now and then [a youth possibly spent as part of the Anarcho-punk tribe] grows into 30 years plus, [1983 – 2013] our memories begin to fail and are eroded bit by bit until we are left with only the core memories we do have.

Is this where the ghosts begin to haunt us?

The ghosts of half-remembered memories?

Did we record what we were doing?

Some did some didn't. Did we diarise life or were we too busy living life to create diaries.

Is our memory a relevant historical tool?

Can memories really be used to form a "history" or should we only use source documents from the time?

With the recent upsurge in the study of Anarcho-punk are we [as ex-activists] haunted by our own failings to smash the system?

Are we haunted by the failures of our dreams for a fairer and more equal society?

Do we feel guilty that we have pushed the ghost of peace, freedom and unity into a wardrobe and kept it locked up there for 30+ years and are now revisiting it because Igs is back on the road and we want to believe we can make a change to society for the better?

Maybe we are haunted by the small things we do in life that help to perpetuate the system we so despise[d] we maybe bank with a non-ethical company, buy the odd item from Amazon, drink the odd cup of coffee from Starbucks, eat the occasional veggie offering from the global Multi Death Corporation that we sang along to when MDC toured the UK in the 1980s.

Some of us may be creating our own ghosts as part of the rise in nostalgia and the reforming of a whole raft of Anarcho-punk bands such as The Mob, Antisect, The System and more. We are reminded by their insistence on continuing the attack on the same targets as they did all those years ago that nothing has changed. And we still go and see them and smile and enjoy the music, the spirit, the desire for change, the old balding men with expanding waists and the characterful aging faces of those punk heroines who we, as young men, so looked up to and admired.

And are we haunted by the fact that we fell asleep politically or gave up the struggle or turned our backs on Anarcho-punk sometime in the past?

Was this a conscious decision due to having children, having a career, buying a house, getting a job, growing up and becoming responsible?

And now can we return to the revolution because the children have grown up and left home, leaving us to our thoughts again after 20 years and we know we failed, or rather, that we stopped trying? And will we now have time to do all those things we promised ourselves so long ago? Are we going to demonstrate against austerity in London with our black and red armbands on, black balaclavas covering our faces, afeared of the state getting a pretty picture and use this to terrorise us with later?

There is nothing wrong with this. Remember there is no authority but yourself – do what you will. There are no rules and as we age disgracefully we can shout at coppers, spit in the face of the system and really try and make a change from the inside out, as part of the system, revolutionaries from within.

Is it the rantings of the old angry punks on social media and sitting in the pub that force us to recapture the spirit of Anarcho-punk to feed our own lost years spent in limbo?

For my own part I don't have any ghosts haunting me [there are some very minor regrets; I didn't spend enough time talking at gigs to band members of say,

Flux of Pink Indians, I didn't engage with Annie Anxiety when I had plenty of opportunities to do so, I didn't engage with the squatting scene at Vauxhall Grove, I didn't go to more gigs at The Ambulance Station, I didn't go on the 1984 Crucifix/Antisect Tour, I didn't get to either London Stop The City demo for no particular good reason, I missed out on Stonehenge 1984 for no good reason I can remember.] because whilst Anarcho-punk died for me [us?] externally I continued to live my life by the same ideals as much as possible, like I guess we all did/do?

My vegan shoes arrived today. They were less than £10 including delivery. But did I research who made them and how much the workers are paid for putting them together?

No.

For all I know they are made by child slaves in a factory working for a dollar a day in Cambodia [note to self to look into this further]. So on one hand I have saved the life of a cow that won't die to make leather for my boots but on the other maybe I am committing a far worse atrocity?

And of course I do wear leather boots and have bought leather shoes and wear wool, and eat dairy products and until the other year bought factory farmed eggs.

Are any of us living the perfect anarchist lifestyle now?

I am still amazed when I hear of old Anarcho-punks who have "made it" and who are living the safe upper-middle-class lifestyle that we once were trying to pull apart.

But were we wrong?

Is there anything wrong with living a safe middle class lifestyle if we can live it ethically and responsibly?

What about the old Anarcho Punks who holiday in far off places four times a year at a cost of thousands of pounds, whose wives now drive their second generation of children to school safely in their Chelsea tractors and who complain on Facebook about the scroungers and immigrants coming over here to ruin our economy...

We're Old and We are F**king Angry: Haunted by Post Post-Punk

Lucy Robinson

It probably says more about my life than theirs, but I seem to be haunted by old punks propping up the bar telling me stories about the Clash, or showing off their badge collection on Ebay. There's certainly a lot of punk ghosts around. Virgin's use of Jamie Reid's images for their credit cards feels like an act of defilement to our memories of what punk was, or could have been. The memories marketed as punk nostalgia aren't the useful type of ghosts. Some ghosts are raised up as icons– Sid and Nancy spring to mind immediately. Some ghosts mark our own ageing process, the deaths of those who were still a part of the Anarcho-punk community – most recently Paco the stalwart drummer with Conflict, for example. I've learnt more about my Facebook friends by noting which musician's deaths they comment on, sharing their stories as a sort of memorialization to mark both the loss of a punk idol, and the loss of their own youth.

But what are the ghosts for? And why are they following me round all the time?

Ageing subcultures work.

Although the original academic work on subcultures associated subcultures as forms of resistance with the energy of youth, it is no longer possible to make the easy assumption that subcultures and youthful or that youths are subcultural.

Work on ageing subcultures, or subcultures and ageing has helped us unpick some of the obsession with youthful rebellion in subcultural lives. The history of academic work on subculture is wrapped up in the move to reclaim youth, popular culture and subcultures from associations with 'deviancy' and claim them instead as a form of resistance.

Since then the battles over whether subcultures are or are not ticking the box of 'resistance through rituals' have been run and re-run, with generations of subculturalists assigned a pecking order as to whether they qualify as resistant, and radical or even important (which usually means working class boys are probably important as long as they appeal to a middle class aesthetic)

Recent work on growing up and growing older with a subcultural identity has shaken this up a lot. Andy Bennett and Paul Hodkinson's edited collection Ageing and Youth Cultures: Music, Style and Identity gives up on the youthful ghost and looks at the ways in which subcultural identities can be carried around in and on ageing bodies. In the process however, it seems as though the radicalism assigned to the original subcultural generation, youth, has been withdrawn. The subcultural capital only goes around so far. If the ageing get assigned some subcultural capital, it is usually by default because the current youth of today have let us down. Their pick n mix, virtual fluidity just can't be so easily shut in a box and labelled as 'resistance'.

I've often thought that the sort of subcultures getting taken seriously by academics, or uncovered by documentary makers, is partly about the generation who write about subcultures or make films about them, as much as what happened to the generation that they write about. As a generation of researchers, we've have mapped our own life cycle stages onto the chronology of subcultures. The more distant we are from our teenage years the more we refuse to recognise current young people's dissidence, transgression and resistance. The more we age the more we drag the tropes (or ghosts) of our subcultural pasts with us. I spend a lot of my most enjoyable bits of my work collaborating with a group of academics from different disciplines called The Subcultures Network. We love what we do, but we also tend to relive it. If you come to any of our academic or public events, for example, you will see more DMs and Harringtons that at the average Ace Café Reunion. You can spot us a mile off.

But if we look to Anarcho Punk it lets go of an obsession with youth, partly because Anarcho was ostensibly much more about who you were and how you lived than it was what your wore, or where you shopped (Not that there wasn't something of a tribal uniform, just that it self-consciously eschewed consumption as identity work) Work on Anarcho-punk is interesting right now because not only does it avoid focusing on 'the kids' alone, it also avoids worrying about whether youth is deviant, resistant, tribal or consumer led. Anarcho Punk had, and has, an explicitly personal and public political agenda. We don't need to do the tricky work of working out whether something is, or isn't political, because the Anarcho Punks have already worked that out for themselves.

Academic work on Anarcho Punk like Rich Cross's There is No Authority But Yourself, Pete Dales' in Anyone Can Do It, and Matt Worley and Mike Dines' forthcoming book, all take Anarcho Punk seriously as a way to think about politics, history, culture and experience. As a subfield of a subfield Anarcho Punk (or post-punk) Studies have started to flourish. There is even a new academic journal dedicated to work on Post-Punk. This isn't just about an abstract academic trend. This tells us something about how academic work in the past is a response to the present. I'd argue that we are beginning to see so much good work on Anarcho Punk from historians and others, not least because we can see so many of its traces in contemporary activism: focus on the personal politics, direct action, types of democratic organization, thinking through consensus, DIY and parallel cultures, emotional networks and self care for example. UK Uncut, Occupy, People's Assembly all have the legacies of Anarcho Punk running through them. In a world where traditional models of political organization don't seem to have the answers, or even know how to work, memories of Anarcho Punk are just what we need.

So I'm trying to suggest that a few things are coming together – we've worked out subcultures might not only matter when we are young, we understand that Anarcho Punk might have an important history and that that history might be speak to us, shouting in our ear, in the present.

So I wanted to think about what we do with this attachment to the subcultural past in our older here and now. Can we still wield subcultural resistance in our 40s and 50s – and if so can we do it without negating the creative agency of the youth? Can we act on the future, remembering our youths but without defining ourselves against the current generation of young people?

I've bemoaned the omnipresence of punk nostalgia elsewhere, often for its insistence on set piece narratives around big London slebpunks and an obsession with authenticity. I've listened to old and ex-punks bemoan the youth of today as apathetic and apolitical despite what I see as overwhelming evidence all around them to the opposite. Since when was punks' dream to grow up and tell of young people for not being young properly? I think I've spent too many nights in pubs, with too many men I really like, ranting on about their top trump punk collections and encyclopedic knowledge of punk factoids. I've got to say it's put me right off.

Recently I've felt a lot of old punk hanging about – largely self inflicted, teaching a course on Post-Punk Britain, being married to one, and hanging out with the Subcultures Network will do that to you. But the ghosts of old punk, or particularly post post-punk, appear to be doing more than hanging about, they appear to be actively haunting the present.

Just like punk, there's quite a lot of thinking about 'Haunting' going around at the moment too. I'd read Avery Gordon's book Ghostly Matters: The Haunting and the Sociological Imagination when it first came out in the late '90s and to be honest hadn't really got it. Or couldn't quite see what it could do for me. Maybe I just needed to grow up a bit, but the penny suddenly dropped while I listened to some of my favourite sociologists (Nicola, Ingham, Lisa Mckenzie, and Tracey Jensen) actively wield haunting as an analytical tool at the Working Class Studies Association conference in Washington this year. Jensen, for example took Gordon's work and used it to explain, and take inspiration from the recent campaigns by the E15 young mother's, among others, taking on privatization of social housing and social cleansing of London. By reclaiming the ghosts of communities, solidarity and victories, these haunting memories, are ways into the real power at play:

"Haunting is an animated state in which a repressed or unresolved social violence is making itself known, sometimes very directly, sometimes more obliquely. It describes those singular yet repetitive instances when home becomes unfamiliar, when your bearings on the world lose direction, when the over-and-done-with comes alive, when what's been in your blind spot comes into view." [Avery Gordon quoted by Jensen.]

Described as a the inhabitants of a sink estate, the backdrop to numerous cutting edge dramas on TV and the epitome of broken Britain, instead the E15 mothers and East London estates like Carpenter's Estate in Stratford, are remembering a different version of themselves, for themselves.

The WCSA conference is one that brings together academics, activists, activist academics, and academic activists to think about why class matters and what to do about it. I realized that I should probably look at Gordon's work again. Just because it hadn't spoken to me then, didn't mean it couldn't help me out now.

Thoughts on Haunting?

The idea of haunting helps us get rid of some of our hang ups about memory. I'm not even going to bother thinking about reliability or selectivity of memory because that stuff is seriously dull, especially when we've got more interesting ways to think about memory; public memory (there is a politics to what is and isn't formally and collectively remembered), the cultural circuit (we fit our own stories into the big stories we see around us in film, the media and popular culture more generally), composed memory (we structure ourselves and our stories through the process of sharing narratives about the past), or trauma (the impossibility of reconciling the past becomes written into fragmented traumatic memories), or nostalgia, (the warmth of a romanticised past is really a way of criticising the present). But all of these don't quite get us to where we need to be. Memory is either collectivised to the extent that our individual sense of experience is flattened out, or our memories are shaped in ways that speak only of the present. Above all these concepts of memory as history often lack a materiality – what is it is a given context that means that some versions of the past speak of the present rather than others?

For me the strength of haunting as a historical lens is that it is explicitly not bounded by ideas of nostalgia, or trauma. In practice Gordon's ideas help to get us out of the immateriality of memory in the now. "[T]he very tangled way people sense, intuit, and experience the complexities of modern power and personhood has everything to do with the character of power itself and with what is needed to eradicate the injurious and dehumanizing conditions of modern life. " p194

Haunting can let go of the old questions about resistance, rejection or celebration of the past because haunting is in itself a form of knowledge. The Haunting, and the haunted, allows the past to trouble the present. For anyone looking back on their lives, let alone on a history of activism and subcultural utopianism, we need to work out what we do with our failures and losses (and our lost dreams). Haunting shows us that they can still work for us now, even from the past, even from our defeats.

"haunting is an encounter in which you touch the ghost or the ghostly matter of things: the ambiguities, the complexities of power and personhood, the violence and the hope, the looming and receding actualities, the shadows of our selves and our society" (Gordon, p134)

The haunting ghosts demand that the present should be upset by the past, but it should also be inspired by it, on a joint enterprise. Here memory is more than a measurement of an individual loss, of youth, of hope, of politics, of battles, it is about claiming a collectivity to those losses which can be reclaimed to enact in the now. "yearning for a something that must be done" (Gordon, p184) We know it can be, because we tried before, we failed, or were failed, 'but we got up again'. So when how does that help make sense of the post post-punks hanging around?

Alongside the commercial 'sell out' of Sex Pistols perfume (it smells of pepper) and Virgin's credit card, there is a very different spectre haunting our now: the Anarcho memory in the present. I've written before about the recent growth in really good academic work on the Anarcho Punk scene, and the development of ideas around teaching as punk as well as teaching about punk. It looks like we don't need to look only to the past for inspiration, there is an Anarcho haunting the now. Community projects, activist groups and movements like UK Uncut or Occupy re-animated ideas from earlier countercultural groups. But right now the Anarcho musicians and performers, seem to be taking up a more active haunting, beyond re-enactment, that 'yearns for something that must be done'. The resurgence of 80s stalwarts Class War and their warrior queen Lisa Mckenzie have taken the haunting to the street – with pitch forks. Mckenzie, a working class sociologist at LSE and author of the brilliant book Getting By: Estates, Class and Culture in Austerity Britain, recently stood as Class War candidate against Ian Duncan Smith in the Chingford and Wood Green constituency. Since then her involvement in the Poor Door campaigns against social segregation in housing has drawn some very clear lines between who can say what should be done, when and where. McKenzie's academic book is engaging, analytical and blisteringly clear in its political interventions. It has been rightly applauded in the academic and liberal media circles. But when Mckenzie carried a well recognized class war poster (black and white graphics of gravestones with the words 'We've Found New Places for the Rich to Live') on a No More Poor Doors demo she was charged with three Section 5 Public Order Offences. It acted as a good reminder. However much our academic work might feel important in a very small world, it is in our lives and on the street that it really counts. This is where the ghosts of the past can really help us out. If we are going to make a difference today, we've got to learn some lessons of previous successes, defences and failures.

Anarcho Punk gives us a style, slogans and some great moments to remember, but it has always been about using music, thinking about culture as a site of resistance and building our own space. Sleaford Mods, and Crass's Steve Ignorant, and my new favourite band Interrobang!? are using their past to haunt the music they produce today for themselves. These post post-punks are doing something very different from reunion gigs (although I should be clear that I'm not opposed to a reunion gig). These post post-punks are very much based in the now, with an active reflection on what can be learnt from the failure and from the dreams and energies expended in the past. I love the Sleaford mods, I love everything about them, but not as much as I love Interrobang!? Interrobang!? put the haunting to the front and remind me that as impressive as the academic work on ageing, haunting and Anarcho memory might be, there's nothing like taking your lead from those who are doing being haunted in the now. Not only are these clearly older performers, not chasing a youth market, they are explicit about what is and isn't political in the present and how their pasts can be used to make trouble in the present. By seeing current bands as musical ghosts I think it helps us learn some lessons in the past, whilst letting go of some of our old hang-ups.

As usual, I've relied on Dunstan Bruce (ex-Chumbawamba) to do the thinking for me in the now. I interviewed him as part of his visiting lecture for this year's second year History module at the University of Sussex, '1984:Thatcher's Britain'. Dunstan has been an important ally to the History department. Students have interviewed him for their masters and undergraduate dissertations. He lectures the second year for me every year, has shared his personal collection with our archive and contributed to the digital open access project Observing the 80s. Dunstan has always been more than a 'source' of the past to be listened to or studied from the present. He has always provided an active analysis of the present for us, showing how his past can be used in the present to mess things up, and remember to change the future.

Interrobang!? are Dunstan, and Harry from Chumbawamba and Griff from psychedelic rock band Regular Fries. The Interrobang, a combination of the exclamation mark and the question mark, is the grammatical equivalent of WTF? It challenges, questions, but it also exclaims. Interrobang !? don't need to borrow resistant rituals from youth culture today. They write, sing and shout about what it means to be turning fifty in the now. Haunting finds a way to take inspiration from faded youthful dreams, and of lost past successes and allows our past to unsettle and trouble the past rather than offer the warmth of nostalgia as a distraction from what is to be done. If we map the biographical ageing process onto a broader marker of historical continuity and change than Interrobang!? haunts the present. Interrobang!? are asking and answering an important question 'How do I express anger in my fifties' in the now?

"Think Eight Rounds Rapid meets Sleaford Mods and Dr Feelgood but with some Crass and some early Chumbawamba (the distinctive vocal you see) in the mix and I'm possibly still way off the mark" (Yorkshire Evening Post Review, 09/04/15)

Interview with Dunstan Bruce [DB]

DB: People go talk about 1976 as year zero as though there was nothing before that…. I don't know why everybody is looking back to that era all time, but there is a thing from my point of view, in music where there seem to be a lot of bands around at the time in the 70s and early 80s who were saying something that was relevant or interesting or challenging and there doesn't seem, to me, … that you can only find that sort of thing in underground subcultures now. I don't see it in the mainstream, and I think what's fascinating about the 70s and early 80s was that a lot of that stuff was mainstream and you were aware of it and people were quite happy to say stuff.

We were at Kate Tempest the other day at the Concorde and what was interesting was that she was saying stuff that could have come straight out of the 80s, but it was weird because I found it really rewarding to hear someone saying that to a new generation.

Lucy Robinson [LR]: She was quite uncertain about how to say it … even as a wordsmith and a poet, so there was a sense that there's a new generation learning how to do it for themselves

DB: Is it just our generation? Maybe its just our generation that are looking back to that time, because that's the time that we thought a lot of stuff was going on… its interesting watching those old episodes of Top of The Tops from the 70s and 80s. I had this idea that punk was huge and it was all over everything and you watch them episodes and it wasn't at all. You watch all those episodes and you see who was in the charts… I thought we'd wiped all this out with punk.. but we hadn't at all. Its still this monster rolling on?

LR: and what about old punks when they grow up?

DB: We'd just been talking about that. That was something that's been a massive problem for me over the last few years. There's been a massive thing about nostalgia and about bands reforming. For people of my generation that's become the go-to gig, that everybody just goes to see Buzzcocks .. to me there's too many bands reforming and they're not doing stuff that says something new. They're doing what they were doing in the 70s – which is fine up to a point, but I find that really frustrating, there's not enough people talking to your generation [to the students], there's not enough people talking to my generation, saying, something about our experience of the now. There's a lot of people talking about their experience of the past. Or just regurgitating some old shit from forty years ago, I've sort of had enough of that really. So I got a new band together and I'm trying to do something that's saying something to people of my generation. Like, what do you do when you've come through all that punk, all that rebellion, all that thing of being your generation when we thought we could change the world and that something amazing was going to happen. And then realising that that's not going to happen and you think well right, but I'm still angry about stuff. I've still got something to say. How do I channel that?

What you do is put a vest on and some braces.

The importance of the mainstream matters here. Rather than settling in the authentic vs the mainstream binary, Chumbawamba grasped the opportunities offered to them by a surprising chart success with Tub Thumping. They subverted their profits into activist groups, talked about anarchy on light entertainment shows, and took money from multinationals who used their music in advertising and fed it back to the same campaign groups challenging the multinational's work practices. Unlike Crass, Chumbawamba thought it mattered to be heard in the mass market. When Chumbawamba signed to EMI in 1997 it was a situationist prank, but it was also the ultimate sell out in Anarcho folk lore. Chumbawamba famously lived collectively, shared their money, resources and skills, which made for a very slow decision-making processes. But this extended beyond the politics of the personal to the politics of the politics. Alice recently talked to Dunstan for a short film he made to promote the Kick Starter for his forthcoming documentary 'I Get Knocked Down (The Untold Story of Chumbawamba)'. The ghosts of the sell out went out and did all sorts of disorderly things she explained; 'the stuff we did with the money had invisible repercussions, that no-one would ever connect to Chumbawamba'. They financed the May Day conference that 'kick started the Anti-Capitalism Movement'. Money from the inclusion of one of their tracks in an Italien Pontiac commercial went to an Italian Pirate Radio station. The band took $70,000 from General Motors and handed it to Corp Watch and IndyMedia – who used it to campaign against GM. All of these decisions implicated every one at every stage. IndyMedia debated taking the money, Chumbawamba's fans cried sell out. The only player that didn't seem to have a problem with it was GM.

Alice Nutter explained the importance of being heard, leaving a trace in an interview for Indy File in 1997 Alice now a writer, has always nailed it when it comes to what matters, when and why.

Alice: You see, that's great, the idea that catalysts like Chumbawumba ….and the idea that we're in people's houses and on karaoke machines. Popular culture is what shaped us. Punk rock led us towards politics, punk rock led us towards music. Then you want to be part of popular culture. The fact that little children are singing our songs, just makes us think, "great, this is how we've always wanted to be."

Tubthumping as children's singalong, karaoke soundtrack and mobile phone ringtone liberated ghosts to come and haunt us later. When we need them.

So where does this get me and my ghosts?

When they're not being smug and showing off their badge collection, the ghosts of Anarcho Punk can do some of the work that we need doing. Post post-punk can be an arsey ghost, rather than a smug romanticised memory of youth. That is, as long as its not the ghost of a old punk at the bar banging on about Joe Strummer, but is a man, in his fifties, in a [vest, braces and] nice suite suit shouting through a megaphone.

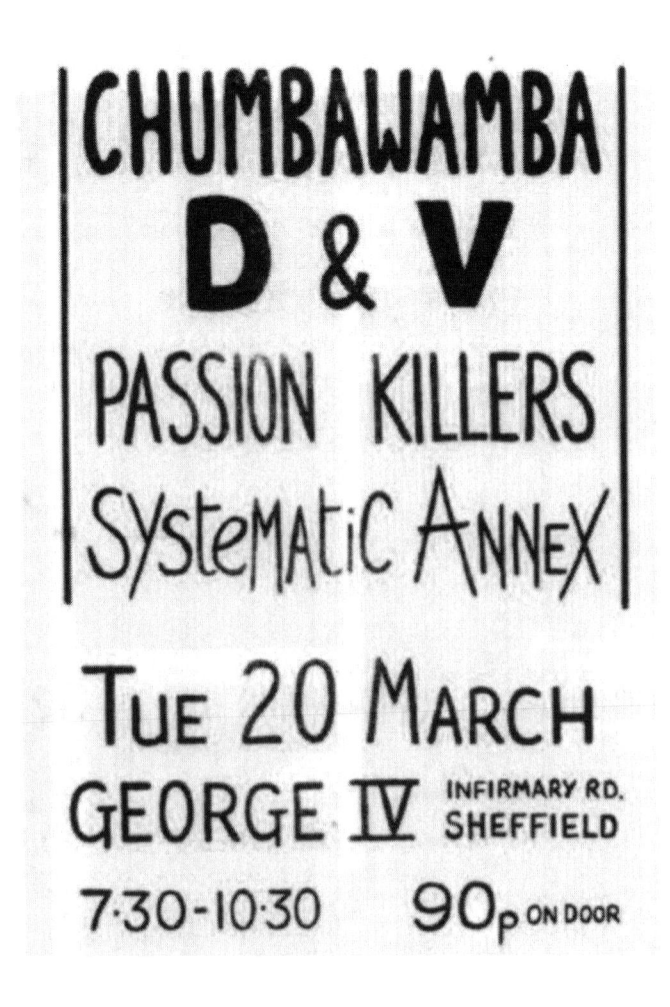

Various Handouts

Courtesy Greg Bull Collection

FUCK PEACE. WE'RE ENJOYING OURSELVES

THE HORROR PERPETRATED BY THATCHER AND REAGAN IS OUR HORROR. THEY ACT FOR US BECAUSE OF US. THE BOMB WASN'T FORCED UPON US – WE ASKED FOR IT. UNABLE TO ACCEPT THE LIMITLESS AND BOUNDLESS POTENTIAL THAT EACH OF US HAVE, WE CREATE A LIMIT TO CONTAIN OURSELVES WITHIN PERCEPTABLE PARAMETERS. WHY ARE WE SO SCARED OF OUR POWER THAT WE NEED TO CREATE GODS OR BOMBS TO ACT AS "LIDS" TO CONTAIN THAT POWER. WHY ARE WE SO SCARED OF OUR OWN BEAUTY THAT WE NEED TO CREATE SOMETHING THAT CAN DESTROY THAT BEAUTY. THATCHER AND REAGAN ARE MEANINGLESS LACKEYS DOING JOBS WE HAVE GIVEN THEM. WE ARE THE REAL PROBLEM AND THEY ARE JUST SYMPTOMS OF THAT PROBLEM – WHILE WE REMAIN UNCHANGED SO WILL THEY – AS SOON AS WE REMOVE THEM NEW LEADERS WILL BE CREATED BY US TO CONTAIN US. THE ONLY WAY THAT WE CAN ACHIEVE REAL FREEDOM IS TO COME TO TERMS WITH OURSELVES AND ACCEPT THE PERSONAL RESPONSIBILITIES THAT WE HAVE BEEN AVOIDING BY CREATING DIVERSIONS LIKE THE BOMB. THE SOONER WE STOP HIDING FROM OURSELVES THE SOONER WE CAN BE OURSELVES.

ALL THE ARMS WE NEED

PLEASE DON'T HURT ME

SO WHAT IF EVERYONE STOPS EATING MEAT?
SO WHAT IF WE MANAGED TO BAN CRUISE?

WHAT DIFFERENCE WILL IT MAKE - WE SHOULD BE WORKING WITHIN A PHILOSOPHY NOT A DOCTRINE.
THE REASON MANY EXTREMIST GROUPS HAVE NEVER POSED ANY REAL THREAT IS BECAUSE THE MAJORITY OF ITS FOLLOWERS ARE INDOCTRINATED IDIOTS, THEY HAVE NO COMPREHENSION OF THEIR GROUPS PHILOSOPHY. FOR EXAMPLE THE SWASTIKA EMBELISHED BOOT BOY SIEG HIELING KNOWS HE HATES BLACKS BECAUSE HE'S BEEN TOLD HE DOES, BUT HE DOESN'T KNOW WHY. JUST LIKE THE POLICEMAN (ANOTHER BOOT BOY IN A DIFFERENT UNIFORM) WHO DEFENDS AMERICAN CRUISE MISSILES BECAUSE HE'S BEEN TOLD TO - HE DOES AS HE'S TOLD ALTHOUGH HE DOESN'T UNDERSTAND WHY, JUST LIKE HE DID IN BRIXTON, ON THE PEACE MARCH AND ON THE PICKET AT WARRINGTON. JUST WHO THE HELL DOES THE POLICEMAN THINK HE IS PROTECTING - DOES HE EVEN CARE?
DENY THOSE SORT OF SHEEP THEIR LEADER AND THEY ARE LEFT FLOUNDERING. THEY ARE CAPABLE OF LITTLE ELSE BUT FOLLOWING AND AS SUCH MAKE USEFUL CANNON FODDER FOR THE "REAL THREAT" WHO PLAN THE NAZI CAMPAIGN.
UNLESS WE ARE CAREFUL THE PEACE/PROTEST MOVEMENT IS GOING TO FALL DOWN THE SAME HOLE. IT'S SO EASY TO MOUTH THE SAME OLD SLOGANS LIKE "FIGHT WAR NOT WARS", "FUCK THE SYSTEM", "GIVE PEACE A CHANCE" AND ALL THE OTHER FASHIONABLE RHETORIC THAT HAS BECOME SYNONYMOUS WITH THE CIRCLED 'A' SIGN.
EATING MEAT, NUCLEAR WEAPONS, WAR AND RAPE ARE ALL SYMPTOMS OF THE DISEASE THAT IS INFESTING OUR LIVES - OF WHICH EACH OF US IS AN INTEGRAL PART.
HOW MANY TIMES HAVE YOU SEEN PEOPLE ON A PEACE MARCH STOP AT A HAMBURGER STALL AND BUY A BEEFBURGER? CAN'T THEY SEE THE CONNECTION BETWEEN THE WAR IN THE SLAUGHTERHOUSE AND THE SLAUGHTER ON THE BATTLEFIELD?
HOW MANY TIMES HAVE YOU SEEN PEOPLE ON AN ANTI-VIVISECTION DEMO WEARING LEATHER AND FUR AND EATING MEAT? - ISN'T ALL ANIMAL EXPLOITATION UNECCESSARY?
I AM NOT NEGATING THE VERY IMPORTANT AND VALUABLE WORK THAT THOSE SORT OF PEOPLE ARE DOING, BUT I AM TRYING TO LEARN FROM THEIR MISTAKES.
IT'S SO EASY TO GET CAUGHT UP IN PERIPHERAL ISSUES, AND IN SO DOING LOSING SIGHT OF THE REAL GOAL.
WE EACH NEED TO DEVELOP OUR OWN PACIFIST, HUMANITARIAN AND ANARCHIST PHILOSOPHY AS WELL AS TRY TO DEVELOP OUR OWN PERSONAL COURAGE AND CONVICTION TO APPLY WHAT WE BELIEVE TO OUR EVERYDAY LIVING. - WHY DO I DO WRONG WHEN I KNOW WHAT IS RIGHT?
IF WE DONT WANT TO BE KILLED WE SHOULDN'T SUPPORT THE MURDERERS, BE THEY BUTCHERS SELLING MEAT OR GOVERNMENTS SELLING WAR.
IF WE DON'T WANT TO BE OPPRESSED WE SHOULDN'T SUPPORT THE OPPRESSORS, BE THEY GOVERNMENTS SELLING THE OBSCENITY OF DEMOCRACY WHICH GIVES ONE GROUP OF PEOPLE THE RIGHT TO CONTROL ANOTHER - OR THE SYSTEM THAT FORCES CHILDREN TO PRAY TO THEIR GOD IN THE SCHOOL ASSEMBLY AND SING THE NATIONAL ANTHEM.
YOU DON'T HAVE TO LOOK FAR TO FIND SOMETHING THAT IS CONSIDERED NORMAL AND ACCEPTABLE. FOR EXAMPLE - WHY IS IT ACCEPTED AS NORMAL THAT OVER A THIRD OF THE WORLD IS DYING FOR THE WANT OF FOOD WHILE THE OTHER TWO THIRDS THROW AWAY FOOD AT THE END OF EACH MEAL? WHILE STARVATION IS A KILLER IN THE THIRD WORLD, OBESITY IS A KILLER IN THE CIVILIZED WORLD. SOME FUCKING CIVILIZATION.
THIS SORT OF DISTORTED NORMALITY WILL CONTINUE TO BE ACCEPTED AS NORMAL UNTIL A SUFFICIENT NUMBER OF PEOPLE QUESTION THAT NORMALITY. ONLY THEN WILL THINGS CHANGE - AND EVENTUALLY THEY WOULD AS THERE WOULD BE NO DEFENCE FOR THEIR CONTINUANCE - IF, AND ONLY IF, EACH OF US IS AWARE OF OUR PHILOSOPHICAL BELIEFS RATHER THAN INDOCTRINAL ISSUES.
THE BIGGEST PROBLEM WITH DIVIDING THE PROBLEMS THAT WE ARE FACED WITH INTO ISSUES IS THAT IT IS DIVISIVE.
IT IS EASIER TO IGNORE A MASS OF DIFFERENT VOICES CALLING OUT FOR PEACE, ANTI-VIVISECTION, EQUAL RIGHTS ETC RATHER THAN A UNITED VOICE CALLING FOR AN END TO ALL OF THAT SHIT.
IN BRITAIN THE PEACE MOVEMENT WOULD PROBABLY CRUMBLE IF THE GOVERNMENT GAVE IN TO ITS DEMANDS TO GET RID OF CRUISE. THE PEACE MOVEMENT HAS ALLOWED ITS "PACIFIST PHILOSOPHY" TO BE CHANNELLED INTO ONE PERIPHERAL ISSUE - CRUISE, WHEN IN FACT CRUISE IS JUST ONE OF MANY DEMANDS.
THE GOVERNMENT COULD AGREE NOT TO ACCEPT CRUISE AND INTRODUCE OTHER FORMS OF WEAPONS BEFORE THE PEACE MOVEMENT COULD GET ITSELF TOGETHER AND BECOME SUFFICIENTLY ORGANISED TO GAIN ENOUGH MOMENTUM TO PUT FORWARD ANOTHER DEMAND THAT THAT THE GOVERNMENT WOULD TREAT SERIOUSLY.
THE TIME HAS COME TO START REALLY DEMANDING RATHER THAN ASKING.
THE RECENT CND MARCH WAS A GOOD EXAMPLE OF THE INEFFECTIVENESS OF ASKING OR REQUESTING - WHILE WE ALL MARCHED ALONG A ROUTE APPROVED BY THE GOVERNMENT AND CONTROLLED BY THEIR POLICE THE CRUISE MISSILES WERE UNLOADED AT FELIXSTOWE HARBOUR - THE GOVERNMENT MAINTAIN THE PRETENCE OF DEBATE BUT ALL THE TIME THEY IGNORE US.

Flux of Pink Indians Handout

WHILE WE ASK – AND WHILE WE WORK WITH THE AUTHORITIES THAT OPPRESS US THEY WILL CONTINUE TO IGNORE US. THE VERY ESSENCE OF THEIR POWER LIES IN US ASKING. JUST LOOK HOW SUCCESSFULLY THEY MANAGED TO HERD A HALF A MILLION OF US INTO HYDE PARK DURING THE CND RALLY WHERE WE CAUSED LITTLE OR NO NUISANCE AND HAD LITTLE OR NO EFFECT.

WHAT WOULD HAVE HAPPENED IF WE HAD ALL CONFRONTED THEIR AUTHORITY AND MARCHED TO DOWNING STREET AND DEMANDED PEACE AND DEMANDED AN END TO THE WAR MACHINERY IN THIS COUNTRY.

A HANDFUL OF WOMEN AT GREENHAM HAVE SHOWN THE VERY REAL POTENTIAL WE HAVE – THEIR ACTIONS WILL EITHER BE A CATALYST SPARKING OFF REAL DEMANDS AND ACTION WITHIN THE PEACE MOVEMENT – OR ELSE THEY WILL BECOME MARTYRS TO A LOST CAUSE. WILL WE SIT BACK ON OUR ARSES AND WATCH THE GOVERNMENT REMOVE THEM?

WE NEED TO STOP BEING SO FUCKING REASONABLE AND STOP MAKING EXCUSES FOR OTHERS AS WELL AS OURSELVES. RELIGION IS NOT OKAY BECAUSE A FEW GOOD PEOPLE HAVE BEEN DRAWN INTO ITS GAME. IT IS A VICIOUS BLOOD SUCKING LEECH PLAYING ON PEOPLES FEARS, SUCKING THEM DRY. "MAN WAS MADE TO SUFFER AND THROUGH HIS SUFFERING HE WILL RECIEVE HIS REWARD – A PLACE IN HEAVEN NEXT TO HIS LORD" IS ALL RUBBISH.– THERE IS NO "GODS WILL". THROUGH MANS SUFFERING THE CHURCH HAS LINED ITS OWN POCKET – FILLED ITS OWN BLOATED GUT – FINANCED ITS OWN HEARTLESS BLACKMAILING MACHINE – A MACHINE THAT ROLLS ON AND ON CRUSHING AND RECRUITING.

THE ROYAL FAMILY IS NOT A NICE HARMLESS BRITISH TRADITION, IT IS JUST ANOTHER PERNICIOUS TOOL USED TO JUSTIFY THEIR LIES. ANDREW WAS IN THE FALKLANDS FIGHTING FOR HIS COUNTRY – CHARLES AND DI SHOW US WHAT A LOVING MARRIAGE CAN MEAN – SMILING FATHER, MOTHER AND CHILD. THE REAL HAPPY FAMILY WHERE MEN ARE STRONG AND DOMINANT, THE WOMAN PETITE AND SUBMISSIVE. THAT HAPPY FAMILY IS A LOATHSOME JUSTIFICATION FOR ALL THE PATRIARCHAL AND MATRIARCHAL BIGOTRY THAT RULES OUR LIVES.

THE RICH DO NOT DESERVE WHAT THEY HAVE – EVEN IF THEY WORKED FOR IT – THEIR EXCESS IS ANOTHERS DEPRIVATION –THE CAVIAR THEY LEAVE ON THE SIDE OF THEIR PLATE BECAUSE THEIR STOMACH IS TOO FULL TO TAKE ANOTHER MOUTHFULL WAS SNATCHED FROM THE MOUTH OF STARVING CHILDREN DYING FOR THE WANT OF FOOD – ANY FOOD. IT WAS STOLEN FROM THE PATIENT IN THE HOSPITAL DYING BECAUSE THERE WASN'T ENOUGH KIDNEY MACHINES TO GO ROUND.

CORONATION STREET, WOMENS OWN, JACKIE, THE SUN ARE NOT OKAY, THEY ARE NOT HARMLESS FUN THEY ARE ALL OBSCENE VILE DEGRADING TOOLS JUSTIFYING OUR MISERY. THE DISTORTED IMAGE ON PAGE THREE IS A REFLECTION OF YOU – AND YOU ARE A REFLECTION OF ME.

THE SMILING BOBBY ON THE BEAT WILL ALWAYS BE SMILING – ON THE STREET CORNER. IN HIS RIOT GEAR HE LINES US UP AGAINST THE WALL – HE'S ONLY DOING HIS JOB.

THE SOLDIER THE SAILOR THE TINKER THE TAILOR THE HANGMAN AND THE BUTCHER ARE ALL DOING THEIR JOBS – ARE YOU DOING YOURS?

ALL AUTHORITY IS OPPRESSION AND POSSESIVE – ALL INSTITUTIONS ENFORCE THAT OPPRESSION – UNLESS WE BREAK IT DOWN IT WILL CONTINUE TO EXIST. THEY CAN'T OFFER EXCUSES FOR THEIR EXISTANCE BECAUSE THERE ARE NONE – SO WHY DO WE?

WHAT IT BOILS DOWN TO IS THAT WE EITHER SIT DOWN AND LET THEM FUCK UP OUR LIVES MORE AND MORE EACH DAY OR WE GET OFF OUR ARSES AND TRY TO DEFEND OURSELVES. WHAT HAVE WE GOT TO LOOSE?

Flux of Pink Indians Handout

Distortions and crawling damp hands
shades of greyness, throwing out sweat
Decomposition of limbs and facial
  qualities ripped.
    Fake tanned
  preening bird-like strutting features
    Packed into sweaty stadiums
       of circus animals.
       Packed cling film glue bags
         uniformed bondage
           in straight
              jackets.

Asphyxiated on false hopes.
Rawness, Coldness, Naked.

sterile
promoting Images
suiting the time of life
Blindness staring
  you in the face
stretched out and
  pinned to a bloody
              board
They stare at my bright wings
  Relations
              Unnatural
Greed sets its bittern
         Rusty nails
and seeps up torn spaces
  where love could have bred.

Enflamed Institutions
Daily Sick, Piss, Shit.

Daily Blindness
But deliver us from evil.

Flux of Pink Indians Handout

Biographies

Irene González Frizzera [artist]

Irene González Frizzera was born in October 26th, 1983 in Montevideo - Uruguay.

Started drawing and painting at a very early age and never stopped.

In 2006 she graduated from Escuela Universitaria Centro de Diseño (Universitiy of Industrial Design in Montevideo) in the field of Textile Design and attended further studies at University of Arts - London College of Fashion in England.

Worked as a fashion and pattern designer in a few Uruguay-based textile trading companies for some years but became a freelancer illustrator and Pattern designer since August, 2014.

See online porfolio at: www.behance.net/Irene_ene

Tom Laimer-Read

Tom Laimer-Read is the author of the punk novel *Needles & Pins*, which you can find at various online resources.

He went to various state schools in various states of conscience during the '80s and '90s and there learnt a healthy disrespect for authority - so at least schools do teach you something!

http://www.needlesandpinspunknovel.co.uk

http://www.letsrockpublishing.co.uk

for more details.

You can also find him on Facebook at

http://www.facebook.com/letsrockpublishing

http://www.facebook.com/needlesandpinspunknovel if you're interested.

Willie Rissy

Willie Rissy returned to Birmingham in 1984, to attend another Crass gig at Digbeth Civic Hall - during which he was battered in the side of the head by a drunken arsehole.

He still judges that this was a better evening than the one he experienced in 1983.
Willie has passed through Digbeth many times in the intervening years, but has opted not to return to the venue since.

He still listens to *Yes Sir, I Will* on a regular basis.

Unlike many things from the 1980s, he thinks that the album has actually improved with age.

Paul Platypus

Paul Platypus played in several bands, produced fanzines, compiled charts, organised gigs, ran record labels and a music publisher – all from 1978 to 1984.

He mixed in a variety of different circles over that time, from postpunks to anarchopunks to the founders of Creation Records – he also knew a lot of people who went on to become rich and/or famous, unlike him.

He now works in university research management, whilst trying to make sense of his past.

The Sounds Obscurist Chart can be found at

http://obscuristchart.wordpress.com

www.obscurist.net

may occasionally be updated (or not).

Contact paul@obscurist.net.

Marcus Blakeston

Marcus Blakeston is an unashamed writer of trashy pulp fiction. With titles like *Punk Rock Nursing Home*, *Skinhead Away*, and *Biker Sluts versus Flying Saucers*, his books are populated by an assortment of punks, skinheads, biker gangs, and the occasional football hooligan.

Born in Northumberland in the 1960s, he emigrated to Yorkshire with his mother a year later and has remained there ever since.

https://marcusblakeston.wordpress.com/

Andrew J. Wood

Activist, writer, musician, and teacher Andrew J. Wood holds a B.S. in Political Science from the University of Tennessee — Chattanooga, and an M.A. in Social Sciences from the University of Chicago.

He is currently a Ph.D. candidate in Politics, with a designated emphasis in the History of Consciousness, at the University of California — Santa Cruz.

Drawing from his lifetime engagement and dedication to punk rock cultures, his dissertation from which this essay is derived, is titled "Makers & Breakers: Pre-Raphaelites, Punk Rockers, and the Political Imagination" focuses on the philosophy of aesthetics and politico-aesthetic movements ranging from William Morris to contemporary punk cultures, and the effects and affects such movements have on our (political) imaginations.

Influenced by an eclectic amalgamation of philosophy, political thought, music, poetics, economics, literature, and aesthetics, his work broadly addresses radical social change through visual, sonic, and affective registers often disregarded by traditional social scientific paradigms.

He lives in California with his wife/life-partner and their two dogs.

anjwood@ucsc.edu

Darren Johns

Born, raised and content to die in Plymouth, Darren Johns is a middle-aged, working class man trapped in a crust punk kid's psyche.

Entering the fray in 1968, he had an enjoyably normal childhood, either playing in Southway woods with friends or studying diligently, yet begrudgingly, in school.

He got '50s rock'n'roll at 8 years old; his first guitar at 10; punk at 11; Crass at 13; left school at 15; got his first and only tattoo (of a tiger) at 16; turned vegetarian then vegan at 17; gave up alcohol the same year (after three years of pretending to like scrumpy cider); left home at 18; and got laid and arrested (not consecutively) for the first time the same year. Then adulthood took over and the rest is a blur.

For the past decade he has fronted/ran roots-punk band, Crazy Arm. When he's not doing that he writes for music magazines or drives for other bands or designs band/show posters, album artwork and T-shirts or plays acoustic shows (as Sawtooth) or does a spot of grassroots activism or cycles or reads or cuddles his beloved cat, Smudge, a lot or spends many hours worrying about a) his waistline spreading, b) his hairline receding and c) his lifeline deteriorating.

Ted Curtis

Ted Curtis was an up and coming young writer working in all fields, but not advertising. At the time of his disappearance in the Warminster triangle he was working on a collection of vignettes about Swindon in the 1980s, when everything was free, as well as a novel about valentines day and the end times.

His dad could have beat up your dad, easy, but only on a Sunday: the rest of the time he was busy.

Random samples of his shit can still be found at http://antsy-pantsy.blogspot.com/

During the 1990s he had some success in the small press, but everything is connected and nothing means anything, so he concentrated on his drinking instead.

He was very good at it too, for a while.

Then there was that business with the carrots.

Anyway, just read the story, although it doesn't mean anything either. The others will be better.

Rich Cross

In February 1979, Rich Cross had to pick up his copy of *The Feeding of the 5000* from the Post Office in town, because the Small Wonder package arrived while he was at school.

Luckily everyone was out when he got it home, so he could immediately play it on the family's hi-fidelity stereogram.

More than 35 years later, he cannot shake off his preoccupation with the explosive, formative years of anarchist punk rock.

He runs the *Hippies Now Wear Black* website [http://thehippiesnowwearblack.org.uk] site and can be contacted at info@thehippiesnowwearblack.org.uk.

Anth Palmer

I grew up in a small market town in northern England called Hebden Bridge.

Throughout the seventies this small town became somewhat of a mecca for left wing and free thinking individuals, writers and musicians.

It seemed no surprise that a burgeoning punk scene of its own would begin to thrive and from that became my initial interest of the bands and their politics.

By 1987, with the anarcho-punk scene somewhat on it's hind-legs, I finally moved to the big bright lights of Leeds, moved into an all vegan communal house and continued the political activism, fanzine publishing, home-brewing, skating and general mischief.

Twenty-eight years on and my involvement in bands, writing and publishing, upholding my ethics and the old adage of growing older and more cynical has peaked and flowed throughout all of those years. Halcyon days.

Paul Davies

After attending several free festivals in the 1980s, campaigning against nuclear weapons in Nottingham and blockading nuclear bases in England, Paul (aka Oddie) served time as a conscientious objector and lived at Menwith Hill Peace Camp before setting off to hitch hike around England.

He read Archaeological Theory and Social Anthropology at University of Wales, Lampeter, and went on to complete an MA in the Anthropology of Religion at the University of Durham.

Oddie worked alongside many other people to bring the issue of ancestry and specifically the reburial of human remains at Avebury, into the public domain.

He spent 9 years living on a narrowboat in Bath and Northampton, experiencing, at 1st hand, the social exclusion experienced by many liveaboard boat owners with no home mooring.

He is a (sometimes) Green Anarchist, Independent Druid, a Quaker and that, of course, means he is, fundamentally, an absolute pacifist.

Lucy Robinson

Lucy Robinson teaches Modern British History at the University of Sussex.

She works on sexuality, popular culture and protest since the 1960s. She is currently working on the 1980s and helped create the open digital archive 'Observing the 80s'. She works in collaboration with musicians, artists, journalists, activists, film makers, young people and students.

Most recently, Lucy has been publishing work around teaching punk, digital pedagogy, and feminism and fandom, and is currently writing a book about popular culture and politics in the 1980s.

Her innovative history course 'Post-Punk Britain' has been awarded a number of teaching awards. She loves shit telly, Kathleen Hanna and Elvis.

She tweets as @DrLucyRobinson and blogs at https://drlucyrobinson.wordpress.com/

Gerard Evans

Gerard Evans was the singer in Flowers in the Dustbin and indeed remains so since they reformed in 2014. During this period he also helped organise the first Stop The City demo in 1983.

After Flowers, Gerard went on to write for Sounds and Amnesty International, using the psuedonym George Berger. Using this name, he wrote biographies of the Levellers (Virgin publishing) and Crass (Omnibus), before releasing the *All The Young Punks* series of books, where people who weren't in bands got to tell their story for the first time. There is an anthology of his punk writings published called 'Let's Submerge', which features his popular columns for 3ammagazine.com and a sample chapter of 'Horse-Drawn And Quartered' - his unpublished book about life on a horse-drawn wagon in Ireland. New books are in the pipeline.

Since 1999, Gerard has been running a Web Consultancy called Abisti (named after his punk fanzine *Ability Stinks* - not suitable in full of course!) and he also makes guided meditation tapes to help people cope with the everyday stresses of modern life.

He lives in Lewes, East Sussex. Still seeking.

Web Consultants:abisti.co.uk

Guided Meditations: abisti.com

Punk: flowersinthedustbin.co.uk

Chris Butler

Having taken up the rallying cry from the punk movement to pick up a guitar and make a noise - Chris did just that.

He ran with the idea and hasn't stopped running since. Where he's headed is anyone's guess for this acoustic singer songwriter...

Since writing the article about his first Conflict gig in 1985, Chris recently achieved a career highlight in 2015 when he shared a bill with Conflict at the Another Winter Of Discontent North festival. Chris's latest CD called *If Not Now, When?* is available from his gigs and via his online shop at

www.etsy.com/shop/chrisbutlersongs

and more information can be found at

www.facebook.com/chrisbutlermusic.

Meanwhile, Chris still hopes to change the world for the better.

Vincent G Learoyd

Vincent G Learoyd a.k.a Vomit (musician/ artist). Founding member and bassist with the anarcho punk band 'D.I.R.T.' and subsequent guitarist with day-glo punksters 'Rubella Ballet'.

Touring extensively with Crass, Flux, The Mob and Conflict during the early eighties with his brother Fox. The brothers were formerly from the Enfield punk band The Gutterats. Their emblem, a three horned skull created by their father Leo. This was later to become the emblem for D.I.R.T.

After recording *Object, Refuse, Never Mind Dirt* and the *Mother/Ripper* single on Crass records, Vince left the band and formed the neo pagan band 'Earth Culture' with ex Rubella bassist Dave Slight.

After a few years of recording music with the band and composing music for theatre companies he returned to writing and illustrating, (his other great passion) and released his debut novel 'The Laila Mythology', creating a video trailer with DT Films and a little help from Crass founder Penny Rimbaud and Sid from Rubella Ballet. His second book was 'The comic book guide to Botany' which he illustrated whilst studying Arboriculture in London.

Currently on his third comic book he lives with his wife Sara and son Rocco in leafy Surrey.

Stephen Spencer-Fleet.Fleaty.Shonk Set.

Former editor of *Freedom Construction* fanzine and the bands Disturbance From Fear, Le Pendu and Winged Demons.

Now producing music as Bludgeon Club Sound using forgotten sounds and redundant technology.

DJ's infrequently.

bludgeonclubsound.bandcamp.com

Ruth Gasson

Excluded from school at fifteen for being 'stupid' and having the wrong colour hair. She went on to have an exciting and varied professional career; working overseas, at the famous residential recording studio 'Rockfield' and organising/hosting large scale music and sporting events.

In 2005 she was diagnosed as dyslexic: a catalytic moment which gave her the confidence to follow her dreams and in June 2010 she graduated with a First Class Honours Degree in Creative Writing.

In 2012 she was elected as the fourth Bard of Northampton by the people of Northampton. During her year as Bard, she worked to introduce Spoken Word to children and young people by running workshops in schools and libraries and developed the young Bard competition.

In December 2013 she was awarded, one of only ten, National Literacy Heroes, by the National Literacy Trust and HRH the Duchess of Cornwall for her work with young people and overcoming her personal learning difficulties.

She is now a writer, teacher and creative practitioner with a keen interest in Arts and Mental Health, and wants to make a difference to individuals and communities.

She volunteers and is a director of the Umbrella Fair Organisation and is a regular contributor on BBC Radio Northampton.

http://www.ruthgasson.co.uk/

https://ruthharveygasson.wordpress.com/

https://uk.linkedin.com/in/ruthgasson

Nick Hydra

Nick Hydra was born in 1965, and has always lived (and will almost certainly die) in South East London. He discovered punk in 1978.

In his spare time, he makes noisy post-industrial anarcho punk in Hydra, slightly less noisy industrial in A.I.M., and audiovisual industrial as No Man

He writes occasional reviews for the DSO Audio website and designs badges and the odd flyer.

He also spends quite a lot of time gardening, but in an angry punk way, obviously.

https://www.facebook.com/SlainoftheHydra,

https://www.facebook.com/Advanced-Idea-Mechanics-AIM-202543906452572/

https://www.facebook.com/noman

http://www.dso.co.uk/indexa.htm

Lance Hahn 1967-2007

"A certain glib brand of postmodernism might point to how there was not one Lance Hahn, but many. There was Lance Hahn, the singer-songwriter and driving force behind the band J Church, but also Lance Hahn the punk historian, Lance Hahn the San Franciscan, Lance Hahn the Situationist, Lance Hahn the Asian-American, Lance Hahn the baseball fanatic, etc. Still, this kind of a description overlooks a simple but somehow elusive fact: these were not separate identities united by the same body, but facets of the same prismatic whole.

Lance Hahn defied convention at every turn. He offered class analysis at a time when it had been eclipsed by a cloud of floating signifiers and debates over language and representation.

He was nominally a punk, but he harbored as much admiration for Albert Ayler as Ian MacKaye. And in an era when punk became more thoroughly commodified than ever before, Hahn stayed doggedly faithful to the DIY ethic without ever losing his sense of humor, as he noted in 2000 regarding J Church's lack of commercial success: "First off, we're ugly, and secondly, I'm Chinese." [http://www.popmatters.com/feature/faded-reflection-lance-hahn-1967-2007/]

The article included here will be included in the full book of punk history 'Let The Tribe Increase' which will be published by PM Press (www.pmpress.org)

Gail Hart

I am a 51 year old female punk. I was born in London and lived mostly in and around London throughout my life. At 16 after discovering punk and dying my hair blue, I put an advert in Sounds music paper and my life changed. I met new people, joined a band, in fact to date I have been in 5 bands including Adventures in Colour, The Lost Cherrees, Word of Mouth, The Pukes and Flowers in the Dustbin.

I lived in various squats and bedsits and apart from my passion for designing and sewing, developed my interest in the paranormal and now work as a full time psychic, appearing in magazines and on TV. I still sing backing vocals for Flowers in the Dustbin and also raise my 14 year old son who was born deaf with global development delay.

Flowers in the Dustbin are about to release an EP on red vinyl and CD version called 'I am an Artist, your rules don't Apply.'

My psychic website is www.gailhart.co.uk and I hope to publish my autobiography about my life aged 17- 30 , soon.

Watch this space!

Alastair 'Gords' Gordon

Alastair "Gords" Gordon likes all things DiY punk rock and always knew he was out of step with the world.

He's been involved in the punk scene for longer than he'd like to remember. He became a 'punkademic' via an early, total rejection of formal schooling and its traditional teaching methods. He completed a doctorate on Authenticity and DiY punk under the supervision of Professor Mike Pickering (Loughborough University). Gords informs his academic research through playing in bands and remains active in the UK and international DiY punk scenes.

He currently vents anger at the world singing, touring and recording with the band Geriatric Unit and playing bass in Endless Grinning Skulls.

He is currently a senior lecturer in Media and Communication and De Montfort University, Leicester.

He also co runs the Punk Scholar Network with Mike Dines, Pete Dale, Russ Bestley & Matt Worley.

Gords fucking hates Tories of all political colours.

Russ Bestley

Russ Bestley is a graphic designer and writer, currently employed as Reader in Graphic Design at the London College of Communication.

He has written a number of books and articles on design methods, punk graphics and punk history, and has contributed articles to publications including *Eye, Zed, Emigré, The National Grid, Street Sounds* and *Vive Le Rock*. His book *The Art of Punk*, co-authored with Alex Ogg, was published by Omnibus Press (UK), Voyageur (North America), Hannibal Verlag Gmbh (Germany) and Hugo et Compagnie (France) in 2012.

He is co-editor of the academic journal *Punk and Post Punk*, published by Intellect Ltd, and he leads the *Graphic Subcultures Research Hub* at the London College of Communication. His PhD thesis, *Hitsville UK: Punk Rock and Graphic Design in the Faraway Towns, 1976-84,* was completed in 2008 and led to several publications, a website, www.hitsvilleuk.com, and a range of post-doctoral research.

He has curated exhibitions on a variety of themes connected with punk and punk graphic design in London, Southampton, Blackpool, Leeds and Birmingham. He has also designed books, posters, pamphlets, programmes and other material for the Punk Scholars Network, Active Distribution, Viral Age Records and other DIY and independent labels, publishers and producers.

Matthew Worley

Matthew Worley is a historian at the University of Reading. He has written widely on British politics between the wars and, more recently, on the relationship between youth culture, politics and social change in 1970s-1980s Britain.

His work has been published in journals such as *Contemporary British History, History Workshop Journal* and *Twentieth Century British History*, as well as in magazines such as *Street Sounds*.

He is a co-founder of the Subcultures Network, which published *Fight Back: Punk, Politics and Resistance in 2015*.

He supports Norwich City.

Tim Voss

Tim Voss first heard the sounds of punk through the headphones of his big brother stereo; The Clash, The Pistols, The Damned alongside Bowie and Bolan filled his head. Then, old enough the buy records with his bus fare he loved the next wave of punk, the Subs, the Ruts and most importantly the unique and uncompromising band Crass. This turned his thoughts and the music he listened to forever, looking to the power of independent music made by bands that had something to say, that crafted their songs in an uncompromising and expressive way.

Tim played drums in a number of 'local' bands, formed with mates at school and people who knew mates from school, -often these bands never formed beyond bedroom dreams. He put gigs on with the same mates including the legendary Hartham Common peace festival with Flux.

For Tim the music was only a part of what he got from the punk movement, the politics that forged life long opinions, the friendships, the ability to think and act freely and the people were at least, if not more, important.

Punk was just the beginning – its what we in everyday life that counts.

Mike Dines

Originally from a working-class, market-trading background, Mike joined the West Sussex Institute of Higher Education in the early 1990s, gaining a first class Honours degree in Music and Related Arts.

Although a performer throughout his degree (he is a classical pianist by trade), he decided the road of musicology and analysis was for him; and so embarked on a Masters degree at the University of Sussex.

After writing a thesis on Crass and the anarcho-punk scene of the 1980s, Mike continued his research at the University of Salford, completing a PhD entitled The Emergence of the Anarcho-Punk Scene of the 1980s.

Mike continues to write about punk and has recently co-edited the volume *Tales From the Punkside* (2014) with Greg Bull and has also written on punk pedagogy and Krishnacore.

His forthcoming co-edited *The Aesthetics of Our Anger: Anarcho-Punk, Politics, Music* is due out in early 2016 from Autonomedia.

Tony Drayton

Original 1976 mover and shaker in the punk world with his fanzine *Ripped And Torn*, followed up in 1980 with the ground breaking fanzine *Kill Your Pet Puppy*.

Tony lives with his family in Leytonstone and works in Walthamstow organising the market stall permits.

Going under the name Tony De La Fou, Tony continues to juggle, breath fire and perform in other circus disciplines. Tony started and continues to own the *Kill Your Pet Puppy* blog;

www.killyourpetpuppy.co.uk.

Greg Bull

Greg Bull heard the Sex Pistols as a 12 year old and liked the noise they made. He liked their energy. He liked their attitude. And he liked their dress-sense and their rejection of authority. He didn't really know or understand this at the time as he just felt these things without understanding them. But he didn't become a punk then.

Later, in the early 1980s Greg met up with like-minded individuals who turned him on to "Black and White" bands such as Crass, and he met and went to see Antisect quite a few times as well.

He listened to a wide-range of music though and avoided proper "work" until the mid 1990s.

He is writing things down now from his memory of those times.

Co-editor of *Tales From The Punkside, Not Just Bits of Paper* and now *Some of Us Scream... Some of Us Shout* he is still working on the final part of his punk/sci-fi novella trilogy which began with *Perdam Babylonis Nomen*, continued with *Deus Magnus Timor Mortuum* and will one day conclude with a novella with an equally obscure latin title..

Darren Pike (Pikey)

Coming from Sunderland, and forming in 1984, Hex consisted of Pikey (vocals), Golly (guitar and vocals), Lainy (bass) and Cubby (drums). Looking back we were really keen and enthusiastic and full of ideas living the band 24/7.

Practising in a local youth club twice a week, we would store the gear in Lainy's mams and use an old shopping trolley to hump the gear backwards and forwards, it used to take ages then after practising reverse the process.

After a few months of practising we did a few gigs, went into Desert Sounds studio and recorded the first of 5 demos, made our own tapes with covers and put an add in Sounds advertising the demo and sold quite a few. One of the people who got hold of a copy was Karl who then formed his own label-Words of Warning- and in 1986 released You Are Not Alone four-track E.P. which featured Hex (our track being 'Is This To Be?'), Oi Polloi, Stalag 17 and Symbol of Freedom.

We did a few more gigs around the North East and enlisted 2 more members Sharon and Cas, both on vocals. Sharon and Cubby left the band and after recording our 4th demo with Lainy reverting to drums with Dickie Hammond joining on bass. In early 1988 Lainy left and was replaced on drums by Anth Irwin from the Famous Imposters, we recorded our 5th and final demo in the spring of that year. We did a few more gigs then Golly decided to leave, we continued on for a while but finally called it a day in late 1988.

Footnote: Since writing this biog our dearest friend and brother Dickie Hammond passed away. He was a living legend and will be sorely missed by everyone involved with Hex.

Matt Grimes

Matt has had a colourful and varied life as a punk, Traveller, activist, performer, art technician, landscape gardener, DJ, parent and more recently an educator. He is a Senior Lecturer in Music Industries and Radio at Birmingham City University. Matt has written on anarcho-punk, punk 'zines and radio as a tool for inclusion and change. A member of the Punk Scholars Network, Matt is currently studying for a doctorate on anarcho-punk, memory, ageing and legacy.

Passionate about equal access to media, Matt has worked with a number of marginalised groups such as Gypsies and Travellers and isolated teenagers in rural communities; using radio production techniques as a way of giving a voice to the voiceless and enabling them to create media and counter-media.

Born into a West Ham United supporter's family Matt swapped allegiance to their arch-rivals Millwall at the age of 12, coincidentally at the same time he discovered punk rock. His dad and granddad never forgave him. He has remained committed to Millwall ever since-probably because no one likes them and he don't care.

He spends a lot of time cycling, rock climbing, gardening and trying to live as ethically as possible-though at times failing miserably.

ATTENTION. Piss to the Parties, the politicians, the military and their slaughter games

ATTENTION. Labour/Tory/Liberal - you stink and kill this Earth for your powerful silk-purse morality

ATTENTION. It's fucking stupid to let so few run our lives into death.. Don't let them do it

ATTENTION. Why the fuck do we allow this world to slowly die from self-inflicted wounds?

ATTENTION. In every country on the street the police and army protect the stage thats set for the holocaust

Stand up and fight. Choose life or destruction. Go Forward. Get out on the streets. Snap the rules. Creep through the net. Fuck their diseased system.

THE BUCK STOPS HERE - Antisect

Is life better than death?
If so, then surely peace must be better than war
If suffering is something that nobody wants
then why should it escalate more?
Are we really so afraid we have to close our eyes
And ignore these things exist
Until people are prepared to cast away their greed
War and poverty will always exist
Some of us believe that it's more important
To feed the banker before the poor
And some are not quite sure just what they want
But they're positive that they want more
Conflict in the name of peace
As we declare war again and again
Seems to be that the politics of power
Are brutal murder equals material gain
Why are we content to ride the wave?
Whilst forgetting about the storm
And why must the hand that delivers the child
Seek to strangle the unborn
Some people bath in affluence
Wealth in wallet but not in mind
Divorced from want and oblivious to
The unfortunates of humankind

And meanwhile, half a world away
A baby cries dying of hunger
Its tiny body ravaged with disease
An old man falls to his knees
Embracing a blood stained corpse that once carried life
The battered corpse is his wife
A grief stricken mother turns silently from a window
As she awaits her son who'll never return
Another victim of another's cause
Obscenity....War
In the playground wide eyed children play war games
Whilst on the other side of the street real war continues
Guns and bombs as toys
Or the real macoy
Men pointing rifles out of armoured cars
Creates tension, causes bloodshed
And we fool ourselves, as some of us believe that this is peace
A grain of rice a day
Keeps malnutrition at bay....Bollocks!
Most, so called, aid to the third world
Comes in the form of weapons
Well I'm sorry mate but something's gone wrong
If we seriously believe that guns and bombs preserve life
Seems to us that the opposite is true
Weapons create wealth only for the arms dealers
And not those existing in the third world
Is it really ok to make money out of death
Civilisation? We're but a fucking joke
We'll never find peace unless we find ourselves

But it's late and it's getting very dark outside

When we are confronted with obstacles in our path towards a more compassionate and wholesome way of life. Too often, we pass the blame onto someone or something else. We do this in order to remove the burden from ourselves and thus We distort the problem rather than solve it. The ends we reach for cannot be achieved unless we find in ourselves what we desire to see throughout the world. An awareness of what we are doing and where it is leading us is the first major obstacle we must overcome. Not until we have reached this stage and found our own way through it can we further our own personal progress. It is then that we may reflect on what we see and if necessary, make efforts to change ourselves. When we have learnt to recognise the strength that lies within each and every one of us, the foundations for a truly harmonious world will have been laid.

When we have learnt to use this strength to its full advantage.

When we have learnt to share it with those who have not yet found it within themselves, we may then and only then, begin to pull ourselves up from this quagmire of carnage and really set forth on the path towards a peaceful co existence for all to share.

Together we can change the world, but time is running out and the buck stops with

you

Printed in Great Britain
by Amazon